GENESIS 1–4

A LINGUISTIC, LITERARY, AND THEOLOGICAL COMMENTARY

C. JOHN COLLINS

PUBLISHING

P.O. BOX 817 • PHILLIPSBURG • NEW JERSEY 08865-0817

Page design and typesetting by Lakeside Design Plus

Printed in the United States of America

Library of Congress Cataloging-in-Publication Data

Collins, C. John, 1954–
    Genesis 1–4 : a linguistic, literary, and theological commentary / C. John Collins.
        p. cm.
    Includes bibliographical references and index.
    ISBN-10: 0-87552-619-5 (paper)
    ISBN-13: 978-087552-619-5 (paper)
    1. Bible. O.T. Genesis I–IV—Commentaries. I. Title: Genesis one–four. II. Title.

BS1235.53.C65 2006
222'.11077—dc22

                                             2005048866

CONTENTS

ANALYTICAL OUTLINE

ACKNOWLEDGMENTS

To think over how much I owe to so many people is to realize afresh how blessed I am, so writing these acknowledgments is a happy task.

The Templeton Foundation's Science and Religion Course Program and the Discovery Institute's Center for Science and Culture have given me grants over the years that have encouraged and supported my studies. Steve Meyer of the Discovery Institute told me nice things about my first paper on Genesis, and life has never been the same since; Jay Richards, also of the Discovery Institute, has given me helpful advice and instruction on matters of philosophical theology (and so much more): beyond that, these have become cherished friends.

The administration of Covenant Theological Seminary has been unflagging in their support for my work: notably Bryan Chapell, the president, and Donald Guthrie, the dean of faculty. My faculty colleagues have done much to shape and correct my thinking: in particular, Mike Williams, Robert Peterson, Jay Sklar, Hans Bayer, and David Chapman have made an enormous impact on me—and not only with their ideas but also with their genuine friendship and kindness. My former colleagues Dan Doriani, Phil Long, and Bob Yarbrough have also given me much encouragement.

Many fellow teachers, ministers, and elders, as well as former students, have given me much. I am grateful to Brian Aucker, Doug Doll, Howard Griffith, Rob Rayburn, Max Rogland, Robert Rogland, Ron Youngblood, and Bruce Waltke; and to Mike Farley, Charles

Kuykendall, Joshua Moon, and Julie Siverd. Special thanks go to Vi Coulter, my student assistant, who helped me manage the bibliography and gave me feedback on the work, and to Joel Hathaway, who also made comments.

This commentary owes its origin to the urging of the students in my fall 2002 Hebrew class, with Mr. Brig Jones as the chief instigator. I pray that they find their efforts rewarded.

To reflect on God's work of creation, and his instituting of marriage and family, is to renew my gratitude to the Lord for his kindness in surrounding me with the wife and children he has. These remind me that God's blessings are free and gracious:

> Better is a dinner of herbs where love is
> than a fattened ox and hatred with it. (Prov. 15:17)

Thank you, Lord, for the love in my house!

ABBREVIATIONS

AV	Authorized (King James) Version
BDAG	Bauer, W., F. W. Danker, W. F. Arndt, and F. W. Gingrich. *A Greek-English Lexicon of the New Testament and Other Early Christian Literature*, 3d ed. Chicago, 2000
BDB	Brown, F., S. R. Driver, and C. A. Briggs. *A Hebrew and English Lexicon of the Old Testament*. Oxford, 1906 (cited by page and column)
CEV	Contemporary English Version
ESV	English Standard Version
JOTT	*Journal of Translation and Textlinguistics*
LSJ	Liddell, H. G., R. Scott, H. S. Jones, *A Greek-English Lexicon*. 9th ed. with revised supplement. Oxford, 1996
LXX	Septuagint
MT	Masoretic Text
NAB	New American Bible
NASB	New American Standard Bible
NBD	*The New Bible Dictionary*. Edited by I. H. Marshall et al. Downers Grove, Ill., 1996 (cited by page and column)
NEB	New English Bible

NIDOTTE *New International Dictionary of Old Testament Theology and Exegesis.* Edited by W. A. VanGemeren. 5 vols. Grand Rapids, 1997 (cited by volume and page)

NIV   New International Version

NRSV   New Revised Standard Version

OPTAT   *Occasional Papers in Translation and Textlinguistics*

REB   Revised English Bible

RSV   Revised Standard Version

RV   Revised Version

1

INTRODUCTION

How can anyone ever get tired of studying the opening chapters of Genesis? It is true that many controversies swirl around these chapters. Who wrote them, and why? What use did the author make of sources? Do they have any value as history? How do they square with science?

The list goes on, but it gets tedious fast. But when one turns from the controversies to the Hebrew text, the tedium vanishes and the fascination returns. These chapters are front-loaded with all manner of vital topics, such as God's work of creating the world and mankind; what it means to be human; why our present experience is so different from what we find in Genesis 2; how we come to know God and to be sure of his love.

This book is a commentary on the first four chapters of Genesis. I aim to provide pastors and students with an academically rigorous treatment of the biblical text that explores the connections of the parts of the Bible and the impact of the Bible on life today. My vision of academic rigor includes a literary-theological method informed by contemporary discourse analysis, in order to arrive at an integrated reading of each segment. In order to explore the connections of the Bible's parts, I will look at how the passages from Genesis have shaped subsequent material—especially in the Old Testament, Apocrypha, and New Testament.

The most common way to use a commentary is to skip the introductory chapters and dip into its comments on individual passages. But my approach is governed by a methodology that stresses the passages' role in a coherent literary production, so I urge you not to skip the chapter on method or the integrated literary-theological expositions.

My vision of academic rigor also includes responsibly reading and weighing what others have written; hence the bibliography. However, if I were to transcribe all my marginal notes on everything I have read into footnotes here, you would find that unbearably tedious. In other words, I found myself pulled both to write something that reflects this academic rigor and to write something that people would read. For this reason I have presented my arguments, giving reasons for my positions and noting where needed representatives of competing positions.[1]

I believe my most important contribution is the method that I describe and apply. This method involves us in paying attention to linguistic and literary details, as well as in arriving at an overall integrated reading of a passage within its larger context. It also grapples with the fact that these passages are intended to be Scripture, which means that they have a theological function in the life of both their original audience and their subsequent audiences, including us. I have therefore been explicitly theological in relating my expositions of the individual passages to themes in biblical and systematic theology and in tracing the impact of these passages on other texts in the Old Testament, the intertestamental period, and the New Testament. In the last two chapters I have also outlined how I would relate my conclusions about these chapters to questions of history, science, and worldview formation. I believe these passages in Genesis equip us to live faithfully in today's world, with a passionate devotion to God and a vigorous Christian mind.

There are many topics in these chapters about which people disagree. I believe that the methodology I have offered gives us a set of tools to evaluate competing views with sound critical thinking.

---

1. In order to make my discussion as accessible to the intended audience as I can, without sacrificing rigor, I have cited the underlying Hebrew and generally supplied as well a simplified transliteration based on *The SBL Handbook of Style* (Peabody: Hendrickson, 1999), 28. I have not thought it necessary to do the same with the Greek.

Scholarly commentaries on Genesis, or on parts of it, usually begin with a great deal of time and space on matters of special introduction—source and redaction criticism, authorship, date, canonicity, and so on. These matters are important, and I have postponed that discussion until after I have carried out the literary and theological discussions. Such criticism depends on discerning the seams between literary units of presumably disparate origins, but this discernment should be the product of careful study. I believe my discourse-oriented literary approach gives us tools for greater rigor in this topic, as well.

The book proceeds, therefore, as follows. First, in chapter 2 I will describe and illustrate the methodology; then in chapter 3 I will put Genesis 1–4 into its literary context. Then come the four exegetical chapters, taking each of the four pericopes in turn (chapters 4–7). In chapter 8 I take up the question of sources and unity. Chapters 9–11 focus on applying the text: chapter 9 deals with the communicative purpose of Genesis 1–4 in its original setting; chapter 10 addresses questions of history and science in Genesis 1–4; and chapter 11 looks at how we can appropriate Genesis 1–4 today, by focusing on the worldview these chapters inculcate.

In the exegetical chapters, my standard format is to begin with the pericope boundaries and structure and then to move on to the annotated translation. The translation is the English Standard Version (ESV), and the notes are primarily linguistic. Following that, I offer extra notes on points that need more discussion (some are linguistic, and some are more general). Then I move to the literary-theological exposition. The last section considers other reverberations, namely, echoes of the passage that have not already been treated.

When I cite a commentary, I ordinarily do so using the author's last name only. Other materials get a fuller reference in the footnote, and they all appear in the bibliography at the end.

The obvious question is, why stop at chapter 4? Why not go on through chapter 11? To begin with, we must admit that no part of Genesis makes any sense without the rest. For example, the special choice of Abraham's offspring (Gen. 12–50) requires that we understand the unity of mankind and its common accountability to its Creator—otherwise, the promise of universal blessing (Gen. 12:1–3) has no foundation. However, there are still natural subunits to the book, and thus we must decide whether the first subunit is Genesis

1–3 or Genesis 1–4; I have given my reasons for thinking that it is Genesis 1–4 in the chapter that examines Genesis 4.

I have found much benefit in the commentaries I have read, and among these the most prominent are those by Leon Kass, Bruce Waltke, Yehuda Kiel (in Hebrew), Victor Hamilton, Gordon Wenham, Claus Westermann, Franz Delitzsch, and S. R. Driver. In addition, there are several special studies on Genesis 1–3 or parts of it, such as Henri Blocher, *In the Beginning*; Hugh Ross, *The Genesis Question*; David Hagopian, *The Genesis Debate*; James Barr, *The Garden of Eden and the Hope of Immortality*; and Howard J. Van Till, Robert E. Snow, John H. Stek, Davis A. Young, *Portraits of Creation*. I have found that each of these has its merits, but I dare to offer my work to accompany theirs, in view of the features that I have described above.

My usual English Bible for citations is the English Standard Version (ESV of 2001; or ESV Update of 2006).[2] For the Apocrypha, I have used either the RSV or the NRSV (rarely the RV), occasionally modifying it to suit the original better. Likewise for other Greek writers (such as Herodotus, Plato, Philo, or Josephus), I have used the Loeb translation but modified it to be closer to the Greek.

I have been studying, teaching from, and writing on Genesis 1–4 for many years now. I have done more than simply rework older material for this book; I have taken the opportunity to examine everything afresh. I am grateful for the privilege of such study, and I pray that you, the reader, will use the best tools available to you to grapple with God's Word.

---

2. For my views on translation philosophy and why I prefer this version, see my appendix, "Without form you lose meaning," in Leland Ryken, *The Word of God in English: Criteria for Excellence in Bible Translation* (Wheaton: Crossway, 2002), 295–319.

2

A DISCOURSE-ORIENTED
LITERARY APPROACH

I n this chapter I will describe the method I intend to use in studying
these biblical passages. In the method I aim to achieve "ancient
literary competence":[1] that is, I seek to read the text the way a competent reader in the original audience would have done, to the best
that we can reconstruct that competence.

Of course this raises questions about who the original audience
was, and whether we can reconstruct its competence—not to mention
the question of whether such an aim even matters to today's reader.
I will wait until chapter 8 (on authorship) before giving my answer
to the first question, who was the original audience? For now it will
be enough to say that it was ancient Israel, before the Hellenistic
period. As to the second question, whether we can reconstruct their
competence, the proper response is: try it and see. The third question has to do with authors, texts, and intentions; we can break it
into two subquestions: Can we speak of texts expressing an author's
intent, and do we care?

The communication model that I develop below shows why we
naturally suppose that an author expresses intention by way of a text.

1. The term comes from V. Philips Long, *The Art of Biblical History* (Grand Rapids:
Zondervan, 1994), 33.

He might be only partially successful, depending on his own ability or on the level of overlap between his world and that of the audience. To the question of whether we care, one might simply say, "Well, *I* do even if *you* do not." But our answer will probably take us deeper into matters of the soul: we ask not simply, Do we respect this particular author enough to make the effort to listen to him on his own terms? but also, Does his intention have any bearing on what I ought to believe? The traditional doctrine of biblical inspiration indicates that the believing community cooperates with God by cooperating with the intention of his authorized spokesmen. (I do not say that this exhausts our cooperation, but let us see how that develops as we go.)

I have developed the approach that I advocate under the influence of the disciplines of discourse analysis and literary studies. In the discussion that follows, I will focus on what these disciplines have done for our study of biblical narrative. I argue that careful use of these tools will help us to arrive at critically defensible readings of the biblical texts, which will mean that we are listening to the authors—and this will have its payoff in exegesis, in expounding and applying these texts and in using these texts in our theological formulations. Given that narrative is such a major form of biblical material and that it is notoriously easy to abuse it, the help from such methods should be welcome.

A. What Is Discourse Analysis?

The field of discourse analysis starts from the notion that a text is an act of communication. So let us reflect briefly on what takes place in acts of communication. It is far too simple to say that we have a speaker, an audience, and a message that connects them. Rather, we should see that the speaker and audience have a picture of the world that to some extent they share between them: that picture includes, for example, knowledge, beliefs, values, experiences, language. For example, I am writing this book in English, and I assume that you know what I mean by "the Hebrew Bible." A *text* is a means by which the speaker (or *author*) operates on that shared picture of the world to produce some effect (the *message*) in the audience. Perhaps the author adds new things for them to know or corrects things that they thought they knew; or draws on some part of it, such as their experience of God's love, in order for them to act upon it; or evokes some aspect of it for celebration or mourning; or even radically revises their orientation to the world (their worldview). The authors and their audiences also share linguistic and literary conventions, which indicate how to interpret the text; for example, everyone who is competent in American English knows what to expect when a narrative begins with "once upon a time." For an audience to interpret a text properly, they must *cooperate* with the author as he has expressed himself in his text.

When we describe things this way, we see that we can talk about authorial intent without getting lost in the supposed psychological states of the author or even the structure of his thought; instead we can look at the effect this text is used to produce in the audience.[2] We can ascertain this effect from the standard uses that the genres and the rhetorical features of the text have, as well as from observing the ways in which people close to the audience's culture have responded to the text. (By the way—and this is helpful when we are uncertain as to whether a single person wrote the whole work—this also means that, for the purpose of ascertaining intent, it matters little whether the author is a single individual or a committee.)

In order to be true to experience, we have to add a nuance to this description; namely, we should recognize that the author's picture of the world overlaps with that of the audience, but the overlap is never entire (unless the author is speaking to himself). An author who wants to be understood, then, will take pains to stay within the overlap or else to equip the audience to deal with the nonoverlapping part. We ought also to add a moral component: not all authors speak in good faith (they may use deceptive means to achieve their goals), and not all audiences are inclined to cooperate with the author. Of course we must also be willing to apply this qualification to ourselves; we all have our own world pictures, interests, and agendas, and these affect how well we cooperate with any author, ancient or modern. This does not mean that we *cannot* get a good idea of what the author meant; it only means we have to be careful, honest, and humble.

Discourse analysis studies how texts accomplish their communicative purposes. This means understanding their genre and their information structure, as well as their rhetorical features. Discourse grammar analyzes grammatical structures, such as verb tense and

---

2. This bears some resemblance to Mark Brett's distinction between "motives" (what moved the author to write) and "communicative intentions" (what the author is trying to say), in "Motives and Intentions in Genesis 1," *Journal of Theological Studies* n.s. 42 (1991): 1–16, at 5.

aspect, to find patterns of usage that indicate authorial intent. There are different schools of discourse analysis (also called textlinguistics), and I do not intend to describe or evaluate them here; my goal is instead the practical one of pressing their insights into the service of interpretation. Our aim is to say what good readers in the receptor audience do when they receive a text.[3]

Discourse analysis as applied to biblical interpretation owes much of its impetus to linguists associated with the Summer Institute of Linguistics (SIL). These linguists, with experience analyzing the communicative patterns of non-Western languages around the world, began asking similar questions of the Hebrew and Greek of the Bible. A seminal paper by Robert Longacre appeared in 1976, "The Discourse Structure of the Flood Narrative."[4] Longacre summarized his concerns:

> Contemporary discourse analysis is interested in questions of genre classification . . . ; the articulation of parts of a discourse such as formulaic beginnings and endings, episodes, and high points in the story (called peaks); the status of discourse constituents such as sentences, paragraphs, and embedded discourses; the cast of participants in a given discourse . . . ; author viewpoint and author sympathy as indicated in the text; the main line development of a discourse . . . ; the role of tense, aspect, particles, affixes, pronominalization chains, paraphrase, and conjunctions in providing cohesion and prominence in a discourse; ways of marking peak in a narrative; and the function of dialogue in discourse.

This is doubtless quite a complicated description, but its relevant parts should become clear as we proceed. Essays that reflect these interests have appeared in publications sponsored by SIL, and only rarely outside of such venues.[5]

---

3. Consult the helpful article by Bruce Hollenbach and Jim Watters, "Study Guide on Pragmatics and Discourse," *Notes on Translation* 12, no. 1 (1998): 13–35.
4. Robert Longacre, "The Discourse Structure of the Flood Narrative," in *Society of Biblical Literature 1976 Seminar Papers*, ed. G. MacRae (Missoula: Scholars, 1976), 235–62. See also Robert Longacre, "Interpreting Biblical Stories," in *Discourse and Literature*, ed. Teun A. van Dijk (Amsterdam/Philadelphia: John Benjamins, 1985), 169–85. A book-length work is Longacre, *Joseph: A Story of Divine Providence* (Winona Lake: Eisenbrauns, 2003).
5. E.g., Barbara D. Heins, "From Leprosy to Shalom and Back Again: A Discourse Analysis of 2 Kings 5," *OPTAT* 2, no. 1 (1988): 20–31; Calinda Hallberg, "Storyline and Theme in a Biblical Narrative: 1 Samuel 3," *OPTAT* 3, no. 1 (1989): 1–35. In 1993 the Summer

My focus is on Old Testament prose narrative here, although we shall see that the ideas apply to New Testament narratives as well. Narratives involve characters and events. Events can be part of the main storyline (what the author wants the reader to attend to), or they can be part of the background (what the audience needs to know in order to appreciate the storyline).

The discourse grammarians have observed that the verb tenses denoting events tend to fall into a consistent pattern. There is a tense (or a set of tenses) used to denote the backbone or basic storyline of the narrative; while other verb forms, when part of the narrator's presentation (as opposed to the reported speech of participants), are used for supplying background information: that is, to say what happened before the story got under way or what was happening as the story got going. Thus a basic distinction is between what is on the storyline and what is off the storyline.

Recognizing this will help us to ascertain the information structure of a narrative, such as how it breaks down into paragraphs, how the paragraphs relate to one another, and how characters are introduced.[6]

B. What Is a Literary Approach?

A literary approach starts from recognizing that authors use aesthetic devices to a greater or lesser extent, both to make their works interesting and to help the audience focus attention on the main communicative concerns.

Institute of Linguistics hosted a conference on discourse linguistics and Biblical Hebrew in which I participated, and some of its papers appeared in Robert Bergen, ed., *Biblical Hebrew and Discourse Linguistics* (Dallas: Summer Institute of Linguistics), 1994, or in the *Journal of Translation and Textlinguistics* (the successor to *OPTAT*). Summer Institute of Linguistics has produced similar works on the New Testament, such as David Alan Black, ed., *Linguistics and New Testament Interpretation* (Nashville: Broadman, 1992); essays using these tools for New Testament interpretation appear more widely, including such journals as *Filologia Neotestamentaria* and *Novum Testamentum*.

6. The critique of Robert L. Thomas, "Modern Linguistics versus Traditional Hermeneutics," *The Master's Seminary Journal* 14, no. 1 (2003): 23–45, seems to me to be based on misunderstandings of linguistics, Greek grammar, and hermeneutics. Further, when he makes a valid point, he fails to distinguish what particular linguistically oriented scholars might say from the discipline of linguistics itself. He refuses to allow linguistic study to refine traditional hermeneutics. But of course, the best reply to such critique is to show the positive benefits of the methodology, which the rest of this book hopes to do.

A wide variety of literary approaches have been applied to the Bible, and these vary in their emphases on the author, the audience, and the text. I am here sticking with what we may call conservative literary approaches: namely, those which focus on the text having a meaning, as opposed to the modern kind, which are primarily interested in the process by which the text came about, and as opposed to the postmodern kind, which locate meaning only in the reader or in the reader's interpretive community or which deny the possibility of communication altogether.[7]

Perhaps I need to give some warrant for this preference. Writing in the *Encyclopaedia Britannica*, Frederick Crews observed, "The totality of Western [literary] criticism in the 20th century defies summary except in terms of its restless multiplicity and factionalism."[8] But this means that there is no single literary method, and one must decide what to do. The basic choices in biblical studies revolve around what it means to explain a biblical work: do we aim to explain how the work came to be as it is, or do we aim to explain how that work should function as a religious text? While not rejecting the former out of hand, I am seeking the latter. I am grounding my sense of how a text should function in the communication model that I described above.

Conservative literary approaches to biblical narrative share some of the same concerns as discourse analysis and add some of their own. These methods stem from the observation that the biblical narratives

---

7. Because of this orientation of my work, there is little to be gained from extensive critique of alternative kinds of reading: for example, there is the kind that has little grasp of biblical exegesis, such as Sam Dragga, "Genesis 2–3: A Story of Liberation," *Journal for the Study of the Old Testament* 55 (1992): 3–13; there is the kind that follows a preset ideological agenda, such as the "ecojustice"-based essays in N. C. Habel and Shirley Wurst, eds., *The Earth Story in Genesis* (The Earth Bible, vol. 2; Sheffield: Sheffield Academic Press, 2000); and there is the "deconstructive" kind that undercuts the idea of a message at all, such as Edward L. Greenstein, "Deconstruction and Biblical Narrative," *Prooftexts* 9 (1989): 43–71. The goals of these works are so different from mine that all one can do is compare the presuppositions and the finished products. In general I agree with N. T. Wright, *The New Testament and the People of God* (Minneapolis: Fortress, 1992), who notes in his chapter 2 that "the problems which we encounter in the study of literature, history and theology all belong together" because "each reflects . . . the basic shape of the problem of knowledge itself." Wright proposes "critical realism" as the best epistemology. My only reservation about Wright's discussion is that he seems to speak as if we can "propose" an epistemology: it seems far better to say that we must offer an account of what we do unreflectively, and show that it explains our known-to-be-rational behavior.

8. Article "The Art of Literature," in *Encyclopaedia Britannica*, ed. Philip W. Goetz (Chicago: University of Chicago Press, 1989), 23:86–224; Crews wrote the section "Literary Criticism," 203–7; the quotation comes from 206.

are *stories* and hence involve characters, events (plot), and scenes. To call them stories is not to downplay whatever historical claims they might make (indeed, if the genre is one that tells history, then of course one must address these); instead it directs our attention to the narrator's ways of portraying characters' good and bad traits and of displaying or hiding his own point of view. A helpful survey of these approaches for the uninitiated is the Ph.D. dissertation of V. Philips Long, *The Reign and Rejection of King Saul*.[9] Some of the features we find in the Old Testament narratives include the following:

- The narrator is *reliable* and *omniscient*: that is, he serves as the voice and perspective of God.[10]
- The narration is *scenic*: that is, the emphasis is on direct action and interaction of the characters rather than on descriptive detail of the environs.
- The narratives are *sparsely written*: that is, they focus on what is essential for the narrative.
- The author will use *Leitwortstil*: that is, he will repeat a key word or word root to draw attention to thematic issues.
- The author employs *wordplay*, such as words or roots used with different meanings or words that sound alike; these are generally used for ironic contrasts.
- The author signals *heightened speech* using poetic diction: that is, elevated diction of a speech is evidence of its significance;[11] often oracular, it may even be divine speech.
- The author uses *repetition*, such as of similar kinds of events, and even of scenes, in different circumstances.
- The author employs *analogy* and *contrast*, where the characters and scenes are like and unlike one another.

The result of these features is that, generally speaking, the author communicates his point of view by indirect and laconic means. The

9. V. Philips Long, *The Reign and Rejection of King Saul* (Atlanta: Scholars, 1989). He has a section on "Selected Features of Hebrew Narrative Style" (21–41). The classic is Meir Sternberg, *The Poetics of Biblical Narrative: Ideological Literature and the Drama of Reading* (Bloomington: Indiana University Press, 1985); see further Robert Alter, *The Art of Biblical Narrative* (New York: Basic Books, 1981); Jean-Louis Ska, *Our Fathers Have Told Us: Introduction to the Analysis of Hebrew Narratives* (Rome: Pontifical Biblical Institute, 1990).
10. Traditionally the narrators are called "prophets"—that is, spokesmen for God.
11. This will often include poetic devices such as parallelism, chiasmus, artistic word order, and vocabulary choice.

emphasis will be on *showing* (displaying the heart by action and speech) versus *telling* (the narrator telling us explicitly what kind of person the character is).

Hence, if we want to be good readers of Old Testament narratives, we will pay attention to, for example, the way people speak. We will look for the relation between what they say and what they do, or between what the narrator has reported and what the character reports (if the character adds or deletes things, how does this reflect spin?), or between what someone says (or is told) he will say and what he does say. The biblical narrators are fully aware that humans are sinful and that even the best of us have mixed motives and imperfect morality. Very few important biblical characters get off with a purely positive portrayal,[12] since the authors rarely intend to make heroes out of their characters.

If we bring these disciplines together, we can arrive at a methodology that is based on empirical studies of linguistic and literary conventions, and this entitles us to a level of confidence in our reading. David Cotter, in his recent commentary on Genesis that employs literary methods, nevertheless falls into pessimism when he admits:[13]

> Are these structures really "in" the text we are studying? Has their author purposefully organized his material in this way so that we can discover it many years later? I think not. These structures are generally speaking more in the exegete than in the text. In other words, whenever we study a text we necessarily organize our reactions in some manner. We note beginning and end, we find a middle point of high emotional drama and so on.

If this is so, then we have no ground for saying that one reading is better than another, and this runs counter to our experience as authors and readers.[14]

---

12. Boaz in the Book of Ruth is one of these rare exceptions, and this has to do with the narrator's plan of using Boaz to embody aspects of God's own character; see C. John Collins, "Ambiguity and Theology in Ruth: Ruth 1:21 and 2:20," *Presbyterion* 19, no. 2 (1993): 97–102. Of course New Testament authors uniformly portray Jesus as having no flaws, because that reflects their notions of his sinless character.

13. Cotter, xxix.

14. Perhaps this explains why Cotter's commentary has little critical discussion assessing competing ways of reading the passages.

C. What about History?

It is common to call the Old Testament narratives historiography; that is, to acknowledge that they aim to describe real events. Most think that the category of history is crucial to the way the biblical narratives work; as Edmund Fryde wrote:[15]

> The Jews were the only people of antiquity who had the supreme religious duty of remembering the past because their traditional histories commemorated the working out of God's plan for his chosen people. By contrast, no Greek ever heard his gods ordering him to remember. It was the duty of every Jew to be familiar with the Jewish sacred writings, which were ultimately gathered into what became the Old Testament. The writers of these biblical books only gave an authoritative version of what everybody was supposed to know, and they were only concerned with the selection of such facts as seemed relevant in interpreting God's purpose.

I shall save the discussion of what kinds of claims we actually find in Genesis 1–4, and what value these claims have, for chapter 10; in this section I shall simply reflect on what impact this should have on how we read the texts.

In order to ask what is the place of history, we have to face a difficulty right up front: namely, not everyone agrees on just what the word *history* means.[16] In ordinary English, when we call a narrative or poem "historical" we mean that it refers to things that actually happened. Technical discussions by professional historians, however, do not always use the ordinary meaning. They may think of an account that aims to show the causal connections of the events they describe; they may judge historicity by how detached the historian is; and they may even reject any account that includes the actions of deities as historical (even if they do not deny that the event might have happened!). This is confusing, and I prefer to keep to the ordinary language sense.[17]

15. Article "The Study of History," *Encyclopaedia Britannica* 20:621–85; Fryde wrote the section "History of Historiography," 621–35.

16. For a fuller discussion, I refer the reader to the fine chapter, "History and Fiction: What Is History?" in Long, *The Art of Biblical History*.

17. It is important to note that if we say an account makes a historical truth claim, that does not settle every question we might ask about whether, for example, things are narrated in the order in which they occurred; or whether the description is complete; or

Further problems with history appear if the historian under study is partisan or if he is recording his events to teach some lesson. But—just to take a simple example—the fact that Stephen Ambrose admired the men of the 101st Airborne in World War II, and Meriwether Lewis in his voyage of discovery, hardly undermines the historical truthfulness of *Band of Brothers* and *Undaunted Courage*. Further, I have told my children a story called *How I Got That Big Scar on My Left Knee*. It recounts a stupid action of mine when I was a teenager, riding on the hood of a moving car at dusk while looking for snakes on a gravel road beside a swamp in southern Illinois[18]—can you guess what happened when I spotted one and asked the driver to brake? (Hint: It has to do with the low friction between my trousers and the metal hood of the car.) It even includes an apparent angelic interference: I cannot recall any conscious thought of moving out of the way of the right front wheel of the oncoming car, nor can I explain why I rolled right, off the road, and not left. But these events really happened (even if you think my rolling right was just luck), and, despite my obvious moralizing motive—I want my children to think before they act, unlike their father—the story is historical. I might be able, after all these years, to locate the fellows I was with; but even if I cannot, the story is still true.[19]

Some advocates of literary methods have thought it proper to bracket out questions of history: that is, we need not delay our literary study over questions about whether these events actually happened.[20] Some will even go so far as to say that what matters is how the narrative functions *as a story*, not whether its events are in some sense "real."[21]

---

whether we must interpret the account without reference to metaphor, hyperbole, literary devices, etc.

18. This particular swamp was known for its snake population and is mentioned in Raymond L. Ditmars, *Snakes of the World* (repr., New York: Macmillan, 1960), 103.

19. This story is also an *etiology*, explaining a feature of the world by a narrative (compare Josh. 7:26). Again, the etiological motive cannot be said to undermine the fundamental historicity of the tale.

20. For example, Tremper Longman III, "Biblical Narrative," in Leland Ryken and Tremper Longman III, eds., *A Complete Literary Guide to the Bible* (Grand Rapids: Zondervan, 1993), 69–79, at 78, though he suggests it only for limited purposes.

21. For example, see R. W. L. Moberly, "Story in the Old Testament," *Themelios* 11, no. 3 (1986): 77–82, though he does acknowledge the importance of history in general to the Old Testament. He does not say what criterion distinguishes those tales which must be historical from those which need not be.

As a strategy for winning an academic hearing for one's literary reading, this may have some merit; but as a reading of the biblical passages, it raises serious questions. If it is part of an author's intention to have his readers believe that his events actually took place, and we bracket out such matters, then we cannot claim that we are reading what the author wrote. If we say that the "happenedness" of the events in a story does not matter, we are making an ideological prejudgment about what kind of message the Bible gives us. We are also failing to consider whether believing the happenedness is part of the way that at least some biblical stories work as stories.

The ancients were capable of telling the difference between stories whose function lies in their happenedness and those whose function lies in their "story-ness," at least as early as the fifth-century-B.C. Greeks. For example, Thucydides (c. 460–400 B.C.), in his *History of the Peloponnesian War* 1.21, asserted the truthfulness of his account, as opposed to those concerning which poets have made songs, adorning them, and concerning which chroniclers have composed recitations for pleasing the ear more than for telling the truth. He recognized that one must sift differing accounts (1.20) in order to get the truth; he also felt that one can supply the speech some person would have given at a particular occasion, even when memory cannot be perfectly accurate, and still be telling the truth (1.23). He had an object in telling his tale: to persuade us that this war was the most important thus far among the Greeks (1.21.2).[22]

For Thucydides' purpose, "history" was better than "poetry"; but Aristotle (384–322 B.C.) had another perspective. In his *Poetics* 9.1–3 he wrote:

> A poet's object is not to tell *what actually happened* (τὰ γενόμενα), but rather what *would and could happen* according to either probability or necessity. The historian and the poet differ, not because one speaks in prose and the other in meter—for the writings of Herodotus might be put into meter and would still be no less a kind of history, with meter or without it. But the difference is in this, that one says what happened, and the other what might happen. Therefore poetry is a thing more philosophical and serious than

22. See also Herodotus (c. 484–425 B.C.), who declares that he has set forth what he has learned by inquiry (1.1) and notes that, for example, Persians and Phoenicians give different accounts that one must sift through (as in 1.5). His goal is to preserve the memory of the past, especially the tale of the "great and marvelous deeds" (1.1).

history: for poetry speaks rather of general things, while history
speaks the particular.

Aristotle had his reasons for preferring the general over the particular, but they need not concern us here. The point is that he knew the
difference between history and edifying fiction (which is what he
means by "poetry").

These Greeks have left us their reflections on the ideas, but there
is no reason to suppose that they were the first to think of them. Much
later than the OT, in the first century AD, Jewish authors show the
same awareness: 2 Peter 1:16 distinguishes between "cleverly devised
myths" (σεσωφισμένοι μῦθοι) and what the apostles told as "eyewit-
nesses" (ἐπόπται); and Josephus describes the Pentateuch narratives
as "history" (ἱστορία, *Antiq.* 1.1), and distinguishes these from "un-
seemly mythology" and "false inventions" (ἀσχήμων μυθολογία, ψευδῆ
πλάσματα, *Antiq.* 1.15–16).[23]

Hence, at some point we will have to address the question of history: Does the text claim it, and should we believe it? This has more
than academic interest: it determines how we should read the text.
For example, the recent commentary of Leon Kass regularly advocates that we read Genesis "anthropologically" and "philosophically"
(echoes of Aristotle) rather than "historically": that is, as a record not
of what *did* happen, but what *might* happen, and what *always* happens. This, he contends, gives us a much richer way of reading. S. R.
Driver, who concluded that we cannot give much historical credence
to Genesis, sought to reassure us that this does not undercut the
theological and moral utility of these texts. He could do so because
in his view Eve and Cain "still stand before us, the immortal types of
weakness yielding to temptation, and of an unbridled temper leading its victim he knows not whither." Other stories "exemplify the
ways in which God deals with the individual soul, and the manner
in which the individual soul ought,—or ought not,—to respond to
his leadings."[24]

---

23. These points show that Moberly is mistaken when he tells us that "prior to the rise
of modern thought . . . the significance of historicity played a small role in most Christian
and Jewish use of the Old Testament" ("Story in the Old Testament," 81). The ancients
grasped the issues as well as we do.

24. S. R. Driver, *The Book of Genesis* (Westminster Commentaries; London: Methuen,
1904), lxviii–ix.

By contrast, any kind of redemptive-historical reading of the narratives requires that they be real history—particularly, the real history of God's dealings with his people. These historical dealings instantiate God's faithfulness, his commitment to having a holy people, and they also ground the confidence of all the heirs of that people that God will continue to display his faithfulness and forgiveness.

The redemptive-historical approach seems to lie behind the various historical sections in the Psalms, such as Psalm 77:10–20;[25] 78; 105; 106. There the focus is not on the individual soul as such, though it is not left out; rather, it is on the people as a corporate entity with real existence. God has called, preserved, and purified this people all the way through. As I said, this does not leave out the individual soul but puts it into perspective. Each member of the people of God can thus see himself as a player in a great story that began with Adam and will end with God's ultimate self-vindication. This is morally invigorating; as William Kirk Kilpatrick put it:[26]

> It is the point of Christianity that we each do play an irreplaceable part in a cosmic drama, a story in which some of the strands only come together in eternity. In such a story, what you do counts infinitely. But even non-Christians and pre-Christians have shared this sense of storied lives. They all believed that the best incentive to moral behavior was this conviction that we are part of a story that begins before us and goes on after us, but whose outcome we may influence.
>
> The important thing, then, is to play our part well.

He went on to say:

> The main reason—and it is a difficult one for non-Christians to grasp—that you cannot extract ethical principles from Christianity and set them up on their own is that Christianity is *not* an ethical system. It is not meant to be a prescription for good behavior, although good behavior is one of its side effects. It is a story. Christians believe that it is a true story but a story, nonetheless.

This last comment captures how great the exegetical difference is between reading these narratives as a true story of which one is a

---

25. Note the appeal to "the years of the right hand of the Most High."

26. William Kirk Kilpatrick, *Psychological Seduction* (Nashville: Nelson, 1983), 109–10; the second quotation comes from 117.

part and reading them as descriptions of what always happens (and hence as moral lessons). Of course, it is possible that a true history may also have the side benefit of being moral lessons of things that happen in such circumstances, gaining their power from the fact that it actually *did* happen. (We must avoid unnecessary antitheses.)

As it turns out, both the discourse and literary approaches often result in rejecting conventional source- or redaction-critical results. This is because, while they agree with the source critics about the existence of certain difficulties in the texts, they explain them as literary devices rather than as seams between (incompatible) sources. And if the sources tell contradictory stories, then of course the resulting edited narrative is unlikely to be of much historical value. But if we can see a unity to the stories, then we open up the possibility that the story is true. So the methods have played a role in apologetics; the contribution of these methods to the task of theological exposition of the books, however, has not been explored as much.[27]

D. The Expositional Questions

We can combine the insights of these approaches into a method for theological exposition of Old Testament narrative; we can apply the same method to studying New Testament narrative. The method, such as it is, consists of a set of questions for the text. I will illustrate the method using 1 Samuel 3 (the call of Samuel) and Matthew 4:1–11 (the temptation of Jesus). One disadvantage to calling this approach a "method" is that someone might suppose that I am suggesting that we can isolate these questions from one another and simply answer them in sequence. It will be clear from these examples, and from the expositions that follow, that no one could possibly do that; rather, these questions advance us along the hermeneutical spiral.

1. What is the pericope, and who are the participants?

We want to identify the boundaries of our pericope; for example, by noticing places where the location changes, or where a new set

---

27. An attempt to do so, but without a clearly articulated method, is C. John Collins, "From Literary Analysis to Theological Exposition: The Book of Jonah," *JOTT* 7, no. 1 (1995): 28–44.

of participants is introduced, or where there is some grammatical expression of discontinuity, or where some problem is introduced at the beginning and then resolved at the end. We also list the cast of characters and note when they enter and when they leave.

Consider, for example, 1 Samuel 3.[28] Verse 1 begins with *waw* + subject ("Now the young man Samuel"), shifting the focus from the previous material, where a man of God had pronounced judgment on Eli and his house; also, none of the verbs (or quasi-verbs if we include אֵין, *'ên*, "there was no") in this verse are in the *wayyiqtol*, which means that its three clauses are background to the new section. The pericope ends not with the chapter break but with 1 Samuel 4:1a, "and the word of Samuel came to all Israel." This is an example of "problem-resolution": the pericope opens with a "problem" (3:1, "the word of the LORD was rare") and tells the story of how the situation was alleviated (4:1a, the word of the Lord coming by way of Samuel). This envelope sets off the pericope.[29]

The main participants in 1 Samuel 3:1–4:1a are Samuel, Eli, and the Lord, all of whom are active throughout; "all Israel" carries out a storyline action in 1 Samuel 3:20 (they knew that Samuel was established as a prophet). This cast of characters, with the prominent place it gives to Samuel, also sets the pericope off from the ones before and after it: 1 Samuel 2 mentions Samuel only sporadically, and 1 Samuel 4:1b–7:2 does not mention him at all.

In Matthew 4, it is easy to see that the pericope is verses 1–11.[30] Matthew 4:1 makes a transition from the place where John was baptizing; Matthew 4:11 wraps up the action with a verb in the imperfect describing the outcome of the pericope. Matthew 4:12 changes the location from the wilderness of Judah to Galilee. The main participants are only two: Jesus and "the tempter." Actors mentioned briefly are the Spirit (4:1) and angels (4:11).

---

28. I will use this passage as an example here and draw on Hallberg, "Storyline and Theme." Though in several places I differ with Hallberg (for example, on the limits of the pericope), and though she has not ventured into much theological reading, I consider this a seminal paper.

29. See also Josh. 7, where the envelope is nicely visible in the ESV: in 7:1 "the *anger* of the LORD *burned* against the people of Israel," and in 7:26 "the LORD turned from his *burning anger*."

30. A useful source here is Daniel Akin, "A Discourse Analysis of the Temptation of Jesus Christ as Recorded in Matthew 4:1–11," *OPTAT* 1, no. 1 (1987): 78–86.

2. What is the paragraph structure of the pericope (including peak)?

Here we outline the broad structure of the events described in our passage. A paragraph would consist, for example, of a single exchange between two characters or a connected set of actions. The "peak" is that part of the narrative that has the maximum interest: for example, when God finally makes his opinion known or when the narrative tension is at its climax; it is often the communicative focus of the pericope.

Consider again 1 Samuel 3. As we observed, 1 Samuel 3:1 is background and sets out the problem to be resolved by the events in this pericope. Then verses 2–3 crystallize this background into one particular evening, when Eli and Samuel were lying in bed: only the very first verb, וַיְהִי (wayehî, "and it came about"), is wayyiqtol, which means that the author is still setting the stage. The next three paragraphs describe the way that the Lord tries three times to call Samuel without success. In the next paragraph the Lord at last gets to give his message to Samuel, and then Samuel reports the message to Eli. Finally, the author wraps it all up by speeding up elapsed time ("and Samuel grew, and the Lord was with him") and indicating that the problem is now resolved.

We may chart it this way:[31]

3:1	**problem**
3:2–3	specific setting
3:4–5	first call
3:6–7	second call
3:8–9	third call
3:10–14	fourth call
3:15–18	Samuel tells Eli
3:19–4:1a	**resolution**

The peak comes in 1 Samuel 3:10–14, where God reveals his plan to punish Eli and his house. We can see this from the way the "call" progresses in intensity: "then the Lord called Samuel" (v. 4); "and

31. It is possible to put 1 Sam. 3:15 with the previous paragraph and to begin the next paragraph with "called" (as the four event paragraphs had done). However, 1 Sam. 3:15 takes the timeline to the morning and thus sets the stage for Eli's call.

the LORD called again, 'Samuel!' " (v. 6); "and the LORD called Samuel again the third time" (v. 8); "and the LORD came and stood, calling as at other times, "Samuel! Samuel!' " (v. 10). Further, in this section the Lord gives his opinion—an opinion that not only matters more than any other, but also explains why the rest of 1 Samuel works out the way it does (the rationale for rejecting Eli also applies to rejecting Saul).

We can map the structure of Matthew 4:1–11 in this way:

	Description	Participants
4:1–2	setting	Jesus the only subject of the event line
4:3–4	interchange$_1$	tempter, then Jesus (ὁ δέ)
4:5–7	interchange$_2$	devil, then Jesus
4:8–10	interchange$_3$	devil, then Jesus
4:11	resolution	devil, then angels

The peak is Matthew 4:8–10, with verse 10 the highest part, which we see from Jesus saying, "Be gone, Satan"; the paraphrase of Deuteronomy in verse 10 (while verses 4, 7 were direct quotations); the dismissal results in the devil leaving in defeat (4:11).

3. What is the basic sequence of events?

In a Biblical Hebrew narrative, the function of the *wayyiqtol* verb form (also improperly called "the *waw*-consecutive with imperfect") is as "the backbone or storyline tense of Biblical Hebrew narrative discourse."[32] Hence, if we want to find the main sequence of events in a narrator's presentation, we should begin by looking for the *wayyiqtol* verbs.[33] Other verb forms, when part of the narrator's presentation (as opposed to the reported speech of participants), are used for supplying background information: for example, the "perfect" (*qatal*) is used to denote events off the storyline, while the "imperfect" (*yiqtol*),

32. Robert Longacre, "Discourse Perspective on the Hebrew Verb: Affirmation and Restatement," in *Linguistics and Biblical Hebrew*, ed. Walter Bodine (Winona Lake: Eisenbrauns, 1992), 177–89, at 178. See also Randall Buth, "The Hebrew Verb in Current Discussions," *JOTT* 5, no. 2 (1992): 91–105.
33. Of course, since this verb form can be used for embedded storylines, we cannot mechanically identify the occurrence of the verb form with this function.

"converted perfect" (*weqatal*), and participle (*qotel*) denote activities with process aspect ("something *was happening*").[34]

Normally, in New Testament Greek narrative the aorist (*both* indicative *and* adverbial participle) gives the event line.[35] In Matthew and John we have the historic present as well.[36] Although the historic present is often said to be for the sake of greater "vividness," this explanation is unlikely, since the feature appears so often.[37] Off the storyline, imperfects are often used to provide background, as the present participle can be; subordinate clauses (such as relative clauses), which are grammatically marked as off the storyline, can use any of the tenses; but the time reference is typically with respect to the storyline. One special use of the imperfect is when it is near the end of the pericope and on the storyline: this typically denotes the outcome of the events.[38]

We may include here questions of the order of events, which may or may not be the same as order of narration,[39] and historical truth claims our narrator is making. I consider it important to raise this question and invalid to bracket it out; after all, such claims, when made, are part of the communicative intent of the narrative.[40]

The comments above show how the verb tenses in 1 Samuel 3 function in structuring the account. In verse 1 we have a general condition that crystallizes into a particular day that is the setting for

34. "Process aspect" has a number of contextually inferred nuances, such as habitual action, repeated action, one action in process, inceptive action.

35. We can see this from the way the Septuagint typically renders the *wayyiqtol* with καί or δέ with the aorist, or else by an aorist participle (as in Gen. 3:6; 4:1, 17, 25; 12:18).

36. There is also the special case of the imperfect ἔφη ("said," Matt. 4:7), from a verb that lacks the full range of tense forms.

37. This classic explanation comes from Longinus, *On the Sublime*, §25. When the historic present is frequent in English narrative, this typically reflects artlessness (colloquial speech) rather than literary art.

38. The impact of this varies with an author's own style. Mark often uses a verb form with process aspect at the end of a pericope to highlight the result.

39. For a grammatical discussion of when the event denoted by a *wayyiqtol* verb form is not directly sequential to the previous event, see C. John Collins, "The *Wayyiqtol* as 'Pluperfect': When and Why," *Tyndale Bulletin* 46, no. 1 (1995): 117–40.

40. Joseph Pipa Jr., in "From Chaos to Cosmos: A Critique of the Non-literal Interpretations of Genesis 1:1–2:3," in *Did God Create in Six Days?* ed. Joseph Pipa Jr. and David Hall (Taylors, S.C.: Southern Presbyterian Press, 1999), 153–98, at 198, expresses the fear that an approach to biblical narrative based on these methods will lead to the downplaying of historical truth claims; he seems to think it is inherent in the methodology. But since this methodology recognizes that historical claims are part of the communication event, and since the expositor should address the question, that fear is seen to be unfounded.

the events of this pericope (vv. 2–3). Then the events follow in their proper sequence, with the four calls from the Lord to Samuel in the night and the one call from Eli to Samuel the next morning (vv. 4–18). But then the closing paragraph moves ahead quickly, summarizing how Samuel grew up and became known as a prophet.

And what of the next pericope, starting in 1 Samuel 4:1b: does it follow sequentially from 4:1a? The answer is, probably not: Samuel is absent in a way that 1 Samuel 3:19–4:1a would not have led us to expect. We may explain this on source-critical grounds, but that is not explanation enough in light of the wordplay on כבד (kabed, "heavy") that begins in 1 Samuel 2:30 and runs through these chapters, which indicates that someone has integrated the texts together.[41] Hence we can see 1 Samuel 4:1b–7:2 as being concurrent with 1 Samuel 3:19–4:1a, and it is there to show the audience what happens when God's people do not honor God's covenant from their hearts—and thus to show why they need the ministry of Samuel and eventually the leadership of a king like David. It took the discipline of losing the ark to make Israel willing to hear Samuel's message.

If we see the text this way, we then are relieved of all pressure to doubt the historical veracity of the account—unless we doubt supernatural events altogether, but that is another matter.

In Matthew 4:1–11, we can discern the storyline with the aorist indicatives and participles. We also have storyline historic presents in verses 5 ("took"), 6 ("said"), 8 ("took . . . showed"), 8 ("said"), and 11 ("left"). We also have an imperfect, διηκόνουν ("they were ministering," v. 11), as the last verb of the pericope, giving the outcome: "and so they proceeded to minister to him."

This presents a difficulty in that Luke's account arranges the temptations differently: namely, it has the order 1, 3, 2. Do the two accounts disagree? Only if the genre conventions imply a strict sequence in the storyline verbs. It is clear that Matthew and Luke use their verb tenses differently and present different perspectives on the event; it is quite conceivable therefore that they have differing assertions about sequence. If the actual sequence is not a strong part

41. See V. Philips Long, "Scenic, Succinct, Subtle: An Introduction to the Literary Artistry of 1 and 2 Samuel," *Presbyterion* 19, no. 1 (1993): 32–47; this also appears as "First and Second Samuel," in Ryken and Longman, eds., *The Complete Literary Guide to the Bible*, 165–81. Additional linguistic discussion appears in C. John Collins, "כבד," no. 3877 in *NIDOTTE* (Grand Rapids: Zondervan, 1997), 2:577–87.

of the historical truth claims of the narrators, the chief problem for historicity remains the supernatural element.

4. How do those events follow causally from what comes before and affect causally what comes after?

This concerns the relationship between our pericope and its context. The events in our passage may be influenced by choices the characters made in earlier passages, while the choices the characters make in our pericope may influence events later. This reflects the biblical position that, under divine sovereignty, our choices are freighted with unimaginable significance and effect.

In the case of 1 Samuel 3, verse 1a ("the young man Samuel") links up with 1 Samuel 2:11, 18, 26, each of which uses the same term ("young man, lad") for Samuel, and each of which is off the main event line. Samuel, the foster son of Eli, is contrasted with Hophni and Phineas, the natural sons of Eli—but just as they did not "know the LORD" (2:12), neither did he—*yet* (3:7); this is probably a reproach on Eli. The decree against Eli's house (3:11–14) picks up the message from the man of God (2:27–36). This decree is worked out in what follows, as the sons of Eli die at the hands of the Philistines, as Eli falls over and dies, and as the ark goes into exile. Similarly, in 1 Samuel 7:3 and elsewhere, we can see how Samuel rises to prominence.

The episode in Matthew 4:1–11 directly follows Matthew 3, where John was in the "wilderness" (3:1, 3)—and Jesus was led into the wilderness (4:1). In Matthew 3:13–17, at Jesus' baptism, we find the Spirit descending on him (3:16)—the same Spirit who led Jesus into the wilderness (4:1). Finally, the voice from heaven declared Jesus "my beloved Son" (3:17), and this is what the devil tests (4:3, 6).[42]

Thematically, we see Jesus as the one who resisted temptation and who is therefore qualified for his ministry (as the ideal Israel). We also see the contest over how he will inherit his universal kingship over the Gentiles (a messianic mission): in Matthew 28:18 we see that he has gone about it the right way, in contrast to the offer in Matthew 4:9.

---

42. Jesus as God's "Son" in Matt. 2:15 (citing Hos. 11:1); 3:17; 4:3, 6; 8:29; 11:27; 14:33; 16:16; 17:5; 24:36; 26:63; 27:43, 54; 28:19. In some of these passages he is clearly the ontological "Son" (as in Matt. 28:19); in others, he is the redemptive-historical "son" (as Israel, Exod. 4:23; Hos. 11:1; as the king, 2 Sam. 7:14; Ps. 2:7, 12). It lies with the reader to discern which is in view in Matt. 3:17.

5. *Are there repeated key words or roots (both within this pericope and across several pericopes)?*

Repeating key words can bind passages with a theological unity, as well as give them a unity across pericope boundaries. Further, repetition of roots within a pericope can provide anaphora (back reference to something mentioned previously) or can be used for irony.

For example, 1 Samuel 2:30 is a controlling principle for the first part of 1 Samuel: "Those who honor me I will honor, and those who despise me shall be lightly esteemed." Here, the word *honor* is from the Hebrew root כבד (*k-b-d*), from which other forms are derived meaning "heavy," "harden [the heart]," and "glory." The word *lightly esteemed* is from the root קלל (*q-l-l*), the natural antonym of כבד. Use of words from these roots serves to remind the reader that 1Samuel 2:30 is the relevant interpretive principle. This appears in 1 Samuel 3:13, where Eli's sons were "blaspheming [מקללים, *meqa-lelîm*] God."[43]

Within the pericope, the key repetition is דבר (*dabar*, "word, thing"), found in 1 Samuel 3:1, 7, 11, 17, 18, 19, 21; 4:1a. The related verb דבר (*dibber*, "to speak") appears in 1 Samuel 3:9, 10, 12, 17; and other terms in the same semantic realm are "word of the LORD was revealed" (3:7), "tell the vision" (3:15), and "the LORD revealed himself" (3:21). All of these together remind us of the work of the prophet, to which Samuel is now called.

This shows us that the call of Samuel restores divine revelation. Samuel's work is a paradigm for all true prophets, who must insist on covenant faithfulness and must not hide a single word of God's revelation (1 Sam. 3:17).[44]

Matthew 4:10 has Jesus saying, ὕπαγε, σατανᾶ ("Be gone, Satan!"). Compare this with the similar words in Matthew 16:23, ὕπαγε ὀπίσω μου, σατανᾶ ("Get behind me, Satan!")—but this time addressed to

---

43. So the ESV, following the scribal *Tiqqûn*; the Masoretic Text has "blaspheming for themselves," but the point made here is still the same.

44. Note the chiastic structure of Eli's speech in 3:17:

a	what was the word that he spoke to you
b	do not hide it from me
x	may God do so to you and more also
b′	if you hide from me
a′	any word from all the word that he spoke to you

The curse is in the middle, and is thus highlighted, focusing attention on the prophet's responsibility to convey God's word.

Peter, who would dissuade Jesus from his path to the cross. These are the major temptations to enter his kingship by pragmatic means.

Within the Matthew 4 pericope, we find προσέρχομαι ("came," vv. 3, 11): this is a contrast, because in one case the tempter came, and in the other angels came. We also find γέγραπται ("it is written") in verses 4, 7, 10, where Jesus cites from Deuteronomy; contrast this with verse 6, where the devil uses it to introduce a quotation from Psalm 91 (which he distorts). Other repetitions include πειράζω ("tempt," vv. 1, 3) and διάβολος ("devil," vv. 5, 8, 11) as the one who tempts.

6. How does the author present the characters?

For example, look for the ways in which the characters' action and speech reveal their hearts; the way they describe events as compared with the way the narrator does (their spinning of events); the ways people develop or deteriorate; and the ways an author may create sympathy or suspicion.

The author of 1 Samuel is clear on why it took so long for Samuel to respond to God's call: "Samuel did not yet know the LORD." Something this explicit should control our reading of the rest. This is similar to 1 Samuel 2:12, where Hophni and Phineas did not know the Lord, but it is also different—because the "not yet" in 1 Samuel 3:7 leads us to expect a change. Samuel's reluctance to tell the vision (3:15) is understandable given its content and his youth, but his obedience to Eli's solemn charge (3:18) shows what kind of prophet he will be and justifies Israel's confidence in him.

Eli comes across as a kindly figure, of genuine piety: he is gentle with Samuel when the boy comes to his bedside three times (most parents can appreciate how much kindness this would take); he recognizes the Lord's call; and he enjoins Samuel to deliver the message in full. All of this makes his parental failure stand out even more—his piety cannot make up for failure to initiate his children into knowing the Lord (something at the heart of covenant faithfulness—see Gen. 18:19—and Eli's task is to be an example of such faithfulness). Sadly, this character defect shows up in Samuel as well (1 Sam. 8:3).

The Lord is patient, too, in his willingness to call Samuel four times. He never chides Samuel. Nor is he limited by Eli's failure to lead Samuel into a proper relationship with God. Theologically, we can see his freedom, as well: he calls Samuel but not Hophni and

Phineas. But his freedom is never caprice: Hophni and Phineas have debased themselves and cannot blame God.

In Matthew 4 we see that Jesus is presented as the one who resists temptation by citing the hortatory section of Deuteronomy (Matt. 4:4 from Deut. 8:3; Matt. 4:7 from Deut. 6:16; Matt. 4:10 a paraphrase of Deut. 6:13). By fasting forty days and forty nights he is like Moses (Matt. 4:2; compare Exod. 34:28; Deut. 9:9, 18, 25; 10:10). We see his humanity in Matthew 4:11: after the contest he is weary and receives ministration. He proves his true sonship by resisting temptation.

We see Satan as a real and malevolent person: a clever tempter who addresses a felt need (Matt. 4:3), distorts Scripture (v. 6), and offers a shortcut (vv. 8–9). He is overcome by faithfulness to Scripture.

7. What devices does the author use to communicate his point of view?

For example, sometimes he gives an explicit evaluation of characters or events (this is rare); sometimes he allows us to see contrasts between characters (for example, between the chaste Joseph and the lustful Judah, Gen. 38–39); sometimes he uses ironic foreshadowing or back reference; sometimes he omits the mention of things we would have expected.

In 1 Samuel 3, the author favors us with an explicit evaluation: "Samuel did not yet know the LORD" (3:7). He also reports God's speech a great deal, and, for a biblical author, this indicates the view that the audience should adopt. We see further that the Lord "let none of [Samuel's] words fall to the ground" (3:19) and that "the LORD revealed himself to Samuel" (3:21)—hence the "word of Samuel" that "came to all Israel" (4:1a) is in fact God's word, and reliable.

In Matthew 4:1–11, the author is explicit with πειράζω and the names of the parties. We already know what Matthew thinks of Jesus (3:17), so we resent anyone calling that into question or urging him to use his sonship for selfish purposes. We should also recognize the misuse of the psalm text.

8. What is the passage about?

Once we have answered these questions, we are in a position to summarize what the pericope is about: that is, what is the key event, what is its significance, and how does the author want his audience to think about it? The focus here is on the author's intent as embodied in the text itself—in its genre conventions, discourse features, rhetorical devices, and point of view.

The study of 1 Samuel 3 enables us to see that the author is presenting the call of Samuel to be a true prophet of God; he is to be a true prophet, never hiding any of God's word. Samuel's reliability matters because he is the one who will anoint the first two kings of Israel: Saul, who proves a failure, and David, who, with all his faults, is nevertheless the headwaters of an everlasting dynasty (2 Sam. 7). And just as the true prophet makes known God's words, the right response for faithful Israel is to heed that word with repentance, faith, and obedience.

If we study Matthew 4:1–11 in this way, we can see that the passage aims to present Jesus as the messianic king promised in the Old Testament: he is qualified to call the Gentiles to submit to his empire (Matt. 28:18–20). He is also the ideal Israel, and hence the ideal Israel*ite* (see the use of Deut. texts)—which makes him the ideal *Man* (which would contrast him to Adam).[45]

We also see Satan as the tempter, the enemy of God's purpose and people; nevertheless Jesus meets and defeats him, and this he does as the champion and representative of God's people.[46]

9. How are covenantal principles on display here?

For example, how does this passage demonstrate God's grace; or how do we see the tension between the conditionality and unconditionality of covenant participation; or how do we see divine sovereignty at work; or the success or failure of covenant succession (i.e., the promise in Gen. 17:7; 18:19); or the function of the mediatorial kingship (e.g., David's combat with Goliath)? Under this heading we should also consider the ways in which later Scripture refers to the passage we are studying. For example, the historical psalms (such as Pss. 78, 105, 106) lead us in our theological reflection on the history

45. See below, chapter 6, section E.6, which argues that this pericope about Jesus' temptation evokes Gen. 3 about Adam's temptation.

46. It is common in Christian preaching to see Jesus primarily as the believer's model in resisting temptation: "*We* should quote Scripture like *he* did." Whereas this captures some of the truth, it misses the point of the passage, which is about Jesus the champion. It also misses the important aspect of New Testament teaching on *how* to resist the evil one, as described below.

of Israel, and Paul's reference to Abraham (Rom. 4:3–5) should lead us to find a religious kinship between Christians and their forefather in the faith.[47]

Answers to these questions can provide the jumping-off point for theologically sensitive application to ourselves, whether in discerning the covenantal principles by which God deals with his people or in the examples of individuals who act faithfully or unfaithfully toward God's gracious covenant and what happens as a result.

In the case of 1 Samuel 3, we might explore how Eli's chief flaw is his failure as a father, and we might consider how diligent parenting is a crucial aspect of honoring the Lord (2:30). We might also reflect on how this is to be especially true of the priesthood of the covenant people, who are to embody covenant faithfulness for the sake of the whole people. We might also pursue the notion of a true prophet and see how important it is to discern one and listen to his words (as in the case of Jeremiah and Ezekiel, whose words are so unwelcome).

In the case of Matthew 4:1–11, themes include the Old Testament prophecies of the Messiah's rule over the Gentiles and the New Testament texts that take this up (as Rev. 11:15; Rom. 15:8–12). Christians are able to see their obedience to the Great Commission of Matthew 28:19–20 as the means by which Jesus conquers the Gentiles and incorporates them into his worldwide empire.

There is also the theme of Jesus' victory over Satan on behalf of his people. It is the "prince of the power of the air" who keeps mankind—Jews and Gentiles—in thrall and prevents them from giving themselves to Christ. As Genesis 3:15 foretells (see discussion in chapter 6 below), Jesus wins a victory over the tempter *for his people*—and therefore Christians lay hold of his strength and triumph (in the New Testament, see 1 John 3:8; Heb. 2:14–15; Col. 2:15). This is why the key to spiritual warfare in Ephesians 6:10–20 is to "be strong in the Lord and in the strength of his might," which comes from "putting on" the armor of God—and, since the way Paul describes the armor of God comes from Old Testament messianic prophecy, this is another

---

47. One must be careful, though: it does not follow that the later reference exhausts all the possible applications of the earlier one. For example, the fact that Heb. 2:6–8 uses Ps. 8:4–6 does not require us to conclude that the psalm is exclusively messianic; instead the psalm lends itself to the context of Hebrews because Jesus is an ideal representative of human nature.

way of saying "putting on Christ/the new man" (as in Eph. 4:24; Rom. 13:12, 14; Gal. 3:27; Col. 3:10, 12; 1 Thess. 5:8).

E. Allusions, Echoes, and Reverberations

In connection with the last expositional question, we should comment on criteria for recognizing how the passage we are studying uses earlier texts and how later texts use our text. This is an important part of exegesis, for at least two reasons. First, in view of the communication model I have advocated, we must note how competent readers have taken our text, as well as what aspects of their shared experience of the world the author operates on. Second, the biblical material is self-consciously in development, with its parts in organic relationship to one another: Moses foretells a line of prophets (Deut. 18:15–22) but also requires that their message be in harmony with his (Deut. 13:1–5).

One scholar who has tried to posit criteria for detecting these uses is Richard Hays, in his study entitled *Echoes of Scripture in the Letters of Paul*.[48] He distinguishes an "echo" from an "allusion," but the distinction is primarily in how obvious the "intertextual reference" is. He offers seven tests for weighing claims about such references:

(1) *Availability.* Was the proposed source of the echo available to the author and/or original readers?

(2) *Volume.* The volume of an echo is determined primarily by the degree of explicit repetition of words or syntactical patterns; how loudly does it evoke the alleged precursor?

(3) *Recurrence.* How often does Paul elsewhere cite or allude to the same scriptural passage?

(4) *Thematic coherence.* How well does the alleged echo fit into the line of argument Paul is developing?

(5) *Historical plausibility.* Could Paul have intended the alleged meaning effect? Could his readers have understood it?

(6) *History of interpretation.* Have other readers, both critical and precritical, heard the same echoes?

48. Richard Hays, *Echoes of Scripture in the Letters of Paul* (New Haven: Yale, 1989), especially 25–33.

(7) *Satisfaction.* With or without clear confirmation from the other criteria listed here, does the proposed reading make sense?

This list does not give as much weight as I would to explicit verbal echoes as the first criterion, nor does it indicate where the burden of proof lies when such explicit echoes are missing. However, it does serve as a place to begin, and we can benefit from the criteria.

A good example that shows how important it is to have criteria comes in Calum Carmichael's book *The Story of Creation*, which argues that the seven creation days of Genesis underlie the first five chapters of John.[49] This book raises all manner of questions, especially about what constitutes a reference or evocation—but Carmichael never addresses that and hence never provides criteria by which we may evaluate his proposals.

Carmichael's book shows why we should give priority to the criterion of *volume*; namely, to look for vocabulary and syntax (the Masoretic Text for Old Testament echoes, and Greek versions for New Testament evocations of the Old Testament).[50] Of course there will be times when we must appeal to the evocation of ideas, and we do best when we give reasons for our parallels.

These chapters from Genesis are a special case: to speak of what biblical materials they use is to make a judgment about the date of the materials. And further, the impression we get is that the influence is *from* Genesis *to* other texts. So in this study I will examine ways in which the material from Genesis has been taken up into other texts. Rather than distinguish between citations, allusions, and echoes, I will simply refer to reverberations.

The texts in which I will look for echoes are the rest of the Old Testament, intertestamental Jewish literature (especially the Apocrypha, Philo, and Josephus), and the New Testament. This reflects my interest in the Christian appropriation of the Old Testament as Scripture, of course.

Students of the New Testament have considered this matter, but from the other end of the stick: namely, starting with the New Testa-

---

49. Calum M. Carmichael, *The Story of Creation: Its Origin and Its Interpretation in Philo and the Fourth Gospel* (Ithaca: Cornell University Press, 1996).

50. The New Testament authors commonly use the Septuagint. In a few places, however, the New Testament text seems to use its own rendering of the Hebrew: for example, Eph. 4:30 (Isa. 63:10); Jas. 1:11 (Isa. 40:6); and John 1:14 seems to evoke Exod. 34:6.

ment itself. Indeed, students of the Old Testament seem to have left it to the New Testament students; Wernberg-Möller put it this way:[51]

> So the use of the Old Testament in the New is the concern of the New Testament scholar, and not of the Old Testament scholar; the latter should not go to the New Testament, except in isolated instances for the purpose of textual criticism, and should never for a moment forget that, as far as he is concerned, it is the original meaning of the text that matters, and not the use which was made of it in the New Testament.

This author is clear that "a theological task along the lines of Christian systematic theology can be accomplished in the case of the Old Testament taken as a whole only by imposing upon the latter interpretations different from the plain meaning of the text—interpretations which are either typological or allegorical."

There are several reasons why we should reject Wernberg-Möller's strictures. First, it fails to acknowledge the role of considering what other readers have seen: that is, what I think to be the plain meaning of the text may be plain to me, but I may be wrong if a competent reader sees otherwise. Second, it presupposes that later authors are unreliable—and thus reflects the Enlightenment uncritically. Third, it assumes what it ought to prove: both that the Old Testament is inconsistent in itself and that the only New Testament uses are typological and allegorical (and why are these necessarily contrary to the original intent?).

Even though this attitude cannot stand careful examination, it is nevertheless firmly engrained. I will venture into this territory, allowing that it is just possible that reading the New Testament in the light of the Old Testament may shed interpretive light on the New Testament as well as on the Old Testament.

---

51. P. Wernberg-Möller, "Is There an Old Testament Theology?" *Hibbert Journal* 59 (1960–61): 21–29, cited from 29.

3

GENESIS 1–4 IN ITS
LITERARY CONTEXT

I n order to study these chapters in their current context, we must first clarify their literary relation to the rest of the Pentateuch, to which these chapters are the front end. At this point I am only setting out the *literary* context: addressing what communicative impact this will have, what historical claims it makes, and what authorship conclusions we should draw. I shall save for the chapters that follow my detailed examinations.

It is commonly held that the Pentateuch has a composition history: namely, someone or some group produced it by stitching together materials from a variety of sources. These sources may or may not be compatible with each other, though often incompatibility is a criterion of separate origin of the sources. Nevertheless, the form in which we have it has some kind of unity—at least the one or group who gave us the final edition thought so.

It should not need any argument to show that the Pentateuch is about the Mosaic covenant. The events of the exodus lead up to Israel at Sinai receiving the covenant from God (Exod. 19–20), and the rest of Exodus, Leviticus, and Numbers spell out the obligations and privileges of the covenant. Deuteronomy presents itself as the speeches of Moses as Israel is on the verge of crossing the Jordan to take the promised land. The purpose of the Mosaic covenant is to constitute Israel, who are already the people of God and heirs of his promises to Abraham, as what Josephus called a "theocracy":[1] that is, the covenant specified the operations of the civil and social as well as the religious spheres; we might call it a "church-state nexus." This will be the context in which the people of Israel are to live out their privilege as the people of God.

The Mosaic covenant carries forward the covenants made with the patriarchs. The pattern we find is that each successive covenant *builds on* (rather than *replaces*) those before it. In Genesis 12, 15, and 17 we find the basic promises that God made to Abraham: land, offspring, blessing, privilege. The Mosaic covenant does not replace these but provides a setting in which they are to be realized; for example, Genesis 17 institutes circumcision as the required rite of entry into the visible people of God, and Exodus 12:44–49 make it a requirement for participation in the Passover meal. Hence later writers speak of God's "covenant*s*" (for example, Wis. 18:22; Sir. 44:12, 18; 2 Macc. 8:15; Rom. 9:4; Eph. 2:12), seeing all of them as applicable.[2]

We are now in a position to see how the whole Pentateuch hangs together, if we start from Genesis 12: there we have the call of Abram to be God's covenant partner, and the following chapters describe the ups and downs of his immediate descendants, leading to their sojourn in Egypt. But the Pentateuch begins in Genesis 1; how do these earlier chapters factor in?

The best way to answer that is to consider the mission statement that the Pentateuch assigns to Israel, Exodus 19:3–6 (as Israel has just come to Sinai):

> [3]while Moses went up to God. The LORD called to him out of the mountain, saying, "Thus you shall say to the house of Jacob, and tell the people of Israel: [4]You yourselves have seen what I did to the

---

1. Josephus, *Against Apion* 2.165, apparently coining the term θεοκρατία, which he describes as a polity that attributes its authority and power to God.

2. Reformed systematic theology, as represented in the Westminster Confession of Faith 7:6, speaks of a single covenant of grace with different administrations. This need not be wrong, but we should at least recognize that the Bible itself does not speak this way. Harold Hoehner, *Ephesians: An Exegetical Commentary* (Grand Rapids: Baker, 2002), 357–59, misunderstands the force of the plural in Eph. 2:12, apparently because he did not consider the intertestamental usage. Hoehner thinks that the Mosaic covenant is left out of Paul's reference, but this makes no sense in light of this usage—nor does it do full justice to Paul's use of Pentateuch language for Gentiles, such as "strangers and aliens."

Egyptians, and how I bore you on eagles' wings and brought you to myself. ⁵Now therefore, if you will indeed obey my voice and keep my covenant, you shall be my treasured possession among all peoples, for all the earth is mine; ⁶and you shall be to me a kingdom of priests and a holy nation. These are the words that you shall speak to the people of Israel."

We have here the theme of election to privilege: Israel is to be the Lord's "treasured possession among all peoples," at the same time that "all the earth"—and hence all its peoples—"is mine." There is also election to service: Israel is to be "a kingdom of priests," which is best taken to mean that they will serve to mediate the knowledge of the true God to the other peoples (see also Gen. 12:3; 18:18; 22:18; 26:4; 28:14).[3] We further see the character of the Lord, especially his power ("what I did to the Egyptians," whom you reckoned so powerful) and his faithfulness (the Lord kept his promises to Abraham in the way he dealt with the Egyptians and brought his people out, Gen. 15:13–14).

Thematically, then, Genesis 1–11 set the stage for this mission of Israel to live as God's treasured people and thereby to be the vehicle of blessing to the rest of the world. There is one God, who made all that there is, and who made man in his own image (Gen. 1); he entered into a special relationship with the first human beings, a relationship that was broken (Gen. 2–3). Mankind began to spread over all the earth (Gen. 4–5). The stories of the flood and the tower of Babel have similar import: all mankind is accountable to the one God who made them and not to any fancy of their own devising, and God is fully capable of bringing his judgment down on any people anywhere. But judgment is really only the backcloth: all mankind belongs to him, and the Pentateuch focuses on God's merciful and persistent efforts at recovering not just one ethnic group but the whole of mankind.

Thus the Pentateuch is both particular and universal: particular with its stress on the Mosaic covenant, which is for Israel, and uni-

---

3. See, for example, C. F. Keil, *The Second Book of Moses (Exodus)* (Grand Rapids: Eerdmans, 1981), 98: "As a priest is a mediator between God and man, so Israel was called to be the vehicle of the knowledge and salvation of God to the nations of the earth." Compare also the Israeli commentaries of Cassuto and Hakham at this phrase: Umberto Cassuto, *A Commentary on the Book of Exodus* (Jerusalem: Magnes, 1967), 227, and A. Hakham, *Sefer Shemot* (Exodus, Da'at Miqra; Jerusalem: Mossad Harav Kook, 1991), שׁוֹא. The Septuagint of this phrase appears in 1 Pet. 2:9, but it is not something new for Christians.

versal in putting this covenant in the context of God's larger plan for the whole human race.

Now consider the architecture of Genesis itself. It is well known that the expression "these are the *generations*" (using the Hebrew word *toledot*) structures Genesis, appearing at Genesis 2:4; 5:1; 6:9; 10:1; 11:10, 27; 25:12, 19; 36:1, 9; 37:2, and in each case introducing the material that follows. Alexander observes that these headings serve two functions:[4]

> First, they are like chapter or section headings in modern books. Some of them introduce major narrative sections, indicating a new stage in the development of the plot. . . .
>
> Second, the *toledot* headings function like a zoom lens on a camera. They focus the reader's attention on a particular individual and his immediate children.

Hence we may say that, generally speaking, they mark things related to the plot as it moves through the characters and their descendants.

If we look at Genesis this way, we see immediately that the first pericope, Genesis 1:1–2:3, stands prior to the first of these: it is a sort of prologue to the whole. Hence it is not surprising that its narrative style, which is exalted and formulaic (as I shall discuss in the next chapter) is different from that of the rest of the book, which is more like what we find in the rest of the Old Testament narrative books.

As I have indicated, the question of authorship must await the details. But at this point a distinction from the literary theorists will supply us with interpretive help. The distinction is between the two kinds of authors and audiences: the *real* and the *implied*. The real author is the person who actually composed or edited the final form of the work, and the real audience is the one for whom the real author wrote. The implied author, however, may or may not be the same person, and the implied audience may or may not be the same as the real audience. A good reader will try to put himself into the sandals of the implied reader.

For example, the real author of *The Lord of the Rings* was an Oxford don named J. R. R. Tolkien, but the implied author is someone who found the *Red Book of Westmarch*. Likewise the real audience was the modern Western world after World War II, while the implied

---

4. T. Desmond Alexander, *From Paradise to the Promised Land: An Introduction to the Pentateuch* (Grand Rapids: Baker, 2002), 102.

audience are folk who live in a world in which hobbits were "more numerous formerly than they are today."[5]

The Pentateuch has Moses as its implied author, and the generation who followed him out of Egypt as its implied audience. This is the uniform testimony of the other authors: for example, Joshua 1:7–8; 8:30–35; 1 Kings 8:53, 56; 2 Kings 14:6; Nehemiah 1:8; 8:1, 14; Malachi 4:4; Daniel 9:11, 13; 1 Esdras 1:6, 11; Matthew 19:7–8. This means we read the books best when we read *as if* they record the words of Moses to Israel.

In the chapters that follow I will make use of these observations with a view toward reading Genesis 1–4 with ancient literary competence.

---

5. J. R. R. Tolkien, *The Fellowship of the Ring: Being the First Part of the Lord of the Rings* (Boston: Houghton Mifflin, 1965), 10.

4

GENESIS 1:1–2:3:
THE CREATION WEEK

The opening pericope of Genesis—indeed, of the whole Bible—describes God's work of making the world and everything in it, in six days of work followed by a Sabbath.

Many refer to the first two pericopes of Genesis as the creation accounts, meaning that they see the two accounts as giving different (contradictory or complementary, depending on the author's perspective) narratives of the creation. From this will follow such questions as whether the final editor of Genesis used sources for his work and how he used them; what literary genre or genres the two narratives employ; what significance the change in divine name (from "God" in the first narrative to "the LORD God" in the second) conveys; and whether history is a proper category for discussing these chapters.

These two pericopes have played a major part in science and religion controversies as well: that is, does the text claim anything about the nature of the six workdays, and does this lead to a claim about the age of the earth and the development of life?

The advantage of the discourse-oriented literary approach that I am advocating is that it gives us a critical procedure for addressing these questions without using them as the focal point of our investigation. That is, we have a way of examining the literary features of the text to see how they convey a message with which the text calls us to cooperate—and to do this well, we must allow that these matters of controversy need not be the main burden of the text.

A. Pericope Boundary, Structure, and Genre

As we consider the first pericope, we immediately notice that the chapter boundary is not a good guide to the pericope boundary: Genesis 1 ends with the sixth day being complete, but Genesis 2:1–3 goes on to describe the seventh day of that extraordinary week.

The Masoretic Text has an end-of-paragraph marker (פ) after Genesis 2:3, which would lead us to see the first pericope as 1:1–2:3: that is, the narrative ends once it finishes describing the seventh day.

A large number of scholars, however, take Genesis 2:4a ("These are the generations of the heavens and the earth when they were created") as the conclusion of the pericope, arguing that "the heavens and the earth" and "created" point us back to 1:1 ("In the beginning, God created the heavens and the earth"), and round off the account. By this reckoning, 2:4b ("in the day that the LORD God made the earth and the heavens") begins the sentence that runs through 2:7 and hence is part of the setting for the forming of the first man (see NRSV). Hence verse 2:4b introduces the new divine name, "the LORD God" (Hebrew יהוה אלהים, *yhwh 'elohîm*), which contrasts to the simple "God" (אלהים, *'elohîm*) of the first pericope.[1]

A small number of others suppose that the first pericope contains all of Genesis 2:4, arguing that we should not break 2:4 apart and that the wording of the verse points us primarily to the first pericope.[2]

In my judgment, the features of the text decisively favor taking Genesis 2:3 as the end of the pericope. To begin with, we notice that "these are the generations of" (אלה תולדות, *'elleh tôledôt*) is a recurring feature in Genesis: besides 2:4, it appears in 5:1;[3] 6:9; 10:1; 11:10, 27; 25:12, 19; 36:1, 9; 37:2.[4] In these other cases, it functions

---

1. Many who take this approach argue that the preference for the divine name is a feature of the different sources behind Genesis (P and J)—though many others do not.

2. See, for example, A. Niccacci, "Analysis of Biblical Narrative," in *Biblical Hebrew and Discourse Linguistics*, ed. R. D. Bergen (Dallas: Summer Institute of Linguistics, 1994), 175–98, at 183–84, though he gives no critical discussion.

3. Actually, here it is a slight variant: זה ספר תולדת אדם (*zeh seper tôledôt 'adam*, "this is the book of the generations of Adam").

4. See also Num. 3:1; Ruth 4:18; 1 Chr. 1:29.

as a heading that introduces new material.[5] We would need a good reason, then, to find it serving another function here.

Next, we notice that the structure of Genesis 2:4 is highly patterned, which tells against any effort to divide the verse. The chiastic structure is widely recognized:[6]

These are the generations
   a   of the heavens
   b   and the earth
   c   when they were created
   c´   in the day that the LORD God made
   b´   the earth
   a´ and the heavens

The terms *heavens* (a) and *earth* (b) are in reverse order in the second line, while the time expressions (c and c´) correspond syntactically: בהבראם (*behibbare'am*, "when they were created") is a preposition with an infinitive construct, and ביום עשות (*beyôm 'asôt*, " in the day [he] made") is an idiomatic time phrase with an infinitive construct.[7]

If we find a chiasmus of two corresponding elements (a-b // b´-a´), we still need to show that it was authorial art rather than chance that produced it. When there are three corresponding elements as we have here, however, there is rarely any need to show that it was art. Typically, the effect of a chiasmus is to have the reader see its parts in some kind of unity, with the context allowing us to infer just what kind of unity the author has in view. Since in my judgment Genesis 2:4 belongs to the following pericope—or serves as a hinge between the first and second pericopes—in the next chapter I will propose a way of reading it that cooperates with this authorial intent.

It is certainly true that the use of ברא (*bara'*, "create") in Genesis 2:4a, as well as the mention of "the heavens and the earth," links up with 1:1; it is equally true that the new divine name in the second line ("the LORD God") links up with the material that follows. However, in

---

5. This is also true of Num. 3:1 and Ruth 4:18. The case of 1 Chr. 1:29 is more complicated, since the section heading is verse 28 ("the sons of Abraham: Isaac and Ishmael"). Then verse 29a continues with אלה תלדותם (*'elleh tôledôtam*, "these are their genealogies"). If we take verse 29a as the end of the introductory sentence in verse 28, we then have a clear introduction to the genealogical material that follows, in which case this verse fits our pattern as well.

6. For bibliography, see my "Discourse Analysis and the Interpretation of Gen. 2:4–7," *Westminster Theological Journal* 61 (1999): 269–76, at 271 n. 8.

7. Compare BDB 400a, s.v. יום 7d.

the next chapter I will argue that we can recognize these links without breaking the chiasmus apart; I will also offer a grammatically sound reading of 2:5–7. Hence these links are not in themselves sufficient reason to ignore the chiasmus.

I conclude, therefore, that the text as we have it makes the first pericope Genesis 1:1–2:3.

The structure of this pericope is well known: six workdays followed by a seventh-day Sabbath. Further, the refrain ("and there was evening, and there was morning, the nth day," Gen. 1:5, 8, 13, 19, 23, 31) clearly indicates the end of each workday, and its absence from the seventh day is so striking that an adequate reading must account for it.

What is not so clear, however, is the function of Genesis 1:1–2: does it begin the first day or stand outside of the days? And if the latter, where does the time reference fit in with the days?

To answer this, we begin by noticing the verb tenses: Genesis 1:1–2 has four clauses, none of which contains a *wayyiqtol* verb. The first clause, verse 1, has its verb in the perfect (בָּרָא, *bara'*, "he created"); while the next three clauses are all stative: verse 2a uses the perfect of "to be" (הָיְתָה, *hayetâ*, "it was"), verse 2b is a verbless clause ("was" is supplied for translation), and verse 2c has a participle describing ongoing action (מְרַחֶפֶת, *merakhepet*, "was hovering"). Verse 3 gives us the first *wayyiqtol* in the account (וַיֹּאמֶר, *wayyo'mer*, "and he said") and begins the main sequence of events, a main sequence indicated by the *wayyiqtol* form in the rest of the pericope.

In fact, each of the other workdays begins with the same *wayyiqtol* verb: that is, each workday begins with God saying something, in each case expressing a wish.[8] It follows from this that we should expect the first workday to begin with God's speech in Genesis 1:3, and this makes good sense in view of the clause types.

Since the backbone of a narrative, as we have already discussed, uses the *wayyiqtol*, and since Genesis 1:1–2 does not use the *wayyiqtol*, we conclude that these verses stand outside the main stream of the narrative. The most common usage of the clause types that we find in verses 1–2 is to provide background material for the narrative. More specifically, the perfect of verse 1 ("created") may be either an event that precedes the main storyline or else a summary of the entire pericope;

---

8. The wish is denoted by the volitional form, which is clearly distinct from the imperfect in Gen. 1:3, 6, 14, and 24. In verses 9 and 20 the verb uses a form that could be either volitional or imperfect, and we infer volitional from the analogy of the other days.

the stative clauses of verse 2 describe the conditions as the first day gets under way. As I argue below (section C.1), the perfect in verse 1 is more likely an event that precedes the storyline than a summary of the account. This suits the syntax of the clauses and the theological point that later writers found here a doctrine of creation from nothing.

All of this enables us to see the following structure in this pericope:

1:1–2	preface: initial creation event, and conditions of the earth just before day 1 gets under way
1:3–5	day 1: light and darkness
1:6–8	day 2: sea and sky
1:9–13	day 3: land, sea, vegetation
1:14–19	day 4: light-bearers in the heavens
1:20–23	day 5: sea animals and flying creatures
1:24–31	day 6: land animals and humans
2:1–3	day 7: God's Sabbath (no refrain)

Finally, we can identify the genre. We have called the passage a narrative, and this is proper because of the prominent use of the *wayyiqtol* to denote successive events. But we must acknowledge that this is an unusual narrative indeed: not only because of the unique events described and the lack of other actors besides God, but also because of the highly patterned way of telling it all.[9] The material that begins in Genesis 2:5 is much more like "ordinary" prose narrative even though those events are also quite exceptional.

Other features of this narrative draw our attention as well: first, the narrative is exceedingly broad stroke in its description. That is, in Genesis 1:12 we find plant life falling into two categories, small plants and "trees"; and in 1:24 land animals falling into three categories, "livestock" (domesticable stock animals), "creeping things" (small creepy-crawlies such as mice, lizards, and spiders), and "beasts of the earth" (larger wild animals).[10] One has to believe that the first users of this text, had they been looking for a useful taxonomy, would have wanted some-

9. The Greek author called "Longinus" takes features of this text (paraphrasing the Greek of 1:3, 9) as examples of "sublime" style (*On the Sublime*, 9:9). Since Longinus uses the aorist *middle* of γίνομαι, while the Septuagint uses the aorist *passive*, it may be that Longinus is responding to some account like that of Josephus (who also uses the middle, *Antiquities* 1.27).

10. For the exegetical details, see discussion below.

thing more specific—unless taxonomic utility was not the purpose or proper use of the text. No single species, other than man, gets its proper Hebrew name; nor do we learn *how* the earth "brought forth vegetation" or how the animals appeared in their respective environments. Similarly, in 1:16 the sun and moon are called by unusual names, the "greater light" and the "lesser light," names not otherwise used in the Old Testament.[11] Finally, consider the "expanse" in verse 6, which seems to be a rhetorically "high" name for the heavens or sky.[12]

All of this leads us to conclude that the genre of this pericope is what we may call exalted prose narrative. This name for the genre will serve us in several ways. First, it acknowledges that we are dealing with prose narrative, and thus its purposes will be related to other uses of prose narrative—which will include the making of truth claims about the world in which we live. Second, by calling it exalted, we are recognizing that when we come to examine the author's truth claims, we must not impose a "literalistic" hermeneutic on the text. Further, to call it exalted points us away from ordinary narration and leads us to suppose that its proper function extends well beyond its information to the attitudes that it fosters. Finally, this name is far better than the term some use, "poetry," since that term is ambiguous; if we say Hebrew poetry we might go on to speak of parallelism, which is absent.[13]

B. Translation and Notes

Preface (1:1–2)

¹In the beginning, God created the heavens and the earth.[14]
²The earth was without form and void,[15] and darkness was over the

11. Psalm 136:7–9 clearly echoes our pericope; there the author speaks of the "great lights" (v. 7; אורים גדלים ['ôrîm gedolîm]; compare Gen. 1:16, המארת הגדלים [hamme'ôrôt haggedolîm]). In the reverberations discussion below (E.1) we will see more of how the psalm reflects the Genesis text.

12. Elsewhere used in this sense in Pss. 19:1; 150:1; and Dan. 12:3. The "expanse" also appears in Ezekiel (Ezek. 1, 10), as part of the prophet's near-ineffable vision.

13. Currid, 38–42, discusses these questions as if the only options are "poetry" and "(ordinary) prose narrative," but the idea of "exalted prose narrative" solves the problems.

14. On the proper translation and interpretation of this verse, see section C.1, "Genesis 1:1 and creation from nothing."

15. This is not an expression for "chaos" but rather refers to the earth as "an unproductive and uninhabited place," as argued in David Tsumura, *The Earth and the Waters in Genesis 1*

face of the deep.[16] And the Spirit of God[17] was hovering[18] over the face of the waters.

Day one (1:3–5)

[3]And God said, "Let there be light,"[19] and there was light.[20] [4]And God saw that the light was good. And God separated the light from the darkness. [5]God called the light Day, and the darkness he called Night.[21] And there was evening and there was morning, the first day.[22]

Day two (1:6–8)

[6]And God said, "Let there be an expanse[23] in the midst of the waters, and let it separate the waters from the waters." [7]And God

---

and 2: A Linguistic Investigation (Sheffield: Sheffield Academic Press, 1989), 41–43. The two terms appear together in Isa. 34:11 and Jer. 4:23, where they describe a land that has been returned to an unproductive and uninhabited condition because of God's judgment.

16. The Hebrew rendered "the deep" is תהום (*tehôm*), which some connect with Akkadian *Tiamat*, a chaos deity whom Marduk fights, and from whose corpse he makes the world in *Enuma elish*. See Tsumura, *The Earth and the Waters*, 45–47; and Alexander Heidel, *The Babylonian Genesis* (Chicago: University of Chicago Press, 1951), 98–101, where this idea is refuted. The Hebrew word simply means "the depths of the sea."

17. This is the usual interpretation of the expression רוח אלהים (*rûakh 'elohîm*). Attempts to see it otherwise, such as Wenham, 16–17, who takes רוח as simply "wind" ("wind of God"; cf. New Jerusalem Bible, NRSV), or those which take "of God" as an intensifier ("mighty wind"; cf. NEB), all overlook contextual factors that support the conventional rendering. These would include (1) the fact that we are not considering the meaning of רוח by itself or of אלהים as a genitive, but the *composite* expression רוח אלהים, whose consistent Old Testament usage is "Spirit of God"; (2) the verb מרחפת (*merakhepet*, "hovering"/"brooding") more properly takes "Spirit" as its subject than "wind"; and (3) the association of the Spirit and the dove (a bird, which "hovers" or "broods") in, e.g., Matt. 3:16.

18. This verb, the Piel of רחף (*r-kh-p*), also appears in Deut. 32:11 for a mother bird "fluttering" over her nest. The Syriac cognate, in the equivalent Pael theme, secures the sense here.

19. In 2 Cor. 4:6 Paul paraphrases this (perhaps using the Septuagint): the same kind of power displayed here has been at work in the hearts of believers to deliver them from their spiritual blindness to the light of the gospel (4:3–4).

20. This need not denote the creation of light as such; see section C.3.

21. The chiasmus *called-light-darkness-called* expresses simultaneous action; compare Shemaryahu Talmon, "The Presentation of Synchroneity and Simultaneity in Biblical Narrative," in *Studies in Hebrew Narrative Art*, ed. J. Heinemann and S. Werses (Scripta Hierosolymitana; Jerusalem: Magnes, 1978), 9–26, at 11.

22. See the extra note, "The proper rendering of the refrain" (section C.2).

23. ESV margin: "Or a *canopy*; also in verses 7, 8, 14, 15, 17, 20." See BDB, 956a; Delitzsch, 85–86. The word translated "expanse," רקיע (*raqîa'*), is related to a verb that means "to beat out" or "to spread out" (cf. Job 37:18); hence the word here conveys the

made the expanse and separated the waters that were under the expanse from the waters that were above the expanse. And it was so. ⁸And God called the expanse Heaven.²⁴ And there was evening and there was morning, the second day.

Day three (1:9–13)

⁹And God said, "Let the waters under the heavens be gathered together into one place, and let the dry land appear." And it was so. ¹⁰God called the dry land Earth,²⁵ and the waters that were gathered together he called Seas. And God saw that it was good.

¹¹And God said, "Let the earth sprout vegetation,²⁶ plants²⁷ yielding seed, and fruit trees bearing fruit in which is their seed, each according to its kind,²⁸ on the earth." And it was so. ¹²The earth brought forth vegetation, plants yielding seed according to their own kinds, and trees bearing fruit in which is their seed, each

---

idea of the atmosphere "as the semi-spherical vault of heaven stretched over the earth and its water" (Delitzsch, 86). We could translate it "vault" or "canopy" if we wanted. We have here a prime example of *phenomenological description*; that is, things are described as they appear, and not "scientifically." (That this is clearly *not* a description of a "vapor canopy" or cloud cover as such, is seen from the use of this term in Ps. 19:2 and Dan. 12:3, denoting what we see now; and the fact that in Gen. 1:8 God names the extended surface "sky," with which we are familiar.) Note further the development of this phenomenological description in 1:14–18. The traditional English "firmament" comes from *firmamentum*, the Latin rendering of the Septuagint στερέωμα, "firm or solid thing." Sir. 43:1, 8 describes it as a "clear" solid; Philo, *On the Creation* 36, tells us it is called "firmament" because this body is by nature "firm" (στερεόν). The Hebrew does not require Philo's level of literalism, however. See further chapter 10, section C, "World Picture, Worldview, and Good Faith Communication."

24. ESV margin: "Or *Sky*; also in verses 9, 14, 15, 17, 20, 26, 28, 30; 2:1." Note that Hebrew שָׁמַיִם (*shamayim*) was more generally "heavens" (in contrast to earth) in 1:1; while here it is more specifically "sky," as is seen by the thing referred to. Similarly אֶרֶץ (*'erets*) in verses 10–12 is "land," while in verses 1–2 it was "earth." Recognizing this relieves us of the problems in Paul Seely, "The Geographical Meaning of 'Earth' and 'Seas' in Genesis 1:10," *Westminster Theological Journal* 59 (1997): 231–55, who takes אֶרֶץ as the entire earth, a flat disk of ancient conception.

25. ESV margin: "Or *Land*; also in verses 11, 12, 22, 24, 25, 26, 28, 30; 2:1." This is similar to what happens with שָׁמַיִם (*shamayim*, "heaven/sky").

26. As Delitzsch, 90, points out, the grammatical construction (as well as the Masoretic accent) indicates that דֶּשֶׁא (*deshe'*, "vegetation") is the general term, while עֵשֶׂב (*'eseb*, "[small] plants") and עֵץ (*'ets*, "trees") are the particular kinds of vegetation. That is, some of the vegetation is "plants" (the KJV "grass" is too specific and potentially misleading), that is, low vegetation; and some is fruit trees, that is, large, woody vegetation. These are obviously representatives, not exhaustively listed. It makes the most sense to suppose that the author chose his representatives because of their relevance to his intended audience.

27. Or *small plants*; also in verses 12, 29.

28. See extra note, "The meaning of '*kind*' " (section C.4).

according to its kind. And God saw that it was good. [13]And there was evening and there was morning, the third day.

Day four (1:14–19)

[14]And God said, "Let there be lights in the expanse of the heavens to separate the day from the night. And let them be for signs and for seasons,[29] and[30] for days and years, [15]and let them be lights in the expanse of the heavens to give light upon the earth." And it was so. [16]And God made[31] the two great lights—the greater light to rule the day and the lesser light to rule the night—and the stars.[32] [17]And God set them in the expanse of the heavens to give light on the earth, [18]to rule over the day and over the night, and to separate the light from the darkness. And God saw that it was good. [19]And there was evening and there was morning, the fourth day.

Day five (1:20–23)

[20]And God said, "Let the waters swarm with swarms of living creatures,[33] and let birds[34] fly above the earth across the expanse

---

29. ESV margin: "Or *appointed times*." It is possible that this word מוֹעֵד (*mô'ed*, "appointed time") simply refers to the seasons of the year; but more likely (as Kiel, יי, notes) it has the more specific nuance "appointed (liturgical) time" (as the word has in Exod. 13:10 etc.); see further David J. Rudolph, "Festivals in Genesis 1:14," *Tyndale Bulletin* 54, no. 2 (2003): 23–40. From this it follows that the "days and years" being marked are the days and years of the liturgical calendar. If this is accepted, then it becomes likely further that "signs and appointed times" is a hendiadys meaning "signs marking appointed (liturgical) times."

30. Probably a *waw*-explicative: "*namely* for (marking) days and years."

31. ESV margin: "Or *fashioned*." A matter for discussion is whether this must refer to creating the lights, and in section C.3 below I argue that it need not. Rather, the stress is on God appointing the lights to their task of marking the liturgical calendar for man.

32. It seems likely that this passage, with its mention of sun, moon, and stars, as well as the varieties of animals, birds, and fish, provided Paul with the framework for his discussion in 1 Cor. 15:39–41.

33. It is difficult to give a good literal translation of this term (נֶפֶשׁ חַיָּה, *nepesh khayyâ*, ESV "living creature": see also Gen. 1:21, 24, 30; 2:7, 19) and still have elegant English: "living animated being" might capture the nuances. Delitzsch, 94, points out that since a נֶפֶשׁ (*nepesh*, often rendered "soul") animates a body, the expression denotes "animated material beings, bodies having souls." Perhaps we might take this as "animal"; and in 2:7 we shall see that man is one of them.

34. ESV margin: "Or *flying things*; see Lev. 11:19–20." Traditionally it is rendered "birds," and perhaps that is the correct referent. But the word (Hebrew עוֹף ['*ôp*]) just means "flying thing" and can denote other flying creatures, such as insects and bats (as in Lev. 11:19–20); hence the ESV note.

of the heavens." [21]So God created the great sea creatures[35] and every living creature that moves, with which the waters swarm, according to their kinds, and every winged bird according to its kind. And God saw that it was good. [22]And God blessed them, saying, "Be fruitful and multiply and fill the waters in the seas, and let birds multiply on the earth." [23]And there was evening and there was morning, the fifth day.

Day six (1:24–31)

[24]And God said, "Let the earth bring forth living creatures according to their kinds—livestock and creeping things and beasts of the earth according to their kinds." And it was so. [25]And God made the beasts of the earth according to their kinds and the livestock according to their kinds, and everything that creeps on the ground according to its kind. And God saw that it was good.

[26]Then God said, "Let us[36] make man[37] in our image, after our likeness. And let them have dominion[38] over the fish of the sea and over the birds of the heavens and over the livestock and over all the earth and over every creeping thing that creeps on the earth."

> [27]So God created man in his own image,
> in the image of God he created him;
> male and female he created them.

[28]And God blessed them. And God said to them, "Be fruitful and multiply and fill the earth and subdue it, and have dominion over the fish of the sea and over the birds of the heavens and over

---

35. Wenham's "great sea monsters" makes them sound like mythical beasts. Others simply use (as G. S. Cansdale, in *NBD*, 43) "giant marine animals." The word is תנין (*tannîn*), cognate to a term that appears in Ugaritic. In chapter 9, section A, I shall consider whether the passage is making any comment on its surrounding cultures. Be that as it may, in this account the emphasis is on creatures that the Israelites might have some experience with; as Heidel, *Babylonian Genesis*, 104, argues, here it refers to "such sea monsters as the whale and the shark."

36. See discussion in section C.5 below, "Genesis 1 and the Trinity."

37. ESV margin: "The Hebrew word for *man* (*adam*) is the generic term for humanity and becomes the proper name Adam." Richard Hess, "Genesis 1–2 and Recent Studies of Ancient Texts," *Science and Christian Belief* 7 (1995): 147, points out that this term אדם (*'adam*, "man") can be either "human" (as it is here), or "man" as distinct from woman. See further my comments at 2:7.

38. Note that the phrase *have dominion* is different from that of 1:16–18, *rule*.

every living thing that moves on the earth." [29]And God said, "Behold, I have given[39] you every plant yielding seed that is on the face of all the earth, and every tree with seed in its fruit. You shall have them for food. [30]And to every beast of the earth and to every bird of the heavens and to everything that creeps on the earth, everything that has the breath of life,[40] I have given every green plant for food." And it was so. [31]And God saw everything that he had made, and behold, it was very good. And there was evening and there was morning, the sixth day.

Day seven (2:1–3)

[1]Thus the heavens and the earth were finished, and all the host of them.[41] [2]And on the seventh day God finished[42] his work[43] that he had done, and he rested[44] on the seventh day from all his work that he had done. [3]So God blessed the seventh day and made it holy, because on it God rested from all his work that he had done in creation.

39. As Max Rogland, *Alleged Non-Past Uses of Qatal in Classical Hebrew* (Assen: Royal Van Gorcum, 2003), 114 n. 154, notes, this is likely a performative use of the perfect: "Behold, I hereby give. . . ." (See also Paul Joüon, *A Grammar of Biblical Hebrew*, trans./ rev. Takamitsu Muraoka; Subsidia bibilica 14 [Rome: Pontifical Biblical Institute Press, 1991], §112f, g).

40. In place of "everything that has the breath of life," it might be better to say, "everything in which is life." The Hebrew has, "to every beast of the earth and to every bird of the heavens and to everything that creeps on the earth, in which is a חיה נפש [*living soul*, see note on Gen. 1:20]." Thus the phrase *everything that has the breath of life* further describes the land animals and birds, rather than extending the categories.

41. The "host" denotes the inhabitants of the land and sky that the account has just described: it describes them as if they were an ordered array (witness the Septuagint rendering here, κόσμος "orderly arrangement"). The "heavenly host," which some think of, do not even come into this narrative at all. Hence this passage does not answer the question of when the angels were created. The word צבא (*tsaba'*) expresses the idea of a "serried host" and can of course denote the angels as God's army. But it has wider usage (cf. BDB, 838b). For the same thought with different words, compare Exod. 20:11, "heaven and earth, the sea, *and all that is in them*."

42. As Delitzsch notes, 106–7, "Not that on the seventh day God continued and ended his as yet uncompleted work, but that he made an end . . . of the work, because it was now finished."

43. Delitzsch, 107, notes, "When the name 'work' [מלאכה, *mela'kâ*] is given to God's six days' creation, human work [designated by the same word, Exod. 20:9–10] is ennobled to the highest conceivable degree, as being the copy of this model." As pointed out in section E.3 below, the Sabbath commandment, Exod. 20:8–11, reflects much of the wording of Gen. 2:2–3.

44. Hebrew שבת (*shabat*), hence the noun שבת (*Shabbat*, "Sabbath rest").

C. Extra Notes

1. Genesis 1:1 and creation from nothing

Christians have held to the notion that God created all things out of nothing (Latin: *creatio ex nihilo*). They have often appealed to Genesis 1:1 in support of this position; however, controversies around the proper interpretation of that verse have led some to claim that the doctrine is a later development and that the Christian church did not commit itself to that belief until it had to respond to Gnosticism in the second century.[45] Hence we must first assess the grammar and sense of this verse and then go on to see what role it plays in the pericope. From that we can discern whether creation from nothing is a proper inference from that verse.

The ESV rendering of Genesis 1:1 is conventional for English translations: "In the beginning, God created the heavens and the earth." This follows the accents of the Masoretic Text[46] and agrees with the oldest versions, the Greek and Latin:

Ἐν ἀρχῇ ἐποίησεν ὁ θεὸς τὸν οὐρανὸν καὶ τὴν γῆν.

In principio creavit Deus caelum et terram.

More recently,[47] however, it has become common to render it differently:

When God began to create the heavens and the earth . . .[48]

This takes the opening expression "in the beginning" (בְּרֵאשִׁית, *bere'shît*) as a construct, with the next word as a genitive: "in the beginning of God's creating. . . ." The problems with this approach fall into the textual, grammatical, and theological categories.

---

45. See the discussion in Paul Copan, "Is *Creatio ex Nihilo* a Post-Biblical Invention? An Examination of Gerhard May's Proposal," *Trinity Journal* n.s. 17 (1996): 77–93.

46. The accent on בְּרֵאשִׁית is disjunctive.

47. I refer to it as "more recent" with respect to the ancient versions and the English translation tradition. Kiel, א, notes that, among others, Rashi (1040–1105) held to this analysis; Rashi's comments are included in Kiel's commentary.

48. See NEB and the margins of NRSV and CEV. For the alleged grammar, see Joüon, *Grammar of Biblical Hebrew*, §129p.

On the textual level, this newer rendering would be worth considering if the verb *create* were an infinitive construct rather than a perfect. But the early versions offer no support to this; ought we to dismiss them without some other evidence?

Grammatically, as I will argue below, the normal use of the perfect in the opening of a pericope is to designate an event that took place before the main storyline got under way. It is grammatically possible, though not likely (see below), that the perfect verb here denotes a summary of the account—but that is not consistent with the newer rendering, either. Further, the noun רֵאשִׁית (*re'shît*, "beginning") does not appear in the construction alleged in support of the newer reading. On the other hand, Hosea 1:2 uses the synonym תְּחִלָּה (*tekhillâ*, "beginning") in the construction "when the LORD first spoke through Hosea" (ESV):

the beginning of the Lord's speaking by Hosea	תחלת דבר־יהוה בהושע

However, this does not support the rendering suggested for Genesis 1:1, because it does not use the combination רֵאשִׁית + בְּ (*be* ["in"] + *re'shît*). Further, the noun תְּחִלָּה is clearly in the construct,[49] while רֵאשִׁית is not: the article is missing because the word is definite on its own, as it is in Isaiah 46:9–10.[50]

The verb *created* in Genesis 1:1 is in the perfect, and the normal use of the perfect at the very beginning of a pericope is to denote an event that took place before the storyline gets under way. Most narrative pericopes in the Pentateuch actually begin with a *wayyiqtol* verb, as in Genesis 12:1, וַיֹּאמֶר יְהוָה (*wayyo'mer yhwh*, "now the LORD said"). A number do begin with a verb in the perfect, and they do so in order to describe an event that precedes the main storyline. For example, consider Genesis 24:1:[51]

---

49. It is also possible that the form דבר (*dibber*) in Hos. 1:2 is a noun, as it is in Jer. 5:13 and in Rabbinic and Modern Hebrew.

50. See Bill Arnold, "רֵאשִׁית," *NIDOTTE* 3:1025–28, at 1025. Heidel, *Babylonian Genesis*, 92, notes that "terms like *rêshîth*, 'beginning,' *rôsh*, 'beginning,' *qedem*, 'olden times,' and *'ôlâm*, 'eternity,' when used in adverbial expressions, occur almost invariably *without* the article, and that in the absolute state."

51. See also Gen. 3:1; 4:1; 15:1; 16:1; 21:1; 39:1; 43:1; Exod. 5:1; 24:1; 32:1; Num. 32:1.

Now Abraham was old, well advanced in years. And the LORD *had blessed* Abraham in all things.	ואברהם זקן בא בימים ויהוה ברך את־אברהם בכל

The action of *blessing* took place prior to the main action.

All of the other examples in the Pentateuch are of this sort, with the apparent exception of Exodus 19:1–2:

¹On the third new moon after the people of Israel had gone out of the land of Egypt, on that day they *came* into the wilderness of Sinai. ²They set out from Rephidim and came into the wilderness of Sinai, and they encamped in the wilderness. There Israel encamped before the mountain.	בחדש השלישי לצאת בני־ ישראל מארץ מצרים ביום הזה באו מדבר סיני ויסעו מרפידים ויבאו מדבר סיני ויחנו במדבר ויחן־שם ישראל נגד ההר

Here, "they *came*" in Exodus 19:1 gets ahead of the storyline, while verse 2 backs us up and then narrates (using ויבאו, *wayyabo'û*, a *wayyiqtol* verb) the same event. So we may call the opening verse a title or heading of the pericope, but in any case it is not true that this verse denotes a summary of the entire account.

An example of an initial clause that uses a perfect to convey a summary of an account is Genesis 22:1:

After these things God *tested* Abraham and said to him, "Abraham!" And he said, "Here am I."	ויהי אחר הדברים האלה והאלהים נסה את־אברהם ויאמר אליו אברהם ויאמר הנני

Notice that the verse actually begins with ויהי (*wayehî*, "and it came about"). Interestingly enough, of the other examples of this pattern in the Pentateuch, this is the only one that is a summary; the others describe an antecedent event.[52]

On the theological level, it seems plain that later Jewish writers had a doctrine of creation from nothing, and if they did not get it here, no one can say where else they could have got it. In the Apocrypha, we have 2 Maccabees 7:28–29 (RSV), where a mother encourages her son to stand fast and endure martyrdom at the hands of Antiochus:

52. See Gen. 14:1–2; Lev. 9:1; Num. 10:11.

²⁸I beseech you, my child, to look at the heaven and the earth and see everything that is in them, and recognize that *God did not make them out of things that existed* [οὐκ ἐξ ὄντων ἐποίησεν αὐτὰ ὁ θεός]. Thus also mankind *comes into being* [or, *is made*: γίνεται]. ²⁹Do not fear this butcher, but prove worthy of your brothers. Accept death, so that in God's mercy I may get you back again with your brothers.

To say that God did not make the heaven and the earth from things that exist is to say that he made them from nothing.

Hebrews 11:3 is similar: "By faith we understand that the universe was created by the word of God, so that what is seen was not made out of things that are visible." "What is seen" and "things that are visible" are material things, so this author is denying that the world was made from preexisting material.

Finally, consider Revelation 4:11:

> Worthy are you, our Lord and God,
>   to receive glory and honor and power,
> for you created all things,
>   and by your will they existed and were created.

As the last line asserts, all things get their existence from God's will, and God created them at some time; hence they did not exist before then, which means they were created from nothing.

The closest these verses come to asserting creation from nothing is in 2 Maccabees 7:28, while in the other texts the notion is an inference. One does not have to accept 2 Maccabees as canonical to support the notion; it represents the way that pious Jews understood the origin of things. Nor does one need to read the New Testament texts back into the Old Testament; rather, they depend on this notion as part of the shared picture of the world between author and audience—that is, they too represent the shared way of accounting for origins. It is hard to find another place besides Genesis 1:1 on which these could be depending, and thus we do well to suppose that they were reading Genesis 1:1 to imply creation from nothing.⁵³

---

53. Some have supposed that Wis. 11:17, "thy all-powerful hand, which *created the world out of formless matter*" (RSV) (κτίσασα τὸν κόσμον ἐξ ἀμόρφου ὕλης), actually denies creation from nothing; perhaps the term *formless* (ἄμορφος) deliberately recalls Plato's use (*Timaeus* 50D, 51A). It seems best to interpret this author in light of biblical ideas, since he follows them pretty closely (as in Wis. 9:1); and we may note that he does not say that the "formless matter" is eternal, and we need not press the word κτίζω too strongly

The strongest case for taking Genesis 1:1 as a title that summarizes the whole pericope comes from Bruce Waltke.[54] The argument to which he attaches the most weight is the observation that the combination "the heavens and the earth" is a merism for "the organized universe, the cosmos," and "this compound never has the meaning of disorderly chaos but always of an orderly world." He supposes that "disorder, darkness, and deep" present "a situation not tolerated in the perfect cosmos and never said to have been called into existence by the Word of God." This argument founders, however, on just this point: "without form and void" (Gen. 1:2) is not a term for "disorderly chaos" but pictures the earth as "an unproductive and uninhabited place." There is no indication that the "deep" is any kind of opponent to God; indeed, in the rest of the Bible it does his bidding and praises him (compare Gen. 7:11; 8:2; 49:25; Pss. 33:7; 104:6; 135:6; 148:7; Prov. 3:20; 8:28). And since God names the darkness (Gen. 1:5), there is no reason to believe that it opposes his will, either.[55]

When we add these observations to the normal discourse function of the perfect tense at the beginning of a pericope, and the search for a source for the idea of creation from nothing, we find that taking Genesis 1:1 as a background event, prior to the main storyline, is the best way to read it. These discourse grammatical conclusions support the way that Heidel described the first two verses (writing before "discourse grammar"):[56] "The first verse of Genesis briefly records the creation of the universe in its essential form, and the second verse singles out a part of this universe, viz., the earth, and describes its condition in some detail."

(see C.7 below). J. A. F. Gregg, *The Wisdom of Solomon* (Cambridge Bible for Schools and Colleges; Cambridge: Cambridge University Press, 1909), comments (110–11): "The use of *create* here is non-committal: it leaves the origin of matter out of sight, and deals merely with the arrangement of matter"; see also Joseph Reider, *The Book of Wisdom* (New York: Harper & Brothers, 1957), 145.

54. Waltke wrote a series of articles for the journal *Bibliotheca Sacra* 32 (1975) on "The Creation Account in Genesis 1:1–3": Part 1, "Introduction to Biblical Cosmogony" (25–36); Part 2, "The Restitution Theory" (136–44); Part 3, "The Initial Chaos Theory and the Precreation Chaos Theory" (216–28); Part 4, "The Theology of Genesis 1" (327–42). The syntactical arguments relevant here (and which he restates elsewhere) appear in Part 3.

55. Waltke appeals to texts such as Rev. 21:1, 25, where the new heavens and new earth will have no sea or night, but it better fits the nature of the Revelation to suppose that the seer used these as symbols for what fallen man fears rather than as comments on the moral status of sea and night in themselves.

56. Heidel, *Babylonian Genesis*, 93.

All of these considerations also tell against another way of translating that has become popular (as NRSV, NAB):

> ¹In the beginning when God created the heavens and the earth, ²the earth was a formless void. . . .

This fails to account properly for the clause and verb-type analysis that we have seen above.

The result of all this is that the ESV rendering stands and that "created" denotes an action prior to the main storyline—that is, prior to the beginning of the first day. Does it follow from this that creation is said to be *from nothing*? The answer is yes, but not for the reason that some give. Some find the "doctrine" in the verb *created* itself, as if that settles the question. But this is clearly wrong: after all, the same verb appears in Genesis 1:27, where God "created" the man; and, as we will see in the next chapter, this description is parallel to that in 2:7, where God "formed" the man *using dust from the ground*. That is, man's "creation" was not "from nothing," though it is of course extraordinary.

However, the sentence of Genesis 1:1 taken as a whole does in fact imply creation from nothing. "The heavens and the earth" likely refers to "everything in the material universe," and "in the beginning" tells us what time the author is speaking of. Hence, if God created everything at the beginning, then "before the beginning"—whatever that might mean—there was nothing. Therefore Genesis 1:1 clearly *implies*, though it does not explicitly *state*, that God created from nothing and that the material universe has an absolute beginning.

2. The proper rendering of the refrain

The days are marked off by a refrain, which the ESV (and most modern versions) has rendered: "And there was evening and there was morning, the nth day." Readers of the AV, however, are accustomed to something different: "And the evening and the morning were the nth day."

Of the ancient versions, the ESV agrees with the Septuagint, while the likely antecedent of the AV rendering is the Latin Vulgate:

> LXX: καὶ ἐγένετο ἑσπέρα καὶ ἐγένετο πρωί, ἡμέρα δευτέρα
> *and there was evening and there was morning, (the) second day*

Vulgate: et factum est vespere et mane dies secundus
and so of the evening and morning was made the second day
(Tyndale)

The AV rendering fails properly to represent the grammar of the refrain. In Hebrew it runs (1:8),

ויהי־ערב ויהי־בקר יום שני

That is, we have successive events, each denoted by the verb ויהי (*wayehî*, "and there was"), and we have the evening followed by the morning. Grammatically, the AV rendering compresses the two *events* into a *sum*, namely, the evening plus the morning were a day.[57] Logically, this is nonsense: to get a day we must describe twenty-four hours, or at least the period of daylight. To add the evening and the morning means nothing, but if we simply allow the verbs to indicate two events, we find that they mark the end points of the nighttime.[58]

The ESV rendering of the refrain allows us to see what it is doing: marking the end points of each of the workdays. The overall reading of the pericope should take this into account.[59]

3. *The fourth day*

Many refer to the events of the fourth day (Gen. 1:14–19) as the *creation* of the heavenly lights. Similarly, we find scholars referring to verse 3 ("and there was light") as the *creation* of light. This presents a serious problem to those who want to correlate this account

57. Some have even gone so far as to claim that the refrain "defines" the days, with a view toward making sure that we take them as the twenty-four-hour kind.

58. Compare Num. 9:15–16, "On the day that the tabernacle was set up, the cloud covered the tabernacle, the tent of the testimony. And at evening it was over the tabernacle like the appearance of fire until morning. So it was always: the cloud covered it by day and the appearance of fire by night." From evening until morning (v. 15) is paraphrased as "night" (v. 16).

59. Another question lies in the use of אחד (*'ekhad*, "one") for "first" in Gen. 1:5. In my judgment there is no problem with the conventional acceptance of this as "first." On this point and a fuller discussion of the refrain, see C. John Collins, "The Refrain of Genesis 1: A Critical Review of Its Rendering in the English Bible" (forthcoming), which assesses and rejects the arguments of Andrew Steinmann, "אחד as an ordinal number and the meaning of Genesis 1:5," *Journal of the Evangelical Theological Society* 45, no. 4 (2002): 577–84, who favors something like the Vulgate and AV.

with a scientific description, because we assume that day and night are marked off by the heavenly lights—but how could that happen on the first three days? Depending on the scholar's perspective, he will either come up with something like "God provided light through some other means," or he will abandon attempts to follow sequence in the account, or he will simply see in this proof that the account is either "poetry" or "prescientific." Another approach is that of what are called the concordists (those who seek a strong level of agreement between Genesis and scientific findings): these take the "making" or "setting" of the lights as their appearing when the cloud cover (their interpretation of the "expanse") of the early earth began to clear. This runs into trouble when we recognize that the account does not present the "expanse" as something different from our experience.

However, if we look closely at the Hebrew, we must conclude that the words used do not *require* that we take them as describing the *creation* of the lights (if by "creation" we mean the beginning of their being)—though it is true that the words allow such a reading. First, consider Genesis 1:14: "And God said, '*Let there be* [יְהִי, *yehî*] lights in the expanse of the heavens to separate the day from the night, and let them be for signs and for seasons, and for days and years.'" Then in Genesis 1:16: "And God *made* [עָשָׂה, *'asâ*] the two great lights . . . and the stars." The verb *made* in Genesis 1:16 does not specifically mean "create"; it can refer to that, but it can also refer to "working on something that is already there" (hence ESV margin), or even "appointed."[60] Verse 14 focuses on the function of the lights rather than on their origin: the verb *let there be* is completed with the purpose clause, "to separate." Hence, the account of this day's work focuses on these lights serving a function that God appointed for the well-being of man—and that they serve that function by God's command, which implies that it is foolish to worship them.[61]

Likewise, the verbs in Genesis 1:3, "let there be . . . and there was," do not of themselves imply creation. If God created the universe (1:1) and then at some unspecified time afterward the first day began (1:2–3), then we should read "let there be light" as summoning the light for the first day. After all, the volitional form "let there be" does not of itself require the sense of coming into existence; compare Psalm

---

60. Rashi (on 1:14; text in Kiel, שׁם) thought that God created the lights on the first day, while on the fourth day he commanded that they be hung in the expanse.

61. As Kiel, יד, observes.

33:22, "*let* your steadfast love, O LORD, *be* upon us," which hardly suggests that the steadfast love had not previously been with them![62]

We also note that we need not see Genesis 1:3, "let there be light," and 1:14, "let there be light*s*," as describing the same event; the word in verse 3 is "light" (אוֹר, *'ôr*), while that in verse 14 is "light*s*" (מארת, *me'ôrôt*), that is, " light-b*earers*." We can take these verses as describing God calling for the "dawn" of the first day and appointing the heavenly lights to their function in service of mankind on the fourth day. God's activity may be supernatural, but that is not the same as *creation*.

4. The meaning of "kind"

The word מִין (*mîn*, "kind") appears in days 3, 5, and 6, each time in the construction לְמִין + suffix ("according to the kind of it/them"):

> And God said, "Let the earth sprout vegetation, plants yielding seed, and fruit trees bearing fruit in which is their seed, *each according to its kind*, on the earth." And it was so. The earth brought forth vegetation, plants yielding seed *according to their own kinds*, and trees bearing fruit in which is their seed, *each according to its kind*. And God saw that it was good. (Gen. 1:11–12)

> So God created the great sea creatures and every living creature that moves, with which the waters swarm, *according to their kinds*, and every winged bird *according to its kind*. And God saw that it was good. (Gen. 1:21)

> And God said, "Let the earth bring forth living creatures *according to their kinds*—livestock and creeping things and beasts of the earth *according to their kinds*." And it was so. And God made the beasts of the earth *according to their kinds* and the livestock *according to their kinds*, and everything that creeps on the ground *according to its kind*. And God saw that it was good. (Gen. 1:24–25)

Some suggest that the word *kind* is roughly equivalent to "species" and that the text is opposed to any notion of new species developing from old ones.[63]

---

62. Other examples include 1 Sam. 20:13; Pss. 90:17; 119:76.
63. Some creationists hold this view; but the claim more commonly comes from opponents of all forms of creationism, such as those cited in my *Science and Faith: Friends or Foes?* (Wheaton, Crossway, 2003), 400.

There are two problems with such statements. First, the meaning of מִין does not support it; and second, it is not what Genesis actually says. As to the semantics of מִין, the term here is not as technical as "species"; it rather means something like "category" or "variety," and its basis for classification is the appearance.[64]

Second, consider what the text actually says. It simply says that these first plants bore their fruit according to their kinds and that the first animals were created according to their kinds. This does not say that these are the only "kinds" that ever were or could be.

Let us relate this to the genre and message of the text. It takes for granted the everyday experience of its audience, namely, that wheat grains produce more wheat, barley makes more barley, and so on. (The text does not say that camels produce more camels; it leaves the reader to draw the inference.) The reader will get the idea that the things he is familiar with work the way they do because God intended them to work that way: there are edible plants and domesticable animals—every farmer knows this, and Genesis explains why it is so. This, as we shall see in chapter 10, provides the philosophical ground for a confident, and even scientific, approach toward the world, even though it is not what we call a philosophical or scientific statement in itself. It does not assert, however, that under some circumstances one cannot get varieties of wheat so different that they are different species; it does not comment on the topic at all.

5. Genesis 1 and the Trinity

In Genesis 1:26 God says, "Let us make man in our image, after our likeness." Who or what is the "us" to whom God speaks? Several possibilities have been offered:

(a) It reflects an originally polytheistic account insufficiently sanitized.

(b) God is speaking to his heavenly court, that is, to the host of angels.

(c) It is a "we" of self-address (which can open the way for plurality of persons in the Godhead).

---

64. See Mark Futato, "מִין," no. 4786 in *NIDOTTE*, 2:934–35; Paul Seely, "The Basic Meaning of *Mîn*, 'Kind,' " *Science and Christian Belief* 9, no. 1 (1997), 47–56.

The first option is popular with those who think of the origin of Genesis in myth; the second dates back at least as far as Philo of Alexandria.[65] We cannot say that option (b) is distinctive of Jewish scholars, while option (c) goes to the Christians: many conservative Christian authors support (b), such as Delitzsch, Wenham, and Waltke, while there are faithful Jews who support (c), such as Cassuto.

The main reasons for adopting (b) is the feeling that anything approaching the Trinity is either ill-suited to the Old Testament, or at least anachronistic, and the fact that there is certainly an idea of an angelic council that surrounds God's throne (e.g., Isa. 6:8; Ps. 89:6–8; 1 Kgs. 22:19–22; Job 1; Dan. 7:9–13; Luke 2:9–14; Rev. 4–5). In fact, we find God asking Isaiah to go up *for us* (Isa. 6:8), that is, for himself and his angels.

However, option (c) is surely the best supported of the three. To begin with, the possessive "our" in "our image" should refer to the same person(s) as the "us" that is the subject of the verb: "Let *us* make man in *our* image, after *our* likeness." Then God carries this out in Genesis 1:27, "God created man in his own image"; that is, only God is the subject of the verb, and only God is the referent of the possessive. In fact, man is only said to be in *God's* image, not in the image of any other heavenly being (as also Gen. 5:1). Second, the verbs *make* and *create* have only God as their subject throughout this account: no one joins him in the work. Third, we have a parallel in Genesis 11:7, where the Lord says, "Let *us* go down and confuse," with its fulfillment in Genesis 11:8, where the Lord is the only actor.

Finally, it is certainly plain that there is a heavenly council, as the verses cited show, but this is a far cry from saying that the council includes counselors or even co-makers with God. In Isaiah 6:8, Isaiah is asked to go for *us*; but there is no evidence in the text that Isaiah goes for anyone besides the Lord. (Even if he does go for the whole host, that does not make the host God's co-makers.) In Psalm 89:6–8, none of the heavenly beings is like God in power and authority; in 1 Kings 22:19–22, a lying spirit volunteers to entice Ahab to death, but there is no "us" in the text. In Job 1 the angels ("sons of God") present themselves to God strictly as subordinates; in Daniel 7:9–13 there are thousands upon thousands who serve God, but only the

65. I leave it to students of Philo to decide whether he found this plausible in the light of Plato's *Timaeus* 42D, where God leaves the task of forming mankind to the younger gods.

"Ancient of Days" and the "one like a son of man" have dominion and authority. In Luke 2:9–14, the angels act as messengers for God but not as counselors; and in Revelation 4–5 the heavenly hosts worship at God's throne but are not called his counselors.

I conclude, then, that the "us" in Genesis 1:26 has God speaking to himself. I think we can go further and say that God is deliberating with himself; after all, we have already seen the Spirit of God in verse 2.

Does this lead us to the Trinity? No, not of itself. But if there is a place for any kind of *sensus plenior* ("fuller sense"), this is it. The kind of *sensus plenior* that I can accept occurs when a later passage amplifies an earlier one in a way consistent with the intent of the earlier one. If the Christian doctrine of the Trinity is true, then the referent was present in Genesis 1. This is not the same as claiming that the author or a pious Israelite reader must have been able to see it, only that the narration allows it. As mentioned, the Spirit of God in Genesis 1:2 is closely associated with God himself in the Old Testament. The Christian doctrine allows us to make good sense of all the elements in the text, as well as of the elements of other texts (those which speak of Christ as the one through whom the world was made).

6. The image of God

In Genesis 1:26 God plans to make man "in our image, after our likeness." What is the image and likeness? Are they different? Are they constituent parts of human nature? If so, what is their relation to the soul?[66]

---

66. Important bibliography, besides the commentaries and manuals of theology, includes James Barr, "The Image of God in the Book of Genesis—A Study of Terminology," *Bulletin of the John Rylands Library* 51 (1968): 11–26; David Clines, "The Image of God in Man," *Tyndale Bulletin* 19 (1968): 53–103; J. M. Miller, "In the 'Image' and 'Likeness' of God," *Journal of Biblical Literature* 91 (1972): 289–304; J. F. A. Sawyer, "The Meaning of בצלם אלהים ('in the Image of God') in Genesis I-XI," *Journal of Theological Studies* n.s. 25, no. 2 (1974): 418–26; Raymond Van Leeuwen, "Form, Image," in *NIDOTTE*, 4:643–48; and the painstakingly detailed Gunnlaugur A. Jónsson, *The Image of God: Genesis 1:26–28 in a Century of Old Testament Research* (Coniectanea Biblica, Old Testament Series 26; Lund: Almqvist & Wiksell, 1988). Jónsson concludes that what I am calling the "representative" view is not only the right one but also the most common one among Old Testament scholars; he mentions a few scholars who take the "relational" view and calls this the only tenable alternative. He does note that neither Sawyer nor Barr in the articles cited side with either of these two (and Sawyer seems to favor the "resemblance" view).

Many earlier Christian theologians have taken the image and likeness as separate components of created human nature—often with the idea that one was lost by the fall of Genesis 3, while the other remains. Since about the time of the Reformation, scholars have recognized that this does not suit the text itself. First, there is no "and" joining "in our image" with "after our likeness." Second, in Genesis 1:27 we find simply "in God's image"; and finally, in Genesis 5:1 God made man "in the likeness of God." The best explanation for these data is to say that "in the image" and "after the likeness" refer to the same thing, with each clarifying the other. This will allow us simply to speak of the "image" of God in this discussion.

Theologians after the Reformation commonly thought of the image of God as some property of human nature that is like God in some way, and they came to speak of the wider sense of the image and the narrower sense. In the wider sense, man has reason, will, and relationships, as God does. In the narrower sense, man's abilities are completely in harmony with God's own purity and wisdom. Thus by this construction, in the fall the image-in-the-wider-sense was badly damaged but still remains in every human being. The image-in-the-narrower-sense was lost, and the process of sanctification is the restoring of that image.

I will call this traditional view the *resemblance* view: namely, the image consists in some aspect of man that resembles God. In the twentieth century many theologians came to reject this in favor of two other positions. Generally speaking, theologians in the twentieth century felt that the Bible focuses on *function* rather than *ontology*: that is, on what people *do* rather than what they *are*. The resemblance view is highly ontological, since it speaks of an actual part of human nature, and the two views that have come to replace it are functional. Speaking generally, there is great merit in recognizing the distinction and in realizing that ordinary language—which predominates in the Bible—is likely to concentrate on function. However, it is a fallacy to suppose that ordinary language cannot address ontology, either directly or by implication. Hence we must examine the case carefully.

The first of the functional views can be called the *representative* view: man was made to represent God in his activity of ruling the world on God's behalf. This position appeals to the second sentence in Genesis 1:26: "Let us make man in our image, after our likeness. *And let them have dominion* over the fish of the sea and over the birds of the heavens and over the livestock and over all the earth and over every creeping thing that creeps on the earth." According to this position, the dominion defines the image. Advocates find further support in Psalm 8, which celebrates man's position in the world and in God's mind, basing itself on the creation account (see section E.1 below for more discussion of the psalm).

The second functional view I will call the *relational* view: that is, man is fully man when in relationship with God and the human community. This appeals to the structure of Genesis 1:27:

> So God created man in his own image,
> in the image of God he created him;
> male and female he created them.

The third line, which adds something to the first two (and lacks the word *image*), shows that it is mankind as male and female that gives us the image of God. This can be broadened to all manner of relationships: man and God, man with fellow man and with the human community.

Scholars will advocate one of these three over the others, but we will note that they need not be mutually exclusive. Perhaps none is right, or some combination is right, or maybe we simply cannot come to a firm conclusion.[67]

We will consider the question in two parts. First, we will look at the other biblical passages that speak of the image or likeness; then we will carry out a lexical study of the two Hebrew nouns.

The other biblical texts that speak of the image or likeness fall into three categories: those which speak of mankind as made in God's image; those which speak of Christ as the perfect image of God; and those which speak of believers being molded into the image of God.

The first group of texts speaks of mankind as made in God's image. Genesis 5:1 looks back to Genesis 1:26–27, but it says that God made man in the *likeness* of God—suggesting, as noted above, that the two terms "in the image" and "after the likeness" refer to the same thing. Genesis 9:6 simply repeats the idea that God made man in his image—this is the reason why "whoever sheds the blood

---

67. Westermann, 149–50, lists a number of authors who thought that the emphasis was on physical form itself. This is not considered a major contender today—and the discussion here, by providing a lexically based interpretation, will show why we need not spend time on it.

of man, by man shall his blood be shed." Wisdom of Solomon 2:23 says that God "made man as the image of his own eternity"—that is, he was made to live forever like God. Sirach 17:3, speaking of man's creation (see v. 1), says:

> He endowed them [mankind] with strength like his own,
>   and made them in his own image.

Finally, James 3:9 marvels at how we use the tongue: with it we bless God, and with it we curse others, "who are made in the likeness of God." James 3:9 and Genesis 9:6 affirm that there is a sense in which man is still in God's image; the other passages are not decisive on this point.

The second group of texts describe Christ as the image of God. In Colossians 1:15 Paul calls Jesus "the image of the invisible God," without saying just what that is. The context, though, describes his primacy in the creation: "all things were created through him and for him" (Col. 1:16). Similarly, in 2 Corinthians 4:4 he calls Christ the image of God—which probably links back to 2 Corinthians 3:18, where believers "are being transformed into the same image." The image is the way that Christ is, which shows what God is like; this becomes the target for the believer's moral transformation.[68]

This leads to the third group of texts. According to Colossians 3:10, believers "have put on the new self, which is being renewed in knowledge after the image of its creator"; likewise, Ephesians 4:24 says that believers have been taught "to put on the new self, created *after the likeness of God* [Greek, *according to God*] in true righteousness and holiness." The image of God is the norm and goal into which the Christian believer is being molded. Two more texts speak of the image *of Christ* in the same way: in Romans 8:29, "those whom he foreknew he also predestined to be conformed to the image of his Son"; and in 1 Corinthians 15:49, believers will "bear the image of the man of heaven [that is, *of Christ*]."

It is easy to see from these verses why traditional theologians have thought of the image in terms of resemblance of some kind,

---

68. It is possible that this usage hints at the idea of Christ as a new Adam. Typically in the Septuagint, man is said to be "according to the image of God" (κατ᾽ εἰκόνα θεοῦ; Gen. 1:26–27; 5:1, 3; Sir. 17:3) or "in the image of God" (ἐν εἰκόνι θεοῦ; Gen. 9:6), that is, it uses a preposition. However, in Wis. 2:23 we find the term without a preposition, where man *is* the image of God's eternity.

since—to the extent we can tell one way or another—that is how these texts use it. Now the question is, does this suit the lexical and contextual demands of Genesis 1?

The term *image* (צֶלֶם, *tselem*) is generally used for a solid representation of something: for example, in 1 Samuel 6:5 the Philistines make *images* (figurines) of their tumors and of the mice; in Ezekiel 23:14 there are "men portrayed on the wall, the *images* of the Chaldeans in vermilion"—these images were relief carvings. Often the *image* is an idol, as in Numbers 33:52; 2 Kings 11:18; Amos 5:26; Ezekiel 7:20 (and probably 16:17). The Aramaic cognate appears in Daniel 2:31–33; 3:1, describing colossal statues.[69]

"Likeness" (דְּמוּת, *demût*) is a more general term for "resemblance," without saying what kind of resemblance is in view (that is inferred from the context). It is common in comparisons, as in Isaiah 13:4, where "as of a great multitude" is literally "the *likeness* of a great multitude." In Isaiah 40:18 we find, "what *likeness* will you compare with" God (see also Ezek. 1:5, 10). Consider also Daniel 10:16, where "one in the *likeness* of the children of man" touched Daniel's lips: the angel looked like a man. In 2 Chronicles 4:3, the likeness is a carved one, "*figures* of gourds."

Outside of the Bible, the Aramaic equivalents for both our words "image" and "likeness" appear in a remarkable statue found in 1979 at Tell Fekheriyeh in northeast Syria. The statue was put up in the ninth century B.C. and has an Assyrian inscription and an Aramaic paraphrase. The Aramaic refers to the statue as a "likeness" in lines 1 and 15 and an "image" in line 12. This agrees quite well with the pattern we find in the biblical material itself.[70]

But we must not stop with this kind of lexical study. We do not have just the words themselves in Genesis 1:26; we have them with

---

69. Problematic uses are Pss. 39:6; 73:20. In Ps. 39:6, "surely a man goes about *as a shadow*," the word *shadow* may instead be a "lifeless statue," or it may be "a mere semblance." In Ps. 73:20 "their *phantoms*" may be "their very semblances." (See BDB, 854a, sense 3.)

70. Publications on this inscription include A. Abou-Assaf, P. Bordreuil, and A. R. Millard, *La statue de Tell Fekherye* (Paris: Editions Recherche sur les Civilisations, 1982); A. R. Millard and P. Bordreuil, "A Statue from Syria with Assyrian and Aramaic Inscriptions," *Biblical Archaeologist* 45, no. 3 (1982): 135–41; S. A. Kaufman, "Reflections on the Assyrian-Aramaic Bilingual from Tell Fakhariyeh," *Maarav* 3, no. 2 (1982): 137–75; T. Muraoka, "The Tell-Fekherye Bilingual Inscription and Early Aramaic," *Abr-Nahrain* 22 (1983–84), 79–117; V. Sasson, "The Aramaic Text of the Tell Fakhriyah Assyrian-Aramaic Bilingual Inscription," *Zeitschrift für die Alttestamentliche Wissenschaft* 97, no. 1 (1985): 86–103.

prepositions: "*in* the image" and "*after* the likeness," and it is the prepositional phrases that amplify each other. We find this construction in a few places: for example, Psalm 58:4, "they have venom *like* the venom of a serpent," is literally "they have venom *after the likeness of* the venom of a serpent." Daniel 10:16, cited above, has "one *in the likeness of* the children of man"; this could easily be rendered, "one *after the likeness of* the children of man." And in Genesis 5:1 we read of man being made "*in* the likeness of God"; compare that with 1:26, which uses "*after* the likeness." And 5:3 has "*in* the likeness" and "*after* the image" (reverse of 1:26 prepositions).

All of this implies that "A is *after the likeness of* B" is equivalent to "A is *like* B." Further, it does not seem that the prepositions matter much: "*in* the image/likeness" seems to be pretty close to "*after* the image/likeness." From the usage of "image" we can see that to say "A is *in the image of* B" is equivalent to "A is *a concrete resemblance of* B."

Thus we can paraphrase Genesis 1:26: "Let us make man to be our concrete resemblance, to be like us." This supports a version of the resemblance view: man is a bodily creature who is like God in some way.

When it comes to determining the way in which man is like God, we are left to infer that from the context. To appeal to the sentence in Genesis 1:26, "and let them have dominion," as defining the image is to mistake the grammatical function of that sentence; as Delitzsch put it, "the *dominium terrae* . . . is not . . . its content but its consequence."[71] Further, it is quite a leap from "male and female he created them" to claim that this *defines* the image, and a much greater leap to find in this a paradigm of all relationships. It is much simpler to see that mankind consists of both males and females, both of which are in the image of God and both of which are necessary to carry out the commission to "be fruitful and multiply."

In this pericope and the next, God displays features of his character: he shows intelligence in designing the world as a place for man to live; he uses language when he says things; he appreciates what is "good" (morally and aesthetically); and he works and rests. He is also relational, in the way he establishes a connection with man that is governed by love and commitment (Gen. 2:15–17). In all of this God is a pattern for man.

---

71. Delitzsch, 100; the syntax is *waw* followed by a volitional form, which commonly indicates a purpose or result clause (Joüon, *Grammar of Biblical Hebrew*, §116a).

As Kidner put it in his commentary,[72] man is "an expression or transcription of the eternal, incorporeal creator in terms of temporal, bodily, creaturely existence." These features of God which are present in man distinguish him from the other creatures; and in man newly made, they were fully in accord with God's own purity. We conclude then that the wide sense and narrower sense distinction is a valid one and allows us to make sense of the various biblical texts. We can also see that the *resemblance* view does not exclude the *representative* or *relational* views: rather, these features of human nature form the basis for man's rule and relationships. By organizing things this way we recognize the valid points of all three positions and see how they relate to one another.

7. *The use of the words* create *and* make

The verb ברא (*bara'*, "to create") appears in Genesis 1:1, 21, 27; 2:3, 4. The verb עשה (*'asâ*, "to make") with God as subject appears in 1:7, 16, 25, 26, 31; 2:4 (and in 2:2, 3 as "to do"). They often denote the same activity, as we can see from the way that 1:26 ("make") is paraphrased in 1:27 ("create"). Perhaps the best way to describe their semantic relationship is to say that "to make" is the broader term of the two: that is, "to create" is "to make," but "to make" might or might not be "to create."[73] Hence to say that God is the "Creator" (as in Isa. 40:28) is also to say that he is "Maker" (as in Isa. 44:24).

Seen this way, the author uses "create" in this passage when he wants especially to stress that the product is some kind of fresh start. Hence the material universe (Gen. 1:1; 2:4) is a fresh start because it came from nothing; the sea creatures (1:21) are new in that they are the first of what our account calls "living creatures" (נפש חיה, *nepesh khayyâ*); and mankind (1:27) is a fresh start because the image of God is unique.[74] The term *make* focuses more generally on God's activity of working; just what the manner is we must infer from the context. Hence when God "made" the expanse (1:7) or the lights (1:16), this does not necessarily assert the origin of their being; instead it says that God carried out some operation on them, without saying just

72. Kidner, *Genesis*, 51.
73. The word for this relationship is *hyponymy*: "create" is a hyponym to "make."
74. As Delitzsch, 101, notes: "The essential characteristic of creation is not the exclusion of existing material, but the achievement, and indeed the miraculous achievement, of something hitherto non-existent."

what it was. When God "made" the man (1:26), he did so by "creation" (1:27); the second verse is more specific about God's activity.

When we consider how this pericope shapes the worldview of the covenant people (chapters 9–11), we will see that the vocabulary variation has nothing to do with how "supernatural" the author presented events to have been—indeed, that question does not normally rely on specialized vocabulary.[75]

We can see how close the two terms are in meaning from the way the Septuagint renders them both with the verb ποιέω ("to make") throughout this pericope. Readers of the New Testament might have expected κτίζω for "create"; but perhaps, at the time the Septuagint of Genesis was made, that verb in Greek had not yet acquired its special meaning of "create": in the wider Greek literature it meant "to found, establish."[76]

8. Genesis 1:28 and environmental ethics

Genesis 1:28 has God commissioning the first human couple with the charge, "Be fruitful and multiply and fill the earth and subdue it and have dominion over the fish of the sea and over the birds of the heavens and over every living thing that moves on the earth." It has become common to charge this passage with instilling an ethic of exploitation toward the earth and its resources. "Subdue" drums up notions of conquest by destruction, while "have dominion" is taken as "dominate."[77]

75. For the general discussion, see C. John Collins, *The God of Miracles* (Wheaton: Crossway, 2000), especially chapters 4 and 9.

76. See LSJ, 1002b–1003a. The Septuagint Pentateuch uses κτίζω only six times: Gen. 14:19, 22, to render קנה (*qanâ*, "get, possess"); Exod. 9:18, for יסד (*y-s-d*, "to found"); Lev. 16:16, in the passive to render שכן (*shakan*, "to dwell"); Deut. 4:32, for ברא (*bara'*, "to create"); Deut. 32:6, for כונן (*kônen*, "to establish"). The specific sense "create" is most prominent in the Prophets and Apocrypha, which were translated later than the Pentateuch. (And Wis. 2:23, which refers to Gen. 1:27 using κτίζω, shows that the author of Wisdom of Solomon is not solely reliant on the Septuagint for his terms, which uses ποιέω.) In the New Testament, the sense of the verb and cognates is typically "create," except once in the noun κτίσις: in 1 Pet. 2:13 it refers to "every human *institution*." Philo, *On the Creation*, uses κτίζω only in 17, 19, 24—all in the sense "found" (a city). The only place in Josephus's account of creation is *Antiquities* 1.27, his rendering of Gen. 1:1—but he may mean only "founded."

77. Useful bibliography includes Michael B. Barkey, ed., *Environmental Stewardship in the Judeo-Christian Tradition: Jewish, Catholic, and Protestant Wisdom on the Environment* (Grand Rapids: Acton Institute, 2000), with its own bibliography; Colin Russell, *The Earth, Humanity and God* (London: University College of London Press, 1994); Lynn

Just on the face of it, the charge is nonsense: the most successful destroyers and polluters of the environment have been societies that repudiate biblical ethics, such as the Iron Curtain countries of the twentieth century. It is possible, though, that some believers have taken the texts this way, so it is important properly to understand the commands in context.

To begin with, we must note where the command comes, namely, just after the man and woman have been created, while they are still in their pristine condition—which means they govern themselves by holiness and wisdom. Once they fall into sin, they do not lose their position as head of creation, but they have lost the perfect purity, sensitivity, and good sense that they need to carry it out well. The careful reader of this text will see that in this arena, too, all mankind displays both desperate badness and deep longing for repair; and seeing that is part of the function of these passages in Genesis.

Next we note just what the commands are. As Delitzsch pointed out,[78] "The authorization and vocation to dominion over the earth employs such strong expressions as כבש [*subdue*] and רדה [*have dominion*], because this dominion requires the energy of strength and the art of wisdom."

As we shall see in the following chapters, mankind's original task was to begin from Eden, work their way outward, and spread the blessings of Eden to all the earth. This would mean managing all of its creatures and resources for *good* purposes: to allow their beauty to flourish, to use them wisely and kindly, and to promote well-being for all.

9. The goodness of creation

This pericope has God seeing what he made, that it was "good"— that is, pleasing to him, answering his purpose (Gen. 1:4, 10, 12, 18, 21, 25, 31). The only day that lacks this is day 2; perhaps in some way the mere expanse is not satisfactory. As we shall see in the next chapter, the fact that 2:18 has God saying that something is "*not good*" therefore stands out.

White, "Historical Roots of Our Ecological Crisis," *Science* 155 (1967): 1203–7 (and available on the Internet).

78. Delitzsch, 101. This is significant because Delitzsch wrote long before environmental concerns became fashionable, and therefore one cannot simply dismiss him as apologetically motivated to soften biblical teaching.

A later text that reflects on the goodness of creation is Sirach 39:16, "All the works of the Lord are very good" (note the allusion to Gen. 1:31);[79] and in 1 Timothy 4:1–5 Paul applies the original goodness of creation to a particular ethical question:

> [1]Now the Spirit expressly says that in later times some will depart from the faith by devoting themselves to deceitful spirits and teachings of demons, [2]through the insincerity of liars whose consciences are seared, [3]who forbid marriage and require abstinence from foods that God created to be received with thanksgiving by those who believe and know the truth. [4]For *everything created by God is good* [πᾶν κτίσμα θεοῦ καλόν], and nothing is to be rejected if it is received with thanksgiving, [5]for it is made holy by the word of God and prayer.

Paul uses the term *good*, found in the Septuagint of Genesis 1, and seems to have thought that the creation retains its goodness even after man's fall into sin.[80] Sinful man is certainly a blemish on the creation, as Psalm 104 notes (see section E.1 below), and the path of salvation is one of people being restored to their original created function. That is why calling evil these created blessings, such as marriage and food, cannot be part of biblical faithfulness.

To affirm that the creation is "good," then, is to affirm that God takes delight in it and that man at his best will do so as well.[81]

10. The unusual seventh day

I have already indicated one way in which the narrator describes the seventh day differently than he does the others: the day lacks the refrain that marks the end of each day. In chapter 5, section C.7, I will look into how we should take account of this in our interpretation. Now I will explore another aspect that sets this day off.

Consider the storyline verbs to see what happens on this day: in Genesis 2:1, the heavens and the earth *were finished*; in 2:2, God *finished* his work and *rested*; and in 2:3 God *blessed* the seventh day

---

79. See also Sir. 38:4, which says, "The Lord created medicines from the earth" (RSV); that is, the creation continues to bear the marks of God's generous provision.

80. In chapter 6, sections C.5 and E.3 below, we will consider Rom. 8:18–25 and the problem of the "fallen world."

81. Compare Wis. 11:24: "For thou lovest all things that exist, and hast loathing for none of the things which thou hast made, for thou wouldst not have made anything if thou hadst hated it" (RSV).

and *made it holy*. These events do not involve strenuous activity; they do not involve work at all. Instead they convey the mental actions of enjoyment, approval, and delight. And that is just what the Sabbath institution in Israel is there to guard and foster. An Israelite shepherd or tiller of the soil who read this would thus be able to enter into his own Sabbath with pleasure rather than with resentment.

This character of God's Sabbath can provide a model for the human Sabbath.

D. Literary-Theological Exposition

I have argued above that the pericope is Genesis 1:1–2:3 and that the genre is exalted prose narrative. The chief character in this pericope is God (אֱלֹהִים, *'elohîm*). He creates, says, sees, separates, names, makes, appoints, blesses, finishes, makes holy, and rests. In fact, God is the subject of virtually every action verb in the *wayyiqtol* tense here—the chief exception being Genesis 1:12, where the earth *brings forth* vegetation (although even that is in response to God's command).

We have seen that the paragraph structure is straightforward:

1:1–2	preface: initial creation event, and conditions of the earth just before day 1 gets under way
1:3–5	day 1: light and darkness
1:6–8	day 2: sea and sky
1:9–13	day 3: land, sea, vegetation
1:14–19	day 4: light-bearers in the heavens
1:20–23	day 5: sea animals and flying creatures
1:24–31	day 6: land animals and humans
2:1–3	day 7: God's Sabbath

We can notice several things further about this structure. We have already seen the unusual nature of the seventh day, namely, the way the refrain is absent (which begs for an explanation, see below) and the way that all its *wayyiqtol* verbs describe glorious inactivity and enjoyment.

We can also see that day 6 gets the longest narration. Its telling is like that of day 3 in that there are two instances of "and God said" followed by a wish (Gen. 1:9, 11, dry land and vegetation; Gen. 1:24, 26, land animals and man), though it goes beyond day 3 with its blessing and commission of man. It further ends with *"very* good" (Gen. 1:31). Thus it is clear that day 6 is getting the most focus in this narrative.

The high point of day 6, and thus of the pericope as a whole, is Genesis 1:27:

> So God *created* man in his own image,
>   in the image of God he *created* him;
>   male and female he *created* them.

The verb *created* appears three times, but only the first is *wayyiqtol*; the second and third are just restatements of the event described by the first. Thus the storyline stops advancing, and the reader is allowed to dwell on this event. Further, this verse represents poetic parallelism, and thus we have an instance of heightened speech signaled by poetic diction. This event is the result of God's self-consultation in Genesis 1:26, which also highlights its importance.

We can also see that the narrator reports the making of mankind differently from how he reports the making of other "living creatures": in Genesis 1:20 God commands the waters to swarm and birds to fly; in verse 24 he commands the earth to bring forth the land animals; compare verse 11 where he tells the earth to sprout vegetation. Man, who is to "have dominion" over the rest of these creatures, "does not come into being by a *fiat* addressed to the earth."[82]

All of these features of Genesis 1:27 indicate that it is the zone of maximum turbulence, the peak of the account. Hence our integrated reading of the pericope should follow this.[83]

The basic sequence of events in this pericope is controlled by the six workdays. However, this simple grammatical and literary observation appears to clash with the subject matter itself, and this in three ways. The first of these ways is the problem that on the fourth day we seem to have the *creation* of the sun, moon, and stars, while we already had light, day, evening, and morning in the previous days. The second clash comes from what seems to be a disagreement between Genesis 1:11–12 (the plants made on the third day) and 2:5–7 (no

---

82. Delitzsch, 97–98.

83. Some have found the Sabbath (Gen. 2:1–3) to be the focus of the narrative, but our result shows otherwise.

plants made when man was formed). We can resolve these apparent clashes by carefully analyzing the Hebrew, and I argue elsewhere in this work that such careful analysis shows that the clashes are only apparent.[84]

The third problem for simple sequence comes from the very structure of the pericope. It looks like the days are organized such that days 1–3 describe locations, while days 4–6 describe the inhabitants of those locations:

Location	Inhabitants
1. light and dark	4. lights of day and night
2. sea and sky	5. animals of water and air
3. fertile earth	6. land animals (including mankind)
7. rest and enjoyment	

We may simply conclude from this high level of patterning that the order of events and even lengths of time are not part of the author's focus; this is at the basis of what is often called the literary framework scheme of interpretation. In this understanding, the six workdays are a literary device to display the creation week as a careful and artful effort.

One version of the framework scheme, however, goes even further: it argues that the reason days 1 and 4 correspond is that they are the same events viewed from different perspectives; likewise days 2 and 5, and 3 and 6. This version is particularly associated with Meredith Kline.[85]

In my judgment, Kline's version of the framework view does not suit the data. To begin with, it would make the workweek of creation into three days (told from two perspectives) instead of six. The fourth commandment, however, refers to this account as follows: "Six days you shall labor and do all your work. . . . For in six days the LORD made heaven and earth, the sea, and all that is in them, and rested the

---

84. See the discussion on the fourth day in section C.3 of this chapter; see the discussion of Gen. 2:5–7 in section C.1 of the next chapter.

85. See M. Kline, "Because It Had Not Rained," *Westminster Theological Journal* 20 (1958): 146–57; "Genesis," in *The New Bible Commentary: Revised*, ed. D. Guthrie et al. (Grand Rapids, Eerdmans, 1970), 79–114; "Space and Time in the Genesis Cosmogony," *Perspectives on Science and Christian Faith* 48, no. 1 (1996): 2–15; and M. Futato, "Because It Had Rained: A Study of Gen. 2:5–7 with Implications for Gen. 2:4–25 and Gen. 1:1–2:3," *Westminster Theological Journal* 60 (1998): 1–21.

seventh day" (Exod. 20:9, 11). Both references to the "six days"—man's and God's—use the Hebrew accusative of time, expressing the extent of time over which the work is distributed.[86]

The other versions of the framework scheme are not as easily rejected, and in my judgment they are right to see the highly patterned form of this pericope as evidence that the reader is invited to sit lightly on sequence and time lengths. However, several factors make me reluctant to abandon sequence altogether.

I have already indicated that the two apparent clashes with sequence seem to me to be only apparent, and resolvable. When I combine this with the prevalent *wayyiqtol*, whose ordinary usage in narrative is to denote discrete and basically sequential events,[87] with the progression of numbered days,[88] I find it easiest to imagine that sequence—of *some* kind, anyhow—matters in the author's presentation of events.

I will argue below that the creation week is indeed a unique one, in that it is God's workweek. This means that though sequence does in fact matter to the author's presentation, it is another question just how strongly the author is asserting exact sequence as a historical matter. I will take up the question of historical truth claims and truth value in chapter 10.

The next expositional question calls on us to consider how these events follow causally from what comes before and affect causally what comes next. Of course, if my conclusion that Genesis 1:1 describes creation *from nothing* stands, then this account cannot follow causally from anything historical; it is the beginning of history, and as far as causes within the created order are concerned, it has none. On the other hand, everything that follows depends on these events. In chapter 5, section C.6, I will examine the relationship between the first three chapters of Genesis; to anticipate that discussion, I will simply say that Genesis 2:4–25 fills out events of the sixth day of this pericope. Further, the lack of refrain on the seventh day leads us to

86. See Joüon, *Grammar of Biblical Hebrew*, §126i.

87. See Collins, "The *Wayyiqtol* as 'Pluperfect': When and Why," *Tyndale Bulletin* 46, no. 1 (1995): 117–40, at 117–18, for a brief statement with bibliography (and recognition that added nuances are needed in a full description of the tense).

88. Compare Kidner, *Genesis*, 54–55: "To the present writer the march of the days is too majestic a progress to carry no implication of ordered sequence; it also seems over-subtle to adopt a view of the passage which discounts one of the primary impressions it makes on the ordinary reader. It is a story, not only a statement."

wonder whether that day is open-ended—which would mean that the rest of human history takes place during God's Sabbath. In any case, this pericope describes the origin of the arena in which mankind will work out its relationship to the world and to God.

Now we come to consider repeated words, and here we will address some that we have not yet considered. Within the pericope, an obvious repetition is "and God saw that the [x] was good" (Gen. 1:4, 10, 12, 18, 21, 25, and especially 31). The effect of this, besides reinforcing the idea that the creation is entirely good, is to drive home the divine pleasure in the material creation: its goodness means that it pleases him.[89] This also, in its present form, prepares us for 2:18, where we encounter something "not good," the man's being alone. Thus when we read 2:18 with a view toward harmonizing, we realize that we are not yet at the "very good" of 1:31; it takes the woman to make it so.

The commission for the human couple to "be fruitful and *multiply*" (Gen. 1:28), making childbearing the arena of blessing, sets up an ironic contrast in 3:16, where the Lord will "surely *multiply*" the woman's pain in childbearing. But the word pair "be fruitful" and "multiply" will echo in later Scripture, as we will see in the reverberations section below.

The only active character in this pericope is God, called אלהים (*'elohîm*) in this account, and we turn to examine how our narrative portrays him. To be sure, one wants to be cautious in drawing a portrait of God from a narrative; he is, after all, far above human attempts to describe him, and those attempts to describe him may turn into attempts to limit him. Nevertheless we may with due caution note a few things.

We will discuss later what to make of the way the divine name changes in Genesis 2:4; for now we can simply inquire whether there is any import to the specific name used here. Delitzsch seems to be right when he says that in this pericope "God is so called as the summary of all that commands reverence, as absolute majesty and power."[90] The name also stresses his relation to the whole of creation as its sole source and owner. Such a deity is in the perfect position to commit himself to caring for everything and to expecting the whole creation to honor and love him. Thus when Israelite faith makes provision

89. See section C.9 above.
90. Delitzsch, 113; see also Cassuto, 86–88.

for Gentiles to know the true God, it is true to its own foundational understanding of God and man; if at any time Israel as a whole, or any of its members, presume on their ethnic privilege, they are denying something fundamental.

Though the divine name here portrays God in his transcendence, the author is far from presenting God as remote or unapproachable. The account allows its readers to enter into the divine experience in at least two ways. The first, in Genesis 1:31, is the expression והנה (*wehinneh*, "and behold"), which in narrative invites one to see the scene from a participant's perspective.[91] The reader is to experience something of God's own delight in "everything that he had made." The second way is in the account of the divine Sabbath in Genesis 2:1–3, which is told with the fourth commandment in view (see section E.3 below). When the Israelite keeps the Sabbath day holy, he is entering into God's enjoyment of his own rest. Indeed, this anticipates one of the ways in which the Bible views the process of human moral formation: as imitating God.

We further see God's absolute power over his world. We have noted that the narrative repeatedly has God saying something, expressing a wish (a volitional form in Hebrew); then the story tells us that the wish was carried out. The account has no comment on how long it took for God's wish to be carried out; it rather focuses on the way that God's wish alone determines what happens.[92] God displays his power by calling the universe into existence and by shaping the earth as a fit place for his human creatures to live. The world did not make itself; rather, *God* made it without any help. The author of Psalm 33 took this feature and made it into a hymn:

91. Bruce K. Waltke and Michael O'Connor, *An Introduction to Biblical Hebrew Syntax* (Winona Lake, Ind.: Eisenbrauns, 1990), §40.2.1 discuss the "Presentative Exclamations" הנה (*hinneh*, "behold!") and והנה (*wehinneh*, "and behold!"), noting that והנה can be used "as a bridge to introduce with emotion a noun clause . . . or perception," but they do not distinguish its role in narrative versus other functions. Consider Gen. 6:12, "And God saw the earth, *and behold*, it was corrupt"; Exod. 3:2, "[Moses] looked, *and behold*, the bush was burning, yet it was not consumed"; Ruth 4:1, "*And behold*, the redeemer, of whom Boaz had spoken, came by." In each case we are brought from the position of observers of the whole scene to sharing the perception of God, Moses, or Boaz.

92. Currid, 72 (see also 61), claims that the text implies that fulfillment was instantaneous, but the text says no such thing. He writes, "To deny the immediacy of creation's completion is to reduce or diminish the power of God that is so greatly invested in the account" but offers no reason why we should think this to be true. Such matters are probably extraneous to the purpose of the narrative.

⁶By the word of the Lord the heavens were made,
  and by the breath of his mouth all their host. . . .
⁹For he spoke, and it came to be;
  he commanded, and it stood firm.

Finally, the structure of the account shows us that our author has presented God as if he were a craftsman going about his workweek. This comes out from the structure of the account, the six workdays followed by a Sabbath. It also comes out from the refrain,[93] "and there was evening, and there was morning, the nth day." The order of the items mentioned is crucial: it is evening *followed by* morning. This means that any effort to find this as defining the days runs counter to the author's own presentation. Evening and morning bracket the night,[94] and this is the daily time of rest for the worker. In Psalm 104:23, when the sun rises, "man goes out to his work, and to his labor until the evening."[95] The seventh day speaks of "his work that he had done," using terms applied to a human worker (Exod. 20:9–10).

When we mention the seventh day, we also see that God is said in Genesis 2:2–3 to "rest" (שׁבת, *shabat*). The verb here may have a broader meaning than simply "rest," such as "cease what he was doing." However, Exodus 20:11 uses a more specific word to describe God's rest (הניח, *heniakh*), and Exodus 31:17 says that on the seventh day God "rested" (שׁבת) and "was refreshed" (הנפשׁ, *hinnapesh*, as if to get his breath back).[96] If God has the kind of power we see in this pericope, then we know not to take this language in any literalistic fashion: God does not get tired as we do (see also Isa. 40:28–31). Hence the language is analogical, and the import is that human work and rest are analogies of God's work and rest.

The author's point of view is one of adoring the God who made everything there is, and of exulting in the variety and fecundity of God's good creation. The clearest way he expresses this is by the repeated way in which God sees that the things he made are good, and especially when the author invites us to see, through God's own

93. See section C.2 above on the proper rendering of the refrain.
94. See Num. 9:15, where "the appearance of fire" was over the tabernacle *from evening until morning*; in verse 16, we find this paraphrased as "the appearance of fire [covered the tabernacle] *by night*." Hence "night" is the period from evening to morning.
95. See also Gen. 30:16; Exod. 18:13.
96. For this latter verb, see Exod. 23:12; 2 Sam. 16:14.

eyes as it were, that it was all "very good" (Gen. 1:31).[97] (I am taking for granted that for any biblical author, God is a "reliable character," whose view of things is the final word.) We further see the author's approval of the Sabbath rest, when God "blessed the seventh day and made it holy" (2:3). The implication is that the pious reader should likewise adore the Creator, exult in the creation, and revel in the Sabbath.

Now we are in a position to draw all the features together and say what the passage is about. Many writers call Genesis 1:1–2:3 a *cosmogony*, meaning a story of how the universe came to be. Though the passage does in fact speak of that, it is not the focus of the text; after all, it tells us of the origin of everything in 1:1 and then narrows its attention as the account proceeds. The first verse, as I see it, narrates the initial creation event; then verse 2 describes the condition of the earth just before the creation week gets under way. These two verses stand outside the six days of God's workweek, and—just speaking grammatically—say nothing about the length of time between the initial event of 1:1 and the first day of 1:3.[98]

Once the workdays begin, attention is wholly on the earth. Whereas in Genesis 1:1 "the heavens" (הַשָּׁמַיִם, *hashshamayim*) and "the earth" (הָאָרֶץ, *ha'arets*) are everything in the material creation, in verse 8 "heavens" gets narrowed to the sky above us (see ESV margin), and in verse 10 "earth" gets narrowed to "land." In verse 14, the author speaks of the heavenly lights solely in terms of their service to mankind—specifically, to man as worshiper, if the ESV margin is acknowledged. The author has gone from the entire universe to the earth alone, and especially to mankind. We further see this in the way that the creation of man is the peak of the account, with the storyline coming to a halt so that the reader can mull over this event. I conclude that man is presented as the crown of God's creation week.

From all of this we may infer that the text has its main interest in telling us that God made the material world as a place for mankind to live: to love, to work, to enjoy, and to worship God. The exalted tone of the passage allows the reader to ponder this with a sense of awe,

---

97. This includes the process of reproduction, which receives God's "blessing" (Gen. 1:28).

98. That is, Gen. 1:1–2 is background to the six days, with verse 1 describing an event that took place before the main storyline got going. The grammar itself tells us nothing about *how long before* the storyline.

adoring the goodness, power, and creativity of the One who did all this.[99] It also shows the human reader why his embodied existence is good in itself and is meant to be received as a gift and blessing. Further, it joins the rest of Genesis in laying the foundation for the Sinai covenant, as we shall see in chapter 9.

One of the key covenantal features in this passage, which is then taken up in later Scripture, is the idea that the God who made the world—who is also the covenant God of Israel—is the sovereign owner and ruler of his creation. This follows from the fact that he made it all from nothing and shaped it by his unopposed power. Hence we find passages such as Psalm 24:1–2 (although the vocabulary is not exactly that of Genesis):[100]

> [1]The earth is the LORD's and the fullness thereof,
> the world and those who dwell therein,
> [2]for he has founded it upon the seas
> and established it upon the rivers.

When a congregation sings Psalm 24, which begins like this and then goes on to reflect on who may ascend the hill of the Lord, they remind themselves what an astonishing privilege it is to enter into this God's presence.

This is what we find in the Bible in general: being a covenantal book, it rarely expounds a doctrine without also showing how it applies to the life of God's covenant people. Hence we also see texts that assure the pious members of the covenant people that the God to whom they are loyal is fully able to provide for them and to protect their community as he has promised: Psalms 136:4–9;[101] 145:5–7;

99. Many have called the passage liturgical in origin: for example, Moshe Weinfeld, "Sabbath, Temple, and the Enthronement of the Lord—the Problem of the Sitz im Leben of Genesis 1:1–2:3," in *Mélanges Bibliques et Orientaux en l'honneur de M. Henri Cazelles*, ed. A. Caquot and M. Delcor (Alter Orient und Altes Testament 212; Neukirchen-Vluyn: Neukirchener, 1981), 501–12. Even though I do not agree with all that lies behind such a statement, I do believe that it captures something about the passage that is really there.

100. Note that Ps. 24:2 uses the verbs יָסַד (*yasad*, "founded") and כּוֹנֵן (*kônen*, "established"), neither of which appears in the Genesis account. Other passages that use "founded" are Pss. 78:69; 89:11; 102:25; 104:5; Prov. 3:19; Job 38:4; Isa. 48:13; 51:13, 16. Some that use "established" (Polel or Hiphil of כּוּן) are Pss. 65:6; 74:16; Prov. 3:19; 8:27; Isa. 45:18; Jer. 10:12; 33:2; 51:15; cf. Pss. 93:1 and 96:10 using Niphal as passive.

101. Closely dependent on the Genesis account; see reverberations below.

147:4–5; 148; 65:5–13; 89:6–14; 93; 95:3–5; 121:2;[102] 123:1; 124:8; Isaiah 40:12–31;[103] 42:5; 44:24–28; 45:7; 11–13, 18; Jeremiah 32:17.[104]

One way biblical authors make this theme explicit is by taking creation terminology and applying it to the creation of Israel, as in Isaiah 43:1, 7:[105]

> ¹But now thus says the Lord,
>> he who *created* [ברא, *bara'*] you, O Jacob,
>> he who *formed* [יצר, *yatsar*] you, O Israel:
> "Fear not, for I have redeemed you;
>> I have called you by name, you are mine. . . .
> ⁷[Bring] everyone who is called by my name,
>> whom I *created* for my glory,
>> whom I *formed* and made."

The Lord created Israel, and his power will see to it that Israel fulfills the purpose for which it was created.[106]

The Bible always acknowledges that there are wicked people in the earth who oppose God's purposes—whether they be the unfaithful among the covenant people or the Gentiles who oppress God's people. These must be warned that their plans are futile, doomed to failure. Hence we find passages such as Amos 4:13; 9:5–6; Psalm 94:8–11; Daniel 2:37–38; 4:34–35 (see also Sir. 23:20).

Further, as we saw above in section C.9, to say that the creation is good is to say that it displays the goodness of its Maker; and more generally, the creation displays aspects of God's character for all to see—especially his greatness and his generosity and his unique regard for mankind. As we will see in section E below, this influences a number of psalms, as well as the creational apologetic of the apostles.

---

102. This describes the Lord as "the one who *made* [עשה, *'asâ*, participle] heaven and earth," using terminology found in Genesis. Compare Pss. 115:15; 121:2; 124:8; 134:3; 146:6.

103. In Isa. 40:22 and elsewhere we read that God "stretched out" (נטה, *natâ*) the heavens. This is an example of phenomenological language, which I will address in chapter 10, section C.

104. Compare also Wis. 9:1–3; 11:21–26; Sir. 4:6; 7:30; 10:12; 32:13; 33:13; 38:15; 39:5, 28; 47:8.

105. Compare also Isa. 45:9, 11 ("form"); Sir. 36:15.

106. It is worth exploring whether this terminology also implies that after the fall of Gen. 3 marred the first creation, Israel is part of the Lord's "new" creation. Perhaps this also explains New Testament "new creation" language, such as 2 Cor. 4:6; 5:17.

Wisdom literature is often said to depend strongly on the doctrine of creation—even more than it does on covenant. I consider this a false antithesis, since the biblical wisdom material represents "covenantal wisdom": wisdom is skill in living in the world, but true skill comes from embracing the covenant.[107] This is why the name *the LORD* plays a prominent role in biblical wisdom material. The Lord by wisdom founded the world (Prov. 3:19; 8:22–31), which is why it is a coherent system; this is the wisdom that is on offer for the pious among the covenant people.[108]

The final topic to treat is the way this account provides a ground for rejecting pagan religion and idolatry. It is the Lord alone who did the whole work of creation; compare Psalm 136:4, "who *alone* [לבדו] does great wonders," the first of which is the making of the world. It also follows from the creation account that the Lord alone rules all aspects of nature, including the weather and the fertility of animals and humans—which means that the other deities do not. This leaves all the other gods with nothing to do. It is also possible that, in a backhanded way, the account "demythologizes" the forces of nature and the lights in heaven: God made them, and we have no reason to attribute divine personalities to them.[109]

Later reflections certainly pick this up. Consider, for example, Romans 1:21–25:

> [21]For although they knew God, they did not honor him as God or give thanks to him, but they became futile in their thinking, and their foolish hearts were darkened. [22]Claiming to be wise, they became fools, [23]and exchanged the glory of the immortal God for *images resembling* mortal man and *birds* and *animals* and *reptiles*.

---

107. Thus I agree with the critique that Craig Bartholomew gives in "Covenant and creation: Covenant overload or covenantal deconstruction," *Calvin Theological Journal* 30 (1995): 11–33, at 32: "The historical covenant literature continues to be set in antithesis to creation-based wisdom literature."

108. This strand in Proverbs likely mediated the creation theology of Genesis to Ben Sira; compare Sir. 1:1–20; 24:8–9. Apparently Sir. 4:6 appropriates the creation theology of Proverbs 14:31; 17:5; compare also Wis. 7:15–8:11. Perhaps this explains the "Wisdom-creation" motif in Col. 1:15–20, as mentioned below in section E.4.

109. I have not said that there is no reason to attribute *any* personality to them; I do not see the account itself as commenting one way or another on this, although other Scripture may do so. Since I am a Westerner with a scientific education, I am not inclined to attribute personality to the heavenly lights. On the other hand, an ancient such as Philo (*On the Creation* 73) specifically calls the heavenly bodies (ἀστέρες) "living creatures endowed with mind" (ζῷα νοερά).

²⁴Therefore God gave them up in the lusts of their hearts to impurity, to the dishonoring of their bodies among themselves, ²⁵because they exchanged the truth about God for a lie and worshiped and served the creature rather than the Creator, who is blessed forever! Amen.

In Romans 1:23 Paul's terms echo Genesis 1 (LXX): "images resembling," literally "the likeness of the image of" (Gen. 1:26); "birds" (1:21); "animals," literally "four-footed animals," the Septuagint for "livestock," and "reptiles," for "creeping things" (1:24). Since from Genesis these are certainly "created things," Paul can pass judgment in Romans 1:26.[110]

Paul also appeals to creation to ground monotheism in 1 Corinthians 8:4–6:

⁴Therefore, as to the eating of food offered to idols, we know that "an idol has no real existence," and that "there is no God but one." ⁵For although there may be so-called gods in heaven or on earth—as indeed there are many "gods" and many "lords"—⁶yet for us there is one God, the Father, from whom are all things and for whom we exist, and one Lord, Jesus Christ, through whom are all things and through whom we exist.

Many authors suggest that this theme of rejecting paganism comes through as well in relation to "the two great lights" of Genesis 1:16, which get this strange name instead of their usual "sun" and "moon."[111] In my judgment, this is probably not the reason 1:16 uses its terminology; rather, the name *light*s—literally, " light-bearers"—matches the "light" of the first day and suits the function of the bodies, "to give light upon the earth" (1:15). The strangeness of the names also reflects the rhetorically high style of the narrative. The wording of Psalm 136:7–9 supports my conclusion: in a song whose wording depends on the Genesis account, we have in verse 7 "the great lights" (אוֹרִים, *'ôrîm*, compare the term מְאוֹרת, *me'ôrôt*, in Genesis), and in verse 8 "the sun" (הַשֶּׁמֶשׁ, *hashshemesh*) and in verse 9 "the moon" (הַיָּרֵחַ, *hayyareakh*). Thus refusing to name the great lights can hardly be

110. See Wis. 14:11 for a similar judgment to Paul's; compare also Bar. 4:7.
111. See for example, Gerhard Hasel, "The Polemic Nature of the Genesis Cosmology," *Evangelical Quarterly* 46 (1974): 81–102, at 89.

necessary in order to declare them creations rather than deities, and we should seek another explanation for this feature in Genesis.[112]

As I mentioned above, many have spoken as if the nature of the six days and the length of the creation period are the main interest of the account; but the literary features direct our attention to other matters. In fact, the closest that any Bible passage comes to reflecting on the length of the creation week is in two texts concerning the Sabbath commandment, Exodus 20:8–11 and 31:12–17.[113] That does not mean, of course, that we may simply dismiss the question of length; it does mean that if our goal is exegesis of the text, we should keep our sense of proportion regarding this question. In section E.3 below I will explore just how the Sabbath commandment uses the six days, while in chapter 5, section C.7 ("How long was the Creation Week?"), I will argue for what I take to be the proper sense of the days.

E. Other Reverberations

1. Psalms 8, 104, 136

The opening pericope of Genesis is exalted indeed, and some have gone on to call it liturgical. I have not used that label, preferring "exalted prose narrative." The pericope has certainly inspired liturgical compositions, such as Psalms 8, 104, and 136, together with quite a few references elsewhere in the psalms.[114]

I will take it as given that the psalms are first and foremost hymns to be sung in public covenantal worship and that therefore their function is to do what hymns do: namely, to shape the affective side of the

112. Compare Wis. 13:2, "They supposed that . . . the lights of heaven were the gods that rule the world," (cf. RSV) which both attests the pagan belief (using the terms of Gen. 1:14 LXX) and rejects it without appealing to any lack of name.

113. I say this based on a survey of all texts in the Old Testament, New Testament, and Apocrypha that have the expression *six days*. I do not find in Philo (*On the Creation*) or Josephus (*Antiquities*) any discussion of this matter, either. (Philo, lines 89–128, does find significance in the *six* days and the *seventh* day, but that is because of the mysteries of the numbers six and seven rather than anything about the days. Further, in his *Allegorical Interpretation* 1.2–3, Philo does seem to suggest that these cannot be ordinary days; once again, the interest is in the number six rather than in length of time.)

114. We should add the magnificently hymnic portions of Sir. 39:12–35 and 42:15–43:33.

worshiper.[115] Of course this does not exclude their role in conveying information and in urging duty; quite the contrary, it shows how the psalms aim to equip the worshiper to embrace the information and give himself to the duty as a loyal member of the covenant people.

Psalm 8 reflects on man's place in the created order:

[1]O Lord, our Lord,
      how majestic is your name in all the earth!
You have set your glory above the heavens.
      [2]Out of the mouth of babes and infants,
you have established strength because of your foes,
      to still the enemy and the avenger.

[3]When I look at your heavens, the work of your fingers,
      the moon and the stars, which you have set in place,
[4]what is man that you are mindful of him,
      and the son of man that you care for him?

[5]Yet you have made him a little lower than the heavenly beings
      and crowned him with glory and honor.
[6]You have given him dominion over the works of your hands;
      you have put all things under his feet,
[7]all sheep and oxen,
      and also the beasts of the field,
[8]the birds of the heavens, and the fish of the sea,
      whatever passes along the paths of the seas.

[9]O Lord, our Lord,
      how majestic is your name in all the earth!

It is generally acknowledged that the psalm evokes Genesis 1, although the wording only has a few points of contact. The "sheep and oxen" of Psalm 8:7 are more specific than the "livestock" of Genesis 1:24–25; the "beasts of the field" in Psalm 8:7 uses the term בהמה (behemâ, "beast") in a different sense (with its qualifier "of the field") than Genesis 1:25 (where it is "livestock"). The term for "have dominion" in Psalm 8:6 (משל, mashal) is different from that used

---

115. I grant that this is controversial; many would read the psalms as devotional literature in the personal prayer journal genre, while others think of the psalms in terms of what they "teach." I do not deny these functions; I only put them in relation to the psalms' place as a hymnbook.

in Genesis 1:26 (רדה, *radâ*). The "setting in place" of the moon and stars in Psalm 8:3 (כונן, *kônen*) uses a different term than Genesis 1:17 (נתן, *natan*).

In the discussion of the "image of God" above I noted that some appeal to this text in order to argue for what I called the representative sense of the image, namely, that man rules the creation as God's representative. I showed there why I think that this is a mistake; we can add to that the simple fact that the psalm nowhere indicates that it is defining the image. (As I argued above, the ruling is a consequence of man's resemblance to God.)

In celebrating the privileged place of man in God's creation, this psalm picks up on the primary communicative point of the pericope, as indicated by the peak at Genesis 1:26–27. It also applies the lesson of the composite divine name in Genesis 2:4–3:24, namely, to identify Israel's God as the universal Creator. That is, it couples majesty with intimacy. This is surprising, since it would be easy to conclude from the magnificent creation that God is too distant and too exalted to have anything to do with mere man. Hence the psalm enables the worshiper to express a sense of wonder, and to delight in the God (the "Lord") who has so ennobled his covenant partners.

Psalm 104 is a long hymn of praise about how the created order reveals God's glory as it provides so abundantly for all living things. As is the case with Psalm 8, it clearly evokes Genesis 1:1–2:3 without repeating its terminology. The works of the six days are reflected in the psalm, as Kidner has set them out:[116]

Psalm 104 verses	
Day 1	2a: light
Day 2	2b–4: the "firmament" divides the waters
Day 3	5–13: land and water distinct
	14–18: vegetation and trees
Day 4	19–24: light-bearers as timekeepers
Day 5	25–26: creatures of sea
Day 6	21–24: land animals and man
	27–30: food for all creatures

116. Kidner, *Psalms 73–150*, 368.

The structure should not be pressed, as we can see from the way that the land animals and man (Ps. 104:21–24) precede the sea creatures (vv. 25–26). Even more, this is not simply a reflection of the Genesis account as an event; rather, it celebrates the way that this created order still continues in human experience. The psalm acknowledges the existence of human sin, but in only one verse (v. 35):

> Let sinners be consumed from the earth,
>   and let the wicked be no more!
> Bless the LORD, O my soul!
> Praise the LORD!

This shapes the worshipers' hearts in two ways. First, it leads them to delight in the world, recognizing that it is a good place that God made (even now, after Gen. 3). Second, it enables them to see that "sinners" and "the wicked"—which probably refer not simply to people who sin but to those who dwell in their sin and refuse the Lord's grace—are a stain on God's world. Hence the worshiper will be glad to be faithful to the God who made the world and keeps it working and will be careful not to identify with those who rebel against the covenant.

Psalm 136 recounts events from Genesis 1 right through the period of the judges. It states its theme in 136:1 and repeats it in 136:26 as an envelope:

> Give thanks to the LORD, for he is good,
>   for his steadfast love endures forever.

The creation (136:5–9), the exodus (136:10–15), the guidance through the wilderness and the conquest of the land (136:16–22), and the many deliverances under the judges (136:23–25) all illustrate how "his steadfast love"—particularly his commitment to his own people—"endures forever." Psalm 136:5–9 reflects the wording of Genesis 1:

> [5]to him who by understanding made the heavens,
>   for his steadfast love endures forever;
> [6]to him who spread out the earth above the waters,
>   for his steadfast love endures forever;
> [7]to him who made the great lights,
>   for his steadfast love endures forever;
> [8]the sun to rule over the day,
>   for his steadfast love endures forever;

⁹the moon and stars to rule over the night,
   for his steadfast love endures forever.

The wording follows that of Genesis 1, with a few additions and modifications: Psalm 136:5 adds "by understanding" (compare Prov. 3:19); Psalm 136:6 speaks of "spreading out" the earth (compare Isa. 42:5); and Psalm 136:8–9 names the sun and moon explicitly.

To speak of the Lord's "steadfast love" in the works of creation is to assert that the creation is the arena in which God pursues his relational purposes for man. Some theologians have drawn a line between creation and redemption; but the biblical text does no such thing.

2. "Be fruitful and multiply" and God's blessing

Genesis 1:28 records God's "blessing" on the human couple, urging them to "be fruitful and multiply." These themes run throughout Genesis and beyond. In Genesis 9:1, Noah is a kind of "new Adam": "And God blessed Noah and his sons and said to them, 'Be fruitful and multiply and fill the earth.'" In Genesis 12:2–3, the Lord will bless Abram and make him a channel of blessing for his own descendants and for the rest of the world (see also 22:17–18).[117] These promises are repeated to Abraham's heirs: to Ishmael (17:20), Isaac (26:3–4), and Jacob (28:3; 48:3–4). The Book of Exodus (1:7) opens by telling us, "But the people of Israel *were fruitful* and increased greatly; they *multiplied* and grew exceedingly strong, so that the land was filled with them." Deuteronomy promises that the people of Israel, when they are faithful, will continue to enjoy this blessing (30:16, compare 7:13):

> If you obey the commandments of the LORD your God that I command you today, by loving the LORD your God, by walking in his ways, and by keeping his commandments and his statutes and his rules, then you shall live and multiply, and the LORD your God will bless you in the land that you are entering to take possession of it.

117. For the view that Gen. 22:18 is messianic and lies behind Paul's statement about "offspring" and "offsprings" (Gal. 3:16), see T. D. Alexander, "Further Observations on the Term 'Seed' in Genesis," *Tyndale Bulletin* 48, no. 2 (1997): 363–67; and C. John Collins, "Galatians 3:16: What Kind of Exegete Was Paul?" *Tyndale Bulletin* 54, no. 1 (2003): 75–86.

All of this allows us to see that Genesis has focused on the ways in which God has made new starts after Adam's sin: with Noah, and then with Abram and his offspring. We are then able to say that Adam enjoyed a covenant, as did Noah and Abram (see further chapter 5, section C.2); we may also say that Noah and Abram are "new Adams."

The Septuagint renders the expression *be fruitful and multiply* (Gen. 1:28) with αὐξάνεσθε καὶ πληθύνεσθε ("increase and multiply"), and Luke has evoked this in Acts. In Acts 7:17, Stephen simply refers to the (LXX) text of Exodus 1:7. However, when Luke describes the impact of the gospel, he writes:

Καὶ ὁ λόγος τοῦ θεοῦ ηὔξανεν καὶ ἐπληθύνετο ὁ ἀριθμὸς τῶν μαθητῶν ἐν Ἰερουσαλὴμ σφόδρα, πολύς τε ὄχλος τῶν ἱερέων ὑπήκουον τῇ πίστει.	And the word of God continued to *increase*, and the number of the disciples *multiplied* greatly in Jerusalem, and a great many of the priests became obedient to the faith. (Acts 6:7)
Ἡ μὲν οὖν ἐκκλησία καθ᾽ ὅλης τῆς Ἰουδαίας καὶ Γαλιλαίας καὶ Σαμαρείας εἶχεν εἰρήνην οἰκοδομουμένη καὶ πορευομένη τῷ φόβῳ τοῦ κυρίου καὶ τῇ παρακλήσει τοῦ ἁγίου πνεύματος ἐπληθύνετο.	So the church throughout all Judea and Galilee and Samaria had peace and was being built up. And walking in the fear of the Lord and in the comfort of the Holy Spirit, it *multiplied*. (Acts 9:31)
Ὁ δὲ λόγος τοῦ θεοῦ ηὔξανεν καὶ ἐπληθύνετο.	But the word of God *increased* and *multiplied*. (Acts 12:24)
Οὕτως κατὰ κράτος τοῦ κυρίου ὁ λόγος ηὔξανεν καὶ ἴσχυεν.	So the word of the Lord continued to *increase* and prevail mightily. (Acts 19:20)

Luke presents the Christian church as the fulfillment of prophecy; see Acts 1:8, "to the end of the earth," which we find also in Acts 13:47 (using Isa. 49:6). These believers are the heirs of the promises to Abraham.

3. The fourth commandment: Exodus 20:8–11; 31:12–17; John 5:17; Hebrews 4:3–11

The rest of the Pentateuch enjoins a Sabbath rest for the people of Israel. The first version of the Ten Commandments, in the fourth commandment, grounds this rest in God's own creation Sabbath (Exod. 20:8–11):

⁸Remember the Sabbath day, to keep it holy. ⁹Six days you shall labor, and do all your work,

זכור את־יום השבת לקדשו
ששת ימים תעבד ועשית
כל־מלאכתך

¹⁰but the seventh day is a Sabbath to the LORD your God. On it you shall not do any work, you, or your son, or your daughter, your male servant, or your female servant, or your livestock, or the sojourner who is within your gates.

ויום השביעי שבת ליהוה
אלהיך לא־תעשה כל־
מלאכה אתה ובנך־ובתך
עבדך ואמתך ובהמתך
וגרך אשר בשעריך

¹¹For in six days the LORD made heaven and earth, the sea, and all that is in them, and rested the seventh day. Therefore the LORD blessed the Sabbath day and made it holy.

כי ששת־ימים עשה יהוה את־
השמים ואת־הארץ את־הים
ואת־כל־אשר־בם וינח ביום
השביעי על־כן ברך יהוה
את־יום השבת ויקדשהו

Exodus 20:11 is an explicit reference to the creation Sabbath, using "the LORD" as the divine name in place of "God" in Genesis 2:1–3. Specific references include "heaven and earth," "the seventh day," "blessed," and "made it holy." The command also uses the term *do work* (עשה מלאכה, *'asâ mela'kâ*) in Exodus 20:9–10, which appears in Genesis 2:2 ("all the work that he had done"); and the name *Sabbath* echoes the verb translated "rest" in Genesis 2:2–3. The Israelite is to pattern his workweek after God's workweek: he is to work for six days as God did, he is to rest as God did, and he is to "keep holy" the day that God "made holy."[118]

On the other hand, Exodus 20:11 uses a different verb to denote God's rest: here it is נוח (*nûakh*), which is more specific than שבת (*shabat*), the verb found in Genesis 2:2–3, which can be generally "to cease." In Exodus 23:12 we find both of these verbs, together with a third, to describe the Sabbath rest: "Six days you shall do your work, but on the seventh day you shall *rest* [שבת]; that your ox and your donkey may *have rest* [נוח], and the son of your servant woman, and the alien, may *be refreshed* [נפש niph.]." This allows us to say that in

118. I take the second masculine singular pronoun ("you") to apply to both men and women, as does Amos Hakham, *Sefer Shemot* (Exodus, Da'at Miqra; Jerusalem: Mossad Harav Kook, 1991), שפה. This is the pattern for the rest of the commandments; otherwise we must suppose that only *men* are forbidden to take God's name in vain or to commit adultery, which is absurd. This explains why "your wife" is not included in the list of Exod. 20:10.

Genesis 2:2–3 the verb שׁבת is used in the narrower sense of "rest," and thus the Sabbath is properly a day of rest.[119]

The second version of the fourth commandment (Deut. 5:12–15), however, grounds Sabbath observance in a different motive—namely, the Israelite remembers his experience of slavery and deliverance:[120]

> [12]Observe the Sabbath day, to keep it holy, as the LORD your God commanded you. [13]Six days you shall labor and do all your work, [14]but the seventh day is a Sabbath to the LORD your God. On it you shall not do any work, you or your son or your daughter or your male servant or your female servant, or your ox or your donkey or any of your livestock, or the sojourner who is within your gates, that your male servant and your female servant may rest as well as you. [15]You shall remember that you were a slave in the land of Egypt, and the LORD your God brought you out from there with a mighty hand and an outstretched arm. Therefore the LORD your God commanded you to keep the Sabbath day.

Theologians will describe the difference by saying that Exodus 20:11 appeals to creation, while Deuteronomy 5:15 appeals to redemption. It would be a mistake to contrast these, however: theologically (as I will argue in chapter 9), one purpose of redemption is to restore man to his proper working order, which was given him at the creation. Further, Exodus itself brings the two together (31:12–17):

> [12]And the LORD said to Moses, [13]"You are to speak to the people of Israel and say, 'Above all you shall keep my Sabbaths, for this is a sign between me and you throughout your generations, that you may know that I, the LORD, sanctify you. [14]You shall keep the Sabbath, because it is holy for you. Everyone who profanes it shall be put to death. Whoever does any work on it, that soul shall be cut off from among his people. [15]Six days shall work be done, but the seventh day is a Sabbath of solemn rest, holy to the LORD. Whoever does any work on the Sabbath day shall be put to death. [16]Therefore the people of Israel shall keep the Sabbath, observing the Sabbath throughout their generations, as a covenant forever. [17]It is a sign forever between me and the people of Israel that in six days the

---

119. Some have denied this, and thus denied that "rest" is the basic idea of the Sabbath: for example, Ian Hart, "Genesis 1:1–2:3 as a Prologue to the Book of Genesis," *Tyndale Bulletin* 46, no. 2 (1995): 315–36, at 325–26.

120. The other differences need not concern us here.

LORD made heaven and earth, and on the seventh day he rested and was refreshed.'"

To call the Sabbath a sign, to refer to the Lord as the one who sanctifies (Exod. 31:13), to threaten to cut a soul off from his people (31:14), and to require this of the people of Israel (31:17) is to evoke the notion of Israel as the covenant people whom the Lord brought out of Egypt and to whom he gave the Sinai code. At the same time the passage explicitly refers to creation as well. Hence the Pentateuch sees no difficulty in holding the two realms, creation and redemption, together.

According to Leviticus 23:3, Israel is to observe the weekly Sabbath as well by gathering for public worship: "Six days shall work be done, but on the seventh day is a Sabbath of solemn rest, a holy convocation. You shall do no work. It is a Sabbath to the LORD in all your dwelling places." This, too, combines what we might call creation and redemption: rest for the body (creation) and for the soul in worship (redemption).

If redemptive covenants have to do with restoring the damaged creation, then it is no surprise that the Old Testament holds out the privilege of Sabbath observance to Gentiles (Isa. 56:6–8):

> [6]"And the foreigners who join themselves to the LORD,
>   to minister to him, to love the name of the LORD,
>   and to be his servants,
> everyone who keeps the Sabbath and does not profane it,
>   and holds fast my covenant—
> [7]these I will bring to my holy mountain,
>   and make them joyful in my house of prayer;
> their burnt offerings and their sacrifices
>   will be accepted on my altar;
> for my house shall be called a house of prayer
>   for all peoples."
> [8]The Lord GOD,
>   who gathers the outcasts of Israel, declares,
> "I will gather yet others to him
>   besides those already gathered."

The Sabbath bestows its gifts upon man—all of mankind—at the deepest places of his created nature.

The New Testament takes up the question of Sabbath observance for followers of Jesus, and I will come back to that in chapter 5, section C.8. Here I want to examine two passages from the New Testament that build on the uniqueness of God's creation Sabbath.

John 5:1–18 records Jesus' miracle of healing a man who had been an invalid for thirty-eight years and the reaction this provoked among the Jewish leaders. Verse 16 tells us that Jesus did this on a Sabbath, and thus he was persecuted. In verse 17 we read, "But Jesus answered them, 'My Father is working until now, and I am working.'" The wording evokes the Septuagint of both Genesis 2:2–3 and Exodus 20:9–10: the phrase *is working* in John 5:17 uses ἐργάζομαι, while the Old Testament verses use the equivalent ποιέω ἔργα for "to do work."[121] Hence the Father is "working" on his Sabbath, which only makes sense if we suppose that his creation Sabbath continues. The point is that God's rest, which is analogical to human rest, is not inactivity; rather, it is with respect to the work of creation. Jesus claims to be doing the same works as the Father does, namely, those which bring salvation to human beings—a point that the Jewish leaders perceive and take as an outrageous claim to deity (John 5:18).

Consider Hebrews 4:3–11:

[3]For we who have believed enter that rest, as he has said,

> "As I swore in my wrath,
> 'They shall not enter my rest,'"

although his works were finished from the foundation of the world. [4]For he has somewhere spoken of the seventh day in this way: "And God rested on the seventh day from all his works." [5]And again in this passage he said,

> "They shall not enter my rest."

[6]Since therefore it remains for some to enter it, and those who formerly received the good news failed to enter because of disobedience, [7]again he appoints a certain day, "Today," saying through David so long afterward, in the words already quoted,

---

121. The Johannine material uses such periphrastic equivalents: κρίνω ("to judge," John 5:22, 30) and ποιέω κρίσιν ("to execute judgment," John 5:27); ἁμαρτάνω ("to sin," 1 John 3:6, 8, 9) and ποιέω ἁμαρτίαν ("to do sin," John 8:34; 1 John 3:4, 8, 9).

"Today, if you hear his voice,
do not harden your hearts."

[8]For if Joshua had given them rest, God would not have spoken of another day later on. [9]So then, there remains a Sabbath rest for the people of God, [10]for whoever has entered God's rest has also rested from his works as God did from his.

[11]Let us therefore strive to enter that rest, so that no one may fall by the same sort of disobedience.

The author is bringing together two passages from the Old Testament, Psalm 95 (see Heb. 4:3) and Genesis 2:1–3 (see Heb. 4:4). They both speak of God's rest; although the Hebrew terms are different,[122] the Septuagint renderings are closely related, using the verb καταπαύω ("to rest," Heb. 4:4, 10; "to give rest," v. 8) and the noun κατάπαυσις ("rest," vv. 3, 5, 10, 11).[123] This rest is both something into which God entered on the creation Sabbath and something into which people may enter through faith (v. 10). Of course the best way for this to make sense is if the author thought that the creation Sabbath continues into the present.[124] But he says much more, namely, that human beings have the opportunity to enter into the peaceful rest that God is enjoying, to which the human Sabbath points (v. 9). Since this author sees his audience as sharing their spiritual opportunities with the generation that left Egypt (see vv. 1, 6, 10), it stands to reason that he saw them as also able to enter God's rest: that is, the rest being available is not a redemptive-historical development, newly available to his audience but absent from previous eras. On the contrary, this rest is an enduring offer for God's people. Further, if the human Sabbath points to the divine Sabbath, we might consider whether the activities of man's Sabbath offer a foretaste of the full experience of that rest. This provides a basis for understanding

122. The Hebrew noun "rest" in Ps. 95 is מְנוּחָה (menûkhâ); the verb in Gen. 2:2–3 is שׁבת (shabat). As we saw in our discussion of Exod. 20:8–11 above, this is not an arbitrary connection due to the Septuagint: Exod. 20:11 uses the verb נוּחַ (nûakh, cognate to the noun in Ps. 95) in place of שׁבת for "to rest." The Septuagint of Joshua uses καταπαύω transitively (see Heb. 4:8) for the Hiphil of נוּחַ (Josh. 1:13, 15; 21:44; 22:4; 23:1).

123. The expression Sabbath rest in Heb. 4:9 renders one word, σαββατισμός.

124. See Donald Guthrie, Hebrews (Tyndale New Testament Commentary; Grand Rapids: Eerdmans, 1983), 116, on this verse; F. F. Bruce, Hebrews (New International Commentary on the New Testament; Grand Rapids: Eerdmans, 1990), 106.

public Sabbath worship as the means by which people are invited to
have a foretaste of their eternal rest.

4. Christ and creation in the New Testament

Several New Testament passages declare that Christ—or the person who became incarnate in Jesus Christ—was the agent of creation:
John 1:1–3; Colossians 1:16–17; and Hebrews 1:3, 10–12.
    John 1:1–5 tells us:

> ¹In the beginning was the Word, and the Word was with God, and
> the Word was God. ²He was in the beginning with God. ³All things
> were made through him, and without him was not any thing made
> that was made. ⁴In him was life, and the life was the light of men.
> ⁵The light shines in the darkness, and the darkness has not over-
> come it.

The opening phrase, "in the beginning" (ἐν ἀρχῇ) echoes the opening
phrase of Genesis 1 in the Septuagint, and that is the most obvious
reference to Genesis. Other echoes include the terms *were made* and
was made in John 1:3 (both ἐγένετο)—this is the passive of the term
used in the Septuagint for both "created" and "made" in Genesis 1
(ποιέω);[125] and the mention of "light," "darkness," and "shine" in John
1:5 (compare Gen. 1:3–5, 17).[126]
    The term *Word* (λόγος) also derives from our pericope, although
by way of several texts in between. The Hebrew text tells us that God
"said" things; then Psalm 33:6 says,

> By the word [LXX λόγος] of the LORD the heavens were made,
>   and by the breath of his mouth all their host.

Then Wisdom of Solomon 9:1 uses "the word" as the supernatural
agency of God,[127] "O God of my fathers and Lord of mercy, who

---

125. For a brief discussion of Greek γίνομαι used as the passive of ποιέω, see John
Collins, "When Should We Translate *Poieô* 'to Make' as 'to Reckon'?" *Selected Technical
Articles Related to Translation* 16 (1986): 12–32, at 26 n. 12. Consider further the Septuagint
use of γίνομαι at times to render the Niphal of עשׂה.
    126. The Septuagint uses σκότος for "darkness," while John uses the equivalent σκοτία;
but this may only mean that John is not tied to the Septuagint wording.
    127. See further Wis. 16:12; 18:15 for similar uses of λόγος as God's supernatural
agency; and for further discussion, see C. John Collins, *The God of Miracles: An Exegetical
Examination of God's Action in the World* (Wheaton: Crossway, 2000), 89.

hast made all things *by thy word.*"[128] But whereas in Psalm 33:6 and Wisdom of Solomon 9:1 the Word may be just a personification, in John it is a person. The person is *distinct from* God ("with God") and at the same time *is* God (John 1:1). Since "God" in Genesis 1 (LXX ὁ θεός) did the making, we can follow John's thought as saying that "God made the world through the Word."

In Colossians 1:15–20 Paul makes a very similar point about Christ:

> [15]He is the image of the invisible God, the firstborn of all creation. [16]For in [see ESV margin] him all things were created, in heaven and on earth, visible and invisible, whether thrones or dominions or rulers or authorities—all things were created through him and for him. [17]And he is before all things, and in him all things hold together. [18]And he is the head of the body, the church. He is the beginning, the firstborn from the dead, that in everything he might be preeminent. [19]For in him all the fullness of God was pleased to dwell, [20]and through him to reconcile to himself all things, whether on earth or in heaven, making peace by the blood of his cross.

To speak of the "image of God" and the "creation" certainly evokes Genesis 1.[129] Possibly so does "the beginning" (Col. 1:18), though this also links with Proverbs 8:22–31, where Wisdom is God's agent in fashioning the world. Another echo of this passage in Proverbs 8 is Paul's "before [πρό] all things" in Colossians 1:17; compare Proverbs 8:23–26. Perhaps Paul could bring together his creation theology and Christology because he read Genesis 1 through the lens of Proverbs 8, and something similar has happened to the personified Wisdom as happened to the Word with John.[130] We can see that Paul, like John, affirms what theologians have called the "deity of Christ" (Col. 1:19); and his notion of creation is similar, too: "God created all things in [or, *by means of*], through, and for Christ." He adds the idea that "in

---

128. Ps. 33:6 uses the dative, and Wis. 9:1 uses the equivalent instrumental ἐν, "*by means of* the word," in contrast to John's "*through* [διά] him." The difference does not seem material.

129. Even though the Septuagint does not use the verb κτίζω, as noted above; but there is no reason to suppose that Paul was limited to the Septuagint.

130. Interestingly enough, the Wisdom of Solomon might also have contributed to this development; compare the vivid and elaborate picture of Wisdom in Wis. 7:22–8:1. For a stimulating discussion on this topic, see N. T. Wright, "Poetry and Theology in Colossians 1:15–20," in his *Climax of the Covenant* (Minneapolis: Fortress, 1993), 99–119.

him all things hold together" (1:17): Christ is the one who sustains all there is.

Hebrews 1:2–3 tells us how Christ is superior to every created thing; it opens thus:

> ²But in these last days [God] has spoken to us by his Son, whom he appointed the heir of all things, through [διά] whom also he created [ποιέω] the world. ³He is the radiance of the glory of God and the exact imprint of his nature, and he upholds the universe by the word of his power. After making purification for sins, he sat down at the right hand of the Majesty on high.

This links up with John and Paul, both in saying that God made the world *through* Christ (v. 2) and in portraying his deity (v. 3).[131] It also agrees with Paul when it says that Christ "upholds the universe" (v. 3; compare Col. 1:17).

The rest of Hebrews 1 applies a number of Old Testament texts to Jesus; in verses 10–12 it cites Psalm 102:25–27:

> ¹⁰You, Lord, laid the foundation of the earth in the beginning,
>   and the heavens are the work of your hands;
> ¹¹they will perish, but you remain;
>   they will all wear out like a garment,
> ¹²like a robe you will roll them up,
>   like a garment they will be changed.
> But you are the same,
>   and your years will have no end.

Jesus is the one who laid the foundation of the earth, and he will outlast the material creation. Hebrews can say this, not because Psalm 102 is messianic but because the author (and the rest of the New Testament) calls Jesus "Lord" (κύριος), which is the Septuagint rendering of the sacred name "the LORD."

5. Creational apologetic: Acts 14:15–16; 17:24–28

The evangelistic message in Acts focuses on the resurrection of Jesus, and all the evangelistic speeches finish with that event.

---

131. It may also be that the term *radiance* (ἀπαύγασμα) signals the idea of personified Wisdom, since Wis. 7:26 (part of Wis. 7:22–8:1) is the only other place that uses the term in the Septuagint or New Testament.

However, the path to that conclusion varies with the audience; most of the audiences are Jewish, and thus the speeches concentrate on Israel's history and prophecy. In two speeches, however, the approach is different, focusing on creation. In both cases the speaker is Paul, apostle to the Gentiles.

The first passage is Paul's visit to Lystra, in the southern part of the Roman province of Galatia (Acts 14:8–18). The speech (14:15–16) is not a full gospel presentation because of what brought it about: Paul heals a lame man, and the locals decide that "the gods have come down to us in the likeness of men!" Since they are speaking Lycaonian, it takes a while for Paul and Barnabas to grasp what is happening, and the people are on the verge of offering a sacrifice to Hermes (Paul) and Zeus (Barnabas):

> [14]But when the apostles Barnabas and Paul heard of it, they tore their garments and rushed out into the crowd, crying out, [15]"Men, why are you doing these things? We also are men, of like nature with you, and we bring you good news, that you should turn from these vain things to a living God, who made the heaven and the earth and the sea and all that is in them. [16]In past generations he allowed all the nations to walk in their own ways. [17]Yet he did not leave himself without witness, for he did good by giving you rains from heaven and fruitful seasons, satisfying your hearts with food and gladness." [18]Even with these words they scarcely restrained the people from offering sacrifice to them.

Luke does not tell us what more Barnabas and Paul said, but we may assume that they tried to show that the God "who made the heaven and the earth and the sea and all that is in them," and who had shown such goodness to all mankind, gave the creation as a witness, that people might want to know him. Then they would, no doubt, have told them of Jesus and the resurrection.

In the second passage, Paul is in Athens, the city that had been home to so much intellectual achievement in the ancient world (Acts 17:16–34). After some vigorous conversations in the marketplace with Jews, devout Gentiles, and philosophers of the Epicurean and Stoic schools, Paul gets a chance to address the entire Areopagus, the council that held jurisdiction over matters of morals and religion. In his speech (17:22–31) Paul gets to finish, leading up to the resurrection by way of creation:

[22]So Paul, standing in the midst of the Areopagus, said: "Men of Athens, I perceive that in every way you are very religious. [23]For as I passed along and observed the objects of your worship, I found also an altar with this inscription, 'To the unknown god.' What therefore you worship as unknown, this I proclaim to you. [24]The God who made the world and everything in it, being Lord of heaven and earth, does not live in temples made by man, [25]nor is he served by human hands, as though he needed anything, since he himself gives to all mankind life and breath and everything. [26]And he made from one man every nation of mankind to live on all the face of the earth, having determined allotted periods and the boundaries of their dwelling place, [27]that they should seek God, in the hope that they might feel their way toward him and find him. Yet he is actually not far from each one of us, [28]for

" 'In him we live and move and have our being';

as even some of your own poets have said,

" 'For we are indeed his offspring.'

[29]Being then God's offspring, we ought not to think that the divine being is like gold or silver or stone, an image formed by the art and imagination of man. [30]The times of ignorance God overlooked, but now he commands all people everywhere to repent, [31]because he has fixed a day on which he will judge the world in righteousness by a man whom he has appointed; and of this he has given assurance to all by raising him from the dead."

It is not my purpose here to give a full discussion of every aspect of these texts, including their use of Old Testament ideas and "natural revelation."[132] For now I will simply point out how important to Paul's arguments is the understanding of creation that Genesis 1 supplies.

Paul tells the people of Lystra about the God "who made the heaven and the earth and the sea and all that is in them" (Acts 14:15); the Greek here is so close to the Septuagint of Exodus 20:11 (and Ps. 146:6) that we may say that Paul has taken it for a summary of what he wants the Lystrans to know. When Paul says that he and Barnabas

---

132. For a start, see C. John Collins, *Science and Faith: Friends or Foes?* (Wheaton: Crossway, 2003), chapters 12 and 18 (with the notes and comments in appendix A).

are men "of like nature with" the Lystrans, he is using a word rare in the Greek Bible[133] but which still echoes the idea of a common human nature derived from common parents. Further, the idea that the idols are "vain" and that there is but one "living God" who rules over all and who has left in the world a witness to himself is an idea that follows from the first pericope of Genesis, as we saw above.

Paul also speaks to the Athenians in Acts 17:24 of "the God who made the world and everything in it," alluding to the same idea as does 14:15, though the exact wording ("made the world") is close to Wisdom of Solomon 9:9. The idea that the Creator is above his world and that he is the source of life and breath for all (Acts 17:24–25) is one of those principles that derive from Genesis 1.[134] So too is the common origin of all mankind in one man (Adam), and the common purpose of mankind to "seek God."

A full treatment of this speech would look into all the allusions Paul makes, whether to Scripture, to other Jewish writings, or to the Greek philosophers. Such a treatment would also put Paul's approach into its context with other Hellenistic Jewish apologetics, especially that found in Wisdom of Solomon, Philo, and Josephus. For our purposes, however, we will simply note that Paul followed a strategy similar to that found in Wisdom of Solomon 13:1, 5:

> [1]For all men who were ignorant of God were foolish by nature;
>> and they were unable from the good things that are seen to know him who exists,
>> nor did they recognize the craftsman while paying heed to his works . . .
>
> [5]For from the greatness and beauty of created things
>> comes a corresponding perception of their Creator.

---

133. In the New Testament, the only other occurrence is Jas. 5:17, "Elijah was a man *with a nature like* ours"; in the Apocrypha of the Septuagint, see Wis. 7:3, where the newborn Solomon "fell upon the *kindred* earth" (either the earth of common properties to the human body, as RV margin; or the earth that all humans share, as REB); 4 Macc. 12:13 (likely first century A.D.), where a Jewish boy denounces the tyrant Antiochus, "As a man, were you not ashamed, you most savage beast, to cut out the tongues of men *who have feelings like* yours and are made of the same elements as you, and to maltreat and torture them in this way?" (NRSV). Since Wis. 7:1 has a reference to origin in Adam being common to all mankind, we can at least say that Paul's terminology evokes the notion of common human nature by virtue of creation.

134. Many of the ideas found in this speech tie in to developments among the Greek philosophers, too; and a full study of the Areopagus speech would examine the way in which Paul sought to use his common ground with his audience.

We also note that Paul seems to have been trying to do just what Josephus says that Moses aimed to do in beginning his book with creation:[135]

> Nothing that he would write regarding virtue would avail with his readers, unless before all else they were taught that God, the Father and Master of all things who beholds all things, gives to those who follow him a happy life, but involves in great calamities those who travel outside the path of virtue. . . . Moses did not, when setting out his laws, begin with contracts and the mutual rights of man, as others have done; rather, [he began by] leading their minds upwards toward God and the constructing of the world, and by persuading them that we men are the fairest of the works of God upon the earth; when he had made them obedient to piety, he easily persuaded them of everything else.

If listeners will follow Paul as to their status as creatures of the one God, then the redemptive history, particularly Jesus and the resurrection, will be intelligible and plausible.

---

135. Josephus, *Antiquities* 1.20–21. See also Philo, *On the Creation* 1–3.

5

GENESIS 2:4–25:
THE GARDEN OF EDEN

This pericope focuses on how God formed the first man and his wife and gave them the garden of Eden as a place to live and work.

In the previous chapter I argued that this pericope begins with Genesis 2:4, because that is the normal function of "these are the generations of X" in Genesis. I further argued that the chiastic structure of 2:4 is reason not to divide the verse. In this chapter I will show why I think that following this division has the happy result of enabling us to read Genesis 1:1–2:3 and 2:4–25 in a complementary way; it also gives us a way to handle the vexing question of the six days and the length of the creation period.

A. Pericope Boundary, Structure, and Genre

If we allow that the pericope begins at Genesis 2:4, where shall we suppose that it ends? We see that in 2:4b we have a shift in the divine name, from "God" (אלהים, 'elohîm) to "the LORD God" (יהוה אלהים, yhwh 'elohîm); this composite name appears throughout Genesis 2–3 and is rare elsewhere in the Hebrew Bible.[1] Hence what I have seen as two pericopes, Genesis 2:4–25 and 3:1–24, have a higher unity with each other than they do with 1:1–2:3. Further,

---

1. In the Pentateuch, it only appears in Exod. 9:30.

the events in Genesis 2 and 3 share a common locale—Eden—and a common list of participants—the Lord God, Adam, and Eve.

The events of these two chapters clearly follow a close causal sequence, and by this standard Genesis 4 is part of the larger unit—although there the deity is simply "the LORD" (except for 4:25, where he is "God"). Actually, once we look at the participants and the causal connections, the rest of Genesis follows close on the heels of these chapters, which is just another way of saying that, on the literary level, the book displays unity.

In order, then, to distinguish pericopes, we must look for signs of discontinuity, which seem to close out the scene. Here we find just such signs in Genesis 2:25 and 3:1. We can see the discontinuity in 2:25: "*And* the man and his wife *were* both naked and *were* not *ashamed*." The first verb, "and . . . were," is in the *wayyiqtol* tense (וַיְהִי, *wayehî*), while the second, "were . . . ashamed," is not; of course the negative cannot take this tense, but the imperfect (יִתְבֹּשָׁשׁוּ, *yitboshashû*) with past time reference, conveying process aspect, draws special attention to itself. We read this best if we take it as wrapping up the pericope by describing its ongoing results; we are left with a feeling of an idyllic scene. The way Genesis 3 begins confirms this sense of having reached an end: instead of a *wayyiqtol* verb we have the "and"-conjunction joined to the subject, with the verb in the perfect:

| Now the serpent was more crafty . . . | וְהַנָּחָשׁ הָיָה עָרוּם |

This discontinuity also introduces a new participant, "the serpent," and a new scene, the temptation. All of this together shows why we are on solid footing when we take the pericope to be 2:4–25.

In order to discern the structure of this pericope, we can start by finding the main sequence of events, usually by looking for the *wayyiqtol* verbs. The first event takes place in Genesis 2:7, where the Lord God "formed" the man, and the event line runs through verse 9. Then in verses 10–14 we have an excursus, where all the verbs have process aspect (participle, imperfect, and *weqatal*). The event line resumes in verse 15, which reiterates the action of verse 8. The event sequence carries on through verse 23, followed by an aside in verse 24 that explains how the first marriage serves as a pattern for every subsequent one, and the summary of verse 25.

This leaves us with the task of deciding what function Genesis 2:5–6 plays. If we suppose that verse 4 stands apart from them (because we do not wish to break the chiasmus), we can see straightaway that they provide background for the first event in verse 7: that is the proper function of the clauses we find, with verbs in the perfect, imperfect, and *weqatal*, and the verbless clause (v. 5, "there was no man"). In other words, these verses describe what the conditions were when the action of verse 7 took place, as the ESV rendering makes clear:

> **5**When no bush of the field was yet in the land and no small plant of the field had yet sprung up—for the LORD God had not caused it to rain on the land, and there was no man to work the ground, **6**and a mist was going up from the land and was watering the whole face of the ground—**7**then the LORD God formed the man of dust from the ground and breathed into his nostrils the breath of life, and the man became a living creature.

(I will take up below the question of why the ESV has done the right thing in rendering אֶרֶץ ['*erets*] as "land" in verses 5–6, rather than the common "earth." I will also examine the communicative function of the chiastic verse 4.)

This discussion allows us to see that the structure of the pericope is as follows:

2:4	hinge/heading
2:5–9	verses 5–6 setting for the events
	verses 7–9 events: formation of man, planting of garden, placing of man
2:10–14	excursus: the four primeval rivers
2:15–17	events: God sets up terms of a relationship with man
2:18–25	events: formation of a complementary helper

Finally, let us consider the genre of this passage. We have already noted that this pericope is causally connected to the rest of Genesis. We also note that here for the first time human activity comes into view, and this activity continues throughout the Book of Genesis, which interleaves human and divine activity. The Hebrew reader has a different feel for the style here: it is more like the normal biblical narrative style found elsewhere in the Bible. For this reason we may simply call this normal prose narrative.

B. Translation and Notes

Hinge/heading (2:4)

⁴These are the generations
   of the heavens and the earth when they were created,
   in the day that² the Lord God made earth and heaven.

Formation of the man (2:5–9)

⁵When no bush of the field³ was yet in the land⁴ and no small
plant of the field had yet sprung up—for the Lord God had not
caused it to rain on the land, and there was no man to work the
ground,⁵ ⁶and a mist⁶ was going⁷ up⁸ from the land and was watering

2. For בְּיוֹם (*beyôm*, "in the day") followed by an infinitive construct in the sense "when," see BDB, 400a; Paul Joüon, *A Grammar of Biblical Hebrew*, trans./rev. Takamitsu Muraoka; Subsidia biblica 14 (Rome: Pontifical Biblical Institute Press, 1991), §129p (A.2).

3. esv margin: "Or *open country*." M. Futato, "Because It Had Rained: A Study of Gen. 2:5–7 with Implications for Gen. 2:4–25 and Gen. 1:1–2:3," *Westminster Theological Journal* 60 (1998): 1–21, at 4, argues that the only legitimate interpretation of שִׂיחַ הַשָּׂדֶה (*sîakh hassadeh*, "bush of the field") must be "wild shrubs of the steppe," in contrast to the עֵשֶׂב הַשָּׂדֶה (*'eseb hassadeh*, "small plant of the field"), which he takes to be cultivated—a possibility mentioned in D. Kidner, "Genesis 2:5, 6: Wet or Dry?" *Tyndale Bulletin* 17 (1966): 109–14, at 109.

4. esv margin: "Or *earth*; also verse 6." On why this is *land*, not *earth*, see additional discussion on Gen. 2:4–7 in section C.1 below.

5. The expression *work the ground* (עָבַד ['*abad*] with אֲדָמָה ['*adamâ*] as object) appears in Gen. 2:5, 15; 3:23; 4:2, 12; Isa. 30:24; Zech. 13:5; Prov. 12:11; 28:19 (compare Ps. 104:14). This is an idiomatic expression, and hence any effort to use the sense "serve" in the verb עָבַד is misguided.

6. esv margin: "Or *spring*." Hebrew אֵד (*'ed*); no one knows for sure what this word means. I see no reason to dissent from Delitzsch, 117, who argues on the basis of Job 36:27 (its only other occurrence in the Bible) and an Arabic cognate for the sense "mist" (that is, "condensed vapor"). The Septuagint rendered the Hebrew with πηγή, "spring," and comparative evidence may favor something like "flood" (see Wenham, 58; Hamilton, 154–56). I do not, however, consider this evidence decisive. Futato, "Because It Had Rained," 5–9, argues strongly and, I think, successfully, against the "flood"/"stream" interpretation and in favor of something like "rain-cloud," that is, along the lines of Delitzsch. Kiel, מַטָר, shows that this is the Targum and Rabbinic tradition. (Futato does not like the rendering "mist" because according to his definition the English word does not quite match the meaning "rain-cloud," but it seems clear that Delitzsch means something close to the sense for which Futato argues.)

7. It is possible to infer from the context that the particular nuance of the process aspect is inceptive action: "It was *beginning to* go up . . . it was *beginning to* water." Bruce K. Waltke and Michael O'Connor, *An Introduction to Biblical Hebrew Syntax* (Winona Lake, Ind.: Eisenbrauns, 1990), §31.2c, support such a possibility, but their examples are not all persuasive (2 Sam. 15:37 is the best; see esv).

8. Taking the verb יַעֲלֶה (*ya'aleh*), as most do, as a simple Qal imperfect with אֵד (*'ed*) as subject. Futato, "Because It Had Rained," 8, argues that we should interpret the verb

the whole face of the ground—⁷then the LORD God formed⁹ the man¹⁰
of dust¹¹ from the ground and breathed into his nostrils the breath
of life,¹² and the man became a living creature.¹³ ⁸And the LORD God
planted¹⁴ a garden¹⁵ in Eden, in the east, and there he put the man
whom he had formed. ⁹And out of the ground¹⁶ the LORD God made
to spring up every tree that is pleasant to the sight and good for
food. The tree of life was in the midst of the garden, and the tree of
the knowledge of good and evil.

---

as a Hiphil imperfect with the "LORD God" as subject of both it and the next verb וְהִשְׁקָה
(wehishqâ, "and it was a mist that he [i.e. the LORD God] was bringing up, and he was
watering"). This is possible, but the reasons he offers do not settle the question. (1) When
the first element of a clause is not the verb, as is here the case, it is more expected for that
element to be the subject. (2) A noun in the semantic category "mist/cloud" can as easily
be the subject of the Qal of the verb (see 1 Kgs. 18:44) as the object of the Hiphil (see Ps.
135:7). (3) Similarly, it is quite proper for a source of water to be the subject of the next
verb, וְהִשְׁקָה, "and was watering" (as in Gen. 2:10). The credibility of his argument that
"God would be the explicit solver of both the problem of no rain and the problem of no
cultivator" (2:8–9) depends in turn on the prior acceptance of his literary reading for the
text and hence cannot establish that reading in opposition to others. Hence I see no reason
not to translate this in the usual way.

9. Note the anthropomorphism here: God is portrayed as a potter (Hebrew יוֹצֵר
[yôtser], which is the participle of the verb used here, יָצַר [yatsar], "to form") who forms
man from moistened dust (so Delitzsch; BDB 427b). Similarly, here God also "blows,"
and in 2:22 he "builds."

10. The Hebrew has a definite article הָאָדָם [ha'adam], "the man," namely, the first
human. I would take the article as anaphoric to the mention of "man" in 2:5, which does
not have the article: literally, "and as for man, there was none to work." Without the article it becomes the proper name Adam in verse 20. In verse 23, using different terms, the
"woman" (אִשָּׁה, 'ishshâ) is taken from the "man" (אִישׁ, 'îsh).

11. That is, loose soil.

12. Wis. 15:11 (RSV) takes this as both a historical event and as a paradigm for
everyone's origin, saying that the idolater "failed to know the one who formed him and
inspired him with an active soul and breathed into him a living spirit."

13. The phrase living creature is נֶפֶשׁ חַיָּה (nepesh khayyâ, "living soul"); see note at
Gen. 1:20. In this respect man is like the other animals, and, like them, is "formed from
the ground" (2:19) and has "the breath of life" (see 7:22; although Kiel, קָצַר, refers the
term to mankind only, I think it summarizes all of 2:21). On the other hand, he is different
from them in the special care that God takes in making him, in the kind of helper fit for
him that he needs, in his rule over the rest of the world, and in his being in the image of
God. If we join the Greek philosophers who called man the "rational animal," we are not
too far away from Genesis.

14. In Collins, "The Wayyiqtol as 'Pluperfect': When and Why," Tyndale Bulletin 46
(1995): 117–40, at 140 n. 75, I reject the NIV's making this pluperfect: "the Lord God had
planted." I think the end of the verse, אֲשֶׁר יָצַר ('asher yatsar, "whom he had formed"),
places the formation of 2:7 prior to the planting of verse 8.

15. Greek παράδεισος ("park, pleasant garden"), which becomes "Paradise" (Luke
23:43; 2 Cor. 12:3–4; Rev. 2:7).

16. Again, nothing in the text requires us to suppose that this happens in the earth
as a whole; the "ground" is the ground of the garden.

Excursus: The four primeval rivers (2:10–14)

[10]A river flowed out of Eden to water the garden, and there it divided and became four rivers. [11]The name of the first is Pishon. It is the one that flowed around the whole land of Havilah, where there is gold. [12]And the gold of that land is good; bdellium and onyx stone are there.[17] [13]The name of the second river is Gihon. It is the one that flowed around the whole land of Cush. [14]And the name of the third river is Tigris, which flows east of Assyria. And the fourth river is the Euphrates.

God establishes his relationship with man (2:15–17)

[15]The LORD God took the man and put[18] him in the garden of Eden to work it and keep[19] it.[20] [16]And the LORD God commanded the man,[21] saying, "You may surely[22] eat of every tree of the garden, [17]but of the tree of the knowledge of good and evil you shall not eat,[23] for in the day that you eat[24] of it you shall surely die."

17. For onyx and gold together, see Exod. 28:20; 39:6, 13 (priest's garments); Ezek. 28:13 (a picture of the king of Tyre when he was "in Eden"); 1 Chr. 29:2 (material laid aside for the temple).

18. The verbs *took* and *put* here look back to "put" (2:8), and hence resume the action after the digression of verses 10–14.

19. It seems to me that Delitzsch is right when he observes, "The world of nature was . . . designed to be tilled and tended, [and] it runs wild without man, who can and ought (as is shown, for example, by corn, vines and date palms) to make it more useful and habitable" (137). Hence this illustrates the caring dominion humans are to exercise. However, when Delitzsch goes on to find here hints that the man "was also to keep it by withstanding the power of temptation, which was threatening to destroy him and Paradise with him," I think he is going beyond the text itself. It is certainly true, though, that humans have horribly failed *lovingly* to "keep" the creation—but this is due to their sinfulness.

20. The two suffixes translated "it" are feminine: they no doubt refer to the *ground* (Hebrew אֲדָמָה [*'adamâ*], feminine noun) of the garden.

21. Delitzsch, 137, suggests that the syntax of the verb צִוָּה (*tsiwwâ*) gives the nuance of "*strictly* commanded": the object "the man" is governed by the preposition עַל (*'al*). In addition to this syntactical argument, which would be debatable if it were on its own, we should consider (1) the highlighting of the prohibition in 2:17a, as mentioned below; and (2) the severity of the penalty "you will surely die" as expressed both in the construction with the infinitive absolute (rendered "surely") and in the semantic content of "die."

22. NASB, NRSV, NIV "freely" is a grammatically unlikely interpretation of the infinitive absolute; see Joüon, *Grammar of Biblical Hebrew*, §123j; Waltke and O'Connor, *Introduction to Biblical Hebrew Syntax*, §35.3.1c.

23. The Hebrew adds "you shall not eat *of it*," thus framing the phrase with "of." The second one, which is redundant, highlights it and therefore shows that this is the strict command of 2:16.

24. ESV margin: "Or *when you eat*."

God makes a complementary helper (2:18–25)

[18]Then the Lord God said, "It is not good that the man should be alone; I will make him a helper[25] fit for[26] him." [19]So out of the ground the Lord God formed[27] every beast of the field and every bird of the heavens and brought them to the man to see what he would call them. And whatever the man called every living creature, that was its name. [20]The man gave names to all livestock and to the birds of the heavens and to every beast of the field. But for Adam[28] there was not found[29] a helper fit for him. [21]So the Lord God caused a deep sleep[30] to fall upon the man, and while he slept took one of his ribs and closed up its place with flesh. [22]And the rib that the Lord God had taken from the man he made[31] into a woman and brought her to the man. [23]Then the man said,

25. A "help(er)" is one who takes a subordinate role (which is why it is so startling to read of God being the "help" of his faithful ones, as in Deut. 33:7 and Ps. 33:20). The article by R. David Freedman, "Woman, a Power Equal to Man," *Biblical Archaeology Review* 9, no. 1 (1983): 56–58, is based on some flawed premises: he posits a homonym meaning "strength" for עזר (*'ezer*, "help"), when this is dubious at best and unnecessary in any other biblical passage; he misinterprets the term *fit for* as "equal to," which it does not mean (see below). Hence we need not give it serious consideration.

26. esv margin: "Or *corresponding to*; also in verse 20." As Delitzsch, 140, noted, the relationship expressed by כנגדו (*kenegdô*, literally, "according to the opposite of him") differs from that of כמוהו (*kamôhû*, "like him"), which the narrator does not use. Hence the proposed "helper" will be "one who by relative difference and essential equality should be his fitting complement." In the interpretive tradition, she is a "help and support," more than simply one with whom he can make children: see Tob. 8:6; Sir. 36:24.

27. esv margin: "Or *had formed*." The esv Update has made the text, "Now out of the ground the Lord God had formed" (reversing text and margin). See Collins, "The *Way-yiqtol* as 'Pluperfect,' " 135–40, justifying this pluperfect rendering. Apparently Josephus represented those who read the order this way; compare *Antiquities* 1.34.

28. esv margin: "Or *the man*." The Masoretic Text, ולאדם (*ûle'adam*), lacks a definite article; hence the proper name in the esv text. Richard Hess prefers to take this as "the man," which would require repointing to supply the article; see Hess, "Splitting the Adam," in *Studies in the Pentateuch*, ed. J. A. Emerton (Vetus Testamentum Supplement 41; Leiden: Brill, 1991), 1–15, at 3. The Septuagint began finding the proper name Adam in 2:16.

29. "There was not found" is literally "he did not find." This could be an impersonal third person (Joüon, *Grammar of Biblical Hebrew*, §155b [n.2]), which amounts to a quasi-passive (thus esv); or it could have God as the subject, "God did not find."

30. Cf. 1 Sam. 26:12; Job 4:13; Prov. 19:15; Isa. 29:10 for this noun (תרדמה, *tardemâ*); and Jonah 1:5–6 for the related verb (רדם, *r-d-m*). The idea is a profound sleep from which it is difficult to awaken.

31. esv margin: "Hebrew *built*." The Hebrew is a vigorous anthropomorphism and reminds us of the overall picture of God as a workman.

"This at last[32] is bone of my bones
    and flesh of my flesh;[33]
she shall be called Woman,[34]
    because she was taken out of Man."[35]

[24]Therefore[36] a man shall leave his father and his mother and hold fast to his wife, and they shall become one flesh.[37] [25]And the man and his wife were both naked and were not ashamed.

C. Extra Notes

1. The meaning of Genesis 2:4–7

The key to understanding how the author or final editor of Genesis wanted his audience to read the first two pericopes together is to grasp the import of Genesis 2:4–7:

[4]These are the generations
    of the heavens and the earth when they were
        created,
    in the day that the LORD God made the earth and
        the heavens.

[5]When no bush of the field was yet in the land and no small plant of the field had yet sprung up—for the LORD God had not caused it to rain on the land, and there was no man to work the

---

32. Expressing the idea of a wait, "finally after numerous tries": "this time" in Gen. 29:34–35; Exod. 9:27; "now" in Gen. 30:20; 46:30.

33. "Bone" and "flesh" together express close kinship: compare Gen. 29:14; Judg. 9:2; 2 Sam. 5:1; 19:12–13; 1 Chr. 11:1.

34. As the ESV margin comments, *woman* (אִשָּׁה, *'ishshâ*) sounds like it is the feminine of *man* (אִישׁ, *'ish*). This is the first occurrence of the term אִישׁ in this account.

35. This last line is also framed (as is 2:17a), beginning and ending in Hebrew with "this one" (feminine; Hebrew זֹאת [*zo't*]): "To this one it will be called 'woman,' because from man was taken this one." Hence it is highlighted.

36. I take this to be the narrator's comment, speaking on behalf of God (typical of the narrator in the Hebrew Bible), and this explains why Jesus in Matt. 19:4–5 attributes this saying to the Creator himself (he had a high doctrine of Scripture).

37. Not primarily a reference to sexual union; as H. C. Leupold points out (137), " 'Becoming one flesh' involves the complete identification of one personality with the other in a community of interests and pursuits, a union consummated in intercourse." Rashi (cited in Kiel, פה) argued that the one-fleshness of a couple is especially visible in their children, who are a mixture of both parents.

ground, ⁶and a mist was going up from the land and was watering
the whole face of the ground—⁷then the LORD God formed the man
of dust from the ground and breathed into his nostrils the breath
of life, and the man became a living creature.

I have already noted the chiastic structure of verse 4, which should
prevent us from breaking the verse apart, and in section A above I
discussed the import of the *yiqtol* and *weqatal* verbs in verse 6 ("was
going up . . . and was watering") as giving the setting for the events
of verse 7 ("formed . . . breathed . . . became"). In this section we will
need to consider what is the communicative function of the chiasmus
and whether ץֶרֶא (*'erets*) in verse 5 should be "land" (ESV) or "earth"
(most other versions). We will find that proper resolution of these
questions will enable us to see how to cooperate with these verses.

We may distinguish between two types of chiasmus, odd (a-b-c-
b´-a´) and even (a-b-c-c´-b´-a´). Genesis 2:4 is an even chiasmus. The
general function of an even chiasmus is to ask the reader to see its
parts in some kind of unity, with the context allowing us to infer just
what unity the author had in view.[38]

The unity here is not hard to find. The word order of Genesis 2:4a,
"the heavens and the earth," together with the verb "created," point
back to 1:1 in the first pericope. Then 2:4b introduces the new divine
name, "the LORD God," which points forward to 2:5–3:24. However,
the divine name is not entirely new: it includes "God" from the first
pericope and adds an element, "the LORD," in order to identify the
God of creation with the God who redeemed Israel.[39] It follows easily, then, that the author or editor wanted his audience to read these
two accounts as complementary.

If we follow the grammatical conclusions regarding the verb
tenses in Genesis 2:6, we see that the first event in 2:4–7 is in verse
7, "formed." If we cooperate with the structure of 2:4, we will see
2:7, 22 as a complementary telling of how God created the first man

38. For more on chiastic structures, see H. Van Dyke Parunak, "Oral Typesetting:
Some Uses of Biblical Structure," *Biblica* 62, no. 2 (1981): 153–68. The odd chiasmus
commonly highlights the middle (or "odd") element.

39. Contrast this with Stephen Kempf, "Introducing the Garden of Eden: The Structure and Function of Genesis 2:4b–7," *JOTT* 7, no. 4 (1996): 33–53, who acknowledges the
chiasmus but supports the division of the verse on the basis of, among other things, the
change in divine name (at 39–41). He is working against the literary form.

and his wife (1:27): the first pericope gives the overview, while the second provides more details.[40]

But Genesis 1:27 takes place on day 6 of the creation week; this would mean that 2:7–25 does as well. (After all, the "not good" of 2:18 puts us prior to the "very good" of 1:31.) Then it follows that 2:5–6, which describes the conditions when God formed or created the man, describes features of the sixth day and not of the creation week.

The common practice of translating אֶרֶץ ('erets) in Genesis 2:5–6 as "earth" makes this hard to do, and under that interpretation it is easy to sympathize with S. R. Driver, who finds in these verses decisive evidence that we have originally two creation accounts that have been joined together:[41]

> The words [of verses 4b–5], taken in connexion with the sequel (v. 7), are intended to describe the condition of the earth at the time when man was created: no shrub or herb,—and à fortiori, no tree—had yet appeared upon it, for it was not sufficiently watered to support vegetation. According to i.11f., plant- and tree-life was complete three "days" before the creation of man: obviously the present writer views the order of events differently.

Authors who do not agree with conventional source analysis must explain the features differently. For example, Mark Futato suggests:[42]

> I understand Gen. 2:5 as having a global reference that would parallel the situation prior to Days 3b [Gen. 1:11–12] and 6b [Gen. 1:26–30], i.e. before God created vegetation and people. . . . Rather than being a second creation account, Gen. 2:4–25 is properly read as a resumption and expansion not of Day 6 but of Days 3b and 6b taken together as a unit.

He uses this to support the conclusion that strict chronological sequence is not a part of the communicative intent of either Genesis 1 or 2, and hence to support a version of the "framework" interpretation of the Genesis days.

40. Richard Hess, "Genesis 1–2 in Its Literary Context," *Tyndale Bulletin* 41, no. 1 (1990): 143–53, argues that this reflects a pattern for the genealogies in Genesis 1–11.
41. S. R. Driver, *The Book of Genesis* (Westminster Commentaries; London: Methuen, 1904), 36–37. See also Gunkel, 4–5; Skinner, 51; Westermann, 197.
42. Mark Futato, "Because It Had Rained," 12 n. 41 and 14.

However, in chapter 4, section D, I argued that the features of Genesis 1 make it hard to do away with sequence as the framework view does, and the discourse analysis of 2:5–7 makes it possible to harmonize the two pericopes without abandoning sequence.

The semantic range of אֶרֶץ ('*erets*) is "the whole earth" (as in Gen. 1:1–2), "land as opposed to sea" (1:10–31), and "land or region" (2:11–13). The common renderings of 2:5–6 assume the first, but the third sense works better, especially if we consider the geography: God made the man in some unnamed "land" and then moved him to the garden of Eden (2:8); after the disobedience in Genesis 3, he banished the man back to the "land" to work it (3:23). It also helps to recall the climate of the western Levant: it rains in the fall and winter, and not at all in the summer.[43] At the end of the summer, and with no man to work the ground (by irrigation), the ground is quite dry and barren; after the rains begin to fall, then the plants may spring up. This makes sense, because the text gives a reason for no bush or small plant: "*for* the LORD God had not caused it to rain" (2:5); this is not at all the same as "he had not yet created them," which is what Driver and Futato seem to require. Rather, it is in terms of the ordinary experience of the Israelite audience.

We are then able to understand just what Genesis 2:5–8 means: in some land, at the end of the dry season, when the "mist" (or rain cloud) was rising to begin the rains, God formed the first man; he then planted a garden in Eden and moved the man there. Some time after that he made the woman.

This way of reading Genesis 2:5–8 has the advantages of (1) following directly from the discourse relations; (2) using ordinary meanings of words; and (3) making it easy to harmonize Genesis 2:4–25 with the sixth day of Genesis 1. But it also has a strong impact on the amount of time that must have been involved. If the time of year and the absence of man are the reasons for why the plants were "not yet in the land," then this means that the familiar seasonal cycle was in effect; and for this to be so, the seasonal cycle must have been in operation for some number of years. If we want to continue to harmonize the two pericopes, we will not be able to maintain ordinary days in Genesis 1—but we shall reserve the rest of this for section C.7 below.

43. See John Bimson et al., *New Bible Atlas* (Downers Grove, Ill.: InterVarsity Press, 1985), 14–15.

In any event, we now see that calling these pericopes two creation accounts does not do justice to the particulars of the text. We rather have an overall creation account (Gen. 1:1–2:3), which focuses on how God prepared the earth as a place for mankind to live, followed by a more detailed account of how God made the first man and woman and entered into relationship with them.

2. Is Genesis 2:15–17 a covenant?

Some theologians have called God's arrangement with Adam (Gen. 2:15–17) a covenant:

> [15]The LORD God took the man and put him in the garden of Eden to work it and keep it. [16]And the LORD God commanded the man, saying, "You may surely eat of every tree of the garden, [17]but of the tree of the knowledge of good and evil you shall not eat, for in the day that you eat of it you shall surely die."

Some have gone even further, calling this a covenant of works, in that Adam's obedience will *merit* life for himself and all his posterity. In our discussion here we must keep the two questions separate: namely, Is it a covenant? is the first question; then we can ask, If so, is it one of works?[44]

The two most common objections to calling this a covenant are that (1) neither the word *covenant* (בְּרִית, *berît*) nor any of its synonyms appears in this context (the first occurrence is Gen. 6:18, dealing with Noah); and (2) biblical covenants involve specific ceremonies of ratification. This second objection can also be connected to the view that to be a covenant it must have something to do with *redemption*. These objections founder once we employ sound lexical method.

To begin with, it is simply false to suppose that the only way the *thing* can be present is if the word is present. For example, the word *Messiah* is rarely used in the Old Testament to mean the promised heir of David who will be anointed, rule forever, and bring light to the Gentiles, but it would be nonsensical to use that fact to deny that the idea is present. Further, in 2 Samuel 7 God makes a promise to

---

44. Useful recent articles include John Stek, " 'Covenant' Overload in Reformed Theology," *Calvin Theological Journal* 29 (1994): 12–41, rejecting the idea that this is a covenant; Craig Bartholomew, "Covenant and Creation: Covenant Overload or Covenant Deconstruction," *Calvin Theological Journal* 30 (1995): 11–33, supporting it.

David of an enduring dynasty; by the objectors' principle we may not call this a Davidic covenant, because that word does not appear in the chapter. However, when Psalm 89 reflects on the situation, it uses the term *covenant* (vv. 3, 28, 34, 39). In my judgment this is precisely analogous to what we have in Hosea 6:7, whose best rendering is "like Adam they transgressed the covenant": the later writer is using the proper word for what he found in the narrative.[45]

The second objection is also based on flawed lexicography: namely, it takes the features of *certain* covenants and makes them normative for *all* covenants. Marriage is a covenant (Prov. 2:17; Mal. 2:14);[46] David and Jonathan made a covenant with each other (1 Sam. 18:3; 20:8; 23:18; Ps. 55:20 mentions a covenant of friendship); and the Lord made a covenant with Phineas (Num. 25:12–13). We do not read of ratification ceremonies accompanying these covenants; hence it follows that these are not essential to a covenant. Instead, we can infer a general description for the notion "covenant": it formally binds the parties together in a relationship; they are to be true to the covenant by keeping their promises of loyalty and commitment. There will be consequences for keeping or not keeping the covenant (benefits or punishments). This description suits the covenants we find in the Bible and allows them to have their own specific features; for example, in the friendship covenant the parties are on an equal level, while in other cases one party is superior and can dictate all the covenantal obligations.

So we can call this arrangement in Genesis 2:15–17 a covenant. It comes from God's initiative; verses 16–17 clearly spell out the condition for the man, namely, obedience to God's command. The punishment for disobeying the command is that Adam will "surely die" (see C.4 below). The text does not tell us what the reward will be for faithfulness, although it implies it: the relationship will continue and Adam will have access to the tree of life (see C.2 below).

At least two later texts call this a covenant: Hosea 6:7 and Sirach 14:17. Hosea describes the northern kingdom of his own day thus, tracing their unfaithfulness back to their first father:

45. This interpretation of Hos. 6:7 is not unanimously accepted, though it rests on sound philology; see Brian Habig, "Hosea 6:7 Revisited," *Presbyterion* (forthcoming). In view of this, we need not concede that this is a difficult, controverted, or indecisive text, as both Stek and Bartholomew do.

46. See Gordon Hugenberger, *Marriage as a Covenant: Biblical Law and Ethics as Developed from Malachi* (Grand Rapids: Baker, 1998).

> But like Adam they transgressed the covenant;
> there they dealt faithlessly with me.

The passage in Ben Sira's book clearly evokes Genesis 2:17:

> All living beings become old like a garment,
> for the *covenant* from of old is, "You must surely die!"

The Greek for "you must surely die," θανάτῳ ἀποθανῇ, echoes the Septuagint of Genesis 2:17.[47]

If we are secure in calling this a covenant, shall we call it a "covenant of works"? Christians have insisted on this, thinking that the analogy of Adam and Christ in Romans 5:12–21 requires it. By this argument, the two covenant heads must be equivalent: just as Jesus *earned* life for those he represents, so Adam must have been able to *earn* life for those he represented. The trouble with this is the fact that Romans 5 depends more on *disanalogy* between Adam and Christ than it does on pure analogy; as Wright points out, Romans 5:15 "denies that there is a direct balance or equivalence between Adam's trespass and God's gift in Christ."[48]

It seems better to think of Adam's action as the work of covenant representation, without introducing the idea of merit. That is, as a representative he acts on behalf of those he represents, in this case his posterity. We will develop this more in the next chapter, but for now we can simply note that the prohibition and threat in Genesis 2:17 ("you shall not eat . . . you shall surely die") is second masculine singular: that is, the "you" is Adam, the addressee.[49] But when Eve appropriates this in 3:3, she uses the plural; she has apparently received the instruction by way of her husband and has accepted him as her representative in receiving the covenant.

---

47. The word in the second line is διαθήκη, as RV recognizes by rendering it "covenant"; RSV has "decree," with a marginal note, "Gk *covenant*." Interestingly enough, the Hebrew does not allude to Gen. 2:17 at all; it reads, "The eternal *statute* [חֹק, *khôq*] is, 'You must surely *expire* [גוע, *gawa'*].' " Hence, if we assume that the extant Hebrew is what Ben Sira's grandson had before him (reasonable, in view of how he renders חֹק elsewhere), it is the Greek version (c. 130 B.C.) rather than the Hebrew original (c. 180 B.C.) that makes the link with Gen. 2:17, but in any case we still have it called a "covenant." Note further that "covenant" and "statute" are at times used in parallel in the Hebrew Bible, as in Pss. 50:16; 105:10; Isa. 24:5.

48. N. T. Wright, *The Climax of the Covenant* (Minneapolis: Fortress, 1993), 37.

49. That is, in the Hebrew (see also Vulgate, Syriac); the Septuagint, on the other hand, has a second singular in 2:16 and switches to a second plural in verse 17.

3. What are the two trees?

Genesis 2:9 speaks of two trees in the midst of the garden of Eden, "the tree of life" and "the tree of the knowledge of good and evil." There are a host of proposals to explain the two trees. For our purposes, the key thing to note is that the author of Genesis does not explain at all the natures of these two trees. From the narrative that follows, though, we can infer the reasons for their names.

The tree of life is apparently some kind of sacrament (that is, there is no reason to believe it is *magical*) that would confirm the man in his moral condition: hence he needed to gain (or retain) access to it by obedience and would have been rewarded by being confirmed in holiness forever. This is why God does not want him to have it after his sin (Gen. 3:22): he would then be confirmed in his sinfulness forever, and this is horrible. This would explain the use of this tree as an image, both in the Old Testament (Prov. 3:18, applied to wisdom; 11:30, to the fruit of the righteous; 13:12, to desire fulfilled; and 15:4, to a healing tongue: they are means to keep people on the path to immortal happiness)[50] and in the New Testament (Rev. 2:7; 22:2, 14, 19, where it functions as a symbol of confirmation in holiness).

To understand the tree of the knowledge of good and evil (to call it simply the tree of *knowledge*, as some do, is quite misleading; a specific kind of knowledge is in view), we must ascertain what is the knowledge of good and evil that it designates.[51] Whatever our theory, it must account for the fact that in Genesis 3:22 God acknowledges that the humans have in fact become like God "in knowing good and evil"; this means that they must have gained some property they share with God. Further, usage of the expression *to know good and*

---

50. Compare Kidner, *Proverbs*, 54.

51. For critical discussion see Hamilton, 163–66; Wenham, 63–64. The explanations most commonly offered for the knowledge resulting from eating this fruit include sexual experience (emphasizing "knowing," Hebrew יָדַע [*yada*ʿ], as in Gen. 4:1); advancement in general knowledge from primitive to civilized; knowledge of everything (taking "good and evil" as polar opposites, hence including everything in between); and moral autonomy (one becomes an autonomous arbiter of good and evil, like God is). The sexual experience interpretation is not worth considering, first because the "knowing" is called "knowing good and evil," not "knowing" simply; and second, because sexual complementarity and reproduction are not presented as things that God would withhold from his human creatures (Gen. 2:18–25; 1:28). The idea of advancement to a civilized state is also to be rejected, among other reasons because it is hard to see why this would be prohibited. Wenham favors the knowledge of everything interpretation, while Hamilton prefers the moral autonomy scheme.

evil elsewhere in the Old Testament carries the nuance of discernment and is "characteristic of maturity and adult life."[52] These point
to the conclusion that the tree is, as Delitzsch argued,[53] the intended
means by which humans were to attain to knowledge of good and
evil—either from above, from the perspective of mastery of temptation, or from below, from the perspective of slavery to sin.[54]

4. What is death in Genesis 2:17?

What is the nature of the "death penalty" with which God threat-
ens the man? Many read this as a threat of physical death as such.[55]

52. R. W. L. Moberly, "Did the Serpent Get It Right?" *Journal of Theological Studies* n.s. 39, no. 1 (1988): 1–27, at 21–22. Compare Keil, 85: "Not to know what good and
evil are, is a sign of either the immaturity of infancy (Deut. i.39) or the imbecility of age
(2 Sam. xix.35); whereas the power to distinguish [using הֵבִין (*hebîn*, "to discern, distinguish") which has partial semantic overlap with יָדַע (*yada'*, "to know")] good and evil is
commended as the gift of a king (1 Kings iii.9) and the wisdom of angels (2 Sam. xiv.17
[using שָׁמַע (*shama'*, "to hear," ESV "to discern")]), and in the highest sense is ascribed to
God Himself (chap. iii.5, 22)."

53. Delitzsch, 138. T. C. Mitchell also endorses this after surveying several other possibilities in "Eden, Garden of" in *NBD*, 289a–290b, at 289b; see also Keil, 85–86. Possibly
Sir. 17:7 supports this, if it is in fact an allusion to this text (the Hebrew original of this part
of Ben Sira is not extant, and its Greek does not exactly match the Septuagint of Genesis):
in making man God is said to have "filled them with the knowledge of understanding, and
showed them good and evil" (RSV). Here to "show good and evil" is to impart discernment.
Compare Patrick Skehan and Alexander DiLella, *The Wisdom of Ben Sira* (Anchor Bible;
New York: Doubleday, 1987), 282, who think this is "a clear allusion to Gen. 2:17."

54. Delitzsch's explanation comports very nicely with some comments C. S. Lewis made
in *Mere Christianity* about the relationship of moral performance and mental acuity. In book
3 (*Christian Behavior*), chapter 4 ("Christianity and Psychoanalysis"), the last paragraph,
Lewis observes that "when a man is getting better he understands more and more clearly
the evil that is still left in him. When a man is getting worse, he understands his badness
less and less. . . . Good people know about both good and evil: bad people do not know
about either." Then in chapter 5 of the same book (on "Sexual Morality"), he comments,
"those who are seriously attempting chastity are more conscious, and soon know a great
deal more about their own sexuality than anyone else. They come to know their desires as
Wellington knew Napoleon, or as Sherlock Holmes knew Moriarty; as a rat-catcher knows
rats or a plumber knows about leaky pipes. Virtue—even attempted virtue—brings light;
indulgence brings fog." The other strong possibility, argued by Moberly in "Did the Serpent
Get It Right?" is that " 'knowledge of good and evil' signifies *moral autonomy*" (24). This,
however, suffers from failure actually to explain what happens in the narrative.

55. The literature is quite extensive. For a sample, cf. James Barr, *The Garden of Eden
and the Hope of Immortality* (Minneapolis: Fortress, 1992), 8–11, who asserts strongly that
immediate physical death was the threat, not mere mortality; and "the serpent was the
one who was right in such matters. They did not die" (8). Wenham, 68, says, "The text is a
straightforward warning that death will follow eating"; while Hamilton, 172–74, concludes
that it is a death sentence that can be averted through repentance.

Those who read the text this way then must say that the snake was in some sense right (see Gen. 3:4), and if they draw back from such a conclusion, it is in the direction of taking the threat along one of the following lines: (1) Adam and Eve will become mortal or come under a death sentence; or else (2) they will physically die immediately, but then in God's grace the threat was not carried out (of which grace the snake would of course not have been a part). But need we go to these explanatory lengths or draw the unwanted conclusion that the snake was right and God was wrong?

It seems clear to me that the right method is (a) to consider the semantic range of the Hebrew word "die" (Hebrew root *m-w-t*) and (b) to use the context to ascertain which part of that range is present in our text. And it seems further plain that cooperation with the narrator requires us to assume that the Lord God is a "reliable character" and the snake is not.[56] This means that we should assume that what happens may serve to identify the meaning of "die."

To begin with, then, what is the semantic range of the Hebrew root *m-w-t*? Whereas its most common referent is physical death (e.g., Gen. 5:5), it can also refer to what we may call "spiritual death," that is, estrangement from a life-giving relationship with God.[57] This appears in Proverbs 12:28:

> In the path of righteousness is *life* [חַיִּים, *khayyîm*],
>   and in its pathway there is *no death* [אַל־מָוֶת, *'al-mawet*]

Since Proverbs does not suggest that righteous people do not physically die (indeed, in 14:32 they take refuge in their death), this "no-death" must refer to a blessed afterlife (that is, it is parallel to "life," which is life in its fullest aspect, life with God forever); which means

---

56. This, I think, is axiomatic. Though biblical writers will wrestle with God, though they express deep perplexity over his dealings, they would never cast aspersions on his truthfulness. Hence when Barr, *Garden of Eden*, 14, concludes, "The person who comes out of this story with a slightly shaky moral record is, of course, God," he should instantly have reexamined his reading of the story.

57. In the interests of clarity of thought we should reject altogether the labels "literal" and "figurative" for these two senses, because in most people's minds, "literal" means "more *real*" than "figurative." In the biblical worldview, not only is spiritual death real, but it is by far the more horrible of the two.

that "death" in this context would be perdition. Similarly, in Proverbs 23:13–14 we read:[58]

> [13]Do not withhold discipline from a child;
>   if you strike him with a rod he will not *die*.
> [14]If you strike him with the rod,
>   you will save his soul from Sheol.

The parallel is between not dying and being saved from Sheol (from perdition).[59] There is of course no question of one's child not *physically* dying; the question is instead, where does his moral orientation take him?[60]

The syntax of the threat is "you shall surely die," using an infinitive absolute with an imperfect.[61] This expression appears in about twenty verses in the Old Testament, and only here and in 1 Kings 2:37, 42 do we find the time element explicit: "For *on the day* you go out and cross the brook Kidron, know for certain that *you shall [surely] die*." The time element in 1 Kings 2:37 says when Shimei will "know for certain," rather than when he will "surely die," so it is not identical to Genesis 2:17, where the time is when the man will surely die. In any case the idea is that the sentence is firm and not likely to be revoked. This makes it harder to argue for an interpretation like "you will surely become mortal" or "you will surely die (but I will revoke the sentence)," and we may hope for something more in keeping with usage.

Now we have the semantic range of the word and syntax of the expression; we can go no further in applying the contextual informa-

---

58. The NASB renders the particle כִּי (*kî*) that introduces the second line of 2:13 as "although," and this is inexcusable in view of the connection with verse 14: כִּי followed by the imperfect here introduces the protasis of a conditional clause (see Joüon, *Grammar of Biblical Hebrew*, §167i).

59. Although some would take Sheol simply as a name for the grave (the policy of the NIV; cf. R. Laird Harris, "The Meaning of the Word *Sheol* as Shown by Parallels in Poetic Texts," *Journal of the Evangelical Theological Society* 4 [1961]: 129–35), the evidence is quite against this interpretation and favors the interpretation that it is the place where the ungodly go: see T. Desmond Alexander, "The OT View of Life after Death," *Themelios* 11, no. 2 (1986): 41–46; Alexander Heidel, *The Gilgamesh Epic and OT Parallels* (Chicago: University of Chicago, 1949), 170–91; Philip Johnston, " 'Left in Hell'?" in *The Lord's Anointed*, ed. P. E. Satterthwaite et al. (Grand Rapids: Baker, 1995), 213–22, at 216–21.

60. See further Kidner's subject study "Life and Death" in *Proverbs*, 53–56.

61. We must distinguish Qal מוֹת תָּמוּת (*môt tamût*, "you shall surely die") from Hophal מוֹת תּוּמַת (*môt tûmat*, "you shall surely be put to death"). Note that the Septuagint renders the expression in Gen. 2:17 θανάτῳ ἀποθανεῖσθε (plural!), using the "cognate dative" for the infinitive absolute.

tion until we have studied Genesis 3, which we will do in the next chapter.

5. Where is Eden?

The question of where Eden might have been rests on how we read Genesis 2:10–14, the excursus.[62] These verses by their process-aspect verb tenses indicate that they do not advance the storyline, as we have already seen.

And what shall we make of these four rivers? Most accept that the Tigris (חדקל, *khiddeqel*) and Euphrates (פרת, *perat*) are the known rivers, but what of the Pishon and Gihon? Scholars have had great difficulties in trying to identify these last two rivers, and some have concluded that this is intentional on the author's part. For example, Radday contends,

> The picture of paradisal beatitude is so idyllic and attractive that a reader who fails to comprehend the sophistication of the story may well decide to set out for this wondrous land.
>
> We are finally coming to the gist of the story of the rivers. It is to him that Torah replies, tongue in cheek: All you have to do in order to reach Paradise is to find the place where four rivers originate from, of which two, famous though in foreign parts, have no common source, the third, also well known, is a little brook across the nearby valley [the Gihon Spring of Jerusalem, see 1 Kgs. 1:33], and the fourth [Pishon] does not exist. *Eden is nowhere.*

This requires that Eden be the source of the four rivers.

Others, such as Harris, suppose that the location is a real one but irretrievable to us—perhaps because the (global) flood has changed the scene.[63]

62. A selected bibliography: R. Laird Harris, "The Mist, the Canopy, and the Rivers of Eden," *Bulletin of the Evangelical Theological Society* 11, no. 4 (1968): 177–79; Yehuda T. Radday, "The Four Rivers of Paradise," *Hebrew Studies* 23 (1982): 23–31; T. C. Mitchell, "Eden, Garden of," in *NBD*, 289a–290b; John C. Munday Jr., "Eden's Geography Erodes Flood Geology," *Westminster Theological Journal* 58 (1996): 123–54; James A. Sauer, "The River Runs Dry," *Biblical Archaeology Review* 22, no. 4 (1996): 52–57, 64; K. A. Kitchen, *On the Reliability of the Old Testament* (Grand Rapids: Eerdmans, 2003), 428–30.

63. Harris is an old-earth creationist and is not quite in the same category as the young-earth flood geologists who are the targets of Munday's article. Nevertheless, Munday's critique applies equally: how can we explain the obvious effort of the text to locate the place?

A recent set of studies has opened up the possibility that the location is real, but the two unknown streams are now dry because of climate changes over the last several thousand years. To appreciate these, we must make some distinctions. First, there is no reason to identify Eden with "the land" in which the man was formed (Gen. 2:5–7), since God moved the man from the land to the garden.[64] Second, we should recognize that "Eden" and "the garden" are not the same: the garden is "in" Eden (2:8).

Now the text looks like it is describing real geography, with its mention of rivers (two of which are known), the land of Havilah and its gold and other stones, and the land of Cush. Cush may be the land in Africa (Sudan), or it may be the land of the Kassites (a people in western Iran). If it is the land of the Kassites, that points us to Mesopotamia; but what then of the gold of Havilah? There is a known source of gold in Arabia, south of modern Medina; and from near those gold fields a now-dry river once arose, flowing toward the Persian Gulf through modern Kuwait. Thus we might have the Pishon. If Cush refers to the Kassites, then the Gihon would be a river flowing down from the Zagros Mountains, such as the modern Kerkheh or the Diz plus Karun Rivers.

And how shall we picture the "four rivers" of Genesis 2:10 (literally, "four heads")? Radday (and many others) takes the text as looking downstream from Eden, with one river dividing into four streams. But what if the text looks *upstream* from Eden and the river "divided" into its four tributaries? As Kitchen suggests, we can suppose ourselves in the garden, looking out into "Greater Eden," from which a single stream enters the garden. Just upstream from us four "head" rivers come together to form the single stream that waters the garden. This would put the garden close to the present head of the Persian Gulf.

The problem, of course, is that the present climate cannot sustain such a picture. But, as recent studies have shown, the climate of the Arabian Peninsula has changed over the millennia, with wetter and drier periods. The potential Pishon dried up somewhere between 3500 and 2000 B.C. If this is so, then the Genesis narrative preserves the memory of a period well before Abraham![65]

---

64. Neither Harris ("Mist, the Canopy," 178) nor Munday ("Eden's Geography," 131) appreciates this point.

65. We might also note, with Munday, that this is incompatible with flood geology, which supposes that an enormously catastrophic flood lies between the events in the

6. Relationship between Genesis 2:4–25; 1:1–2:3; 3:1–24

We are now able to comment on the common practice of calling Genesis 1:1–2:3 and 2:4–25 the two creation accounts in the Bible. Quite simply, our study of 2:4–7 above shows this to be a mistake. The question at this point is *not* whether the pericopes come from originally separate sources; we will save that discussion for chapter 8. Rather, I am looking at the present form of the text.

I argued above that the structure of Genesis 2:4 makes it serve as a hinge, inviting the audience to read the two pericopes together— which means taking them as complementing each other. If we pay attention to the verb tenses and lexical semantics in 2:5–7, we see that we can do just that: in some particular but unnamed land, at the time of year when the dry season was nearing its end and the rain cloud was rising, God "formed" the man. Following the rest of the chapter, we find that after the Lord God placed the man in the garden of Eden he fashioned a woman. Thus the pericope elaborates the very brief narrative of 1:27, declaring that what was presented as a single event in the first pericope actually was spread out over a length of time. Only after he made the woman could God declare the whole thing "very good" (1:31).

Subsequent audiences did in fact read these two pericopes together. Consider, for example, Matthew 19:3–5 (Mark 10:2–8):

> [3]And Pharisees came up to [Jesus] and tested him by asking, "Is it lawful to divorce one's wife for any cause?" [4]He answered, "Have you not read that he who created them from the beginning made them male and female, [5]and said, 'Therefore a man shall leave his father and his mother and hold fast to his wife, and the two shall become one flesh'?"

Jesus here takes Genesis 1:27 (Matt. 19:4) and Genesis 2:24 (Matt. 19:5) together to make his point.[66]

---

garden and the time of Moses and has changed the topography beyond recognition. But Genesis gives fairly straightforward clues to identifying the places, so the flood could not have obliterated them.

66. See also Wis. 10:1–2 ("first-formed" evokes Gen. 2:7; "created" and "rule" evoke Gen. 1:27–28); Tob. 8:6 ("made" evokes Gen. 1:27 LXX; the rest evokes Gen. 2:18).

So the second pericope fills out part of the sixth day of the first pericope. What shall we make of the third pericope, Genesis 3:1–24?[67] (The question is a legitimate one, since Genesis 3 shares much in common with Genesis 2, as we saw above.) It is most likely that the author or editor of the final form of the text wanted the audience to see the events of Genesis 3 as taking place on the divine Sabbath, since the sixth day ends with everything very good, and Genesis 3 introduces evil into human life. Further, as we saw in chapter 4, the author saw the divine Sabbath as God's rest from the work of creating, a rest that continues to the present day. This is just what we see in Genesis 3.

7. How long was the creation week?

In this section we must tackle the questions, What kind of days does Genesis 1 speak about, and does the Book of Genesis actually take a stand on the age of the earth? In my discussion of Genesis 1:1–2:3 I argued that these questions are not at the front of the author's interests, but it does not follow that he says absolutely nothing on the subject.

The way in which these topics have become such points of contention has raised a number of interesting methodological issues, such as: Can we read Genesis 1 and 2 together, and if so, how? What is a genuinely literal reading of the texts, and does that matter? In what sense may we claim that the Scripture is clear, and what role should that play in our interpretation? Do we think that these chapters have any historical truth claims, and may we legitimately harmonize our

---

67. The details presented here show why those who make Gen. 2–3 *as a whole* the complement to Genesis 1 are mistaken; in particular, Gen. 2:4–25 leaves us at the same place as 1:31, while Genesis 3 introduces discord and sin. For example, Leon Kass, *The Beginning of Wisdom: Reading Genesis* (New York: Free Press, 2003), 55–56, does so because he takes "the image of God" (Gen. 1:26) to be the parallel to "like one of us" (Gen. 3:22); but my treatment shows why these two are separate. Philip R. Davies, "Making It: Creation and Contradiction in Genesis," in *The Bible in Human Society: Essays in Honor of John Rogerson*, ed. M. Daniel Carroll R. et al. (Sheffield: Sheffield Academic Press, 1995), says, "I have chosen . . . to read Genesis 1 and 2–3 as two presentations of the same event," without examining whether Gen. 3 moves beyond Genesis 1. He proceeds to find a number of contradictions between the two "presentations" and further refers to "Christian misreading of the account" without argument or even footnote. In his effort to show how the second account undermines the first, he never stops to discuss whether the details of the text require such a reading, or whether ancient authors produced such writings, or whether earlier readers might have seen things that he does not.

interpretation with evidence from outside the Bible? If we are alert to these issues, we may be able to keep our discussion from becoming tedious.

It is probably safe to say that, prior to the rise of the new geology in the eighteenth century, most Bible readers simply understood the creation period to be one ordinary week[68] and the genealogies to be complete; thus the creation took place somewhere in the vicinity of 4000 B.C. Many of the pioneers of the new geology were pious church members, and so they were convinced that neither the Bible nor the evidence of nature could lie. Between 1800 and 1850, exegetes developed most of the major exegetical moves and options available today.[69] One of the first attempts was to find a long gap between the initial creation of Genesis 1:1 and the six days of shaping the earth (these were thought to be normal days): by this view, 1:2 tells us that the earth *became* without form and void as a result of Satan's rebellion. By far the most common harmonizing interpretation was the day-age approach: this aimed to show that Genesis 1 allowed us to read the days as long periods of time ("ages"); this view was widely held among educated Christians by 1900. The *Scofield Reference Bible* combines the gap and day-age interpretations, which tells us that these various interpretive schemes need not be mutually exclusive.

The twentieth century saw several other interpretive efforts, which allow some level of harmonizing between Genesis and geology. The literary framework view sees the days as just that: a literary framework for us to understand the work of creation, without committing anyone to see the days as either sequential or normal. The intermittent day view sees the days as normal ones and sequential, but these normal days are the end points of potentially long periods of creative

68. A major exception is Augustine, who at times declared himself unable to say what kind of days they were and at other times supposed that the creation took place in an instant (this was because he was reading Sir. 18:1 in Latin: *Creavit omnia simul*, "He created all things at the same time"; the Greek is ἔκτισεν τὰ πάντα κοινῇ, "He created all things in common"). In either case he hardly thought the days were ordinary ones, and he had a great influence on other great minds, such as Anselm.

69. See Michael Roberts, "Geology and Genesis Unearthed," *Churchman* 112, no. 3 (1998): 225–55, for evidence that the exegetical moves were developed by 1850. This is significant, because many have claimed that these moves were developed to accommodate Darwinism—but Darwin's *Origin of Species* first appeared in 1859. Further, there is some evidence that some of the best minds of the Middle Ages did in fact read the creation story in a way that was not fully literalistic; see Robert Letham, " 'In the Space of Six Days': The Days of Creation from Origen to the Westminster Assembly," *Westminster Theological Journal* 61 (1999): 149–74.

activity. The view that I shall advocate can be called the analogical days position: namely, the days are God's workdays, their length is neither specified nor important, and not everything in the account needs to be taken as historically sequential. This position found advocates in the American Presbyterian William Shedd and the Dutch Reformed Herman Bavinck, although both can point to precursors in the history of exposition. Such a pedigree matters, because these theologians display marked conservatism and theological astuteness, and they exhibit different stances toward the geology of their day—Shedd accepted it, while Bavinck was skeptical.

These efforts at so-called nonliteral readings of the days have provoked strong reaction, from both the left (scholars who hold to critical views of Scripture) and the right (young earth creationists, primarily conservative Protestants). Scholars from the left, the critical side, argue that such harmonizations simply run away from the conflict between science and faith, with science (and thus, biblical criticism) being triumphant.[70] Those from the right think that the harmonizers compromise the authority and clarity of Scripture, because they depart from the "plain sense" of Scripture simply to satisfy a kind of science that ignores the Bible.[71] There is another group that also decries the harmonizers: these are Christians who think that the biblical creation story speaks to matters of value rather than to matters of historical fact. This group thinks that any attempt to take this story as making historical claims is untrue to the text itself.

It is hard to keep one's head when such reactions are in the air. I will not deceive you by making myself out to be neutral: my sympathies are with the harmonizers. But I hope that I am honest enough to change my mind if the evidence leads elsewhere. The only way to proceed is to keep our focus on the grammar and to keep the hermeneutical issues in plain sight.

Let us begin by tackling the question of the plain sense of a biblical passage. The right response is, "plain" to whom? We are keeping our focus on the act of communication between the author and his first audience and aiming to reconstruct their literary competence;

70. For example, James Barr, *Fundamentalism* (Philadelphia: Westminster Press, 1978), 40–41; Skinner, 21.

71. Recent examples include Douglas F. Kelly, *Creation and Change: Genesis 1:1–2:4 in the Light of Changing Scientific Paradigms* (Fearn, Ross-shire: Christian Focus, 1997); Kurt P. Wise, *Faith, Form, and Time: What the Bible Teaches and Science Confirms about Creation and the Age of the Universe* (Nashville: Broadman & Holman, 2002).

that alone is our criterion for finding the sense of Scripture. I hope to show that the analogical days approach fulfills this requirement, and this is its best commendation. In my judgment the other approaches have severe liabilities, but I will not get into extensive critique; my goal is to follow the text.

I begin by recalling several things that I have already argued. First, Genesis 2:4 invites the reader to read the two accounts together, which means to harmonize them if possible. Second, it best suits the grammar of 2:5–7 if we read these verses as describing the conditions in the "land" when God formed the first man, on the sixth day of Genesis 1. Next, the first day starts in 1:3, and thus our author has not necessarily presented the six days as the first six days of the universe: the author presents the origin of everything, 1:1, as taking place an unspecified amount of time before the workweek. In the previous chapter I gave my reasons for thinking that sequence of the days matters and that the fourth day does not describe the *creation* of the heavenly lights.

We have also discussed the refrain: its effect is to present God as a workman going through his workweek, taking his daily rest (the night between the evening and the morning) and enjoying his Sabbath "rest." To speak this way is to speak analogically about God's activity; that is, we understand what he did by analogy with what we do; and in turn, that analogy provides guidance for man in the proper way to carry out his own work and rest.

The analogy cautions us against applying strict literalism to the passage. I also indicated in the previous chapter that a good interpretation must account for the absence of the refrain on the seventh day. What does God rest from? It must be from his work of furnishing the earth to be a place for mankind to live, love, and worship: he "enjoys" the product of that workweek, which is finished. In other words, this Sabbath rest continues into the present, a notion that underlies John 5:17 and Hebrews 4:3–11.[72]

It follows that this day lacks the refrain because it has no end—it is not an ordinary day by any stretch of the imagination, and this makes us question whether the other days are supposed to be ordinary in their length. Their length makes little difference to the account, which is based on analogy rather than identity between God's work and man's.

72. See chapter 4, section E.3. See also Augustine, *Confessions* 13:36.

If we had only Genesis 1:1–2:3 we could leave the discussion at that: the creation account makes no claim about how old the universe is or about how old the earth itself is, since the author does not specify how long God waited between verses 1 and 2. Further, it makes no claim about how long the creation period was, because it is noncommittal about how long the days were.

But now we come to Genesis 2:4–7 and cooperate with its invitation to harmonize the two narratives:

> ⁴These are the generations
>> of the heavens and the earth when they were
>>> created,
>> in the day that the LORD God made the earth and
>>> the heavens.

> ⁵When no bush of the field was yet in the land and no small plant of the field had yet sprung up—for the LORD God had not caused it to rain on the land, and there was no man to work the ground, ⁶and a mist was going up from the land and was watering the whole face of the ground—⁷then the LORD God formed the man of dust from the ground and breathed into his nostrils the breath of life, and the man became a living creature.

While many versions take הָאָרֶץ (ha'arets) as "the earth" in verses 5–6, the ESV is better in taking it as "the land," referring to some unnamed place where these conditions held. This is clear from the fact that the first account had the plants growing up at God's command on the third day (1:11–12), while here the lack of plants is due to no rain and no man to work the ground (2:5). In theological terms, the sprouting of the plants in 1:11–12 may be called supernatural, while the lack in 2:5 may be called natural: by offering causes within the world as the readers experience it, the author is referring to ordinary providence.

I have claimed that this is what the readers already knew; by this I mean, they were familiar with a land in which the rain falls during the winter and not at all during the summer. This weather pattern makes the ground quite dry and brown by the end of the summer, and the coming of the rains brings about plant growth. The only way to overcome this natural pattern is for man to work the ground, by irrigation in this case. Thus our author points us to a particular time of year, when the rains had not yet come, and hence the plants had not begun to grow (and there was no man who could artificially water the ground); but a mist—or rain cloud—was just rising. At this time of year, in some place called "the land," God formed the man.

Now let us suppose that this is a good faith act of communication and that the author really thought that it was possible to harmonize this event with the sixth day of Genesis 1:1–2:3. What would it take for us to do so? First, we would not confuse anything here with the third day. Second, we would acknowledge that for the causal explanation offered here to have any sense, the climate pattern of rain and drought and its effect on the plant life would have to be established, and this would take several years, at least. Immediately, then, we would conclude that this event on the sixth day took place some unknown number of years after the plants first sprouted on the third day.

There are three ways for this to happen: (1) harmonization is impossible, or at least unwarranted; (2) the days are not ordinary, and at least some of them involve longer elapsed time than twenty-four hours; (3) the days have spaces of time between them. I will resort to the first of these only if I can show that neither of the other two offers a reasonable harmonization.

The second option works the best, as we can see by returning to the picture that Genesis 1:1–2:3 draws for us. There we saw God portrayed as a workman going through his week of alternating work and rest, leading up to his Sabbath rest. The seventh day is not presented as an ordinary day; neither, apparently, are the other six. These are *God's workdays*, and just how long they are does not matter to the act of communication; the audience understands them by way of their own experience of work and rest, and then the analogy serves to direct them in the better performance of their work and rest. Since this is an analogy, we should be cautious about too much literalism, which means that we can call the days and their activities broadly sequential, without requiring that every event be historically sequential; some things might be grouped by logical rather than chronological criteria.[73] The only requirement as to length is that the whole period must be long enough to establish the climate cycle.

73. For example, the fifth day groups what we call invertebrates with vertebrates, and in the latter category it groups fish with aquatic mammals. The logical principle of where they live can easily be the governing principle, rather than the chronological principle of strict historical order of appearance.

Since this way of reading accounts for the details of the text as we now have it without any semantic, grammatical, or literary innovations, we should accept it as cooperating with the author's intention. That in itself should commend it above the competing ways of reading, but I will briefly explain what I take to be the chief defects of the rivals.

The ordinary day reading cannot provide harmonization between the two pericopes, because it does not allow us to take the causal explanation of Genesis 2:5 seriously: it does not allow enough time for the climate cycle to be relevant. Its advocates may or may not acknowledge the force of the missing refrain in the seventh day, but once one acknowledges it, he is in a position to wonder whether the other days are ordinary ones. At the least he should be on his guard against too strict a literalism.

The gap reading requires that we take the opening phrase of Genesis 1:2 as "the earth *became* without form and void" owing to a rebellion of Satan. Genesis itself says nothing about such a rebellion; there is a better explanation of "without form and void," as we saw above (chapter 4, section C.1). Further, the grammar of the verse is also against it:

והארץ היתה תהו ובהו

This does not advance the storyline, because the verb tense is perfect rather than *wayyiqtol*; and the usual idiom for "become" is היה ל (*hayâ le-*), which is not what we have here. Hence this does not describe an event but a state. In my analysis there is a gap between verses 1 and 2, but it is not the gap of the gap reading.

The day-age reading depends on the fact that the word יום (*yôm*, "day") can have several senses: the period of light between dawn and dusk; the whole period of twenty-four hours; and a period of unspecified length, as in "day of the LORD." The day-age approach appeals to this third sense and finds evidence in Genesis 2:4, "in the day that the LORD God made the earth and the heavens": here "day" refers to a stretch of six days. The problem with this stems from its faulty lexical semantics: when "day" has its third sense, it has a qualifying genitive, such as "day *of the* LORD" or "day *of wrath*," and no such a qualifier exists here. Further, the usage in 2:4 is part of an idiom and hence does not come into play. This reading is motivated by a strong impulse to vindicate the Bible by showing how it coordinates so closely with the best findings of the new sciences; I will comment later on whether the impulse is a sound one, but for now I will simply note that this approach seems to miss the communicative intent of Genesis 1–2.

In the previous chapter I gave my reasons for thinking that sequence in Genesis 1 matters to the author and thus for rejecting the literary framework reading in most of its forms. However, by calling the days broadly sequential I am agreeing with the caution about literalism that informs the framework reading, even though I cannot reject sequence altogether.

Let me summarize my conclusions about what Genesis in its present form claims about how long the creation week was:

(1) Genesis 1:1 describes the initial creation of all things, some unspecified time before the first day begins in 1:3. Hence the creation week is not necessarily the same as the first week of the universe.

(2) The days are God's workdays, which are understood by analogy to human work; the analogy in its turn serves to structure the workweek of the covenant people.

(3) The days are broadly sequential, which means they are successive periods of unspecified length; but since this sequence is part of the analogy, it is possible that parts of the days overlap and that events on a particular day may be grouped for logical rather than chronological reasons.

(4) The creation week must be some years long, at least, in order to harmonize Genesis 1 and 2.

(5) The creation Sabbath continues into the present.

I have not yet addressed the question of whether these pericopes make historical truth claims; how we think about this question affects how we would even consider finding a correlation between Genesis and geology. I will come back to this matter in chapter 10.

8. Creation ordinances in Genesis 1–2

I suppose that no one needs to defend the claim that the Pentateuch—which is the front end of the whole Bible—is riddled with ethical requirements for the covenant people. There will be disputes about, say, what is the precise role the Old Testament assigns to ethics and the range of its allowance for forgiveness; or what some of those ethical requirements actually are; or what is the relationship between the laws and ethics; or to what extent the New Testament takes over the ethics of the Old Testament. I will address some of these in this commentary, but at this point I intend to discuss the relationship of ethics to creation.

Many ethicists have spoken of "creation ordinances" found in Genesis 1–2, which define universal human nature. For example, John Murray wrote of "the commandments or mandates given to man in the state of integrity [that is, in the innocent condition in which he was created]"; he said that these commandments are "germane to the most basic interests of life in this world."[74] He listed them: "These creation ordinances, as we may call them, are the procreation of offspring, the replenishing of the earth, subduing of the same, dominion over the creatures, labour, the weekly Sabbath, and marriage." Murray acknowledges that "there is a complementation of these mandates and they interpenetrate one another," and for that reason I prefer to reorganize the list into three simple categories: the family (marriage leading to offspring who will fill[75] the earth and serve as the basis of human society); labor (subduing the earth, exercising dominion, working and keeping the garden); and religion (the Sabbath, as well as the religious bond with the Creator). We may use the mnemonic *wedlock, work, and worship* for these categories.

It is accurate to see these as applying not only to Adam and Eve in the garden but also to all humanity since them. For example, Genesis 2:24 finds in the bond between the first man and his wife a paradigm for every human marriage. The blessing of offspring is closely tied to the covenant as well: it is the means whereby covenant membership is transmitted (Gen. 17:6–7). There is no indication at all that God ever revoked the mandate to fill the earth and subdue it; in fact, God expects man to continue to do just that (as in Gen. 11:1–9, the judgment on Babel). Further, as Paul argued, God "made from one man every nation of mankind to live on all the face of the earth, . . . that they should seek God, in the hope that they might feel their way toward him and find him" (Acts 17:26–27). Every human being needs to know his Maker.

74. John Murray, *Principles of Conduct* (Grand Rapids: Eerdmans, 1957), 27, 26.
75. The AV (which Murray quoted) had "replenish," an English word that, according to the *Oxford English Dictionary*, once meant primarily "fill." In contemporary English that word mostly means "fill up *again*": hence recent versions have "fill."

Each human being fully expresses his humanity when his life is in tune with the creation ordinances. But, as we shall see in Genesis 3, human nature is badly damaged; hence the biblical covenantal religion has to do with redemption, making provision for the covenant member to experience forgiveness for sin and restoration to proper moral conduct. Christopher Wright articulates two crucial aspects of proper moral conduct: imitating "the character and ways of God" and return to the good pattern of creation.[76] As Wright observes, "The purpose of the ethical provisions given in the context of redemption, which include both the covenant law of the Old Testament and the ethics of the kingdom of God in the New, is to restore to humans the desire and the ability to conform to the creational pattern—God's original purpose for them."

We can support Wright's position in a number of ways. For example, one function of Genesis 2:4 is to claim that the God who made his covenant with Israel is in fact the Creator of all that there is—that is, the God who redeems is also the God who created. Further, the Creator declared his creation "very good" in Genesis 1:31; it stands to reason that he does not intend to abandon it.[77] Instead, redemption functions to heal it.

Then if we examine the Ten Commandments we see the aspect of restoring creation at work. Let us take a few of the more obvious ones to illustrate. The first commandment forbids other gods precisely because the creation account has left them no place in God's world; the second commandment forbids images because God transcends his creation; the fourth commandment enjoins a Sabbath observance in Israel that imitates God's creation Sabbath; the fifth and seventh commandments protect the integrity of the family, while the sixth and ninth commandments, in forbidding murder and false witness, protect the fabric of human society; and the eighth and tenth commandments, which protect private property, also promote honest labor as the means of gaining wealth.

Several consequences flow out of this for the lives of the covenant people. First, the fact that the commandments are rooted in creation makes it hard to understand how they could ever be done away with—even if, as Christians believe, they apply differently outside

76. Christopher J. H. Wright, *Walking in the Ways of the Lord: The Ethical Authority of the Old Testament* (Downers Grove, Ill.: InterVarsity Press, 1995), 13–45.
77. Wis. 11:24–26 makes just this point.

of the Mosaic administration that was specifically for the Israelite church-state nexus. For God to abolish any moral principle whose object was to equip people to live out their creational pattern would be cruelty, not love. This line of reasoning should lend clarity to Christian discussions of the continued relevance of the Ten Commandments, and especially of the fourth.[78]

Second, this shows why one of the chief attitudes that the Old Testament cultivates toward the law is astonished gratitude at the awesome dignity it bestows. Human beings at their deepest level need, and even yearn, to live according to this pattern and constantly find their own sin, and the sinful patterns of their cultures, frustrating that yearning.

Third, to speak of covenantal ethics as restorative reminds us how moral demands such as the Ten Commandments properly function among the people of God: not as a list of requirements to which they must measure up (or else be slaughtered), but rather as the shape into which they—as individuals and as a body—are to be molded as they cooperate with the love of their covenant Lord.

Fourth, this guides the people of God in their relationships with those outside the covenant. In their evangelism, they claim that the covenantal message links up with fundamental drives of every human heart—and Paul's speech in Acts 17:22–31 (see section E.5 in chapter 4) employs such reasoning. And in their testimony regarding social justice, they can similarly appeal to creational norms—which, when attended to, can be a step toward those outside the covenant wanting to come inside.

D. Literary-Theological Exposition

The pericope begins with "the LORD God" as the sole actor, as he forms the man, plants the garden, transports the man there, sets up the terms of a relationship with the man, and searches for a helper fit for the man, which culminates in the woman. The man is mostly presented as one who is acted upon, until Genesis 2:20, when he names the animals, and in verse 23 he declares his delight in the woman. The woman appears in verse 22 and is not an actor here at

78. In my judgment, observing the Sabbath on Sunday rather than Saturday for reasons of redemptive-historical development fits under the rubric of "apply differently outside of the Mosaic administration" rather than changing the nature of the commandment.

all—she was naked and not ashamed (this is a state rather than an action), along with her husband.

We have already seen above that the paragraph structure is

2:4	hinge/heading	
2:5–9	verses 5–6	setting for the events
	verses 7–9	events: formation of man, planting of garden, placing of man
2:10–14	excursus: the four primeval rivers	
2:15–17	events: God sets up terms of a relationship with man	
2:18–25	events: formation of a complementary helper	

It is not hard to see that verses 23–24 are the peak of the pericope. First, in them the project of verse 18 is now completed; second, verse 24 describes the enduring consequences of these events; third, the chief characters express their viewpoints—God (v. 24, see note on text) and man (v. 23). We might further notice the rhetorical features of verse 23 that highlight the man's speech (see last note on 2:23).

The basic sequence of events comes through easily if we just look at the structure. The use of the *wayyiqtol* moves the storyline along, with only a few variations. After the events in Genesis 2:7–9, we have an excursus in verses 10–14, which does nothing to move the storyline. Then when the events resume in verse 15, the author helps us to pick up the storyline by repeating the actions of verse 8: "And the LORD God planted a garden in Eden, in the east, and there he put the man whom he had formed. . . . The LORD God took the man and put him in the garden of Eden to work it and keep it." Even though the verbs in Genesis 2:15, "took" (וַיִּקַּח, *wayyiqqakh*) and "put" (וַיַּנִּחֵהוּ, *wayyannikhehû*), are *wayyiqtol*, they point back to "put" (וַיָּשֶׂם, *wayyasem*) in verse 8, which is also *wayyiqtol* (and note how verse 9 had advanced the storyline). This phenomenon, called resumptive repetition, allows the reader to understand how the time of verse 15 relates to the rest of the account; it also indicates that verses 10–14 are in fact an excursus that has been fully integrated into the whole narrative.[79]

79. See Philip A. Quick, "Resumptive Repetition: A Two-Edged Sword," *Journal of Translation and Textlinguistics* 6, no. 4 (1993): 289–316; he mentions Gen. 2:8–15 at 303. Quick argues that "resumptive repetition is a universal discourse feature" in human languages (290), and thus "a natural phenomenon of language such as resumptive repetition cannot be used as a criterion to determine that a text is composed of parts from different

The next verses present us with a problem if we want to read this account with the first pericope: Genesis 2:19 seems to have God forming the animals and birds *after* he formed the man and before he made the woman. At least, that is what the *wayyiqtol* verb in verse 19, "*So* out of the ground the LORD God *formed* [רֶצִיִּּו, *wayyitser*] every beast of the field and every bird of the heavens," normally implies. However, I have argued above that 2:4 invites the reader to read the two pericopes as complementing each other (see section C.1); we cooperate with this invitation if we take the events of 2:7–25 as happening on the sixth day of the creation week. The "not good" of verse 18 tells us that we are at a point prior to the "very good" of 1:31. We further cooperate by taking the *wayyiqtol* in verse 19 as a pluperfect, as in the ESV margin (and text of ESV Update): "the LORD God *had* formed." There are specific criteria that must be met for this to happen, and I have shown elsewhere why I think that this case meets those criteria.[80] Very briefly, the criteria for taking a *wayyiqtol* as pluperfect are the following:

(1) Some anaphoric reference points us back explicitly to a previous event.
(2) The verb begins a paragraph or pericope.
(3) The logic of the referent requires it.

The logic of the referent can be supplied by the literary context, and this is what we have here: the first pericope gives us the broad sequence of events, which enables us to find a rhetorical effect from the different sequence here. The reader knows from Genesis 1 that God made the birds and land animals before he made the man, but when he reads 2:19, he finds that it reinforces the message of 1:1–2:3. Physically, God made these animals *before* man, but conceptually, he made the animals anticipating man's dominion over them—that is, in God's mind the animals were a logical consequence of the man.

Now we consider the causal connections between this episode and what comes before and after it. Genesis 2:7, 22 describes the same

---

authors" (310); see 310–12 for discussion, where he takes Westermann's commentary on Gen. 38 to task for such a failure. Westermann, 215, 219, commits the same mistake, arguing that Gen. 2:10–14 comes from a separate kind of source than its context, and the first sentence of 2:15 is "one of the demonstrable doublets in Gen. 2–3."

80. See Collins, "The *Wayyiqtol* as 'Pluperfect': When and Why," *Tyndale Bulletin* 46, no. 1 (1995): 117–40, at 135–40.

event as 1:27 but with much more detail. This means that 2:5–6, properly understood, tells us what it was like at that point of the sixth day at which God made the man. If we follow the sequence of events, we can also see the geography of Genesis 2–4: in some unknown "land" God made the man, and from there he moved him to the garden of Eden.[81] This is where the temptation of Genesis 3 takes place, until in 3:23 God sent the man out from the garden to work the ground from which he was taken—presumably in the "land" where he was made, a place that will bring forth thorns and thistles instead of the fruits of Eden. The events of Genesis 4 take place outside Eden as a consequence.

In this chapter we learn of the two special trees that are important for Genesis 3. We also find the origin of three activities that define human life ever after: work, worship, and wedlock.[82] But we receive this properly if we recognize the yawning gap between our present experience and life in the garden, and this is a major clue to the communicative purpose of the chapter. If we believe the account has any connection to reality, we will ache as we recognize this gap, and insist on an explanation.

A key repetition is the parallel between Genesis 2:7 and Genesis 2:19: the Lord God *formed* the man *from the ground*, making him a *living creature*, and he *formed* the other *living creatures*, also *from the ground*. As we have seen (Gen. 2:7, note on text), man is presented as like the other animals in some ways and unlike them in others. Further, just as God *brought* the animals to the man (v. 19), he *brought* the woman to him (v. 22). The man gives a name to the woman, just as he gave a name to the other creatures.

The way this account uses the Hebrew word אָדָם (*'adam*) is informative: in Genesis 2:5 it is just a general word for "human being,"[83] while in verse 7 the lack of a man is answered by God forming "*the* man," namely, the first human (who is also male).[84] This person is "*the* man" up through the first part of verse 20; then it appears without

---

81. The "land" is described in terms of the western Levant, and it is hard to know whether this is simply using the reader's familiar experience of the climate for the sake of comprehension or whether this is perhaps a stronger assertion that the man was formed in a place with such a climate.

82. See section C.8 above on "Creation ordinances in Genesis 1–2."

83. It appears without the definite article.

84. I take the definite article here to be anaphoric: 2:5 had said "there was no man," and now verse 7 refers to the afore-mentioned man.

the article again, and we must either suppose that it is the proper name "Adam" or else supply the article.[85] The article reappears in verses 21, 22, and 25.[86] In verses 23–24, this "man" is also called אִישׁ ('îsh)—also rendered "man," but specifically a male.

Genesis 2:23 draws attention to the way that אִשָּׁה ('ishshâ, "woman") sounds like the feminine of אִישׁ ("man"), in order to emphasize their common origin and also the priority of the man.

Many point to the way that the man is called אָדָם ('adam), which sounds like the word for "ground," אֲדָמָה ('adamâ): man was formed from the ground to work the ground and will return to the ground after his sin (Gen. 3:19). However, since the animals too were formed from the ground (2:19), we have little ground for supposing that the author intended such a wordplay.[87]

Genesis 2:9 describes the permitted trees of the garden in a way that foreshadows 3:6:

And out of the ground the LORD God made to spring up every tree that is *pleasant* to the sight and *good* for food. The tree of life was in the midst of the garden, and the tree of the knowledge of good and evil. (2:9)	וַיַּצְמַח יהוה אֱלֹהִים מִן־הָאֲדָמָה כָּל־עֵץ נֶחְמָד לְמַרְאֶה וְטוֹב לְמַאֲכָל וְעֵץ הַחַיִּים בְּתוֹךְ הַגָּן וְעֵץ הַדַּעַת טוֹב וָרָע
So when the woman saw that the tree was *good* for food, and that it was a delight to the eyes, and that the tree was *to be desired* to make one wise . . . (3:6)	וַתֵּרֶא הָאִשָּׁה כִּי טוֹב הָעֵץ לְמַאֲכָל וְכִי תַאֲוָה־הוּא לָעֵינַיִם וְנֶחְמָד הָעֵץ לְהַשְׂכִּיל

The Lord God had supplied the garden with every tree that was "good for food" and "pleasant" or "desirable" (נחמד in both places)—everything the man and woman could have wanted; but the serpent managed to get the woman to ignore that and to see only the forbid-

85. The form is וּלְאָדָם (ûle'adam), and we would then argue that the article is a mere matter of a vowel point under the letter לֹ (le/la); the drawback to this is that there is no textual evidence for the repointing. The Septuagint begins using the name *Adam* in verse 16.

86. The proper name Adam—אָדָם ('adam) without an article—appears again in 3:21 and again in 4:25.

87. Josephus, *Antiquities* 1.34, also explains with a folk etymology: "This man was called Adam; and this, according to the Hebrew tongue signifies 'red' [Hebrew 'adôm], because he was made from the red earth kneaded together, for of such color is the virgin and true earth."

den tree as good and desirable. This is one of several sad ironies that we will explore in the next chapter.

Now we turn to the characters. We have noticed already the way the narration introduces the composite divine name in Genesis 2:4, "the LORD God." It was once common to explain the shift by saying that the first two pericopes come from different sources, which display distinctive patterns for naming God. I am not here discussing whether that is a critically sound move; that can wait until chapter 8. The only canonical text that we have is the one that puts these two pericopes together and invites us to read them as complementing each other. How might we do so? We saw in the previous chapter that the name *God* presents the deity in his majesty, power, transcendence, and ownership with respect to the creation. We have noted in this chapter that the composite name "the LORD God" is rare outside of Genesis 2–3 (only Exod. 9:30 in the Pentateuch); and this rare usage then requires an explanation.

The explanation comes from appreciating what the special name יהוה (*yhwh*, "the LORD") indicates. In Exodus 3:14 God himself connects the name with the verb *to be* when he answers Moses' request for his name by saying, "I am who I am."[88] Many have found in this a simple assertion of his existence, but this hardly does justice to the context; rather, when in Exodus God explains his name, both in 3:12–17 and in 6:2–8, the emphasis is on his faithfulness to his promises, which will result in blessing for his people. For this reason the special name "the LORD" is the name that God is called as the covenant-making and covenant-keeping God, specifically as the God who made promises to the patriarchs of Israel.

Now we are in a position to explain why Genesis 2–3 uses this composite name. First, the focus of the second pericope is on God working personally with the first man (as we have argued, we may even call the relationship a covenant); and second, and perhaps more powerfully, this name makes it clear that the God who has yoked himself by promises to the patriarchs and their offspring (and hence to the first audience) is the transcendent Creator of heaven and earth.

And what do we see of God in the way he acts here? We see that he is a generous provider: he puts the man in a garden that is furnished with an abundance of beautiful trees and delicious food (Gen. 2:8–9);

88. Hebrew אהיה אשר אהיה (*'ehyeh 'asher 'ehyeh*), which might also mean "I am what I am," or "I will be what I will be" (as in ESV margin).

he invites the man to eat from any of these trees (v. 16); he seeks a "helper fit for" the man and does what it takes to find one (vv. 18–22). We see this generosity even when he sets the man in Eden to work the garden and keep it (v. 15): such work, under such conditions, must have been sheer delight for the man![89]

We further see that God is able to do what he wants: he "forms" the man, using mere dust (Gen. 2:7), he makes a garden grow according to his will (vv. 8–9), and he makes animals and at last a woman (vv. 19–22). This continues the portrayal found in the first pericope, where God has absolute power over his creation. Here that power is clearly focused on providing for the well-being of the humans he made.

The final aspect of God's character that we see is his relational side: he has made mankind for relationship—relationship with himself (Gen. 2:15–17) and with other people (v. 18). It is thus no surprise that man—who is in the image of God (1:26–27)—reflects this relational side in his own make-up (2:18, 24).

The passage presents the man as one who receives God's good favor (Gen. 2:7–9, 15–18) rather than one who acquires that favor. We read nothing of the man's accepting the terms of the covenant, although it becomes clear in 3:2–3 (as we shall see in the next chapter) that he did accept them and communicate them to the woman; but it hardly makes sense to think of the covenant as a means by which the man is to *merit* anything.

The man's first recorded action is that of naming the other creatures (Gen. 2:19–20). We assume that in doing so he exercised his faculty of speech, as well as intelligence that discerned the right name for each animal. Naming seems also to be an exercise of authority; after all, the man was given dominion over the other creatures (1:28). It is clear that this dominion is radically different from what we call domination; rather, it expresses the way that man in his created innocence is like God. The man, though he is like the animals in being a living creature who is formed from the ground, is nevertheless different from the animals: none of them is a helper fit for him, and he alone has the capacities needed to assign their names. We never read of animals "holding fast" to one another in the marriage cov-

---

89. "Pain" does not come into man's picture until God banishes them from Eden and withdraws the blessings of Eden (3:17–19).

enant that makes them into one flesh (2:24); this too is distinctive of humans.

Another aspect of the man's character comes through in Genesis 2:23: when he sees the woman newly made, he declares her praise in fine rhetorical form; he is an artist as well as a taxonomist in his speech. Speech, then, is a crucial feature of human nature.

The woman is "a helper fit for" the man: she is not the same as he; she corresponds to him. The text does not say in what way she corresponds; an obvious suggestion is that her anatomy complements his for the sake of begetting and raising children. But there is no reason to stop there; as we shall see in the next chapter, her role complements his.

We can see these first two humans to be innocent as well, as we may infer from their being naked and not ashamed. The narrator has just told us of the man's delight in the woman and of the way in which this is a paradigm for the one-flesh relation; and even though the term *one flesh* is not about their sexual union as such, it does find its consummation in that union. For readers in the receptor culture, to speak of a man and woman naked together is to make them think of sex. But here there is no shame, for there is no reason for it; and that is because there is no sin in their experience. This pristine condition will be shattered in what follows (Gen. 3:10–11).

The author's point of view is uniformly approving in this account. He describes the trees as pleasant and good (Gen 2:9); the lands watered by the rivers are also filled with good things, such as gold, bdellium, and onyx (vv. 11–12). He reports the man's delight in verse 23 so that we can share it, and he further shows his approval by rooting every other human marriage in this first marriage (v. 24): here the author has stopped the event line in order to add his own comment. Genesis 2:25 describes the moral innocence of this couple.

The way the author builds suspense in Genesis 2:18–23 also expresses his approval: God says he wants the man to have a fit helper; he brings all the animals by to get their names, and we learn that none of them is the fit helper. If we are reading this for the first time, we wonder who is the fit helper; and then when we see how far God will go to produce one—anesthesia and surgery, verse 21—we are prepared to agree with the man's satisfied declaration.

All this makes me ache inside at what has been lost; am I not right to suppose that this is because the author ached as well?

The author also equips the reader to see how serious is the moral failure in the next pericope, by casting the "command" of Genesis 2:16–17 in such highlighted terms, as indicated in the translation notes above. The "you" inflections in these verses are all masculine singular, and the woman appropriates the command for herself in 3:2–3, as we shall see. Under no circumstances may these two plead that their disobedience did not concern anything important.

What, then, is this pericope about? The peak shows that the first marriage as a paradigm for every marriage is especially prominent. Let us put this in a larger context of biblical theology.

Everything in this text is good, and worthy of approval; even the "not good" of Genesis 2:18 describes only a temporary situation, which God himself relieves. There are universal features of human nature, which the people of Israel may observe in themselves and everyone else, and these have their origin in the original goodness of God's creation. The impulse to work and to make the rest of the creation serve human ends began with the first man's job in Eden. The impulse to worship God, which gets distorted into idolatry, nevertheless derives from man's creation to be a worshiping creature in covenant with his Creator. And the web of social relationships, especially marriage, was made for man's good, though now it too often brings pain. The covenant God of Israel planted these features into human nature at the very beginning, and, as we shall see in chapter 9, one purpose of the covenants made with the patriarchs and their offspring (culminating in Sinai) is to restore people to experience and enjoy their proper function.[90]

This helps us to see why marriage is especially suited to its prominence here: right at the heart of the promises made to Abraham is the Lord's intention to be a God to Abraham *and to his offspring* (Gen. 17:7), and faithful marriage is the context in which the covenant members find this promise fulfilled.

To reflect on the bounty and goodness of life in Eden makes us wonder about how the temptation in what follows could possibly have worked: how could the serpent have undermined the woman's confidence in her covenant Creator? Genesis 3 will not answer that question; we are left to see disobedience to our Maker as something fundamentally irrational and disruptive, whose consequences can only be harmful.

90. See section C.8 above, on "Creation ordinances."

E. Other Reverberations

1. Man and woman in 1 Corinthians 11:7–12

Paul appeals to the creation narrative to ground his view of complementary male and female relationships in 1 Corinthians 11:7–12:

> [7]For a man ought not to cover his head, since he is the image and glory of God, but woman is the glory of man. [8]For man was not made from woman, but woman from man. [9]Neither was man created for woman, but woman for man. [10]That is why a wife ought to have a symbol of authority on her head, because of the angels. [11]Nevertheless, in the Lord woman is not independent of man nor man of woman; [12]for as woman was made from man, so man is now born of woman. And all things are from God.

Paul is drawing on the account in Genesis 2:18–24, though he meshes that with terms from the first pericope, such as "image" and "created": God made the woman from a piece of Adam's body, to be a helper corresponding to him.[91] Paul's argument does not turn simply on the order in which they were made; otherwise the animals would be over man![92] Rather, the Genesis text itself declares a rationale for the woman: she is not the same as the man but complements him (see notes on Gen. 2:18 above).

For many people in the modern Western culture, this is sexist or discriminatory. This is because for them, to be equal means to have equal access to any role one aspires to. Those who want to defend the Bible must start by insisting on a useful definition of words like "sexist": simply to label something sexist because it sees a difference in men and women does not say anything worth saying, because nature itself is sexist in that sense (since men do not have access to child bearing). Rather, a more useful definition would be one that grounds any differences between men's and women's roles in differ-

---

91. There are also interesting points of contact with 1 Esd. 4:16–17, where men came *from* (ἐξ) women (compare 1 Cor. 11:12), women bring *glory* to men (compare 1 Cor. 11:7), and men cannot exist *without* women (1 Cor. 11:11). However, the 1 Esdras passage is part of an argument that women rule over men and thus are stronger than wine and men—this is a far cry from Paul's ideas!

92. 1 Tim. 2:13 explicitly appeals to order of being formed, and we should probably understand it in the light of this argument in 1 Cor. 11.

ent relative worth of men and women—and there is no evidence that the Bible employs such a rationale in its teaching.

It is clear that Paul does not belittle women here; after all, in 1 Corinthians 11:11–12 he acknowledges his own dependence on them!

For the ethical question, the important thing is that Paul grounds his requirements in the created pattern. If, as I argued above, one goal of the redemptive covenants is to restore human beings to their created functions, we would do well to mind Paul carefully.

2. Marriage: Proverbs; Malachi 2:14–16; Matthew 19:3–9; 1 Corinthians 6:16–17; Ephesians 5:31

Genesis 2:24 sets out a program for marriage, especially if we combine it with 1:26–28. One feature of marriage that stands out in the creation narrative is its covenantal nature: the man is to "hold fast" to his wife, practicing loyalty and faithfulness to her. Though the term *covenant* does not appear here in Genesis, there is no surprise in finding it elsewhere, as in Proverbs 2:17 and Malachi 2:14: the term *hold fast* (דָּבַק, *dabaq*) implies it.

That bond of loyalty is the context in which the other aspects of marriage are to flourish. First, the man and woman are to become "one flesh," a union of interests and pursuits. Thus a good man's wife is called the "delight of his eyes" (Ezek. 24:16), and a woman's husband is "the companion of her youth" (Prov. 2:17).[93] Second, the pair consummate and deepen their unity and companionship in their sexual relation—after all, the most obvious way in which a woman and man correspond to one another is in their complementary sexual anatomy. The biblical picture endorses sexual enjoyment within the marriage commitment as a good part of a good creation, not as a concession to man's fallenness; hence in Proverbs 5:15–19 a father uses a stunning image to encourage his son to find pleasure in his wife's sexuality.

If the husband and wife express and deepen their unity and companionship in sexual relations, they apply that unity in the raising of children. God commissioned the first pair to "be fruitful and multiply," and he promised to make Abraham fruitful (Gen. 17:6). He referred to the offspring not simply as children, but as heirs of the covenant (17:7–8). This reflects the idea that the parents find their fulfillment

93. See also Sir. 26:1–4.

in raising pious children, who embrace the covenant as their own (hence Prov. 10:1; 23:15–26; and many other texts).

These children will be in turn the foundation for their own families, and thus of human society, as Genesis 2:24 indicates by saying that a man will *leave* his father and his mother to form a new entity.

In contrast to this created bliss we can see the pain and pollution that have come in through sin. In particular, other texts appeal or allude to the ideas of Genesis 2 to address some of the most serious threats to marriage fulfilling its purpose, especially adultery, divorce, and polygamy.[94]

Adultery violates the covenant loyalty of marriage, which is why it can be a good image for Israel's unfaithfulness. This lies behind Proverbs 23:27–28 labeling a man who commits adultery a "traitor." Paul brings these together in 1 Corinthians 6:16–17:[95] "Or do you not know that he who *is joined* to a prostitute becomes one body with her? For, as it is written, 'The two will become one flesh.' But he who *is joined* to the Lord becomes one spirit with him." As the ESV margin makes clear, the term *is joined* here is equivalent to "holds fast" in Genesis 2:24 and in Deuteronomy 10:20, where the same expression is used of faithfulness to the Lord.[96]

Malachi 2:14–16 alludes to Genesis to condemn the Jewish men of the restoration community who divorce their Jewish wives in favor of pagan girls:

> [14]But you say, "Why does he not?" Because the LORD was witness between you and the wife of your youth, to whom you have been faithless, though she is your companion and your wife by covenant. [15]Did he not make them one, with a portion of the Spirit in their union? And what was the one God seeking? Godly offspring. So guard yourselves in your spirit, and let none of you be faithless to the wife of your youth. [16]For the man who hates and divorces, says

94. Another obvious threat is for the husband and wife to fail to pursue unity with each other, either by mistreatment or by selfishness; sample texts on this point include Prov. 19:13; 21:9; 25:24; Sir. 9:1–9; 25:13–26. I have not discussed them here because they do not specifically appeal to Gen. 2.

95. See also Sir. 19:2, "The man who *is joined* [κολλώμενος] to prostitutes is very reckless" (cf. RSV).

96. Hebrew דבק (*dabaq*). The Septuagint uses the compound verb προσκολλάω in Gen. 2:24 and the simple form κολλάω in Deut. 10:20; 1 Cor. 6:16–17 uses κολλάω in both places to ensure the connection.

the LORD, the God of Israel, covers his garment with violence, says
the LORD of hosts. So guard yourselves in your spirit, and do not
be faithless.

There are many challenges in these verses, and I will simply say
that I think the ESV has made the best of them.[97] Thus we can see
here that the first marriage is a covenant and that God made them
one, that they might produce godly offspring. The Jewish man whom
Malachi condemns is "faithless" (or "treacherous," as in Prov. 23:28);
he "hates" (or does not love; see ESV Update) his wife and divorces her
(for the sake of the pagan girl, Mal. 2:11), thus staining his character
with violence and giving up the promise of godly offspring (which is
inherent in the covenant, Gen. 17:7).

The Genesis passage is used to address the question of divorce
in Matthew 19:3–9 (parallel to Mark 10:2–9):[98]

> [3]And Pharisees came up to him and tested him by asking, "Is it law-
> ful to divorce one's wife for any cause?" [4]He answered, "Have you
> not read that he who created them from the beginning made them
> male and female, [5]and said, 'Therefore a man shall leave his father
> and his mother and hold fast to his wife, and the two shall become
> one flesh'? [6]So they are no longer two but one flesh. What therefore
> God has joined together, let not man separate." [7]They said to him,
> "Why then did Moses command one to give a certificate of divorce
> and to send her away?" [8]He said to them, "Because of your hard-
> ness of heart Moses allowed you to divorce your wives, but from
> the beginning it was not so. [9]And I say to you: whoever divorces his
> wife, except for sexual immorality, and marries another, commits
> adultery."

Jesus finds in the Genesis texts a principle of unity that man ought
not violate by groundless divorce. The Pharisees, however, want to
know why Deuteronomy 24:1–4, a law regulating divorce, is in the
Bible; they take it as Moses' "command." Jesus replies by calling it
an "allowance," due to human hardness; such an allowance cannot

---

97. For discussion, see Gordon Hugenberger, *Marriage as a Covenant* (Grand Rapids:
Baker, 1994), 48–83; C. John Collins, "The (Intelligible) Masoretic Text of Malachi 2:16 or,
How Does God Feel about Divorce?" *Presbyterion* 20, no. 1 (1994): 36–40.

98. Mark's citation of Gen. 2:24 (Mark 10:7–8) uses the Septuagint, while Matthew's
(19:5) differs slightly. I leave this to others to decide what this means for literary dependence between them.

overthrow the more fundamental ethic of a creation ordinance. Jesus' way of answering the question gains support from recent studies in the role of the various kinds of laws in the Pentateuch, especially studies by Gordon Wenham and Christopher Wright.[99] To put it simply, the civil and family laws, such as that in Deuteronomy 24:1–4, are ethically based in that they enforce a kind of equity, but they do not articulate the ethical ideal for God's people—rather, they preserve the level of civility necessary for the social structure to survive. The ethical ideal comes from the creation account, which is why Jesus cites it.

In my judgment, this way of thinking about the ethical situation is better than the alternatives: for example, N. T. Wright suggests that the law in Deuteronomy "was necessary because of the ambiguous situation, in which Israel was called to be the people of god, but was still a people with *hard hearts*."[100] He goes on to say that Jesus quoted Genesis 1:27; 2:24 "to undermine" Deuteronomy 24:1–3. I cannot imagine Jesus wanting to *undermine* any part of divine law; rather, he honors it by insisting on keeping each part in its proper place.

The Gospels cite a form of Genesis 2:24 that says "*the two* shall become one flesh," while the Masoretic Hebrew simply has "*they* shall become one flesh." The text form in the Gospels agrees with the Septuagint, as well as with the Samaritan Pentateuch ("from the two there shall become one flesh") and Targum Jonathan; the Syriac and Vulgate perhaps reflect the influence of the Septuagint and thus may not be independent witnesses. But the Masoretic Text certainly implies "the two": after all, the man holds fast to his wife (not wives). So this text also insists that marriage, by its creation, is both monogamous and heterosexual.

These features of marriage make it well suited as an image for the relationship of the Lord and his people. We have seen how Paul uses that image in 1 Corinthians 6:16–17; he also employs it in Ephesians 5:31–32 (text very close to the Septuagint of Gen. 2:24).[101]

99. Gordon Wenham, "The Gap between Law and Ethics in the Bible," *Journal of Jewish Studies* 48, no. 1 (1997): 17–29; Christopher J. H. Wright, *Living as the People of God: The Relevance of Old Testament Ethics* (Leicester: Inter-Varsity Press, 1983), 148–73.

100. N. T. Wright, *Jesus and the Victory of God* (Minneapolis: Fortress, 1996), 284–86. Note that Wright incorrectly refers to Gen. 2:4 (rather than 2:24) and Deut. 24:1–3 (rather than 24:1–4).

101. On the passages, see Raymond C. Ortlund, *Whoredom: God's Unfaithful Wife in Biblical Theology* (Grand Rapids: Eerdmans, 1996), 143–46, 152–59.

3. Genesis 2:7 and 1 Corinthians 15:45

In 1 Corinthians 15:42–49, Paul cites Genesis 2:7, contrasting Christ and Adam:

> [42]So is it with the resurrection of the dead. What is sown is perishable; what is raised is imperishable. [43]It is sown in dishonor; it is raised in glory. It is sown in weakness; it is raised in power. [44]It is sown a natural body; it is raised a spiritual body. If there is a natural body, there is also a spiritual body. [45]Thus it is written, "The first man Adam became a living being"; the last Adam became a life-giving spirit. [46]But it is not the spiritual that is first but the natural, and then the spiritual. [47]The first man was from the earth, a man of dust; the second man is from heaven. [48]As was the man of dust, so also are those who are of the dust, and as is the man of heaven, so also are those who are of heaven. [49]Just as we have borne the image of the man of dust, we shall also bear the image of the man of heaven.

The end of 1 Corinthians 15:45, "the last Adam became a life-giving spirit," has puzzled expositors: how does it relate to the Genesis text, and what is the implied connection between Christ and the Holy Spirit (is the statement even properly trinitarian)?

The solution can be found in the role that Genesis 2:7 plays in the whole context. In the Septuagint it reads (with English translation to reflect the passage in 1 Corinthians),

Καὶ ἔπλασεν ὁ θεὸς τὸν ἄνθρωπον χοῦν ἀπὸ τῆς γῆς καὶ ἐνεφύσησεν εἰς τὸ πρόσωπον αὐτοῦ πνοὴν ζωῆς, καὶ ἐγένετο ὁ ἄνθρωπος εἰς ψυχὴν ζῶσαν.	And God formed the man of dust from the earth and breathed into his face the breath of life, and the man became a living creature [*or*, living soul].

The term *natural* in 1 Corinthians 15:44, 46 is ψυχικός ("soulish"), which connects with ψυχή ("soul, being") in verse 45a. It is in contrast to πνευμάτικος ("spiritual"), which connects with πνεῦμα ("spirit") in verse 45b. It appears that the contrast is perishable, dishonored, weak, natural, and earthly, on the one hand; and imperishable, glorious, powerful, spiritual, and heavenly, on the other. Hence the terms *natural* and *spiritual* (and therefore "soul" and "spirit" by implication) refer to man as first created and man as made glorious. Thus "spirit" in verse 45b refers neither to the Holy Spirit nor to a nonmaterial being but rather to a glorious resurrected being. (Note that "life-giving" contrasts to "living" in Genesis and also links us with 1 Corinthians 15:22, "For as in Adam all die, so also in Christ shall all *be made alive*," speaking of the resurrection of believers.)[102]

If we see the passage this way, we will not find any confusion on Paul's part between Christ and the Holy Spirit, since verse 45b, "the last Adam became a life-giving *spirit*," refers to the glorious condition of his body, and not to the Spirit of God. When an author such as Richard Gaffin finds a reference to the Spirit of God here, he must resort to a tortuous and counterintuitive explanation:[103]

> Verse 45c, then, teaches that Christ became life-giving Spirit. . . . This identification is plainly not ontological, as if he were obliterating the personal distinction between Christ and the Spirit. . . . Christ (as *incarnate*) experiences a spiritual qualification and transformation so thorough and an endowment with the Spirit so complete that as a result they can now be equated. . . . This identity is economic or functional.

Attention to the passage in Genesis, and to Paul's usage in context, gives us a far simpler way to read the text; it also relieves the doctrine of the Trinity of a difficulty it did not need!

---

102. For a discussion that emphasizes that "spiritual" does not mean "nonmaterial," see N. T. Wright, *The Resurrection of the Son of God* (Minneapolis: Fortress, 2003), 347–56. At 349 Wright demurs from identifying the distinction between ψυχικός and πνευμάτικος with that between "natural" and "supernatural"; but see my *God of Miracles: An Exegetical Examination of God's Action in the World* (Wheaton: Crossway, 2000), 92–93, 102; (2001 edition: 102, 113–14) for the lexical discussion and a way of handling it that does not fall foul of Wright's concerns about quasi-Deism.

103. Richard Gaffin, *Resurrection and Redemption: A Study in Paul's Soteriology* (Phillipsburg, N.J.: Presbyterian and Reformed, 1987), 78–92, quoted from 87. (This is the fruit of a flawed lexical methodology that relies on "a pattern of word associations," 68–70.) Gaffin makes a similar argument regarding 2 Cor. 3:17, "the Lord is the Spirit," seeing a close functional connection between Christ ("the Lord") and the Spirit. However, it is far simpler to take Paul's remark as indicating that "the Lord" in the passage he cites (v. 16, adapting Exod. 34:34 LXX) is specifically the Spirit (as the ESV margin, "this Lord," suggests). Wright, *The Resurrection of the Son of God*, 355 n. 129, hints at a similar confusion without expanding on it.

6

GENESIS 3:1–24:
THE MAN AND WOMAN DISOBEY

I t has been common to read this pericope as the tale of the fall of the first man and woman through their disobeying God's command of Genesis 2:17. This reading has figured prominently in Christian theology, and some disputes among Christians stem from the implications they draw from the story. Many scholars now dissent from this reading; as James Barr recently put it, Old Testament scholarship "has long known that the reading of the story [of Genesis 3] as the 'Fall of Man' in the traditional sense, though hallowed by St Paul's use of it, cannot stand up to examination through a close reading of the Genesis text."[1]

The methodology that we are using here might bring us the literary competence needed to read this story well. After that we can examine the way that Paul and others used the story.

A. Pericope Boundary, Structure, and Genre

It is easy to discern that the pericope is Genesis 3:1–24. We saw in the previous chapter that Genesis 2:4–25 ends with a summary

1. James Barr, *The Garden of Eden and the Hope of Immortality* (Minneapolis: Fortress, 1992), ix and elsewhere. It is certainly true that a great number of the critical commentaries and articles published in the twentieth century fit this description.

149

("the man and his wife were both naked and were not ashamed"), whose final verb is imperfect, describing their ongoing condition. Further, Genesis 3:1 introduces a new character, the serpent, and its first verb is perfect ("was"), which typically indicates a discontinuity. Similarly, Genesis 4 begins with its subject ("Adam" or "the man"), and its verb ("knew") in the perfect.

We have already seen as well that Genesis 2:4–3:24 is unified by a distinctive divine name ("the LORD God"), location (Eden), the characters, the two special trees, and the command of 2:17.

The paragraph structure is also not hard to see. The action flows from the serpent and Eve conversing, to the human pair eating, to God's arrival on the scene and the humans' unsuccessful effort to hide from him, to God giving his sentence, to Adam and Eve perceiving God's mercy, to God's action of expelling them from Eden.

3:1a	introducing the serpent	
3:1b–5	the serpent and Eve converse	
3:6–7	the human pair eat	
3:8–13	the human pair try to hide from God	
3:14–19	God pronounces his sentence	
	3:14–15	on the serpent
	3:16	on the woman
	3:17–19	on the man
3:20–21	Adam and Eve perceive God's mercy	
3:22–24	God expels Adam and Eve from the garden	

The genre of this pericope, like that of Genesis 2:4–25, is normal prose narrative.

B. Translation and Notes

Introducing the serpent (3:1a)

¹Now the serpent was more crafty² than any other beast of the field that the LORD God had made.

2. Compare Matt. 10:16, where Jesus tells his disciples to "be crafty as serpents."

The serpent and Eve converse (3:1b–5)

He said to the woman, "Did God actually say, 'You[3] shall not eat of any tree of the garden'?" [2]And the woman said to the serpent, "We may eat of the fruit of the trees of the garden, [3]but God said, 'You shall not eat of the fruit of the tree that is in the midst of the garden, neither shall you touch it, lest you die.' " [4]But the serpent said to the woman, "You will not surely die.[4] [5]For God knows that when you eat of it your eyes will be opened, and you will be like God, knowing good and evil."

The human pair eat (3:6–7)

[6]So when the woman saw that the tree was good for food, and that it was a delight to the eyes, and that the tree was to be desired to make one wise,[5] she took of its fruit and ate, and she also gave some to her husband who was with her, and he ate. [7]Then the eyes of both were opened, and they knew[6] that they were naked.[7] And they sewed fig leaves together and made themselves loincloths.

The human pair try to hide from God (3:8–13)

[8]And they heard the sound of the LORD God walking in the garden in the cool of the day,[8] and the man and his wife hid

3. ESV margin: "In Hebrew *you* is plural in verses 1–5." This is interesting, in that Gen. 2:16–17 is in the singular. When Eve cites it (3:3), she makes it plural, thus showing that she has appropriated it through her husband, who is a covenant representative, as we shall see.

4. RSV/NRSV "You will not die" is an undertranslation: the serpent has introduced the infinitive absolute ("surely"), directly contradicting the threat of 2:17.

5. ESV margin: "Or *to give insight*" (להשכיל, *lehaskîl*).

6. When versions such as NIV render this as "realized," they obscure an important repetition (see exposition below).

7. There may be an intentional irony in Luke 24:31. In Genesis their "eyes . . . were opened" and "they knew" (ἔγνωσαν); then in Luke, after Jesus' resurrection, we read of the two disciples on the road to Emmaus, "their eyes were opened, and they recognized [ἐπέγνωσαν]" Jesus.

8. Literally, "at the wind of the day," using a *lamed*-temporal (Paul Joüon, *A Grammar of Biblical Hebrew*, trans./rev. Takamitsu Muraoka; Subsidia bibilica 14 [Rome: Pontifical Biblical Institute Press, 1991], §133d). I take the word רוח (*rûakh*, "wind") in the sense "windy part"; the windy part of the day is the middle to late afternoon when the wind from the west cools the land. Hence it is unnecessary to try to reinterpret, such as Jeffrey Niehaus does in "In the Wind of the Storm: Another Look at Genesis iii 8," *Vetus Testamentum* 44, no. 2 (1994): 263–67, drawing on J. Lust, "A Gentle Breeze or a Roaring Thunderous Sound?" *Vetus Testamentum* 25, no. 1 (1975): 110–15. Niehaus wants to replace "sound"

themselves[9] from the presence of the LORD God among the trees of the garden. **9**But the LORD God called to the man and said to him, "Where are you?"[10] **10**And he said, "I heard the sound of you in the garden, and I was afraid, because I was naked, and I hid myself." **11**He said, "Who told you that you were naked? Have you eaten of the tree of which I commanded you not to eat?" **12**The man said, "The woman whom you gave to be with me, she[11] gave me fruit of the tree, and I ate." **13**Then the LORD God said to the woman, "What is this that you have done?" The woman said, "The serpent deceived me,[12] and I ate."

God pronounces his sentence (3:14–19)

14The LORD God said to the serpent,

> "Because you have done this,
>   cursed are you above all livestock
>   and above all beasts of the field;
> on your belly you shall go,
>   and dust you shall eat
>   all the days of your life.

---

with "thunder," and "in the cool of the day" with "in the wind of the storm," implying a storm-theophany. He contends that "in the cool/breeze of the day" is simply a guess, but it actually fits the climate, and the climatic conditions warrant the Septuagint "at the afternoon." Other aspects of Niehaus's lexical method are problematic as well, but it is enough to refer to Christopher Grundtke, "A Tempest in a Teapot? Genesis iii 8 Again," *Vetus Testamentum* 51, no. 4 (2001): 548–51.

9. This is probably what we have to do in English; but the nuance of the Hebrew is "they heard . . . and the man hid himself [along with his wife]." That is, the second verb is singular, although the subject is, strictly speaking, compound ("the man and his wife"). Cf. E. J. Revell, "Concord with Compound Subjects and Related Uses of Pronouns," *Vetus Testamentum* 43 (1993): 69–87, at 75: when the verb inflection matches only the first element of a compound subject, this puts the spotlight on that first member (in many cases as the leader in the action, cf. 1 Sam. 15:9). Hence the spotlight is on the man as the covenantal representative both of his family and of the race.

10. As the ESV note indicates, "In Hebrew *you* is singular in verses 9 and 11"—that is, God specifically addresses Adam.

11. The Hebrew adds a pronoun, *she*: Adam wants to highlight her part (in order to shift the blame, presumably).

12. Greek ἠπάτησεν. Paul perhaps echoes this (together with Gen. 2:17) in Rom. 7:11, "sin . . . *deceived* [ἐξηπάτησεν] me and . . . *killed* [ἀπέκτεινεν, the causative of ἀποθνήσκω of 2:17] me." This need not imply that Paul's "I" is Adam or Israel; he can recount his own experience using Adam's as a paradigm for temptation and sin. Paul uses the compound verb ἐξαπατάω for this event in 2 Cor. 11:3 and 1 Tim. 2:14.

15I will put enmity between you and the woman,
    and between your offspring and her offspring;[13]
he shall bruise your head,
    and you shall bruise his heel."
16To the woman he said,[14]
"I will surely[15] multiply[16] your pain[17] in childbearing;[18]
    in pain you shall bring forth children.
Your desire shall be for[19] your husband,
    and he shall rule over you."
17And to Adam he said,
"Because you[20] have listened to the voice of your wife
    and have eaten of the tree
of which I commanded you,
    'You shall not eat of it,'
cursed is the ground because of you;
    in pain you shall eat of it all the days of your life;
18thorns and thistles it shall bring forth for you;
    and you shall eat the plants of the field.
19By the sweat of your face
    you shall eat bread,

13. ESV margin: "Hebrew *seed*; so throughout Genesis." See the additional discussions below: section C.2, "Is Genesis 3:15 a protoevangelium?"; E.1, "The 'seed' theme in Genesis."

14. The verb *he said* in both 3:16 and 3:17 is perfect rather than *wayyiqtol*; this is unusual, since the events are certainly part of the main storyline. This disruption of the grammatical norm is best taken as part of the "turbulence" that indicates that we are at the peak.

15. The form is *harbâ*, not *harbeh*; hence I take it as a normal infinitive absolute, "surely," rather than "greatly" (*harbeh* usually means "very much").

16. We have here an ironic contrast: in 1:28 the verb רבה (*r-b-h*) "to multiply" referred to procreation as a sphere in which humans were to experience God's blessing; here the causative form of the same verb is used to denote the malfunction of procreation, so that it becomes an arena of pain, danger, and curse.

17. The word rendered "pain" here is עצבון (*'itstsabôn*), which is related to the word *pain* (עצב, *'etseb*) in the next line. The only appearances of this word in the Hebrew Bible are Gen. 3:16, 17; 5:29.

18. ESV "your pain in childbearing" is more literally, "your pain and your pregnancy." Grammatically, I take the "and" as *waw*-explicative, and "your pregnancy" as an accusative of specification. This is supported by the explanatory clause that follows, using the word *pain* (עצב, related to עצבון, "pain/painfulness"): the clause restates the punishment. This yields "your pain, namely, in regard to pregnancy," which lies behind ESV.

19. ESV margin: "Or *against*; also in 4:7." See additional discussion in section C.3, "What is the woman's 'desire' (Gen. 3:16)?"

20. This "you" is masculine singular, as it was in Gen. 2:16–17; 3:11. God treats Adam as the representative.

till you return to the ground,
>   for out of it you were taken;
> for you are dust,
>   and to dust you shall return."[21]

Adam and Eve perceive God's mercy (3:20–21)

[20]The man called his wife's name Eve,[22] because she was the mother of all living.[23] [21]And the LORD God made for Adam and for his wife garments of skins and clothed them.

God expels Adam and Eve from the garden (3:22–24)

[22]Then the LORD God said, "Behold, the man has become like one of us in knowing good and evil. Now, lest he reach out his hand and take also of the tree of life, and eat, and live forever—" [23]therefore the LORD God sent him out[24] from the garden of Eden to work the ground from which he was taken. [24]He drove out the man, and at the east of the garden of Eden he placed the cherubim[25] and a flaming sword that turned every way to guard the way to the tree of life.[26]

21. Gen. 3:19 looks back to 2:7 on the forming of the first man.

22. ESV margin: "Eve sounds like the Hebrew for *life-giver* and resembles the word for *living.*" In Hebrew the name is חַוָּה (*khawwâ*). There has been some discussion over whether this word is in fact related to the verb חיה (*kh-w-h*), "to be alive," with suggestions such as that it actually is related to an Aramaic word חִוְיָא, (*khewyâ*), meaning "snake," and "the mythological ancestor of Eve was some sort of 'serpent goddess' who was, perhaps, the goddess of life" (Barr, *Garden of Eden*, 65). Fortunately there is a helpful article by Scott C. Layton, "Remarks on the Canaanite Origin of Eve," *Catholic Biblical Quarterly* 59, no. 1 (1997): 22–32. He concludes that "from the perspectives of etymology and morphology, the symbolic name *khawwâ* is derived from the root **khwy*, 'to make alive,' and it may be analyzed as a noun of **qattal* form to be translated 'Life giver' " (31). Hence the Septuagint, which *translates* her name as Ζωή ("Life") rather than following its usual practice of transliteration with Εὔα ("Eva"), is on the right track.

23. This verse is asserting that all humans are descended from Adam and Eve; see further section C.6 below, "Are Adam and Eve the parents of all mankind?"

24. There is a wordplay between "reach out his hand" (3:22) and "sent him out" (v. 23): the first uses the Qal of the verb שׁלח (*sh-l-kh*), while the second uses the Piel. See Collins, "שׁלח," no. 8938 in *NIDOTTE*, 4:121–22, where it is argued that this wordplay actually refutes the source-critical position of Westermann, 271, that verse 23 was originally independent of verses 22–24.

25. It would be a sad mistake to think of the cute cherubs of popular art. These were apparently a terrifying race of warrior angels; compare Ezek. 9:3. In Exod. 25:18 images of cherubim are to overshadow the cover of the ark.

26. Physical access to the tree of life is now closed. Now the humans must work out their salvation through covenantal perseverance under the forgiving grace of God. The

C. Extra Notes

1. Was this a sin?

James Barr claims that we do not have a primeval *disobedience* described in this passage: "It is not without importance that the term 'sin' is not used anywhere in the story . . . nor do we find any of the terms usually understood as 'evil,' 'rebellion,' 'transgression' or 'guilt.' "[27] This is an astonishing claim, because Barr—the scholar who has done so much to introduce exegetes to sound lexical semantics—should of course know that the existence of the referent or concept is not limited to the presence of certain vocabulary. Indeed, God's question in Genesis 3:11, "Have you eaten of the tree of which I commanded you not to eat?" (compare v. 17), could hardly be improved upon as a description of "disobedience."

We might also note that Barr's position makes no sense of Ecclesiastes 7:20, "Surely there is not a righteous man on earth who does good and never sins," compared with verse 29, "God made man upright," which begs for explanation.[28] Other texts referring to this with words such as "sin," "disobedience," and "transgression" include Romans 5:12–19 and 1 Timothy 2:14.[29] The authors of these texts have seen what is really there in Genesis 3.

2. Is Genesis 3:15 a protoevangelium?

Consider verse 15, words that the Lord speaks to the serpent:

I will put enmity between you and the woman,
    and between your offspring and her offspring;
he shall bruise your head,
    and you shall bruise his heel.

We face a number of questions about this verse. Who is the woman's offspring, and who is the serpent's? What is the nature of the conflict between them? Why will the woman's offspring bruise the head

---

special meeting place between God and his people is now the sanctuary, in public worship, with its sacramental rites that address our guilt.

27. Barr, *Garden of Eden*, 6.

28. See also the comments on Hos. 6:7 in chapter 5, section C.2, a topic that Barr does not address.

29. See also Wis. 2:23–24; Sir. 25:24; 2 Esd. 3:6–8.

of the serpent, and not of the serpent's offspring? Is there anything unusual in referring to a *woman's* (rather than a *man's*) offspring? Is it right to take this as a protoevangelium, a first proclamation of good news—and even to go so far as to call it messianic?

Let us begin with the question of the woman's offspring. The first thing to decide is whether the text speaks of a specific offspring or of her offspring in general: the Hebrew word זֶרַע ("seed, offspring") is just as ambiguous as English *offspring*. I have argued elsewhere that in Biblical Hebrew the key signal for a singular or collective offspring is the grammatical number of the pronouns that refer to the word: if the author had a specific offspring in view he would have used singular pronouns; and if he meant posterity in general, he would have used plural pronouns.[30] In this text we have two singular pronouns that refer to the woman's offspring, "*he* shall bruise . . . bruise *his* heel." Thus we are entitled to join the Septuagint in seeing an individual as the referent here.[31]

Some have found it odd to refer to a *woman's* offspring, but this is a mistake. As a matter of statistics the usage is rare, but there is nothing exceptional about it.[32] It is fitting in context, since the serpent had just deceived the woman.

The text tells us nothing about who the serpent's offspring might be, since the mutual bruising is to involve the serpent himself ("your . . . you"), rather than his offspring. How we answer the question of who they are depends on who we think the serpent was. I have given reasons below for seeing the serpent as the mouthpiece of a Dark Power, whom later texts would call Satan; hence I take his offspring to be those who are seduced into his darkness.[33]

---

30. Jack Collins, "A Syntactical Note on Genesis 3:15: Is the Woman's Seed Singular or Plural?" *Tyndale Bulletin* 48, no. 1 (1997): 141–48. T. Desmond Alexander, "Further Observations on the Term 'Seed' in Genesis," *Tyndale Bulletin* 48, no. 2 (1997): 363–67, endorsed this and applied it to Gen. 22:17–18; 24:60. Walton, 225 n. 3, rejects this, chiefly it seems because he takes Gen. 22:17 and 24:60 to be counterexamples (he calls Alexander's work "special pleading"). However, this simple dismissal does no justice to the careful argument of Alexander; and, as I argue in section E.1 below, we can use Alexander's analysis to solve a vexing problem in New Testament interpretation.

31. That is, the Greek noun for "seed" is σπέρμα, which is neuter; while the pronoun referring to it is αὐτός, which is masculine: the mismatch in gender indicates a specific offspring.

32. See Gen. 16:10; 24:60; 1 Sam. 1:11.

33. Perhaps this lies behind Jesus' insult to the scribes and Pharisees who resist him in Matt. 23:33: "You serpents, you brood of vipers."

May we take this as a gospel proclamation? Westermann emphatically denies that we may, for two main reasons: first, because he is confident ("beyond doubt") that "offspring" must be collective; and second, because this occurs in a pronouncement of a punishment: "It is not possible that such a form has either promise or prophecy as its primary or even secondary meaning." Barr calls this a "crushing rebuttal of all such suggestions."[34]

If we analyze Westermann's argument, we will see that it is hardly a crushing rebuttal at all. To begin with, I have already shown why I think that the grammar actually specifies that we have an individual in view. His point about the form carries no weight, either; after all, God speaks these words to the serpent, who has led the human pair into disobedience and shown himself to be the enemy, both theirs and God's. For the serpent to be defeated (the punishment oracle) has the implication that the humans will benefit. In other words, if Westermann is right that it "is not possible that such a form has either promise or prophecy as its primary or even secondary meaning" (though he does not say why it is impossible), that can only apply to the object of the oracle—the serpent!

Hence this is in fact a promise that God will act for the benefit of mankind by defeating the serpent; in that sense we may call it a protoevangelium. But may we go further and call it messianic?

Of course it all depends on what we mean by messianic. We are within our rights to say that this text envisions an individual who will engage the serpent (really, the Dark Power that used the serpent as its mouthpiece) in combat and defeat him, thus bringing benefits to mankind. That is, he is a champion. We are further entitled to say that he will be a human (an offspring of the woman), but one with power extraordinary enough to win.

The rest of Genesis will unfold the idea of this offspring and lay the foundation for the developed messianic teaching of the prophets. We must remember that an author put this text here, and we suppose that he did so with his plan for this unfolding in mind; hence for us to ask whether this particular text is messianic may mislead us: instead, we may say that Genesis fosters a messianic expectation, of which this verse is the headwaters.[35]

---

34. Westermann, 260–61; Barr, *Garden of Eden*, 140 n. 28.

35. See T. Desmond Alexander, "Messianic Ideology in the Book of Genesis," in *The Lord's Anointed: Interpretation of Old Testament Messianic Texts*, ed. P. E. Satterthwaite, R. S. Hess, G. J. Wenham (Carlisle: Paternoster, 1995), 19–39.

If we see Genesis 3:15 as referring to a specific offspring, we can speak this way of "unfolding," and we do not have to appeal to a *sensus plenior*. If, however, we reject the grammatical argument that this refers to an individual, we will need to invoke *sensus plenior* in order to get a messianic sense out of the text; perhaps the way of Calvin (170–71) works best, taking the "woman's offspring" as humanity, which will be victorious because its head, Christ, will win the victory. In view, however, of the grammatical point and its connection with the rest of Genesis, I prefer the individual offspring interpretation.

There are two places in which the New Testament possibly evokes this passage: Romans 16:20 and Revelation 12:17. In Romans 16:20 Paul promises the Roman Christians,

The God of peace will soon crush Satan under your feet.	Ὁ δὲ θεὸς τῆς εἰρήνης συντρίψει τὸν σατανᾶν ὑπὸ τοὺς πόδας ὑμῶν ἐν τάχει.

This, however, is pretty far from the Genesis 3:15 text, which speaks of "wounding" or "bruising" rather than "crushing," and which uses the "heel" rather than the "foot." If this evokes Genesis 3:15, it is quite indirect, and thus it would be a mistake to think of this as defining the "offspring" as the faithful; instead, Paul thought that by their faithfulness they would receive the fruits of Christ's victory (an important part of New Testament teaching about believers: compare Col. 2:15; Heb. 2:14–18; 1 John 3:8).

In Revelation 12:17 we read,

Then the dragon became furious with the woman and went off to make war on the rest of *her offspring*, on those who keep the commandments of God and hold to the testimony of Jesus.	Καὶ ὠργίσθη ὁ δράκων ἐπὶ τῇ γυναικὶ καὶ ἀπῆλθεν ποιῆσαι πόλεμον μετὰ τῶν λοιπῶν τοῦ σπέρματος αὐτῆς τῶν τηρούντων τὰς ἐντολὰς τοῦ θεοῦ καὶ ἐχόντων τὴν μαρτυρίαν Ἰησοῦ.

Here the allusion is much clearer. The "dragon" is "that ancient serpent, who is called the devil and Satan, the deceiver of the whole world" (Rev. 12:9); he had tried to devour the woman's son (vv. 4–5), who seems to be the Christ. But there is imagery here that Genesis does not use—the woman seems to be a figure for the people of God. Hence the author of Revelation is not obligated to keep close to

Genesis. The group in verse 17 is *"the rest of* the woman's offspring," defined as being the genuinely pious. Thus the woman's child (Christ) is the primary offspring, while his followers are her offspring by virtue of their relation to him.

It is just possible that the phrase in Galatians 4:4, "born of woman" (γενόμενον ἐκ γυναικός), evokes the ideas of Genesis 3:15: that is, the Son is "born of a woman" and hence her "offspring." The closest expressions (in LXX and the New Testament) to Paul's usage are γεννητὸς γυναικός (Job 14:1; 15:14; 25:4; Matt. 11:11; Luke 7:28) and γέννημα γυναικός (Sir. 10:18), both of which mean "that which is born of a woman," and both of which stress the humanness of what they describe. If this is Paul's meaning, it is consistent with his connecting the offspring theme of Genesis to the Messiah (see E.1 below). But I must admit that it is difficult to be certain whether or not Paul had Genesis 3:15 in mind.

3. What is the woman's "desire" (Gen. 3:16)?

In verse 16 the Lord God says to the woman:

I will surely multiply your pain in childbearing;
   in pain you shall bring forth children.
Your desire shall be for your husband,
   and he shall rule over you.

It is clear that "pain in childbearing" is a new feature of the woman's life, and an unpleasant one at that: so the first two lines are plainly describing her punishment.[36] But what of lines 3 and 4, dealing with her "desire"? Most commentators find here another aspect of the woman's punishment, namely, the way her husband will dominate her—and perhaps her own sexual desire for her husband makes her a willing accomplice.

There are several reasons why we should reject this common interpretation, however. First, the word *rule over* (מָשַׁל, *mashal*) does not convey the negative associations of "dominate"; if that is present, it comes from the context, not from the word itself (see Gen. 1:16;

---

36. The traditional English "multiply" may suggest to some readers that there already were pains to begin with, and the other versions with "greatly" for the infinitive absolute (see text note) may also lead this way. But the Hebrew verb simply means "to cause to be numerous" and makes no comment about whether there were any to begin with.

2 Sam. 23:3). Second, the noun rendered "desire" occurs in the Bible only here, at Genesis 4:7, and at Song of Songs 7:10. Just because the word is used in Song of Songs does not imply that the word itself carries the idea of *sexual* desire; rather, the word has the sense "craving," with the context telling us what kind of craving is in view.[37]

The third reason comes from the way that Genesis 4:7 is an exact parallel with 3:16.[38] There God tells Cain, "And if you do not do well, sin is crouching at the door. Its desire is for you, but you must rule over it." Compare the two passages:

Your desire shall be for your husband, and he shall rule over you. (3:16)	וְאֶל־אִישֵׁךְ תְּשׁוּקָתֵךְ וְהוּא יִמְשָׁל־בָּךְ
Its desire is for you, but you must rule over it. (4:7)	וְאֵלֶיךָ תְּשׁוּקָתוֹ וְאַתָּה תִּמְשָׁל־בּוֹ

In Genesis 4:7 it is plain that "desire for" someone is "desire to master" that person (hence ESV margin, "against"), while the "ruling" is not a punishment but the necessary remedy. If we apply this to 3:16, we conclude that God describes a condition of human marriages that is all too familiar, namely, competition for control. The proper remedy is a return to the creational pattern of the man's leadership—loving, not dominating.[39]

4. Was Adam made mortal?

In Genesis 2:17, the Lord God had warned Adam, "but of the tree of the knowledge of good and evil you shall not eat, for in the day that you eat of it you shall surely die." Then after his disobedience, the sentence included (3:19),

By the sweat of your face
    you shall eat bread,
till you return to the ground,
    for out of it you were taken;

37. See David Talley, "תשוקה," no. 9592 in *NIDOTTE*, 4:341–42.
38. So far as I can tell, this general line of exposition got its start with an essay by Susan Foh, "What Is the Woman's Desire?" *Westminster Theological Journal* 37 (1975): 376–83. Wenham, 81–82, cautiously endorses it.
39. We have already seen in chapter 5, section E.1, that Genesis presents the man's leadership as the pattern of creation and that Paul follows that. The role of the man as covenant head, as we shall see below in section D, further strengthens this.

> for you are dust,
>> and to dust you shall return.

Most have taken this to imply that death is a new feature of Adam's existence, a punishment for his fall. Were they right in doing so?

We can answer this only if we answer two other questions first: what was the "death" threatened in Genesis 2:17, and what was the nature of the test for Adam?

In the previous chapter I argued that if we assume that Genesis 2:17 speaks simply of physical death—as so many have done—we are guilty of jumping to conclusions. In the literary-theological exposition below (section D), I argue that the passage itself makes it clear that spiritual death is the meaning of the threat, and the experience of the man and woman once they disobey.

It does seem that Genesis 3:19 portrays physical death as a consequence of this fall, although one might reply that its focus is on hard toil for the man until he dies, in place of pleasant labor in the garden until a good death. The difficulty arises from our answer to the second question. In the exposition below, I argue that God did not intend for Adam and Eve to remain in their first condition; they were supposed to attain to a proper knowledge of good and evil by steadfast obedience to God's command and thus to receive permanent access to the tree of life.

Since the created condition was intended to be temporary, then, there is no simple *exegetical* answer to the question of Adam's mortality.[40] But if, as seems to be the case, the passage views physical death as following from the fall, then we may conclude that the first humans were not created mortal. Calvin (127, 180) suggested that Adam's

> earthly life truly would have been temporal; yet he would have passed into heaven without death, and without injury. . . . Truly the first man would have passed to a better life, had he remained upright; but there would have been no separation of the soul from the body, no corruption, no kind of destruction, and, in short, no violent change.

Commentators such as Westermann deny this, but only by disconnecting the command of Genesis 2:17 from the punishment in

---

40. Ps. 90:3 and Sir. 17:1–2 are compatible with either position.

3:16–19, by making the punishments an addition to the narrative
(267, 270).

The passage does not dwell on what might have been, nor even on
the details of the pre-fall existence of Adam and Eve; its function is
to explain how man's current condition came about even though the
Creator is good and holy, and made a world that he declared good.
It also aims at the often inarticulate yearning that is part of every
person's experience, to show why that yearning is there: to prepare
the way for the promises of redeemed life, and to motivate members
of the covenant people to lay hold of the promises of life through the
covenant ordinances.

5. The curses and nature

In Genesis 3:14–19 the Lord God pronounces his sentence on the
serpent, the woman, and the man:

[14]The LORD God said to the serpent,

> "Because you have done this,
>> cursed are you above all livestock
>> and above all beasts of the field;
> on your belly you shall go,
>> and dust you shall eat
>> all the days of your life.
> [15]I will put enmity between you and the woman,
>> and between your offspring and her offspring;
> he shall bruise your head,
>> and you shall bruise his heel."
> [16]To the woman he said,
> "I will surely multiply your pain in childbearing;
>> in pain you shall bring forth children.
> Your desire shall be for your husband,
>> and he shall rule over you."
> [17]And to Adam he said,
> "Because you have listened to the voice of your wife
>> and have eaten of the tree
> of which I commanded you,
>> 'You shall not eat of it,'
> cursed is the ground because of you;
>> in pain you shall eat of it all the days of your life;
> [18]thorns and thistles it shall bring forth for you;
>> and you shall eat the plants of the field.

¹⁹By the sweat of your face
  you shall eat bread,
till you return to the ground,
  for out of it you were taken;
for you are dust,
  and to dust you shall return."

Many have read these verses as implying that these curses describe changes in the way the natural world works—in other words, a fallen creation. Is this what the verses actually say? If we study them carefully, we will conclude that the answer is yes and no.

Let us take the curses in their turn. In my exposition below I argue that the author does not present the serpent as a reptile acting on its own; instead a Dark Power has taken it for its mouthpiece, to deceive the human pair. A good reader who recognized this would not be inclined to see Genesis 3:14 as falling on members of the suborder *Serpentes*, of the order *Squamata*, of the class *Reptilia*: this is too literalistic and would miss the point of the passage. The details of verse 14 add to this: first, because it is rhetorically high (set as poetry in English Bibles), and second because the expression *eat dust* in a curse properly refers to humiliation and defeat.[41] I suspect that most Israelites would also know that serpents do not literally eat "dust," but mice, lizards, other snakes, and so on. Similarly, "on your belly you shall go" refers not to the mode of travel but to cringing. And in view of the discussion of verse 15 above, the "enmity" described is not about serpents as such.

For these reasons a good reader would not have thought of changes in the habits and bodies of reptiles but of the assured victory that God will bring about over this Dark Power.

The first two lines of Genesis 3:16 do seem to introduce "pain" and danger into the woman's experience of childbirth and to imply that an unfallen Eve would have delivered children without them. The text does not say what bodily changes this brought about. Further, we have seen above that the second part of the verse foretells enduring conflict between husband and wife, which only serious self-discipline can overcome.

Just as the woman is to find "pain" in her sphere of labor, childbirth, so too the man will find "pain" in his sphere of labor, working

41. See Mic. 7:17, where the abashed Gentiles will "lick the dust like a serpent" when they see God's deliverance for his people; compare Isa. 49:23 and Ps. 72:9.

the ground for food (Gen.3:17–19). Many have taken these verses as implying systematic changes to the creation: the ground is "cursed" (v. 17) and will yield "thorns and thistles" (v. 18)—which, it is assumed, did not even exist before.

The text, however, does not imply that the pain results from changes in the inner workings of the creation. To begin with, consider the specific expression, "cursed is the ground." It only speaks of the ground, not of the whole creation; that makes sense, because the ground is what the man will "work" (Gen. 3:23). This expression appears only in 3:17, and in 4:11 and 5:29, which look back to it, using this verb (אָרַר, 'arar).[42] But the same verb appears in Deuteronomy 28:17–18, where curses fall upon the basket, kneading bowl, the fruit of the womb, the fruit of the ground, the increase of the herds, and the young of the flock. Then the related noun, מְאֵרָה (me'erâ, "curse"), appears in Deuteronomy 28:20: "The LORD will send on you *curses*, confusion, and frustration in all that you undertake to do, until you are destroyed and perish quickly on account of the evil of your deeds, because you have forsaken me." Verses 38–46 detail the outworking of this. Nowhere does it imply that somehow human sin has distorted the workings of the natural elements: rather, agriculture is the arena in which God brings his chastisement upon human beings.

This will make good sense as we put this in context with the geography. God formed the man in some dry "land" (Gen. 2:5–7), transplanted him to the garden to work it and keep it (2:15), and commissioned him and his wife to multiply and have dominion, which means to bring the blessings of Eden to the rest of the world (1:28). When the man sinned, God banished him from the garden "to work the ground from which he was taken"—a place that naturally produces "thorns and thistles."[43] The account never implies that "the ground" did not produce "thorns and thistles" prior to this point; it instead indicates that working the ground is to be the arena of "pain"—and this is due not to a change in the properties of the ground but to the change in humanity and to God's providential purposes of chastisement.[44] There is no indication that human dominion over the creation

42. Gen. 8:21, where God says, "I will never again *curse* the ground because of man," uses a different verb, קָלַל (q-l-l), which means "to dishonor" (see ESV margin).
43. The problem with "thorns and thistles" is that they cannot feed humans; other creatures may be glad to feast on them.
44. For "thorns and thistles" together, see Hos. 10:8, where "thorns and thistles shall grow up on their altars"; there it is because the altars are overthrown and abandoned,

has been rescinded, but there is every indication that humans will exercise it badly—exploiting and damaging the creation and using it to exploit and damage other people.

Further, nothing here says that animals were never carnivorous until man fell. It is true that Genesis 1:29–30 says that man and animals were given plants to eat, but it does not say that they ate nothing else.[45] And even if we take it as prescribing a vegetarian diet for these animals, it only applies to creatures that live on land; that is, it says nothing about anything that lives in the water, many of which are carnivorous (for example, jellyfish, starfish, crabs, trout, sea snakes, penguins, otters, seals, and orcas). Indeed, Psalm 104—which celebrates the proper functioning of the creation—includes an appreciation for the large carnivores (v. 21):[46]

> The young lions roar for their prey,
>   seeking their food from God.

The psalm concludes the section that includes this verse with (v. 24):

> O LORD, how manifold are your works!
>   In wisdom have you made them all;
>   the earth is full of your creatures.

The predatory lions are not an evil (unless they prey on the flock!), but sinful human beings are, as the psalm finishes with its only mention of evil (v. 35):

> Let sinners be consumed from the earth,
>   and let the wicked be no more!
> Bless the LORD, O my soul!
> Praise the LORD!

In the same way, it is a mistake to read Genesis 2:17 as implying that *physical* death did not affect the creation before the fall. In

---

which supports the view that it is a picture of the land being unfruitful for man. See further along these lines Matt. 7:16 and Heb. 6:8.

45. Calvin, 99–100, did not think that the text of Genesis made a decision possible, but he was not troubled by the possibility of meat-eating before the fall.

46. Compare also Ps. 147:9, where evidence of God's abundant generosity is that "he gives to the beasts their food, and to the young ravens that cry [for food]." God feeds even the carnivorous and scavenging (and unclean, too) birds.

the exposition (see also chapter 5, section C.4) I will argue that the focus of this death is spiritual death; and notice that the threat is addressed to Adam alone (the "you" is masculine singular) and is then appropriated by the woman (3:2–3). It applies to human beings and says nothing about the animals.[47]

From all of this we may conclude that Genesis does say that changes have come into *human* nature as a result of the fall—pain in childbearing, other afflictions of body and soul, death, frustration in ruling the creation—but it does not follow that nonhuman nature is affected in the same way. If one wants to speak of fallen nature, he should mean by that a world fallen *in man*—namely, a world that is ruled by sinful human beings and which is the means by which those humans find toil and frustration.

The most important text offered in reply to this position is Romans 8:18–25, which I will examine in section E.3 below.

6. Are Adam and Eve the parents of all mankind?

Most Bible readers have read Genesis 3:20, where Eve gets her name because she was to be "the mother of all living," as implying that Adam and Eve are to be taken as the parents of all mankind. Indeed, Christian traditions call them "our first parents." Not everyone accepts this, though, so we must review the evidence for this reading.

We begin with the creation of man in Genesis 1:26–27. In 1:26 God decides to make "a man" or "mankind," denoted by the Hebrew word *'adam*—whose normal sense is "human." As the ESV margin points out, this generic term for mankind becomes the proper name Adam in Genesis 2. In 1:27 we find that "man" includes male and female. Then in Genesis 2:18–25, we find the elaboration: there is first a man (*'adam*, 2:7), and then his wife is made from his own body, because there is no other source of a helper fit for him. Their relationship becomes the pattern for every other human marriage (2:24). Does this not lead us to think that Adam is the prototype of *'adam* ("mankind"), by virtue of being the first of them?

This is not decisive, but the simplest reading of Genesis 3:20 takes Eve as the mother of all people who would ever live. Then as Genesis develops, all the people described descend from Adam and Eve.

---

47. This is also Paul's focus in Rom. 5:12–14 and 1 Cor. 15:21–22.

Subsequent readers follow this line. For example, Sirach 40:1 speaks of "much labor" as the common lot of mankind; the name for mankind is "the children of Adam."[48] Further, Wisdom of Solomon 7:1 and 10:1–2 take the pair in Eden as the first human beings, as does Tobit 8:6. And finally, in Acts 17:26 Paul tells the Athenian philosophers that God "made from one man every nation of mankind to live on all the face of the earth."

This makes good sense of what we find elsewhere in the Bible—and indeed, of what we find in ourselves. The Bible looks at Abraham as the one whom God calls in order to bring blessing to all mankind (Gen. 12:1–3), and it presents all human beings as having the same need for God and the same problem of sin. The Pentateuch provides for Gentiles to participate in the life of Israel, and the prophets look ahead to the Gentiles joining themselves to the people of God. The New Testament takes up this strand and sees itself as part of the fulfillment of it. The biblical view, that there is a common human nature, matches what anyone can observe: there are universals in language, ethics, and logic across all the varieties of mankind. The best explanation for this is their common origin in a single pair of parents.

Part of the motivation for disagreeing with this position is the idea that Adam and Eve, as presented in the Bible, are far too recent to be the parents of all mankind, in view of what the sciences have shown. But that presupposes a position on what the Bible presents, including how the genealogies are to be read and what we are to make of the descendants of Cain. We will take up those topics in the next chapter; but it will be enough here to say that the Bible does not commit itself to a too-recent Adam and Eve.

D. Literary-Theological Exposition

The participants in this pericope are (in order of appearance) the serpent, the woman, the man, and the Lord God; they are not all active at the same time. In Genesis 3:1–5, the serpent and the woman converse; in verses 6–7, the woman and the man engage in actions; in verses 8–13, the Lord God makes his appearance and

---

48. The Greek translator is more explicit, putting πᾶς ἄνθρωπος ("every human") in parallel with υἱοὶ Ἀδάμ ("children of Adam"), adding ἄνθρωπος, to explicate what the Hebrew implies.

converses with the man and then with the woman (v. 13).[49] In verses
14–19, however, all the characters are on hand, with only God as the
speaker, to each of the others in turn. In verses 20–21, the man (with
the woman in the background) and God are active, while in verses
22–24 God alone is the actor.

We saw above that the structure falls out as follows:

3:1a	introducing the serpent
3:1b–5	the serpent and Eve converse
3:6–7	the human pair eat
3:8–13	the human pair try to hide from God
3:14–19	God pronounces his sentence
	3:14–15　on the serpent
	3:16　on the woman
	3:17–19　on the man
3:20–21	Adam and Eve perceive God's mercy
3:22–24	God expels Adam and Eve from the garden

The peak is at Genesis 3:14–19, as the following clues make clear:
(1) all the participants are on hand, and God speaks to them in
the order in which they arrived in the earlier verses; (2) it is God's
speech—and his opinion, after all, matters the most; (3) the language
is elevated, set as poetry in English versions; (4) the judgments extend
beyond the time and space of the characters themselves; and (5) the
verbs *said* in verses 16 and 17 are perfect tense and not *wayyiqtol*,
though the events are clearly on the main storyline.[50]

We can see the basic sequence of events from the paragraph
structure above. As we observed in describing the peak, God's speech
acts in Genesis 3:16 and 17 ("said") are part of the storyline, even
though they are reported with perfect verb forms. This is a grammati-

49. As the notes on 3:8 clarify, the woman and the man are the subjects of the first
verb in 3:8 ("heard"), while the second verb ("hid") primarily ranks the woman as an accomplice rather than a main participant. God speaks to the man alone in verses 9 and 11,
as indicated by the singular "you" (see ESV margin).

50. Compare Stephen Kempf, "Genesis 3:14–19: Climax of the Discourse?" *JOTT* 6,
no. 4 (1993): 354–77, at 368–70. This, as Kempf notes, opposes those who find the climax
in 3:6–8, such as Wenham, 75, but that may be due to differing notions of what a "climax" is. In any case, this refutes or at least makes uninteresting the redaction criticism
of authors such as Westermann (256–57), who argue that the judgments are not part of
the original account.

cal signal that the author wanted the reader to attach extra weight to these statements.

When we look for causal connections with what comes before and what comes after, we see, in the first place, that these events flow out of God's settling the man and his wife in Eden and giving them strict instructions regarding one tree (Gen. 2:15–17). We see further that the events of Genesis 3 enable us to understand how Adam and Eve's descendants could so rapidly decline into sin and strife in Genesis 4; it also provides the reason for the pile-driver-like refrain of Genesis 5, "and he died." The promise of a "seed" ("offspring") in 3:15 explains why Genesis as a whole is so interested in the "seed" and in genealogies.[51]

Now we consider repeated key words. There are small ironic word-plays in this pericope, some of which can be obscured in English versions. For example, in Genesis 3:5 the serpent promises that the humans' eyes will be *opened* and they will *know* something, while in verse 7 it is fulfilled: their eyes were *opened* and they *knew* something—but it was just that they were naked! Since they already knew that in 2:25 (and knew it blissfully), we may conclude that their dispositional stance toward that knowledge is different, as becomes obvious right away when they try to cover themselves. Similarly, there is a play between the use of the root *r-b-h* in 3:16 ("I will surely *multiply* your pain in childbearing") and its use in the commission of 1:28 ("be fruitful and *multiply*"). Whereas procreation had previously been the sphere of blessing, now it is to be the arena of pain and danger. Other repeated words and phrases that give thematic cohesion to the pericope include "eat" (אכל, *'akal*, 3:1, 2, 3, 5, 6, 11, 12, 13, 14, 17, 18, 19) and "which I commanded you not to eat from" (vv. 11, 17), and the divine acknowledgment that the humans *are* in fact in some way "like God" (v. 22, compare v. 5). The trees (cf. v. 22) also serve to unite this with 2:4–25. In 3:22, the Lord God is concerned that the man might "reach out" (שלח, *shalakh*, literally "to send") his hand to take of the tree of life, so he "sends him out" of the garden (also שלח [*shillakh*, Piel], "to send away"). This is ironic. Finally, we may mention another set of repetitions that unite 2:4–25 with 3:1–24: in 2:5 there is no man to "work" (עבד, *'abad*) the ground and raise "plants of the field" (עשב השדה, *'eseb hassadeh*). In 2:15 he is put into the garden to

---

51. On which see T. Desmond Alexander, "Genealogies, Seed and the Compositional Unity of Genesis," *Tyndale Bulletin* 44, no. 2 (1993): 255–70.

"work" its ground and to "keep" (שמר, *shamar*) it.[52] Then in 3:23 the man is sent out to "work the ground from which he was taken," and in 3:24 the cherubim will "keep/guard" (שמר) the way to the tree of life. This depicts the reversal that came about from the expulsion: no longer working the ground of the garden, he must work the ground from which he was taken, outside the garden; and now that no man is there to keep the garden, angelic beings must keep it—particularly, to keep the humans out!

The characters, as we observed, are the serpent, the woman, the man, and the Lord God. Consider how the narrator presents them.

The serpent is introduced in a very mysterious way. He is "*the serpent*" (Hebrew הנחש [*hannakhash*], with a definite article): commonly the definite article is anaphoric, that is, referring back to "the serpent we have been talking about," but no such serpent has been mentioned before now. Either this is "the serpent *we* [Moses and his audience] know about" (but we today no longer have the shared cultural heritage), or else it is just plain mysterious, and we readers ask, *which* serpent? and get no answer. This serpent begins by asking in Genesis 3:1, "Did God actually say,[53] 'You shall not eat of any tree of the garden'?" His strategy is to undermine the relationship of trust that is the engine of obedience, by attributing unreasonable motives to God. Hence, when the woman corrects him (vv. 2–3), he responds by denying the threatened outcome (v. 4, "you will not surely die," a direct contradiction of 2:17)[54] and by expounding how selfish God is (3:5, "God knows that in the day you eat of it[55] your eyes will be opened, and you will be like God, knowing good and evil," which he casts as benefits God wants to withhold). After this we hear no

---

52. The Heb. of 2:15 tells us that the man was put in the garden לעבדה ולשמרה (*le'obdah ûleshomrah*): the suffixes are feminine and cannot refer to the garden itself (a masculine noun). As Hamilton, 171 (compare Kiel, ם), suggested, the suffix would refer to the ground (אדמה ['*adamâ*], a feminine noun) of the garden.

53. Hebrew אף כי־אמר אלהים ('*ap kî 'amar 'elohîm*), which Delitzsch, 147–48, calls a "half-interrogatory, half-exclamatory expression of astonishment" which does not express uncertainty as to *whether* God had said it but implies instead that it is so unreasonable that God must be far too restrictive to be trusted. See also Moberly, "Did the Serpent Get It Right?" *Journal of Theological Studies* n.s. 39, no. 1 (1988): 1–27, at 6.

54. In 2:17 we find מות תמות (*môt tamût*), "you shall *surely* die" (RSV omits the infinitive absolute, rendered "surely"); in 3:4 the serpent says לא־מות תמתון (*lo' môt tamût*), "you will not 'surely die'" (again, RSV omits infinitive). In the woman's citation of the warning in 3:3 it is merely פן־תמתון (*pen temutûn*), "lest you die."

55. Hebrew ביום אכלכם (*beyôm 'akolkem*), an echo of 2:17, "in the day that you eat."

more from the serpent. Moberly makes a fine observation:[56] "It is noteworthy that the serpent never tells the woman to transgress God's prohibition. He simply calls into question both God's truthfulness (by denying his warning) and God's trustworthiness (by impugning his motives), and leaves the woman to draw her own conclusions." It is interesting to note that, though the deity throughout Genesis 2:4–3:24 is "the LORD God," the serpent only calls him "God," and he and the woman use only that title in their conversation (3:1b–5). Now, as many have observed, the name *God* designates the deity in his role of cosmic Creator and Ruler (its use in 1:1–2:3), while "the LORD" ("Yahweh") is particularly his name as he enters into covenantal relationship with human beings. By dropping the covenant name, then, the serpent is probably advancing his program of temptation by diverting the woman's attention from the relationship the Lord had established. The woman's use of it shows that she is trapped, and we begin to have a clue as to how she could be led into disobedience: by forgetting the covenant.

Further, even though Genesis never calls the serpent Satan, it is unmistakable that the serpent is not acting as a mere serpent but as the mouthpiece for a Dark Power, as Delitzsch put it:[57] "An animal is intended, but an animal not speaking of its own accord, but as made the instrument of itself by the evil principle. . . . The narrator confines himself to the external appearance of what took place, without lifting the veil from the reality behind it." A number of arguments confirm this. (1) The precise wording of Genesis 3:4 reflects knowledge of 2:17 (the serpent, not the woman, has introduced "surely," the infinitive absolute, into this conversation; he also uses "in the day you eat of it"). (2) Animals do not have the faculty of speech in the Bible; hence there is some supernatural activity here.[58] (3) The evil the serpent speaks (his direct contradiction of God's solemn warning and incitement of disobedience) can only be explained by demonic interference with God's good creation. (4) There is a Jewish interpretive tradition reflected in Wisdom of Solomon 1:13 and 2:24, and in the New Testament in John 8:44 and Revelation 12:9; 20:2, identifying the serpent of this passage with

56. Moberly, "Did the Serpent Get It Right?" 7.
57. Delitzsch, 149–52.
58. In Num. 22:28, when Balaam's donkey speaks, it is because "the LORD opened its mouth," denoting a supernatural action. This is why the notion that we have here a "mythological world" in which animals talk (Gunkel, 15) misses the point badly.

Satan. That is to say, a competent reader from the original audience would have been able to infer that the serpent is the mouthpiece of a Dark Power.[59]

The woman reveals herself through her speech. A major interpretive problem is her reply in Genesis 3:3, where she has "added" the restriction "neither shall you touch it." Is this innocent or is it playing into the hands of the serpent's question of verse 1? I do not know if we will ever be able to know; this may in fact be an intentional "gap."[60] It is also possible to detect a slight deflection of her commitment in her final phrase of verse 3, "lest you die." Does this dilute the solemn warning of 2:17?[61] Again, it is hard to be sure. In 3:6, as she regards the tree and sees that it is "good for food, a delight to the eyes, and desirable for giving insight," the irony of the parallel with 2:9 (there was already "every tree desirable to the sight and good for food" in the garden) should not escape us. She already had everything she could possibly want, and she even had the resources to get everything she thought the tree had to offer. Hence now she is clearly under the sway of the serpent's deception.[62] At this point she is changed completely: she invites her heretofore silent husband to join her in rebellion, responds to her new "knowledge" (3:7), follows

59. Many commentators, such as Westermann, 238 (compare Gunkel, 15–16), suppose that we have here nothing but a serpent, an ordinary reptile. They do not consider these arguments, however. Calvin's position is fascinating for historians of hermeneutics: he takes the declaration of 3:15 in its "simple sense" to be speaking of ordinary reptiles but also finds a "literal anagogy," apparently meaning that the author wanted us to apply this by analogy to the eventual defeat of Satan (167–68).

60. A gap is something left unresolved; when it is intentional, it makes us wonder about it. Since the question here is an obvious one, it may well be the author's intent to say to us, "I know you are curious about this, but since the purpose of the account is elsewhere, I will not satisfy your curiosity." Other gaps in this account include: what is the origin of the evil that possesses the serpent; whence came the woman's willingness to entertain the temptation; and what was the man doing when he was "with her" (3:6)?

61. We should not miss the point that comes from comparing the verb inflections in 2:17 with those in 3:3. In the institution, the Lord God addressed the man only, and the verb is inflected in the second person singular. When the woman refers to it, she cites it with the verb in the second person plural: "lest you all die." This shows that she had appropriated the command of 2:17 via her husband, that is, she accepted him as her covenantal representative.

62. Westermann, 249, says, "It is a case of the general human phenomenon of the attraction of what is forbidden. The prohibition itself fixes attention on what is forbidden, making it in a mysterious way seductively and irresistibly attractive." Besides the fact that this attributes the phenomenon to a good Creator (a possibility the biblical writers would not allow), it misses the obvious fact that, according to the text, it was the serpent who introduced the doubt and desire.

her husband into hiding from God (v. 8), and confesses only when she cannot escape (v. 13).

And what of the man's part? He enters in Genesis 3:6, where we read "she also gave some to her husband [who was] with her, and he ate."[63] If he was "with her," what was he doing when Eve was being led astray? Why did he eat—did he put up no struggle? Again, I do not think our author has given us the wherewithal to answer these questions. Instead, the focus is on other factors: namely, that the couple sinned freely, that is, without any compulsion or pressure from God or their created nature.[64]

The man is presented to us as the leader in this account from this point on: in Genesis 3:8, though "they" heard the sound of the Lord God walking, the man himself is the subject of "hid"; we might render the Hebrew (see text note at 3:8): ". . . and they heard the sound of the LORD God walking in the garden in the cool of the day, and the man hid himself, along with his wife." Then in verse 9 the divine call "where are you?" is addressed to him (masculine *singular* suffix, not *plural*); similarly in verse 11 "you" is masculine singular, and in verses 22–24 the divine actions are taken toward *the man*. All of these factors highlight the man's role as covenantal head, not only for his immediate family but also for his posterity.[65] The sad thing is, though, into what does he lead the way? The making of clothes (v. 7) shows that the blissful innocence about their nakedness of 2:25 no longer holds.[66] To try to

---

63. RSV inexplicably omits the phrase *who was with her*.

64. Compare Sir. 15:14–16.

65. We saw earlier that this is implicit in the way the woman appropriates 2:17.

66. Moberly, "Did the Serpent Get It Right?" 8–9, suggests that this is actually something positive, since "the dislike of nakedness is never considered something negative or sinful in the Old Testament." This assumes too many things: first, that the passage is not about a particular event whose consequences all humans receive; second, that the text *reflects* a "Hebrew outlook" as opposed to trying to *shape* that outlook. Since the action of clothing themselves is in contrast to the unashamed nakedness of 2:25, it is appropriate to find here evidence of a change in their condition. Further, this would be the *origin* of the importance of clothing oneself for subsequent time. Also, as many commentators point out, the fact that their next reaction is to hide in the bushes at the sound of the Lord's approach (3:8) is evidence of a bad conscience. Westermann, 253, objects to such reasoning: "These words express directly neither a consciousness of guilt nor a fear that results from it. Had J wanted to say that, he would have said it clearly and unequivocally." But this is an insistence on *telling* rather than *showing*, contrary to the Hebrew narrative style! Further, he says, the couple hides because of their "fear of being naked before God," but what else is this but a bad conscience? And surely this misses the point of the stark contrast with 2:25.

hide from God is obviously stupid[67]—besides, we should contrast this to what must surely have been their accustomed practice of rushing out to greet him![68] The man explains his actions as due to fear and shame in 3:10, which God directly connects with doing what he had forbidden (v. 11). And instead of owning up to his responsibility in verse 12 the man declares, "The woman that you gave [to be] with me: *she* is the one who[69] gave to me from the tree and I ate." Like the woman's explanation in verse 13 ("the serpent deceived me and I ate"), this is true so far as it goes, but it is not the whole truth. Both humans spin their accounts of what happened to put their own actions in the best light. The pristine condition of delight in God and harmony with one another and with their own consciences has been shattered.[70]

However, in Genesis 3:20 the man's act of naming his wife "Eve," "Life-giver," is likely an expression of faith in the divine words of judgment and grace of verses 14–19.

We have already noted the danger of drawing a portrait of God when he is a character in a narrative. Nevertheless we can say the following: we see him blasphemed in verses 1 and 4, and he makes no reference to it in the account—as if to show that he is not subject to *our* evaluation of *him*, it is the other way around; but also to show that in his mercy he can overlook even such vile insults. We see him taking his own command seriously in verses 11–19. The questions to the humans in verses 9–13, far from exhibiting God's ignorance, instead give the man and woman the opportunity to confess their fault (which opportunity, sadly, they did not take).[71] We see him

---

67. We might compare the idiocy of Jonah, who "feared the LORD, the God of heaven, who made the sea and the dry land" (Jon. 1:9) and yet tried to flee from him across the sea!

68. Josephus, *Antiquities* 1.45, noted this contrast.

69. Note the emphatic use of the pronoun: since he had identified the woman in the first part of the verse, Adam could have simply said נְתָנָה־לִּי (*natenâ lî*, "she gave to me"). Instead he adds the pronoun to focus on her responsibility, הִיא נְתָנָה־לִּי (*hî' natenâ lî*, "she is the one who gave to me"). Westermann, 255, in rejecting the "shifting the blame" interpretation of 3:12, misses the point of the emphatic pronoun, as well as the "spinning" by the man and the woman.

70. Compare the last lines of book 9 of Milton's *Paradise Lost*: "Thus they in mutual accusation spent the fruitless hours, but neither self-condemning; and of their vain contest appeared no end."

71. Compare Keil, 97–98: "Not that He was ignorant of his hiding place, but to bring him to a confession of his sin. . . . In offering these excuses, neither of them denied the fact. But the fault in both was, that they did not at once smite upon their breasts." This is right, and finds confirmation from God's similar questions to Cain in Genesis 4 (see the exposition there).

pronouncing just judgment, which is tinged with mercy in verses 14–19. Rather than rejecting his defiled creatures, he actually provides clothing for them in verse 21: he replaces their pathetic fig-leaf loincloths with something more durable, more suited to the hard lives they will face outside the garden. And the expulsion from the garden is, ultimately, an act of mercy: he cannot stand the thought of their being confirmed in their rebellious state, as suggested by the broken sentence at the end of verse 22, which indicates strong emotion. As we will see below, God also takes upon himself the task of rescuing these people and their descendants from the slavery and degradation they have made for themselves (v. 15). In all of this we see as well the clear marks of God's authority over all his creation, including over humans. He made it all, even the serpent (3:1); he established a relationship with the humans at his own initiative and on his own terms (2:15–17); the humans hid when they disobeyed him (3:8); he had the right to question the parties and to pronounce his sentence (3:9–19); and when he decided to expel Adam and Eve from the garden, out they went (3:23–24).[72]

In the light of this display of God's character and of his reliability, we are now in a position to address the meaning of the death threat of Genesis 2:17. God takes his solemn command with the utmost seriousness and may be relied upon to do as he said. In the light of what happens (the actions and changed attitudes of the humans), we can see that the part of the semantic range of "death" that is present here is spiritual death, estrangement from God. Physical mortality, which 3:19 predicts, is a consequence of the humans' disrupted condition—which even those who have been morally recovered will have to undergo.

What is this passage about? Consider it in redemptive-historical terms. Those who read the idyllic Genesis 1–2 must of course ask, why is my experience not just like that? Genesis 3 explains why. The relationship between God and the humans was a "covenant" (2:17), and Adam acted, not just for himself, and not just as head of his family, but as representative of his posterity: Adam and Eve are expelled from the garden, and neither they *nor their posterity* may return. Their posterity decline into sin in Genesis 4–6, and they like-

---

72. Westermann, commenting on 3:8–10 (253), makes the odd remark, "The following scene presumes that God and human beings are on the same level. This is not to be explained as an anthropological [*sic*; German *anthropomorphe*] presentation of God." But the text says otherwise.

wise die—even though they did not directly receive the stipulation of 2:17.[73] This also explains why any relationship with God, any good that he might intend for us, will have two features: (1) it will depend on divine grace and initiative, not on defiled humans; (2) it will be remedial, that is, directed at removing the polluting and harmful effects of human sinfulness.

We have seen above that the promise of a remedy begins at Genesis 3:15, in the sentence on the evil power behind the serpent. Here we have a promise of a specific human who will do battle with the evil power that spoke through the serpent, and at cost to himself will defeat the enemy, *for the sake of humans* (that is, not for himself). We may conclude the following about this figure:

- While human, he is also a special person (with supernatural *power* to win).
- His work is that of a champion (he fights *on behalf of* others).
- He will inflict a decisive defeat on the Evil One.

Genesis 3:15, then, is a promise of a personal redeemer who will undo the trouble Adam brought us all into, by acting as a *champion* or *representative*. This points the way to Paul's exposition in Romans 5:12–19: the first Adam represented humanity in the first covenant; the last Adam represents his people in the second covenant.

We may summarize the representative character of Adam's disobedience as follows: the test came, not from created human nature

---

73. Moberly, "Did the Serpent Get It Right?" 20, denies this when he says: "The story as a whole gives the impression of being a portrayal of what is generally true, rather than what was true on a particular occasion. . . . The condition of the world, therefore, is presumably to be seen as the result of the constant disobedience of mankind. . . . There [in Gen. 6:5; 8:21] the writer (generally considered to be the same as in Gen. 2–3) stresses that the regular condition of mankind is that of being disobedient to God and deserving of judgment." What Moberly neglects to consider is the possibility that the events of Gen. 3 provide the explanation of the *origin* of the "regular condition of mankind": surely an explanation is required if we are not to suppose that God made man sinful (which contradicts 1:26–27, the humans in God's image, and 1:31, the whole creation was at first very good). Further, the opposition between a particular occasion and the possible paradigmatic nature of the description is a false antithesis: why must we choose one or the other? The reason we can all identify with the workings of temptation here is because our sinfulness is rooted in this particular disobedience. After all, many of the psalms, and many hymns, take their start from the particular experience of the author, and present it in such a way that we can identify with it.

(which was good) but from a demonic enemy; it involved deceit, which then blossomed into desire, which led to disobedience and thus to "death" (first spiritual, then physical).[74] All mankind inherits the results of this action—as guilt and as sinful bent—from conception. The miseries we all do or might experience—lost communion with God, pain, frustration, futility, death, and eternal damnation—derive from this corruption of God's good creation and show why we are at God's mercy if there is to be a remedy.[75]

The author presents this to us as a unique historical event. But that does not mean that there is nothing paradigmatic about it; in fact, there is much to learn about the course of temptation in our present condition. It comes not from our created humanity as such but from the corruption of it. Hence, for example, sexuality is not in itself an evil, but to express it outside of monogamous marriage is. The way to deal with temptations, therefore, is not by attributing evil to our sexuality as such but by finding ways to channel its expression properly. We see further that temptation commonly proceeds by way of deceit: by trying to persuade us either that God is unreasonable to deny us something, or that he has withheld from us some good that we deserve, or that he will not carry out his threats. The key, then, is to hold on to God's truthfulness and trustworthiness. Similarly, if it is the case that the shift of the divine name from "the LORD God" to simply "God" signals a shift away from a focus on relationship, then a strong factor in resisting temptation would be to hold fast to our consciousness of the relationship and of God's loving initiative that established it, and to our desire for its continuing untroubled. We learn from the effects of Adam's sin that we are easily susceptible to temptation, and easily deceived by it; and hence we must be vigilant and studious of our own souls; and we learn from the nature of the "knowledge of good and evil" that the only way to gain skill at resisting temptation is by practice. As members of the covenant

74. As observed earlier, we are left in the dark about the exact psychology of Eve's and Adam's motivation. Neither Moses nor Paul speaks to that. Hence Barr's objection (*Garden of Eden*, 13) to traditional readings, that they introduce the explanation of pride (of which the text says nothing), is a red herring: he himself attributes it to Augustine, which means he has not found it in Paul. Therefore this is useless as a critique of Paul.

75. Contrast these conclusions with what Barr calls his basic thesis: "Taken in and for itself, this narrative is not, as it has commonly been understood in our tradition, basically a story of the origins of sin and evil, still less a depiction of absolute evil or total depravity: it is a story of how human immortality was almost gained, but was in fact lost" (*Garden of Eden*, 4).

people, we must above all lay hold of the resources of the Woman's Seed and his victory, since apart from that we are easy prey to the enemy of our souls.

Consider as well our discussion of the penalties meted out in Genesis 3:14–19. God will see to it that the Dark Power who spoke through the serpent will be defeated and humiliated. Both men and women will experience pain in their normal spheres of labor: the woman in child bearing, the man in working the ground. The alienation that comes from spiritual death has disrupted human nature, both body and soul, and has also disrupted man's relation to the rest of creation. The creation remains good in its own properties and workings but has also become the arena in which God chastens and recalls his sinful human creatures to himself. "Thorns and thistles" are not new in the world (they are food for some creatures, though not for man); the point is that the ground will produce them rather than food for man, with no prospect of Edenic blessings.

E. Other Reverberations

1. The "seed" theme in Genesis

The notion of זֶרַע (*zera'*, "seed, offspring") is a major theme of Genesis. The ESV has made the effort to render it consistently throughout. Alexander laments the policy of the NIV (and really, of most English versions):[76]

> Closely linked to the genealogical structure of Genesis is the frequent use of the Hebrew word *zera'* which is perhaps best translated as "seed." Unfortunately, the NIV translates *zera'* using a variety of terms—the most common being "descendants," "offspring," "seed," "children," "family," "grain," "semen," "line," "people." For this reason the importance of the concept of "seed" in Genesis is easily missed. *Zera'* is a keyword, however, occurring 59 times in Genesis compared to 170 times in the rest of the Old Testament.

As a practical matter, it is difficult for any translation to be good English if it tries absolute consistency with this word; but, since the author has used repetition to indicate his emphases to his readers, it

76. Alexander, *From Paradise to the Promised Land*, 103.

is worth trying to reproduce it, at least when the noun has the sense "offspring." (As it turns out, "offspring" is a good choice, since the English word presents the same challenge as the Hebrew to decide whether it refers to an individual or group.)

In Genesis 3:15 we find the offspring of the woman as the victor over the serpent in combat, and in 4:25 Eve celebrates Seth, "another offspring instead of Abel." Then in 9:9 God establishes his covenant with Noah and with his offspring—a notion that echoes throughout the book and even beyond (12:7; 13:15–16; 15:3, 5, 13, 18; etc.).

I have argued above that Genesis 3:15 refers to a single offspring, as we can discern from the singular pronouns used. There are two other places in Genesis that share this pattern and contribute to the way that Genesis develops its messianic theme: 22:17b–18 and 24:60, as Alexander has argued:[77]

> [17]I will surely bless you, and I will surely multiply your *offspring* as the stars of heaven and as the sand that is on the seashore. And your *offspring* shall possess the gate of his enemies, [18]and in your *offspring* shall all the nations of the earth be blessed, because you have obeyed my voice. (22:17–18)

And they blessed Rebekah and said to her,

> "Our sister, may you become
>   thousands of ten thousands,
> and may your *offspring* possess
>   the gate of those who hate him!" (24:60)

The first use of "offspring" in Genesis 22:17 probably refers to the offspring in general, since they will be numerous,[78] but the second and third uses, and the one in 24:60, refer to an individual (note the singular pronouns). Alexander shows how the specific wording of 22:18 ("all the nations," "be blessed") appears in Psalm 72:17, which warrants the conclusion that this text contributes to the messianic ideology of Genesis. In a further study, I argued that this way of seeing Genesis 22:18 allows us insight into Paul's argument about "offspring"

---

77. T. D. Alexander, "Further Observations on the Term 'Seed' in Genesis," *Tyndale Bulletin* 48, no. 2 (1997): 363–68; *From Paradise to the Promised Land*, 88–90.

78. Although—as Max Rogland kindly suggested to me—it is possible that even the first one is a singular, since it is grammatical to speak of multiplying an individual (17:2, 20; 28:3; 48:4).

and "offsprings" in Galatians 3:16:[79] namely, Paul was referring to Genesis 22:18, and the "offspring" there is a specific individual, who may properly be called messianic (which is what "Christ" means)—in other words, Paul was seeing what was really there in Genesis.

2. Romans 5:12–19

Paul's argument in Romans draws a great deal on Genesis, and in Romans 5:12–19 he especially draws on Genesis 3:[80]

[12]Therefore, just as sin came into the world through one man, and death through sin, and so death spread to all men because all sinned—[13]for sin indeed was in the world before the law was given, but sin is not counted where there is no law. [14]Yet death reigned from Adam to Moses, even over those whose sinning was not like the transgression of Adam, who was a type of the one who was to come.

[15]But the free gift is not like the trespass. For if many died through one man's trespass, much more have the grace of God and the free gift by the grace of that one man Jesus Christ abounded for many. [16]And the free gift is not like the result of that one man's sin. For the judgment following one trespass brought condemnation, but the free gift following many trespasses brought justification. [17]If, because of one man's trespass, death reigned through that one man, much more will those who receive the abundance of grace and the free gift of righteousness reign in life through the one man Jesus Christ.

[18]Therefore, as one trespass led to condemnation for all men, so one act of righteousness leads to justification and life for all men. [19]For as by the one man's disobedience the many were made sinners, so by the one man's obedience the many will be made righteous.

It appears from this study that what Paul found in this text is really there. That is, the tale of Genesis 3 describes how the first man, acting as a representative, sinned and brought sin and death into the world. That death is first spiritual death, or estrangement from God:

79. C. John Collins, "Galatians 3:16: What Kind of Exegete Was Paul?" *Tyndale Bulletin* 54, no. 1 (2003): 75–86. The fact that Paul goes on to call the Galatian Christians "Abraham's offspring" (Gal. 3:29), referring to a plurality, may well imply that he read the first occurrence of "offspring" in Gen. 22:17 as offspring in general (contrast previous note).

80. See also 1 Cor. 15:21–22, 42–49.

see how "death" parallels "condemnation" in Romans 5:15–16, 17–18, while it parallels "made sinners" in 5:19. Likewise, it contrasts with "abounding of grace" in 5:15; with "justification" in 5:16, 18, 19; and with "life" in 5:17. But of course that spiritual death has its consequence, namely, physical death, which explains Paul's observation in 5:14, "death reigned from Adam to Moses" (probably thinking of the genealogies in Gen. 5 with their refrain, "and he died").[81] All of this, by the way, shows that "the world" of Romans 5:12 is "the world of human beings," since only they are in view here; this is another point at which Paul read Genesis carefully.

This physical death of Adam's descendants—who after all did not sin in the specific way that Adam did—shows that the consequences of Adam's sin passed on to his posterity, which means that he acted as their representative. This allows Paul to contrast Adam with Christ, who also acted as a representative of his people. It is certainly the case that Paul has a parallel between Adam and Christ, in that they both act as covenant representatives, but it is also true that Paul emphasizes the differences rather than the similarities beyond that.[82]

In reading Genesis this way, Paul agrees with, among others, Sirach 15:14, which describes the test in Eden and man's responsibility for his own failure, and Sirach 25:24 ("from a woman sin had its beginning, and because of her we all die," RSV).[83] Consider also Wisdom of Solomon 2:23–24 (RSV), which clearly articulates important themes we found in Genesis 3:

> [23]For God created man for incorruption,
>   and made him in the image of his own eternity,
> [24]but through the devil's envy death entered the world,
>   and those who belong to his party experience it.

Some may think that Sirach 25:24 reflects that author's misogyny in blaming a woman, while Paul lays the blame on Adam, and Wis-

---

81. For spiritual death in Paul using θάνατος ("death") and ἀποθνήσκω ("die"), compare also Rom. 6:16, 21, 23; 7:5, 9–11, 13, 24; 8:2, 6; 2 Cor. 7:10. We might further add uses of νεκρός ("dead") in Rom. 6:11; 8:10, 11 (see also Eph. 2:1, 5), as well as the contrast between "death" and "life," but this is enough to establish the point.

82. In chapter 4, section C.6, I noted that perhaps the notion of Christ being "the image of God" (as in Col. 1:15) suggests that Paul presents Christ as a new Adam.

83. Interestingly enough, we have a situation similar to what we found in Sir. 14:17 (discussed in chapter 5, section C.2). The Hebrew uses גוע (gawa', "expire"), while the Greek has ἀποθνήσκω ("die"), and thus evokes Gen. 2:17 more clearly.

dom of Solomon traces it back to the devil. However, that need not be the case; after all, Paul can speak of how "the serpent deceived Eve by his cunning" (2 Cor. 11:3), and "Adam was not deceived, but the woman was deceived and became a transgressor" (1 Tim. 2:14).[84] The difference is that on one side the authors are looking at the events in the story, in which case the woman's being deceived comes into view; while on the other side they are looking at the theological significance of the events, in which case they will focus on the man as covenant head, and the devil as instigator.[85]

3. Romans 8:18–25 and the fallen world

Romans 8:18–25 is often seen as Paul's version of the curses of Genesis 3, describing a world fallen from its innocence, but a number of problems should keep us from reading Paul as telling us how the world is fallen in its very workings:

> [18]For I consider that the sufferings of this present time are not worth comparing with the glory that is to be revealed to us. [19]For the creation waits with eager longing for the revealing of the sons of God. [20]For the creation was subjected to futility, not willingly, but because of him who subjected it, in hope [21]that the creation itself will be set free from its bondage to decay and obtain the freedom of the glory of the children of God. [22]For we know that the whole creation has been groaning together in the pains of childbirth until now. [23]And not only the creation, but we ourselves, who have the firstfruits of the Spirit, groan inwardly as we wait eagerly for adoption as sons, the redemption of our bodies. [24]For in this hope we were saved. Now hope that is seen is not hope. For who hopes for what he sees? [25]But if we hope for what we do not see, we wait for it with patience.

84. For an example of misogyny from this period, see Josephus, *Antiquities* 1.49, where Josephus describes Adam as "yielding to womanish counsels." Louis H. Feldman, *Judean Antiquities 1–4* (Flavius Josephus: Translation and Commentary 3; Leiden: Brill, 2000), (17–18 n. 101) comments on the misogyny here and suggests that Josephus may have deliberately echoed the words of Odysseus in Homer's *Odyssey* 11.436–39.

85. See also 2 Esd. 3:4–11 (from the late first century A.D.), which recounts the events of Genesis 1–9; especially 2 Esd. 3:7, "And thou didst lay upon him one commandment of thine; but he transgressed it, and immediately thou didst appoint death for him and for his descendants. From him there sprang nations and tribes, peoples and clans without number" (RSV).

It may be that Paul had Genesis 3 in mind, though he is not explicitly alluding to it. To begin with, the words of the passage here do not use the terms of Genesis 3:16–19 (LXX). The closest we get is "groaning" (Rom. 8:22, 23), which *may* evoke Genesis 3:16, which in the Greek says, "I will surely multiply your pains and your *groaning*"—but then again, it might not. Since the important term *pain* (Gen. 3:16, 17; עִצָּבוֹן ['itstsabôn] / λύπη) is missing from this passage in Romans, and since the term *groaning* is common in the Septuagint (compare Exod. 2:24), we have very little ground for supposing that Genesis 3:16 influenced Paul's word choice here. Nor is there any mention of a curse. The term *futility* (Rom. 8:20), if it has an Old Testament background, would evoke Ecclesiastes, since that is the Greek term for the refrain-like "vanity of vanities."

On the other hand, the theme of the creation (that is, the nonhuman material world) looking forward to the time when the children of God are revealed in glory—which will happen in their eternal state—certainly runs through the text. Further, the fall of mankind did indeed have its impact on the created world, according to Genesis. Man was made to have dominion over the creation and to bring the blessings of Eden through all the earth, and man has fallen from the task, though not from the dominion. Looked at this way, we should not take "futility" as a reference to Ecclesiastes but "as denoting the ineffectiveness of that which does not attain its goal, . . . so long as man the chief actor in the drama of God's praise fails to contribute his rational part."[86]

The key term in this light is "decay" in Romans 8:21 (φθορά). Another rendering of this noun would be "corruption" (as ESV Update), and the related verb first appears in the Septuagint of Genesis 6:11–13:[87]

> [11]Now the earth was *corrupt* [ἐφθάρη] in God's sight, and the earth was filled with wrong-doing. [12]And God saw the earth, and behold, it was *corrupt* [κατεφθαρμένη], for all flesh had *corrupted* [κατέφθειρεν] their way on the earth. [13]And God said to Noah, "The time of all flesh

86. C. E. B. Cranfield, *Romans* (International Critical Commentary; Edinburgh: T & T Clark, 1975), 1:413–14.
87. The simple verb φθείρω appears in Gen. 6:11 (LXX), while the compound verb καταφθείρω is used in verses 12–13. The word translated "destroy" in verse 13 is actually the same verb, the Septaugint reflecting a wordplay in the Hebrew.

has come before me, for the earth is filled with wrong-doing from them. Behold, I will *destroy* [καταφθείρω] them with the earth.

Seen this way, the creation is "in bondage to decay," not because of changes in the way it works but because of the "decay" (or "corruption") of mankind, and in response to man's "decay" God "brings decay to" (or "destroys") the earth to chastise man. The creation is "subjected to futility" because it has sinful mankind in it, and thus it is the arena in which mankind expresses its sin and experiences God's judgments. No wonder it "waits with eager longing for the revealing of the sons of God," for then the sons of God will be perfect in holiness, and sin will be no more. Paul here sees the resurrection of the sons of God as a blessing not only for themselves but also for the whole creation.

Others take the "decay" to be a feature of the world itself due to human sin; for example, Schreiner asserts: "Slavery entails corruption, decay, and death, which pervade the natural world."[88] The position I have argued, however, is more consistent with Paul's focus on human glorification and with the picture of Genesis, which does not view the created world as changed in its workings but as the arena in which God works out his purposes for mankind.

4. Paul as interpreter of Genesis

Paul made himself out to be an apostle, a messenger from God specially inspired for the task. Theoretically, this could involve him in claiming to reveal hidden meanings in the Old Testament or in reinterpreting it in light of his Christian convictions. At the same time, his office is analogous to the prophet of the Old Testament, who is expected to display his doctrinal continuity with the Pentateuch (Deut. 13). In his apostolic work, he "reasoned from the Scriptures" (Acts 17:2, etc.), which means that he must have appealed to a proper understanding of them in order to establish his assertion that the Old Testament foretold the events of which he was a herald. Further, the Old Testament provided the interpretive categories for Paul as he explained the epochal events of Jesus' death and resurrection.

---

88. Thomas Schreiner, *Romans* (Baker Exegetical Commentary on the New Testament 6; Grand Rapids: Baker, 1998), 436.

In the examples we have discussed, Paul has shown himself a competent reader of the Old Testament. We are in a better position to see how he used his material, and we may strengthen our confidence in his claims for authority. At the same time, we may also find ground for confidence in the methods advocated here. The way Jesus expounds the Pentateuch in Matthew 5 provides an analogy. If we read Matthew 5 in light of sound studies of how the Old Testament law worked—such as those carried out by Wenham and Wright and discussed in the previous chapter—we can see what he was doing, we can see why he was right, and we find ourselves more confident in his authority. And at the same time we can be more confident that Wenham and Wright have given us real insight into Old Testament law.

5. Edenic imagery

In Genesis 3:24 the Lord God "drove out the man, and at the east of the garden of Eden he placed the cherubim and a flaming sword that turned every way to guard the way to the tree of life." This implies that man is forever banished from Eden, never to be allowed back. Certainly no one in Genesis comes back. Nevertheless, Edenic imagery is important for the Bible in general.

Several authors have noted interesting parallels between the description of the garden and the features of the Israelite sanctuary.[89] For example, in the garden the Lord would "walk about" (הִתְהַלֵּךְ [hithallek], Gen. 3:8); and in the sanctuary, the Lord would make his dwelling among Israel, and "walk about" (הִתְהַלֵּךְ) in their midst (Lev. 26:11–12; 2 Sam. 7:6–7).[90] We note further the presence of the cherubim and the entrance on the east as common features of the garden and the sanctuary (Gen. 3:24; Exod. 27:13; Ezek. 11:1). Kiel's conclusion is therefore warranted: "The 'garden' was therefore the first place on earth where the Shekinah dwelt."[91] But even though physical access to the garden and to the tree of life is now closed for mankind, that does not mean that man cannot come into God's presence. In particular, the sanctuary is the way of access to God's

---

89. See for example Kiel, עה–וע, צם, with Rabbinic comments; Wenham, 76, 84, 86.

90. Compare Deut. 23:15 [English translation, v. 14], where the Lord "walks about" (הִתְהַלֵּךְ [hithallek]) in the camp.

91. See Kiel, וע.

presence, in its public worship and sacramental rites that address human guilt.[92] This becomes a foretaste of eschatological glory, where the old wound in man and nature will be healed, and it equips the covenant people for perseverance in the covenant under the forgiving grace of God.

Besides this, Eden (or the garden of God) becomes an image of pristine beauty, usually when the beauty has been lost (Gen. 13:10; Joel 2:3; Ezek. 28:13; 31:8–9). In other cases we find that when God provides salvation, one picture of it is the return to Eden or Paradise (as in Isa. 51:3; Sir. 24:25–28; Rev. 2:7; 22:1–3; Luke 23:43; 2 Cor. 12:3).

6. The temptation of Adam and the temptation of Jesus

According to the literary-theological reading above, we may legitimately say that Genesis tells of how Adam and Eve, the first parents of the human race, were deceived into sinning by a Dark Power that used a serpent as its mouthpiece and thus brought themselves and their posterity into sin and death. God promised a Champion, an offspring of the woman, who would engage the Dark Power in combat and defeat him.

It is clear that the New Testament views the Dark Power as Satan or the devil, and Jesus as that Champion. It even calls Jesus "the last Adam" (1 Cor. 15:45). Hence the obvious question is whether the Gospel writers intended their readers to see the devil's temptation of Jesus in the wilderness (Matt. 4:1–11; Mark 1:12–13; Luke 4:1–13) as any kind of reenactment of the temptation in Eden.

The first thing to say is that on the linguistic level, the connections are quite tenuous. For example, we cannot find the verb πειράζω ("tempt"), or its cognate nouns, used in referring to Genesis 3 in the Septuagint, the New Testament, or Josephus. Mark 1:13 says that Jesus was "with the *wild animals*," employing a term, θηρίον, found in Genesis 1:24–25, 30; 2:19–20; 3:1, 14 (see also 9:2; Sir. 17:4). This would be promising, suggesting Jesus as the new Adam exercising dominion over the wild animals, except for the fact that neither Mat-

---

92. Compare Ps. 22:4 [English translation, v. 3], where the Lord "inhabits [or sits enthroned on] the public praises of Israel" (RV, RSV, NASB, NIV margin; NIV text is inexcusable); Ps. 63:3 [English translation, v. 2], "so I have looked upon you *in the sanctuary*, beholding your power and glory." In this sacramental and liturgical setting God is present in a way not otherwise available.

thew nor Luke uses the term, and Mark's account is exceedingly brief. Both Matthew and Luke have the first temptation beginning with the challenge, "If you are the son of God." This might be significant in Luke, since the previous pericope had ended with "Adam the [son] of God" (Luke 3:38, supplying *son* from v. 23). This might work for Luke, but it will not for Matthew, since Matthew 3:17 uses "son of God" differently.

J. A. Alexander did find a parallel, writing,[93] "As a premonition of the great decisive crisis in the war between the 'seed of the woman' and the 'seed of the serpent' . . . , the heads and representatives of both which parties were now to be brought personally into contact." He identifies the "seed of the serpent" (τὸ σπέρμα τοῦ ὄφεως) with the "brood of vipers" (γεννήματα ἐχιδνῶν) in Matthew 3:7 (see also Luke 3:7), saying, "The mere change of expression, from *seed of the serpent* to *brood of vipers*, is entirely insufficient to outweigh the historical and other arguments in favour of this explanation." In other words, Alexander does not require verbal concord as the decisive criterion for a thematic echo. We might allow this as a theoretical possibility, but we should also acknowledge that such echoes will be highly debatable.

Perhaps, though, Alexander's identification becomes more plausible in view of Matthew 23:33, where Jesus denounces the scribes and Pharisees as "you serpents [ὄφεις], you brood of vipers," combining terms used in Matthew 3:7 with those of Genesis 3:1 (LXX).

However, if this is valid, we still have to modify Alexander's position in the light of this study. The combat is, after all, between the "offspring of the woman" (an individual, not a collective) and the serpent himself—or really, the Dark Power who used the serpent as his mouthpiece. Further, in the light of the New Testament picture, this is not the prophesied combat but only an initial skirmish (Luke 4:13); the cross and resurrection are the consummation.

But with these modifications, we can find in this pericope that the Gospel writers portrayed Jesus as qualified to serve as the "last Adam." His work is not directly parallel to that of the first Adam, because he must represent man as *fallen* and banished from the garden, and provide the way back. Hence, rather than the lush and fruitful setting of the garden, this temptation takes place in the dry wilderness, after fasting, with Jesus hungry. The same tempter aims

93. J. A. Alexander, 77.

to make Jesus doubt not the words of Scripture themselves but the motives behind them. Jesus succeeds at remaining loyal to God, with far more against him than Adam had, because he must do a greater work than Adam was assigned.

A full discussion of the Synoptics' temptation stories would take account of the Scripture quotations and of the purpose of the writers to present Jesus as the promised messianic king who will call the Gentiles into his empire. Of course, to be this kind of king he must be the ideal Israel, and the ideal Israelite, which means the ideal human being—and this brings us back to Adam. (See the examination of Matt. 4:1–11 in chapter 2 above.)

7

GENESIS 4:1–26:
AFTER EDEN

Genesis 4 describes what happened to the first family after their disobedience in Eden. It illustrates both the decline into sin that results from the first disobedience and the enduring faithfulness that God has to his promise.

A. Reasons for Including Genesis 4 in This Work

In this chapter I will first have to show why I think we should include Genesis 4 in this study; after all, it is conventional to treat Genesis 1–3 as the unit depicting creation and fall. However, there are several strong reasons for supposing that our narrator wanted his readers to see the break as coming between Genesis 4 and 5 rather than between Genesis 3 and 4.

First, consider that Genesis 5 begins with, "This is the book of the generations of Adam," which starts a new section of the book; the genealogy acts like a fast forward to bring us to the episode of the sons of God and the daughters of man, followed by the flood.

Second, we have linguistic connections between these chapters. For example, the expression *to work the ground* (עבד ['abad] with אדמה ['adamâ] as object) in Genesis occurs in only Genesis 2–4 (2:5,

15; 3:23; 4:2, 12). As we saw in the previous chapter, the last phrase of
Genesis 4:7 ("but you must rule over it") is parallel to the last phrase of
3:16 ("and he shall rule over you"), and both verses use the rare word
תְּשׁוּקָה (teshûqâ, "desire"), whose only other appearance is in the Song
of Songs. Cain says that God has "driven me away" (גֵּרֵשׁ, geresh) in
4:14, echoing the same verb in 3:24, "he drove out the man."[1] Finally,
the only biblical references to "east of Eden" are in 3:24 and 4:16.

We can also find literary features that connect Genesis 4 with
Genesis 1–3. Genesis 3 ended with Adam and Eve being sent out
from Eden because of their disobedience; in Genesis 4 we see the
result of that disobedience as it spreads through the offspring. A grim
example of this spread-of-sin theme comes from 4:19–24, where the
bigamous Lamech makes a proud boast in front of his wives. This
contrasts with the attractive picture of the origin of monogamous
marriage in 2:18–25.

For these reasons, it seems best to see the macrostructure of early
Genesis as the following:

1:1–2:3	overview of creation week
2:4–4:26	the first human family:
	2:4–25 making of the first man and woman
	3:1–24 the first sin and banishment from Eden
	4:1–26 life begins outside of Eden
5:1–32	genealogy: fast forward
6:1–9:29	Noah and his family

This agrees with Jan Fokkelman's observation:[2]

> The first section of the book of Genesis, also called the Primeval
> History, consists of two such groups [of stories]. They are easily
> distinguishable, as they are marked by a parallelism: both end in a
> genealogical register, Genesis 5 and 11:10–26 respectively. The first
> group, Genesis 1–4, covers the creation as the beginning of every-
> thing, plus two fundamental horizontal relationships in our lives:
> that between man and woman (in the Paradise story, Genesis 2–3)

---

1. In both cases the idea is banishment from God's special presence; when the verb
appears again in 21:10 it refers to driving a wife from the house.

2. Jan Fokkelman, *Reading Biblical Narrative: An Introductory Guide* (Louisville:
Westminster John Knox Press, 1999), 156. We might add that conventional source criticism,
as discussed in chapter 8 below, attaches Gen. 4 to the J source that runs from 2:4–4:26.

and that between brother and brother (and by association: between man and his fellow human beings) in Genesis 4.

B. Pericope Boundary, Structure, and Genre

In the previous section I mentioned the *toledot* marker at Genesis 5:1, which begins a new part of Genesis.[3] Further, in the previous chapter I argued that there is a discontinuity between 3:24 and 4:1. This leaves us with Genesis 4, but the question is, should we take it as a unit?

That the answer is yes comes from noting the structure of the chapter: it consists of three episodes, each beginning with a man "knowing" (ידע, *yada'*) his wife (אשתו, *'ishtô*), who then "bears" (ילד, *yalad*) a son: Genesis 4:1, 17, 25. We note further that the chapter begins and ends with Eve naming a son and giving an optimistic rationale—one that disappoints us, as we shall see (v. 1) and one that holds better promise (v. 25).

The most intricate of these episodes is Genesis 4:1–16; we may divide it up into subunits by following the main events and actors. We may do the same with 4:17–24. This yields (labeling each episode by the person born):

4:1–16	Cain and Abel	
	4:1–2	the two boys born
	4:3–5	the two sacrifices
	4:6–7	God converses with Cain (first time)
	4:8	Cain slays Abel
	4:9–15	God converses with Cain (second time)
	4:16	Cain departs
4:17–24	Cain's offspring	
	4:17–18 genealogy: from Cain to Lamech	
	4:19–24 Lamech and his family	
4:25–26	Seth	

The genre is standard narrative prose, as was the case with Genesis 2–3. However, we do have a difference here: rather than a connected

---

3. We may note also that Gen. 5:1–2 retraces time to before Genesis 4 ("When God created man"), while 5:3 recapitulates 4:25–26.

sequence of events, we have an introduction followed by an unspecified interval ("in the course of time," 4:3). This is followed by an apparently short time span (vv. 3–16) and another unspecified break (v. 8), which is followed by rapid progress through time (vv. 17–22). Only one event stands out of this: Lamech's boast (vv. 23–24). The first action of verse 25, Adam knowing his wife "again," brings us back to the time of verse 16. Then in verse 26 we speed through time again. This reminds us that the narration in Genesis 1–11 is severely selective and impels us to look for the principle governing the selection.

C. Translation and Notes

Cain and Abel (4:1–16)

¹Now Adam knew[4] Eve his wife, and she conceived and bore Cain, saying, "I have gotten[5] a man with the help of the LORD." ²And again, she bore his brother Abel. Now Abel was a keeper of sheep, and Cain a worker of the ground.[6] ³In the course of time Cain brought to the LORD an offering of the fruit of the ground, ⁴and Abel also brought of the firstborn of his flock[7] and of their fat portions. And the LORD had regard for Abel and his offering, ⁵but for Cain and his offering he had no regard.[8] So Cain was very angry,[9] and his face fell. ⁶The LORD said to Cain, "Why are you angry, and why has your face fallen? ⁷If you do well, will you not be accepted?[10]

4. This common euphemism for the sexual relation first appears here. Versions such as NIV ("lay with") and NLT ("slept with") deprive the reader of understanding the idiom and thus of deciding whether it is present in Gen. 19:5 and Judg. 19:22 in debased form. Such an approach "underestimates the reader and loses the force and delicacy of the original," as Anthony Nichols points out; "Explicitness in Translation and the Westernization of Scripture," *Reformed Theological Review* 47, no. 3 (1988): 78–88, at 85.

5. As the ESV margin notes, *Cain* (Hebrew *Qayin*) sounds like the Hebrew for *gotten* (Hebrew קָנִיתִי, *qanîtî*).

6. For "work the ground," compare 2:5, 15; 3:23.

7. There is a chiasmus here: *sheep-ground-ground-sheep (flock)*.

8. The "bringing" and the "regarding" are presented here as simultaneous events; compare Shemaryahu Talmon, "The Presentation of Synchroneity and Simultaneity in Biblical Narrative," in *Studies in Hebrew Narrative Art*, ed. J. Heinemann and S. Werses (Scripta Hierosolymitana; Jerusalem: Magnes, 1978), 9–26, at 12. (Compare note at 1:5.)

9. The Hebrew for "was angry" (4:5) is more literally, "it burned to him"; in verse 6, "why does it burn to you?"

10. ESV margin: "Hebrew *will there not be a lifting up* (of your face)?" Possibly, though, נשׂא here is "forgive": "Will there not be forgiveness?" This might lead to Cain's reply in 4:13 meaning, "my iniquity is too great to forgive."

And if you do not do well, sin is crouching at the door. Its desire is for[11] you, but you must rule over it." **8**Cain spoke to Abel his brother.[12] And when they were in the field, Cain rose up against his brother Abel and killed him. **9**Then the LORD said to Cain, "Where is Abel your brother?" He said, "I do not know; am I my brother's keeper?" **10**And the LORD said, "What have you done? The voice of your brother's blood[13] is crying to me from the ground. **11**And now you are cursed from the ground,[14] which has opened its mouth to receive your brother's blood from your hand. **12**When you work the ground, it shall no longer yield to you its strength. You shall be a fugitive and a wanderer on the earth." **13**Cain said to the LORD, "My punishment is greater than I can bear.[15] **14**Behold, you have driven[16] me today away from the ground, and from your face I shall be hidden. I shall be a fugitive and a wanderer on the earth, and whoever finds me will kill me." **15**Then the LORD said to him, "Not so! If anyone kills Cain, vengeance shall be taken on him sevenfold." And the LORD put a mark on Cain, lest any who found him should attack him. **16**Then Cain went away from the presence of the LORD and settled in the land of Nod,[17] east of Eden.

Cain's offspring (4:17–24)

17Cain knew his wife, and she conceived and bore Enoch. When he built a city, he called the name of the city after the name of his son, Enoch. **18**To Enoch was born Irad, and Irad fathered Mehujael, and Mehujael fathered Methushael, and Methushael fathered Lamech. **19**And Lamech took two wives. The name of the one was Adah, and the name of the other Zillah. **20**Adah bore Jabal; he was the father of those who dwell in tents and have livestock. **21**His brother's name was Jubal; he was the father of all those who play the lyre and pipe. **22**Zillah

11. Or "against"; also in 3:16. Compare discussion in chapter 6, section C.3.

12. This is what the Hebrew says. The Samaritan, Septuagint, Syriac, and Vulgate add, "Let us go out to the field." The verb אמר ['amar] usually focuses on the content of what one says rather than the act of speaking: hence "say" is usually better than "speak" for translation. See, however, Jonah 2:10 [Masoretic Text 11] for a comparable example, which means that ESV is justifiable.

13. The plural for "blood" is typically used for "shed blood."

14. This is conceivably "more cursed are you than the ground" (מן [min] of comparison); the structure is just like that of 3:14a, "cursed are you above all livestock."

15. Or "my guilt is too great to bear." For the syntax, adjective + מן + infinitive construct, see Joüon, *Grammar of Biblical Hebrew*, §141i.

16. Compare 3:24 for the same verb.

17. As the ESV margin notes, the Hebrew name *Nod* means "wandering" (4:12, 14).

also bore Tubal-cain; he was the forger of all instruments of bronze and iron. The sister of Tubal-cain was Naamah.

²³Lamech said to his wives:

"Adah and Zillah, hear my voice;
    you wives of Lamech, listen to what I say:[18]
I have killed a man for wounding me,
    a young man for striking me.
²⁴If Cain's revenge[19] is sevenfold,[20]
    then Lamech's is seventy-sevenfold."

Seth (4:25–26)

²⁵And Adam knew his wife again, and she bore a son and called his name Seth, for she said,[21] "God has appointed[22] for me another offspring[23] instead of Abel, for Cain killed him." ²⁶To Seth also a son was born, and he called[24] his name Enosh. At that time people began[25] to call upon the name of the LORD.

D. Extra Notes

1. What did Eve think she'd got (Gen. 4:1)?

Genesis 4:1 in the ESV reads, "Now Adam knew Eve his wife, and she conceived and bore Cain, saying, 'I have gotten a man with the help of the LORD.'" Eve's declaration has received a number of different interpretations, however, which means that not everyone agrees

---

18. For the word pair שָׁמַע (shama', "hear") and הֶאֱזִין (he'ezîn, "listen, give ear"), compare Exod. 15:26; Num. 23:18; Deut. 1:45; 32:1; Isa. 32:9. The word pair itself does not make this poetry, but it does indicate that we have a rhetorically high style, which poetry uses.

19. See 4:15.

20. For the way the terms שִׁבְעָתַיִם (shib'atayim) and שִׁבְעִים וְשִׁבְעָה (shib'îm weshib'â) express the multiplicative ideas sevenfold and seventy-sevenfold, see Joüon, Grammar of Biblical Hebrew, §142q.

21. The words she said are an addition to show what the force of the conjunction כִּי is here—it is explaining from Eve's perspective why she called him Seth.

22. As the ESV margin points out, Seth (Hebrew shet) sounds like the Hebrew for "he appointed" (shat).

23. Hebrew זֶרַע (zera'), "seed" or "offspring."

24. Eve, not Adam, was the namer in 4:1 and 4:25; now her son Seth names his own son.

25. The Hebrew for "people began" is more literally, "it was begun."

on just what she thought had happened in the birth. The Hebrew of her saying is,

קניתי איש את־יהוה

Each word here involves us in semantic and syntactical questions, as well as larger literary and theological ones.

(1) What is the sense of קנה (*qanâ*) here: "get," "beget," or "create"?

(2) What is the nuance of איש (*'îsh*, "man") here: "man child," "mature man," or "husband"?

(3) What is the syntactical relationship of את־יהוה (*'et-yhwh*) to the rest of the sentence: that is, is the particle את used as the preposition "with," and if so, in what sense? Or is את the marker of the direct object, which would make "the LORD" appositional to "a man": "I have gotten a man, namely, the LORD"?

Let us take each of these in their turn, though of course the answers are interwoven.

The normal sense of the verb קנה is "to get, own"; that is, the focus is on possession ("own") and sometimes the act of coming into possession ("get, buy"). Some claim that it can also have the nuance "to create," that is, "to originate." The evidence adduced for this is the usage in Genesis 14:19, 22; Deuteronomy 32:6; Psalm 139:13; and Proverbs 8:22.[26] Of these verses, though, only Deuteronomy 32:6 comes close to supporting this sense, and it is possible but not necessary in Psalm 139:13, as we shall see.

In Genesis 14:19, 22, Melchizedek and Abram call the Lord "God Most High, *Possessor* [קנה, *qoneh*] of heaven and earth." Some would render the participle קנה as "Creator" instead, appealing to the phrase in Ugaritic, a language and literature closely akin to the background of Melchizedek.[27] However, the attested Ugaritic ideology lacks the

26. See BDB, 888b; I. Cornelius and R. C. van Leeuwen, "קנה," no. 7864 in *NIDOTTE* 3:940–42.

27. As J. C. L. Gibson, *Canaanite Myths and Legends* (Edinburgh: T&T Clark, 1977), acknowledges, the Ugaritic can easily be "owner," using the common sense of the verb (for example, see Aqhat, line 220, page 121; Palace of Baal, 4.1.23, page 55 n. 6). See further Gibson, *Syrian Semitic Inscriptions*, vol. 3: *Phoenician* (Oxford: Clarendon Press, 1982),

notion of "to create" in the sense that the biblical authors use it, namely, "to originate the being of," and "to possess" makes better sense of the context of both the Ugaritic and the Genesis texts.

The Proverbs 8:22 example also fails: there Wisdom (a personification) claims, "the LORD *possessed me* [קָנָנִי, *qananî*] at the beginning of his work." The Septuagint renders קָנָה here with ἔκτισεν (from κτίζω), which most take to mean "created."[28] The Greek is not decisive evidence, however: first, because the Septuagint of Proverbs is not very good, and second, because it is not clear that κτίζω must mean "to create" here; its normal sense in Greek is "to found (as a city)," which became specialized, especially in a Jewish setting, to "to create."[29] The verb קָנָה appears in Proverbs numerous times with an intellectual term (wisdom, knowledge, etc.) as object: Proverbs 1:5; 4:5, 7; 8:22; 15:32; 17:16; 18:15; 19:8; 23:23.[30] The idea in each of these (besides 8:22) is "to *get* wisdom," using the normal sense of קָנָה. The idea of Proverbs 1–9 is to encourage God's faithful covenant members to seek wisdom, and one of the motivations is the claim that the wisdom that God offers is the wisdom by which he made the world (compare 3:19–20 with 8:27). Hence it makes better sense in 8:22 to follow this pattern: *possess* wisdom, and thus imitate God himself.

Psalm 139:13 says to God, "you *formed* [קָנִיתָ, *qanîta*] my inward parts";[31] this activity is paralleled with "you knitted me together in my mother's womb." The context of fetal development under God's watchful care seems to call for something stronger than merely "possessed," going at least as far as "took hold of." Thus the ESV "formed" is warranted, but this does not support the idea of "originated the being of," which is what the sense "created" requires.

Deuteronomy 32:6, however, makes the senses "create" or "beget" possible:

---

63 (on Karatepe A.3.18); the Phoenician evidence is the same. The way to get "creator" in these places is to assume that it exists in Hebrew.

28. This became a hot topic at the Christian Council of Nicea in 325. Both sides, the Arian and the Athanasian, viewed Wisdom here as the Word (Christ before the incarnation). The Arians saw this verse as proof that the Word was a created being, while the Athanasians referred it to the human nature of Christ. Further discussion is available in Philip Schaff, *History of the Christian Church* (repr., Grand Rapids: Eerdmans, 1981), 3:646–49.

29. See LSJ, 1002b–1003a.

30. The typical Septuagint rendering is the verb κτάομαι ("to acquire"), which makes me wonder whether the Septuagint saw some semantic interference with κτίζω at Prov. 8:22 and Gen. 14:19.

31. Familiar in the AV as "thou hast *possessed* my reins [kidneys]."

Do you thus repay the Lord,
    you foolish and senseless people?
Is not he your father, who *created* [קָנָה, *qanâ*] you,
    who made [עָשָׂה, *'asâ*] you and established [כּוּן, *kônen*] you?

The parallels with "made" and "established" can support taking קָנָה as "create" here,[32] though they do not need to; it is also possible that the reference to a father implies that "he begot" is the right sense. It is also possible that the verb simply means God "purchased" them, as is common in reference to his people (compare Exod. 15:16; Pss. 74:2; 78:54; and possibly Isa. 11:11).

The result of all this is that the sense "gotten" is the best established, with "formed" or "begotten" waiting in the wings should "gotten" fail us.

As to the nuance of אִישׁ (*'îsh*) here, there is little difficulty in taking it as referring to a man (anticipating what the child will become), or perhaps as a "man child."[33] This latter gains support from the parallelism in Genesis 4:23, where אִישׁ and יֶלֶד (*yeled*, "young man, boy") refer to the same person. In a few cases, the word אִישׁ, which normally refers to a male, can simply refer to a human being, but since the child is a boy, we naturally read the word in its "male" sense.[34]

Now for the syntax of אֶת־יְהוָה (*'et-yhwh*). From a purely *syntactical* point of view, the interpretation of it as appositional is unexceptionable: "I have gotten a man, namely, the Lord."[35] But though the syntax is fine, the content is jarring, to say the least! To take אֵת as "with," that is, "with the help of," is also quite reasonable, though the parallels are few: 1 Samuel 14:45 uses the virtually interchangeable preposition עִם (*'im*) in the required sense: "for he has worked *with* [the help of] God this day."

---

32. These verbs are used elsewhere to describe God's making the world, as we saw in chapter 4, section D.

33. There is no reason to suppose that the use of אִישׁ (*'îsh*) as an indefinite pronoun "someone" helps us here, since the noun is an object of a verb here, which would be peculiar for the pronominal use.

34. The Septuagint rendered ἄνθρωπον, which often stresses humanity more than maleness, but the Greek word can also bear a masculine overtone, so the Greek is not decisive.

35. For an indefinite object with a definite noun in apposition and marked with the particle אֵת, see Gen. 26:34; Judg. 3:15; Ezek. 4:1; and possibly Gen. 6:10 and Isa. 7:17.

If we were just looking at the number of parallel constructions available to us, we would say that the appositional interpretation is stronger. Christians naturally think of the incarnation, but the question is, what did our author present *Eve* as thinking? With only Genesis 3:15 to go on, even under the strongest messianic reading of it, there is little reason to suppose that this was part of her or the author's thought world.[36]

I propose a different tack: try it from the perspective of the pious Israelite reader. If he entertained the appositional reading, he would likely respond in surprise and say, "She could not mean *that*, could she?" He would then go on to favor "with the help of." But as he reads through the rest of the story, with the surprise in the back of his mind, he will find it clear that Cain is not even *like* the Lord—the "image and likeness" is badly defaced. By the time he gets to Genesis 4:25, which has no such ambiguities, he can conclude that whatever Eve might have meant, "with the help of" is all she had a right to mean. In the process of resolving the question, however, he has had the opportunity to reflect on how the first sin of Adam and Eve has passed on to their son; he has perceived the effects of the fall by way of his imagination.[37]

2. The meaning of נשא ("accept, bear") in Genesis 4:7, 13

The verb נשא (*nasa'*, usually "lift up, carry, bear") appears in verses 7 and 13 with curious variations:

[7]If you do well, will you not be accepted?	הלוא אם־תיטיב שאת
[13]My punishment is greater than I can bear.	גדול עוני מנשא

The ESV acknowledges the difficulties with its alternative readings: for verse 7, "If you do well, will there not be a lifting up [of your face]?" and for verse 13, "My guilt is too great to bear." The existence of literary artistry in this chapter leads us to ask whether the author expected his readers to see a connection.

---

36. To clarify: I do not doubt that Old Testament prophecy does in fact foretell a divine Messiah, notably Isa. 9:6 (to name no others); so the question is only whether it is right to find it here.

37. For a similar use of syntactic ambiguity in Ruth 2:20, see C. John Collins, "Ambiguity and Theology in Ruth: Ruth 1:21 and 2:20," *Presbyterion* 19, no. 2 (1993): 97–102.

The answer appears to be no. The phrase in Genesis 4:7 is in the context of the question of verse 6, "Why has your face fallen?" Hence the likely "lifting" will be a lifting of the face—either applying the idiom "to lift the face, to accept" (ESV text), or perhaps in reference to a more cheerful expression on the face (ESV margin). It is difficult to decide, but in either case the idea is that God sees Cain's heart and invites him to change and improve.

The phrase in Genesis 4:13 uses נשא with a word denoting sin or iniquity—either in the sense "bear the guilt (away), forgive" (as in Exod. 34:7) or "bear the guilt (in one's experience), suffer punishment" (as in Exod. 28:43). Again, it is difficult to decide between these, but in either case it reflects badly on Cain: either he has despaired of forgiveness (even though God has shown him kindness), or he is complaining about God's severity, which fits better with what follows (Gen. 4:14, complaining), and God's mitigation (4:15). Either way, it reveals that Cain's heart is not what an Israelite should want for himself.

Again, I wonder if the ambiguity might not be intentional: the competent reader, in resolving the ambiguity, would see from several angles the tragedy of Cain.

3. Why was Cain's offering rejected?

Interpreters, ancient and modern, have offered quite a variety of explanations for why God rejected Cain's offering and accepted Abel's (Gen. 4:4–5). Josephus, for example, found the reason for the distinction in the things offered: "God was more pleased with [Abel's] offering, because he is honored by the things that grow of themselves and according to nature, but not by things forced from nature by the ingenuity of a covetous man" (*Antiquities* 1.54). Others have suggested that Abel's sacrifice involved blood, while Cain's did not. Some have pointed to the quality of the two offerings—Abel brought the first-born, while Cain brought only the fruit of the ground (not the best); and some have supposed that the fruit of the ground is bad because the ground was cursed. Still others have argued that the distinction lies in the heart attitudes of the two worshipers.

The first thing to notice is that the text does not *say* why God had regard for one offering and not the other, so if there is an answer, we must rely on showing rather than telling. Second, we must remember the audience: whenever this tale was first written, in its present form it serves as part of the front end of the Pentateuch, and this means that it assumes the validity of the various offerings described in Leviticus and Deuteronomy. Both kinds of sacrifice are valid, in this light: the offering of the firstborn (Deut. 15:19–23), a kind of peace offering, which the worshiper eats; and the produce offering (Lev. 2; Deut. 26:2), which feeds the priest alone. Thus we should not look to the type of offering to explain the distinction, for then we would conclude that the one who feeds himself with meat does better than the one who feeds the priests with grain! This will apply both to explanations like those of Josephus and to the "lack of blood" category.

These sacrifices were geared toward expressing consecration to God (produce offering) and fellowship with him (peace offering). But at no stage in Israel's life was the operation of a sacrifice automatic: the sacrifice is effectual only for those who will offer it with a believing and contrite heart, as the prophets had to point out all too frequently. Hence it is legitimate to look at what the narrative reveals about the hearts of the two worshipers. The literary-theological discussion below shows that the condition of Cain's heart is indeed the problem.

4. Where did Cain's wife come from?

Most readers of the Bible have heard the claim that they cannot believe Genesis because it says nothing of where Cain's wife (first mentioned in Gen. 4:17) came from. Others have found room for pre-Adamite hominids in order to harmonize Genesis and paleontology.[38]

The common reply is that the wife is a daughter of Adam and Eve, whose birth is not mentioned but left for us to infer.[39] This reply makes good sense of the text (note how Gen. 5:4 mentions "other sons and daughters"), as well as of the literary technique of the author, who tends to be laconic in style.

This is not the place to deal with objections to the accounts or with the validity of possible harmonizations with science and his-

38. For examples of such harmonizing, see the survey of David Livingstone, "Pre-adamites: The History of an Idea from Heresy to Orthodoxy," *Scottish Journal of Theology* 40 (1987): 41–66.

39. The inference that the first pair also had daughters from whom Cain could find a wife goes back at least as far as Josephus in the first century: after summarizing 4:1–2 he says (*Antiquities* 1.52), "Daughters also were born to them." Presumably this was a common interpretation in his day.

tory; I will take that up in chapter 10. The point here is that literary sensitivity allows us to say that the objection does not stem from a good reading and that the other-hominid harmonization ignores the purpose of the text, which is to describe the behavior of human beings without introducing extraneous issues.

5. What is the relation of Cain's lineage to Seth's?

Several of the names in Cain's genealogy (Gen. 4:17–22) are similar to names in Seth's (Gen. 5), and in the same order. These include the following:

Genesis 4:18		Genesis 5	
Enoch	חֲנוֹךְ	Enoch (18)	חֲנוֹךְ
Methushael	מְתוּשָׁאֵל	Methuselah (21)	מְתוּשֶׁלַח
Lamech	לֶמֶךְ	Lamech (25)	לֶמֶךְ

Of these, only the names Enoch and Lamech are identical. The similarities suggest to some that the genealogies are two versions of the same original. The question is unanswerable without the putative original, of course, so what shall we make of the text as it is now?

We note with Wenham that both lists give more information about Enoch and Lamech than they do about other members.[40] The likely result of this is contrast: the Enoch and Lamech who descend from Seth exhibit piety, while those in Cain's line do not.

And what is the literary effect of this? It leads us to note that the decline we see in Cain's family was not an inevitable outcome of being human; rather it flowed from the moral orientation of the members, which in turn is influenced by the orientation of the head member of the list. We might also suspect that the author saw the orientation of Cain's line as becoming dominant, and perhaps drawing Seth's descendants away from God, so that "the wickedness of man was great in the earth" (Gen. 6:5).

6. How does antediluvian culture fit in with archaeology?

Davis Young offered a discussion in 1995, in which he suggested that a "literal historical understanding of Genesis 4" raises serious

---

40. Wenham, 110.

questions about its historical value.[41] In particular, he concluded that "the biblical and archaeological evidence suggests that Adam and Eve did not live earlier than around 8000 B.C.," and "Genesis 4 seems to describe the cultural achievements associated with the Neolithic revolution, evidence of which is preserved in archaeological sites throughout the Near East." The features of Genesis 4 to which he referred include Cain as a farmer, and Abel as a shepherd; we have a permanent settlement (v. 17), and then, "within a few generations, the descendants of Cain were using musical instruments, working metal, and engaging in the nomadic herdsman lifestyle."

This presents problems for the historical value of Genesis 4, because "there is ample evidence that creatures indistinguishable from anatomically modern human beings occupied much of the world considerably prior to 10,000 years ago."

At this point I am not dealing with the historical value of this chapter, since I will take that up in chapter 10 along with the other pericopes. Rather, I will here examine whether Young is correctly seeing the "literal" reading of Genesis 4. I will simply note in passing the logical problems in Young's conclusions. (1) He is assuming that the archaeological record is so complete that we can be confident that our oldest *evidence* actually dates from the oldest *practice*, and this needs to be warranted. (2) He is assuming that Cain and Abel practiced just what the archaeological evidence suggests. (3) He is making no allowance for the possibility of decline followed by redis-covery, with the archaeological evidence being from the rediscovery period. (4) He is assuming that we can locate Cain and Abel by way of the evidence. The second point is the literary question that I will address.

Let us recall that the implied author of this account is Moses, and the implied audience is the generation that followed him out of Egypt. (The question of whether these are the real author and audi-ence can wait for chapter 8.) It looks like the manner of presentation in these chapters of Genesis is deliberately in terms of the audience's experience—which means that it will hardly be surprising to find anachronism. Further, as Cassuto points out, when 4:20–21 refers to a man as the father of those who practice a craft, it can have the sense that he was the "teacher and founder of the customs, practices and

---

41. Davis A. Young, "The Antiquity and the Unity of the Human Race Revisited," *Christian Scholars Review* 24, no. 4 (1995): 380–96.

ways of life of a given class."[42] Hence it is legitimate to suppose that this means that these men were pioneers in the skills that developed into what the audience would have known as the established crafts. We may apply the same approach to the accomplishments of Cain and Abel, recalling that historical reconstruction of the sort that we are interested in had little place in the author's intent. (There are two further difficulties in historical reconstruction: how far ahead in time the genealogy of verses 18–22 takes us, and whether all the descendants of Cain are thought to have died in the flood. We will take up the first of these in the following section; the second is beyond the scope of this commentary.)

Young's title for his study is an explicit reference to Benjamin Warfield's essay, "On the Antiquity and the Unity of the Human Race."[43] There Warfield had said, "The question of the antiquity of man has of itself no theological significance." Young was suspicious of this claim, but in view of the literary study here, Warfield appears to have been right and Young's qualms are ill-founded.

7. Do biblical genealogies have gaps?

What length of time does Genesis envision from Adam to the events that follow? Can we simply add up the figures for the successive generations? This question is especially acute in Genesis 5 and 11:10–26, which have specific numbers, but it also applies in this pericope. Consider 4:17–22:

> [17]Cain knew his wife, and she conceived and bore Enoch. When he built a city, he called the name of the city after the name of his son, Enoch. [18]To Enoch *was born* Irad, and Irad *fathered* Mehujael, and Mehujael *fathered* Methushael, and Methushael *fathered* Lamech. [19]And Lamech took two wives. The name of the one was Adah, and the name of the other Zillah. [20]Adah *bore* Jabal; he was the father of those who dwell in tents and have livestock. [21]His brother's name was Jubal; he was the father of all those who play the lyre and pipe.

---

42. Cassuto, 235. Cassuto has a similar explanation for the term *forger* (לטש, *lotesh*) in 4:22; see Collins, *Homonymous Verbs in Biblical Hebrew: An Investigation of the Role of Comparative Philology* (University of Liverpool, Ph.D. dissertation, 1988), 232–33 for sympathetic discussion.

43. Benjamin B. Warfield, "On the Antiquity and the Unity of the Human Race," *Princeton Theological Review* 9 (1911): 1–25; reprinted in Warfield, *Biblical and Theological Studies* (Philadelphia: Presbyterian and Reformed, 1968), 238–61, from which I cite it.

²²Zillah also *bore* Tubal-cain; he was the forger of all instruments of bronze and iron. The sister of Tubal-cain was Naamah.

It seems straightforward to read verse 17 as saying that Enoch was the immediate son of Cain and his wife—the language about "knowing," "conceiving," and "bearing" nails that down. And it also seems straightforward to take verses 19–22 as speaking of Lamech's immediate offspring by his two wives, again because the statement about "bearing" leads that way—although, as we discussed above, just how long after these boys the various skills arose is not stated.

Thus we are left with Genesis 4:18, and the important expression translated "A fathered B" (and its passive form "to A was born B"): does this imply immediately successive generations? Some have argued that this is in fact what Genesis means by this term,[44] while others have contended that it is part of the conventions of genealogies to allow gaps of unspecified length.[45] We can only answer this in the light of the conventions for genealogies, and thus we turn to the usages elsewhere.

Consider the formula found in Genesis 5, as rendered in the ESV:

When A had lived X years, he *fathered* B. A lived after *he fathered* B Y years and had other sons and daughters. Thus all the days of A were Z (= X + Y) years, and he died.

44. The most important essay from an Old Testament scholar is Gerhard Hasel, "The Meaning of the Chronogenealogies of Genesis 5 and 11," *Origins* 7, no. 2 (1980): 53–70, which argues that the genealogies do not have gaps, and therefore one purpose of them is to allow time computations. James Barr, *Fundamentalism* (Philadelphia: Westminster Press, 1978), 43–44, insists on this as the "literal" meaning of the words; unfortunately for Barr's case, this equivocates on the word *literal*, because the question is what the words mean *in the context of genealogies* (that is, in view of their conventions).

45. The most important essay in this category is William Henry Green, "Primeval Chronology," *Bibliotheca Sacra* 47 (1890): 285–303, repr. in Walter Kaiser, ed., *Classical Evangelical Essays in Old Testament Interpretation* (Grand Rapids: Baker, 1972), 13–28. Scholars of the ancient Near East who accept Green's conclusions include the following contributors to the *NBD*: Egyptologist Kenneth Kitchen ("Chronology of the Old Testament," see page 187b); Terence Mitchell of the British Museum and Alan Millard, professor of ancient Semitic languages ("Genealogy," see pages 400a–401a). See also Desmond Alexander, who has extensively studied the genealogies of Genesis, in "Genealogies, Seed, and the Compositional Unity of Genesis," *Tyndale Bulletin* 44, no. 2 (1993) at 262 n. 14. Note also K. A. Kitchen, *On the Reliability of the Old Testament* (Grand Rapids: Eerdmans, 2003), 439–43.

The NRSV, however, has a slightly different rendering for this formula:

> When A had lived X years, he *became the father of* B. A lived after *the birth of* B Y years and had other sons and daughters. Thus all the days of A were Z years; and he died.

The NRSV, in saying "after the birth of" in place of "after he fathered," makes the genealogy sound very clearly like a record of immediate descent, but it is inaccurate: the expression in Hebrew is (from Gen. 5:7):

after he fathered Enosh	אַחֲרֵי הוֹלִידוֹ אֶת־אֱנוֹשׁ

The active form of the verb (הוֹלִידוֹ [*hôlîdô*], Hiphil infinitive construct with subject suffix), together with the object marker (אֵת, *'et*) on the name, make the ESV rendering far superior. In other words, we must focus on the lexical semantics of the active forms of the verb ילד (*yalad*; Greek γεννάω) "to father, beget,"[46] using the biblical genealogies.

And what do we find? Matthew 1:8, part of the genealogy of Jesus, tells us, "Joram *fathered* Uzziah," but according to 2 Kings (which Matthew certainly knew), Joram fathered Ahaziah, who fathered Joash, who fathered Amaziah, who fathered Azariah (Uzziah): in other words, at least the Greek equivalent γεννάω can have the sense "fathered (through any number of intervening generations)."[47] Hence it does not appear that biblical genealogies necessarily have the purpose of listing every generation.

Other genealogies in the Bible show signs of being compressed.[48] Consider, for example, Exodus 6:16–20: Jochebed bore Moses to Amram, who was the son (בֵּן, *ben*) of Kohath, who was the son (בֵּן) of Levi (who was the son of Jacob)—that is, the genealogy lists four generations from Jacob to Moses. However, Kohath was born before Jacob took his family down to Egypt (Gen. 46:11). If the Israelites

---

46. Hasel, "The Meaning of the Chronogenealogies of Genesis 5 and 11," fails to address this crucial distinction.

47. It is well known that בֵּן [*ben*] and υἱός ("son") can easily mean "descendant."

48. Hasel, "The Meaning of the Chronogenealogies of Genesis 5 and 11," claims that the formula of Genesis 5 and 11 sets them apart from genealogies elsewhere, but he does not show how that means that therefore the other genealogies will follow different conventions.

spent 430 years in Egypt, as Exodus 12:40–41 claims, and if Moses was eighty at the time of the exodus (Exod. 7:7), then Kohath was born at least 350 years before Moses was. That would be far too long if Kohath was Moses' grandfather (the average Israelite lifespan was around the same as ours, Ps. 90:10—attributed to Moses—and my grandfathers were born fifty to fifty-five years before I was). Further, Kohath's descendants numbered 8,600 males over the age of one month (Num. 3:27–28), and 2,750 of them were between the ages of thirty and fifty (Num. 4:34–37)—just a month after the Israelites left Egypt (Num. 1:1). That is phenomenal fertility if Kohath was Moses' grandfather. (We would expect a number closer to one hundred.)

The solution becomes clear if we look at the genealogy of Joshua—who was something like forty years younger than Moses—in 1 Chronicles 7:23–27. Joshua was the son of Nun, who was the son of Elishama, who was the son of Ammihud, who was the son of Ladan, who was the son of Tahan, who was the son of Telah, who was the son of Resheph, who was the son of Rephah, who was the son of Beriah, who was the son of Ephraim (who was the son of Joseph, who was the son of Jacob). That gives twelve generations from Jacob to Joshua—and we cannot be sure if this is all of them, since only verse 23 is explicit about immediate descent.

This evidence is weighty, since 1 Chronicles 6:1–3 reproduces the genealogical list of Exodus—in other words, the author certainly knew Exodus, and we have no reason to suppose that he felt a tension between these two lists.[49] We are on sound footing, then, if we conclude that Moses' genealogy is compressed, or selective, giving representatives in the line of descent.[50]

A further indication that we have found a valid convention is the simple fact that no biblical author ever reckons up a length of time based on a genealogy.

From this we may conclude that if we use a biblical genealogy to compute a length of time, we are failing to cooperate with the kind

---

49. Barr, *Fundamentalism*, 46, appeals to the apparent discrepancy between the genealogy of Exod. 6:16–20 and the time in Egypt of Exod. 12:40–41, in support of separate sources. His argument only works if the genealogies' conventions *require* immediate descent, but the lists in 1 Chronicles, which surely reflect a native culture way of reading this material, lead to the conclusion that the conventions do *not* require Barr's reading.

50. Hasel, "The Meaning of the Chronogenealogies of Genesis 5 and 11," uses the odd term "discontinuous" for the feature that I am arguing for: it is odd because the list, as I read it, describes a continuous line of descent, without claiming to give every member of the line.

of communicative act that these genealogies perform. Their communicative purpose is to give the line of descent and to emphasize historical continuity. Here in Genesis they also serve to move the event line forward quickly, without stopping for details on particular figures.

If the genealogies allow gaps, then, is there any way to discover how many generations might be omitted and how much time is too much? I do not know of any study that has addressed this question, and it may be unanswerable.[51]

8. What does Genesis 4:26b mean?

The last clause of this pericope "has in it no unusual words and it presents no great problem in translation";[52] it has, nevertheless, presented a variety of difficulties to interpreters.

At that time *people began* [*it was begun*] to call upon the name of the LORD.	אז הוחל לקרא בשם יהוה

These difficulties have included questions over the meaning of הוחל (*hûkhal*, "it was begun"): some have taken it as "to profane," while others have emended the text to "he hoped," as in the Septuagint. Still other problems have to do with the sense of "call upon the name of the LORD": does that refer to public or private religion? And finally, this seems to present a basis for source criticism: here the J source has people knowing the name *the LORD*, while according to the E source (Exod. 3:14–15) and the P source (Exod. 6:3), it was Moses who introduced this name to Israel.

The solution comes from looking at the last question first: to contrast these sources lays a heavier stress on the word *name* than the Hebrew warrants. The Hebrew idiom "to call upon the name of" a deity means to invoke that deity in worship, without stressing the specific name by which the worshiper invokes the deity. "To call upon the name of the LORD" appears elsewhere in Genesis: 12:8; 13:4; 21:33; 26:25, where it is connected with altars and public worship.

51. As Kitchen, *On the Reliability of the Old Testament*, concludes (441), "As for the date of the creation, why waste time number-crunching when Gen. 1:1 says it all: 'In the beginning . . .'—which is soon enough."

52. Samuel Sandmel, "Genesis 4:26b," *Hebrew Union College Annual* 32 (1961): 19–29, at 19.

Thus Genesis 4:26 describes the "origin of regular divine worship"[53] and says nothing about the precise name used; this makes sense in view of the increasing population. The population increase explains as well why this would be the "beginning," since in verses 3–5 there was already sacrificial worship—but presumably not in as highly ordered a fashion as the number of worshipers would now require.

If we look at it this way, we find nothing one way or the other about sources (after all, Eve used the Lord's name in Gen. 4:1), but at least we do not have to conclude that this verse shows that the sources disagree. Further, we see how the traditional Masoretic Text is quite clear, and we lose all reason to correct it.

E. Literary-Theological Exposition

To discuss the participants in this pericope, we have to look at each of the episodes in their turn. In the first episode, Genesis 4:1–16, we have Adam and Eve, Abel and Cain, and then the Lord. In most of the verses only two actors are in view: Abel and Cain or Cain and the Lord. There are two conversations between Cain and the Lord, who takes the initiative in both: verses 6–7 and the longest subunit, verses 9–15.

The second episode, Genesis 4:17–24, consists of a genealogy, which mentions Cain and his descendants fathering successive sons, until we come to Lamech. Then in verses 19–24, Lamech is the chief actor, with his two wives contributing by bearing children, who became pioneers in various crafts: Adah bears in verse 20, while Zillah bears in verse 22. God is notably absent from these verses, except by allusion to his promise of vengeance for Cain (v. 24; compare v. 15).

In the final episode, Genesis 4:25–26, Adam, Eve, and Seth are the actors, albeit briefly. The pericope ends with the vague "people began" (literally, "it was begun").

We saw above that the paragraph structure is as follows:

4:1–16	Cain and Abel	
	4:1–2	the two boys born
	4:3–5	the two sacrifices
	4:6–7	God converses with Cain (first time)

53. Wenham, 116.

	4:8	Cain slays Abel
	4:9–15	God converses with Cain (second time)
	4:16	Cain departs
4:17–24	Cain's offspring	
	4:17–18	genealogy: from Cain to Lamech
	4:19–24	Lamech and his family
4:25–26	Seth	

It is difficult to identify an overall peak, given the loose connection between the episodes. Instead we may speak of subpeaks within the episodes.

The first episode has its peak at Genesis 4:10–12, where the Lord pronounces judgment on Cain in terms that remind us of 3:14, 17, which occurs in the peak of its pericope. This is God's reaction to the first murder and is the longest single speech in the episode. As God's opinion, it is of course especially weighty for the author and his audience. Further, its effects are enduring. An interesting touch is the way that Cain objects to the sentence in verses 13–14; as a result of this God displays his mercy on Cain by marking him.

The second episode has its peak at Genesis 4:23–24, the boastful song of Lamech. Here he addresses the other participants of this subunit, Adah and Zillah, and the speech is in high style, exhibiting parallelism.

If the third episode has a peak at all, it is Eve's speech in Genesis 4:25, "God has appointed me another offspring instead of Abel, for Cain killed him." This looks back to the rest of the pericope and forward to what follows in Genesis with its reference to the seed/offspring theme; also, by acknowledging that neither Abel nor Cain was the promised "offspring" of 3:15, it invites us to look beyond the immediate descendants of Adam and Eve.

We have already seen something of the time relationships between the episodes. The narrator has not specified whether the "knowing" and "bearing" of Genesis 4:1–2 took place before or after Adam and Eve disobeyed God: the verb *know* is in the perfect, which simply signals discontinuity (the same verb is *wayyiqtol* in verses 17 and 25). There is nothing in Genesis that would require us to think that either begetting or bearing children is in itself un-Edenic, so we will be content with the gap. The rest of the first episode proceeds in sequence; since I understand Genesis 3 to present the origin of human sinfulness and alienation, I take these events to be after the disobedience and expulsion. The second episode begins with Cain knowing his wife, and this may have followed his departure but need not have; since the *wayyiqtol* verb begins a new subunit, it can easily be taken as denoting a "pluperfect" (that is, it might have happened before 4:16).[54] The rest of the episode moves in sequence, although verses 17–18 move the clock very fast.[55] The third pericope apparently takes us back from the time of Lamech to Adam and Eve, and hence to somewhere contemporary with verse 17.[56]

If we see the time relationships in this way, then the causal dependence on Genesis 3 is clear. The alienation that had begun in Eden (3:8–13, Adam and Eve alienated from God and from each other) bears its fruit in the strain between Cain and Abel, in the absence of God among Cain's descendants, and in the violent overreaction of Lamech. We see further how men and women will experience the "pain" threatened in 3:16, 17: not simply in the activities of delivering children and working the soil but in the strife that accompanies them. At the same time, there was a word of hope in 3:15, regarding an offspring, and Eve echoes this hope in 4:25, "another offspring."

The genealogy of Genesis 5 takes up the family line of Seth (5:3, 6), but that does not mean that Cain's line is out of the picture. Though Genesis does not mention him again, the crafts his descendants pioneered (4:20–22)—caring for livestock, making music, and working in metals—all play a role in human culture.

We have already noted one of the main repetitions, where a man "knows his wife" and she "bears" a son (Gen. 4:1, 17, 25): this introduces each episode and points to the theme of descendants.

Another term that appears in all three episodes is the verb *kill* or *slay* (הָרַג, *harag*): Genesis 4:8 and 25 use the verb of Cain "killing"

54. In "The *Wayyiqtol* as 'Pluperfect': When and Why," *Tyndale Bulletin* 46, no. 1 (1995): 117–40, at 127–28, I argued for criteria by which we can legitimately appeal to *wayyiqtol* with a pluperfect interpretation. The third of these, "the verb begins a section or paragraph," meets the criteria set down by S. R. Driver, *Treatise on the Use of the Tenses in Hebrew* (Oxford: Clarendon, 1892), 84–88, which are more restrictive than mine.

55. However, the childbearing of Lamech's wives need not be strictly sequential: in 4:20 Adah *bore* (*wayyiqtol*), while in verse 22 it is "and as for Zillah, she too bore" (perfect). It is possible that the bearing took place around the same time; it is also possible that the perfect is there simply to keep us from thinking that Zillah did not bear until after Jubal (v. 21).

56. I say "apparently" because the genealogy does not specify length of time, as discussed in section C.7 above.

Abel; verses 14 and 15 refer to the possible "killing" of Cain; and in verse 23 Lamech boasts of having "killed" a man. The personal name Cain also appears in each of the episodes. All of this contributes to the impression that the disobedience of Genesis 3 has had catastrophic consequences, which is a major theme of this pericope.

The author displays his point of view in several ways. Certainly he considers the Lord's judgment to be decisive; thus the Lord's sentence in 4:11–12, and his disapproval of slaying—even if the victim is the manslayer Cain—display the author's position that such slaying is wrong, an invader of human life. The author does not tell us why the Lord had regard for Abel and his offering and not for Cain and his offering; instead we should be confident that the Lord is just and must have had a good reason. The author shows us that this confidence is warranted when he describes Cain's reaction.

The absence of any divine name in Genesis 4:17–24 illustrates the way that Cain "went away from the presence of the LORD" (v. 16). By quoting Lamech, who appeals to his pride and not at all to any moral principle,[57] the author allows us to draw our own conclusions. But we have already read about the origin of marriage, so the two wives are a deformation; and we have seen that slaying and vengeance come in to spoil the goodness of the original creation, so we can infer that the author wants us to disapprove of this man.

The speeches of Eve also convey something of the author's point of view. Her saying in verse 1, which the ESV renders "I have gotten a man with the help of the LORD," is ambiguous: grammatically it can mean, "I have gotten a man, *namely*, the LORD."[58] If anyone wonders if that was what Eve meant, he will quickly conclude, based on Cain's behavior, that if she did think it, she was wrong. Eve's saying in 4:25, "God has appointed for me another offspring instead of Abel, for Cain killed him," acknowledges the sin of Cain and the kindness of God. It also reflects her appropriation of the offspring promise of 3:15, though it does not say whether she thought that Seth was *the* offspring. There is no ambiguity here about the ultimate origin of the child: *God* has appointed him.

The characters who receive the most development are Eve, Cain, Lamech, and the Lord. We have already discussed Eve's progress from

57. Except maybe to the protection of Cain in an ironic contrast.
58. See discussion in section C.1 above.

the ambiguous verse 1 of Genesis 4 to the clear verse 25; we have also
seen how Lamech is presented. Let us turn to Cain and the Lord.

The author presents Cain as the first child begotten by and born of
human parents, and we would expect him to exhibit greatness. That
he was a "worker of the ground" is no obstacle to that: this is decent
work (compare Gen. 2:5, 15). There is nothing wrong with his offering, either, so far as biblical religion is concerned. Hence the fact that
God "had no regard" for his offering raises questions about what kind
of person he is, since God looks for a clean heart in his worshipers.
We then see Cain as resentful: instead of finding out what it was that
stood between him and God, he got angry, and rather than accept
God's kind offer (4:6–7), he harbored his anger and killed his brother.[59]
When God invites him to confess (v. 9, "Where is Abel your brother?"),
he lies instead and even brushes off the question ("Am I my brother's
keeper?"). But the Lord already knows what has happened and gives
his sentence, much as in Genesis 3. Unlike his parents, however, who
accepted the sentence, Cain actually objects to God's verdict with a
worry about his own safety. There is irony here: he had *killed* Abel (4:8,
הָרַג, *harag*), but he is afraid that someone will *kill* him (v. 14, הָרַג).
When the Lord shows him mercy by granting a protecting mark, Cain
goes "away from the presence of the LORD"; verses 17–24 show that
this departure is not a matter of place but of moral orientation. All of
this is tragic: both times when God addresses Cain (vv. 6–7, 10–12),
there is an offer of grace, if only Cain will accept it. Sadly, he does
not, and this brings ruin not only to his own life but also (and even
worse) to the lives of others: he kills his brother, inflicts grief on his
parents, and leaves offspring who seem to know nothing (or nothing
of any value) of their Maker and potential Redeemer.

We should note in passing that Cain and his offspring, even without
a living connection to God, nevertheless are human, in the image of
God: they develop such important skills as city building (Gen. 4:17),
managing livestock (v. 20), playing musical instruments (v. 21), and
forging tools from metal (v. 22). Even further, Lamech displays a rhetorical flair in his song (vv. 23–24); its artistry is as beautiful as its content
is repulsive. Again, this is tragic: these capacities can do great good if

---

59. If the true text in 4:8 includes Cain saying, "Let us go out into the field," then
the slaying was likely premeditated. Without this, we are left wondering: Did Cain plan it
or did he simply lose control over himself when they were alone together in the field? In
either case he nursed his grudge to the point of slaying.

directed to God-centered ends and great evil if used for selfish ends. In Cain's family, the author presents us primarily with the latter.

The portrait of God here develops what we saw in the previous chapter. In Genesis 4:6, God asks Cain why he is angry, but this does not imply ignorance on God's part, any more than his questions in 3:9–13 do. We can see this in several ways. First, the fact that there is nothing external about the sacrifices to explain why God had regard for Abel's and not for Cain's points us to something about their hearts; but for this to be true, God must know their hearts. Second, God speaks to Cain about the rewards of doing good and the danger of yielding to evil: a remedy for Cain's attitude is on offer here. Again, this must mean that God knows why Cain is angry. And finally, when God asks, "Where is Abel your brother?" in 4:9, he knows full well where Abel is, since his blood "is crying from the ground." Therefore we should consider these questions as God's invitations to Cain to reflect on his heart and his actions and to accept the offer of help. God further shows himself merciful in his sentence upon Cain: there is justice, to be sure, but it is gentle justice. Rather than executing Cain on the spot, he makes him a fugitive, who will be frustrated in his working the ground (v. 12); but this frustration could lead to repentance, if only Cain would receive it. Then Cain complains at the sentence, a just sentence tempered with mercy, and God would have been fully right to destroy Cain or at least to dismiss the complaint—but instead he offers protection! This is a big God; man's spurning of his mercy and sniveling complaints cannot deter God from his pursuit of his fallen human creatures. After the interlude of verses 17–24, we see that Adam and Eve have kept their faith and that God has shown himself faithful to his promise of 3:15.

All of this reinforces the confidence I expressed earlier: God is a reliable and trustworthy character in these narratives. This means that, whatever the reason might have been for distinguishing between Abel's offering and Cain's, it was not caprice.

What, then, is the communicative purpose of this pericope? We can say that our author wanted us to see what happened as a result of the first disobedience in Eden. This disobedience bore its fruit in the disordered lives of Adam and Eve's children. At the same time, the author wants his readers to know that the God who made the world continues in his gracious offer of mercy to his fallen creatures. In this way the pericope serves as a bridge from the pristine and idyllic conditions of Eden to the ordinary experience of mankind, which is so stained and corrupted with sin. The audience needs to know just why their experience is this way, what the remedy is, and what happens if someone turns down the remedy. There is no recourse to the excuse, "I did not sin like Adam"; no one in this chapter did, either, but they still carry forward the consequences of that first sin.

We can identify a number of covenantal principles in this chapter. The first is God's faithfulness and constant offer of mercy, as we have seen. The call to trust him, to embrace his covenant, and to live in repentance and obedience is grounded in God's character. The people who lay hold of his covenant have a right to a kind of optimism about God and the prospects of their lives if they are true to him. The passage also lays the groundwork for a deep distrust of human nature when it is cut loose from its moorings in its Creator and Redeemer. At the same time, it reminds us of the common humanity shared by all, and this means that it is possible to communicate with other kinds of people and that they all retain something of their origin—which includes a need for God.

The original relationship with Adam and Eve involved God's blessing through their offspring (Gen. 1:28). The redemptive covenant with Abraham also included the promise "to be God to you and to your offspring after you" (17:7). Of course, the ideal is that the offspring will grow up loving the Lord, and that they will learn this from their parents. Genesis makes this explicit in 18:19, where the Lord says of Abraham, "For I have chosen him, that he may command his children and his household after him to keep the way of the LORD by doing righteousness and justice, so that the LORD may bring to Abraham what he has promised him." Thus part of covenant faithfulness is the proper nurturing of faith and obedience in the children, and without this there is no prospect for covenant succession. The author never explains why Cain had his problems, but he leaves us to infer why Cain's offspring displayed nothing of a proper relationship to God: Cain went away from the presence of the Lord, and it seems that his children grew up without the Lord. Let not the people of Israel neglect their own duty!

In chapter 5 I argued that Genesis 2:24 supports faithful monogamous marriage as the ideal. Here in 4:19–24 we have a polygamous marriage, and there is nothing attractive in it. This is a recurring pattern in Old Testament presentations of polygamous marriages—they all bring misery.

God had differing reactions to the sacrifices that Abel and Cain brought. I argued above that God distinguished between the motives that each man had; this has a bearing on the view of sacrifice in the rest of the Bible. The worshiper must certainly observe the formal requirements for the sacrifice, but at the same time he must come in a spirit of faith and love toward the God of the covenant. This becomes a chief concern of the prophets.

Finally, we should note the way that Cain allowed his anger to grow, refusing even God's offer of help. The author of the Wisdom of Solomon put it this way (10:3 RSV):[60]

> But when an unrighteous man departed from her [Wisdom] in his
>   anger,
>   he perished because in rage he slew his brother.

The people of the covenant must be different; they have a way of dealing with their anger in the covenantal foundation of God's grace and mercy. Hence Jesus instructed his followers in Matthew 5:21–24:

> [21]You have heard that it was said to those of old, "You shall not murder; and whoever murders will be liable to judgment." [22]But I say to you that everyone who is angry with his brother will be liable to judgment; whoever insults his brother will be liable to the council; and whoever says, "You fool!" will be liable to the hell of fire. [23]So if you are offering your gift at the altar and there remember that your brother has something against you, [24]leave your gift there before the altar and go. First be reconciled to your brother, and then come and offer your gift.

This admonition never loses its relevance if the covenant people are to express the mercy and moral beauty of their God.

F. Other Reverberations

1. Sacrifice and offering

This account is the first mention of a sacrifice in the Pentateuch.[61] If, as I have argued above, the account here was composed with the rest of the Pentateuch in mind and with the generation that followed

---

60. For further references to Cain and Abel, see section F.3 below.

61. Some have appealed to 3:21, where the leather garments required that an animal be slain (note also the mention of "clothing"), as the first sacrifice. However, the text

Moses out of Egypt as the implied first audience, then it stands to reason that one purpose of this account is to pave the way for the sacrificial system of Leviticus. In particular, one function of this account would be to establish the antiquity of the practices—so that the detailed description of Leviticus might be seen as protecting the purity of the rites against the deviations brought in by human sin.[62] In other words, these regulations—which many in the Western world see as burdensome—actually have a humane purpose behind them!

As discussed above, the two offerings are recognizable parts of the Pentateuch system: Cain's is a type of grain offering, while Abel's is a type of peace offering. If the discussion of why God accepted Abel's offering and rejected Cain's is valid, then we also find here guidance for the proper use of sacrifice in the religion of the covenant people. A common failing of the people of Israel was their perversion of sacrifice: supposing that the mere external act of making it, apart from the worshipers' internal disposition of faith and piety, was enough to buy God's favor, or simply presuming on God's grace and favor. But this narrative reminds the people that God looks on the heart; the one who made everything hardly *needs* the offerings of his people—rather, he provides the arrangement for their benefit, that they might enjoy the covenant privileges of being his people.

Neither of these sacrifices is for the sake of "making atonement" (כפר, *kipper*); the first instance of one of these is Genesis 22, which describes a "burnt offering" (עולה, *'ôlâ*). That incident has the effect of bringing substitution right into the ideology of Israelite atonement offerings—compare Genesis 22:13, where Abraham offered the ram as a burnt offering "instead of" (תחת, *takhat*) his son.

2. The line of Seth

We have already noticed how Genesis 5:3 tells of the birth of Seth, returning to the narrative of 4:25. The genealogy that follows details the descendants of Seth, and we leave the family of Cain behind—unless the "daughters of man" in 6:2, 4 were from Cain,

---

says nothing about it, nor does it use any special vocabulary that directs our attention to the question.

62. This is similar to the likely implication of the heavenly lights being appointed "for signs and for seasons, and for days and years" (Gen. 1:14): these markers serve the liturgical calendar of the covenant people. Preserving an ancient tradition from the distortion that comes from transmission is a value commended in Plato's *Timaeus* 22–23.

while the "sons of God" were from Seth (a question outside our scope here). The offspring of Seth feature as well in the postflood genealogies (Gen. 10–11); compare also 1 Chronicles 1:1, Sirach 49:16, and Luke 3:38.[63]

3. Later reflections on Cain and Abel

Outside of Genesis 4, Cain is mentioned in Wisdom of Solomon 10:3 (not by name) and 4 Maccabees 18:11; and in the New Testament, Hebrews 11:4, Jude 11, and 1 John 3:12. Abel is mentioned in 4 Maccabees 18:11, Matthew 23:35 (see also Luke 11:51), Hebrews 11:4 and 12:24, and 1 John 3:12 (not by name).

Of these, the mention in 4 Maccabees is only incidental: the Cain and Abel story is simply a representative event in the Pentateuch. Jude 11 uses "the way of Cain" as a paradigm of those who are unfaithful to the covenant.

The others are more interesting and represent a way of reading the story that lines up with that discussed above. For example, Wisdom of Solomon 10:3 (RSV) describes Cain without naming him:

> But when an unrighteous man departed from her [from Wisdom]
>   in his anger,
>   he perished because in rage he slew his brother.

Wisdom in this book is connected to the saving presence of God, and Cain "went away from the presence of the Lord" (Gen. 4:16), which the author of Wisdom of Solomon takes to be abandoning wisdom, and rightly so (see the literary-theological exposition above).

In 1 John 3:12 we find the two brothers, again used paradigmatically: "We should not be like Cain, who was of the evil one and murdered his brother. And why did he murder him? Because his own deeds were evil and his brother's righteous." John has read between the lines, and done so in a way consistent with the reading above. Cain *showed* himself to have an evil heart by his actions; we may infer that Abel's deeds were righteous, reflecting a pious heart, from the way that God had regard for his sacrifice. Interestingly enough, John's terminology of evil and righteous (πονηρός and δίκαιος), which

---

63. As Sir. 49:16 put it (using the Hebrew), "Shem and Seth and Enosh were honored, and above every living creature is the glory of Adam" (cf. NRSV), Seth joins the most prominent of men.

does not appear in Genesis, is similar to what Josephus, his near contemporary, said of the two: Abel "had respect for righteousness" (δικαιοσύνης ἐπεμελεῖτο), while Cain was "very evil" (πονηρότατος).[64]

Hebrews 11:4 describes Abel as one who "by faith . . . offered to God a more acceptable sacrifice than Cain, through which he was commended as righteous, God commending him by accepting his gifts." Again, this is a legitimate inference from the narrative.

Finally, several texts refer to the "blood of Abel" as that of an innocent victim, which cries for justice: Hebrews 12:24 and Matthew 23:35 (Luke 11:51). These are probably taking their start from Genesis 4:10, "The voice of your brother's blood is crying to me from the ground."

Claus Westermann agrees that Genesis presents Cain and Abel as two individuals but disagrees with the moral evaluation of them found in these reverberations. He argues instead:[65]

> Its [that is, Jewish and New Testament] presupposition that fits Cain and Abel into the contrast-pattern of the just one and the malefactor is not derived from the text; the exegesis proposed here has shown that we cannot support it.
>
> In contrast to the traditional explanation, the narrative sounds quite a different note when Cain is not presumed to be the villain, the malefactor "whose works are evil," but is regarded positively right up to the sacrifice. Cain's crime is his decision to do away with his brother and his execution of it. And so Abel is no longer to be described as the just one. As his very name indicates [Hebrew *hebel* = "breath, vapor"], he is no more than the victim of rivalry in a competition which belongs to human existence as a community of brothers. The Bible at the very beginning includes crime under human existence, and so the possibility of murder. Cain became the outcast, Abel the victim. Before that they were both men like anybody else.

Westermann's conclusion contrasts sharply with what I have found here, and the difference stems from the interpretive approach to the text—that is, from a different view of what we may call "derived from the text." It is true that the narrator does not distinguish the two men morally until he tells us that their sacrifices were regarded differently (Gen. 4:4b–5a). But the very fact that the sacrifices met

64. Josephus, *Antiquities* 1.53.
65. Westermann, 317–20.

different receptions is itself evidence that the two men were in fact morally distinct *prior* to offering the sacrifices. We see further that Cain refuses God's patient offers of help—again, this implies something about his heart. The traditional reading, of course, assumes that there is no reason to believe that murder was intrinsic to the human condition by creation; when the first parents of humanity opened the door to sin by their own disobedience, all manner of other sins came rushing through the crack. Hence the admonition (v. 7) that one must "rule over" sin and its temptation becomes the remedy all mankind must resort to (finding God's help to do so, of course).

It therefore appears that, contrary to Westermann, a literary reading of this chapter commends the tradition that we find in Wisdom of Solomon, Josephus, and the New Testament.

4. Matthew 18:22

Lamech's poetic boast in Genesis 4:23–24 is breathtaking in its arrogance and ferocity: to repay death for a wound or a blow is far beyond justice, and in this light the "seventy-sevenfold" figure is an understatement for extravagant excess. This then provides a proper background for interpreting a statement of Jesus (Matt. 18:22). Consider Genesis 4:23 in the Septuagint:

Ὅτι ἑπτάκις ἐκδεδίκηται ἐκ Καιν,	For Cain's revenge is sevenfold,
ἐκ δὲ Λαμεχ ἑβδομηκοντάκις ἑπτά.	but Lamech's is seventy-sevenfold.

In contrast, consider Matthew 18:21–22:[66] "Then Peter came up and said to him, 'Lord, how often will my brother sin against me, and I forgive him? As many as seven times?' Jesus said to him, 'I do not say to you seven times, but *seventy seven times* [ἑβδομηκοντάκις ἑπτά].' " The evocation is hard to question, and what is its intended effect? Surely it is to encourage those who follow Jesus to practice the same extravagant excess, but this time of forgiveness. That is, just as it would be foolish to take Lamech's "seventy-sevenfold" as a literal measure, so it would be foolish to take Jesus' "seventy seven times" as imposing any limit on forgiveness.

---

66. For ἑβδομηκοντάκις ἑπτά I follow the ESV margin (compare BDAG 269b), though the ESV text, "seventy times seven," is also possible. Either way, the point is not the exact number but the extravagance.

5. Cain in Romans 7?

N. T. Wright has suggested that Paul has "the same kind of allusion to Cain in Romans 7.13–25 as to Adam in 7.7–12, and with the same kind of intent."[67] Now, this is tied to Wright's argument that the "I" in Romans 7:7–12 is Israel as the people who recapitulate the sin of Adam, and evaluating that question is beyond my scope here. Wright offers nine reasons that lead him to his conclusion. Rather than list and assess them here, it is enough simply to show why I find his case unconvincing.

First, Wright acknowledges that there are no real verbal echoes, and this makes for a steep hill to climb.[68] The closest he comes is the fact that Cain says, "I do not know" (οὐ γινώσκω, Gen. 4:9), while Paul says, "I do not know what I am doing" (ὃ γὰρ κατεργάζομαι οὐ γινώσκω, Rom. 7:15), but the Greek parallel is surely accidental. Contrary to Wright, Cain's reply is not "professed ignorance as to what he has done" but an answer to God's question, "Where is Abel your brother?"

Second, Wright takes up the question of Cain's offering being unacceptable: "If the suggestion of my previous chapter [on Rom. 8:3 *concerning sin*] is correct, Paul's matching of the death of Christ, seen as the perfect sin-offering, with the plight described in [Rom.] 7.13–20 means that 'Cain' has at last found an acceptable sacrifice." Unfortunately, this completely overlooks the kind of offering that Cain brought, which is not a propitiatory one—that is, it serves a different purpose than the sin offering.[69] It further overlooks the reason why God rejected the offering.

To argue, then, that Paul expected his readers to catch an allusion to Cain in Romans 7 is quite unwarranted. If a particular exegesis of that text—Wright's or someone else's—then allows us to discern a principle that Cain also instantiates, then it is possible to say that, but this is not the same as allusion and takes us away from exegesis.

---

67. N. T. Wright, *The Climax of the Covenant* (Minneapolis: Fortress, 1992), 226–30 (quoted from 229).

68. Wright, *Climax*, 228 n. 11 on Gen. 4:7 and Rom. 7:21, acknowledges "the fact that there are no obvious verbal echoes in the Greek." See also his discussion on page 226, addressing the question, "How submerged does a reference have to be before it drowns altogether?"

69. I agree with Wright that the sin offering does likely underlie Rom. 8:3, περὶ ἁμαρτίας.

8

Sources, Unity, and Authorship

Until some time in the late eighteenth century, readers of Genesis simply took it as the work of Moses after he had led the people of Israel out of Egypt. But things have changed since then; as Richard Elliott Friedman put it,[1] "For centuries, scholars from many backgrounds have worked on discovering *how the Bible came to be*." Primarily, this means reconstructing the way the final editor handled his sources: knitting them together, modifying them, and imposing unity. There are debates over what kinds of sources these might be: previous documents, orally transmitted stories, an author's free composition, and so on. The dominant theories today are versions of the Documentary Hypothesis associated with Julius Wellhausen, which we will discuss below.

Just what is at stake in this discussion, and what should we hope to get out of it? As I have indicated already, often what motivates this kind of study is the desire to explain a text by explaining the process by which it came into its present form. Scholars suppose that if we can isolate the constituent sources, we might be able to say what their communicative purposes were.[2]

1. Richard Elliott Friedman, *The Bible with Sources Revealed: A New View into the Five Books of Moses* (New York: HarperCollins, 2003), 1 (emphasis added).
2. For example, consider the following studies that focus on the Priestly source: Sean McEvenue, *The Narrative Style of the Priestly Writer* (Rome: Biblical Institute

221

Often what is lacking is a clear notion of what the communicative purpose of the new whole is, but this need not be inherent in the method. An example of someone who accepts the results of the Documentary Hypothesis is Leon Kass, and he wrote, in regard to the accounts in Genesis 1 and 2, which he takes as two creation accounts of separate origin:[3]

> Once we recognize the independence of the two creation stories, we are compelled to adopt a critical principle of reading if we mean to understand each story on its own terms. We must scrupulously avoid reading into the second story any facts or notions taken from the first, and vice versa. . . . Only after we have read and interpreted each story entirely on its own should we try to integrate the two disparate teachings. By proceeding in this way, *we will discover why these two separate and divergent accounts have been juxtaposed and how they function to convey a coherent, noncontradictory teaching about human life.*

(I should note, however, that the exegetical chapters above find a much higher level of consistency between the accounts than Kass does—indeed, I do not agree to call them separate *creation* accounts, but more on this below.)

Nor does identifying sources *of itself* oppose Mosaic authorship; indeed, in the early days of source criticism, the goal was to locate the sources that Moses compiled to form the Pentateuch. Mature forms of the Documentary Hypothesis, however, do reject Mosaic authorship: that is because they posit sources that date much later than Moses' own time.

Press, 1971); Walter Brueggemann, "The Kerygma of the Priestly Writers," *Zeitschrift für die alttestamentliche Wissenschaft* 84 (1972): 397–414; Sue Boorer, "The Kerygmatic Intention of the Priestly Writer," *Australian Biblical Review* 25 (1977): 12–20; John S. Kselman, "The Recovery of Poetic Fragments from the Pentateuchal Priestly Source," *Journal of Biblical Literature* 97 (1978): 161–73; Ralph W. Klein, "The Message of P," in *Die Botschaft und die Boten: Festschrift für Hans Walter Wolff zum 70. Geburtstag* ed. J. Jeremias and L. Perlitt (Neukirchen-Vluyn: Neukirchener, 1981), 57–66; Walter Wifall, "God's Accession Year according to P," *Biblica* 62 (1981): 527–34; Meir Paran, *Forms of the Priestly Style in the Pentateuch: Patterns, Linguistic Usages, Syntactic Structures* (Jerusalem: Magnes, 1989) [Hebrew with English summary]; Jean Louis Ska, "De la relative indépendence de l'écrit sacerdotal," *Biblica* 76 (1995): 396–415; Edwin Firmage, "Genesis 1 and the Priestly Agenda," *Journal for the Study of the Old Testament* 82 (1999): 97–114.

3. Leon Kass, *The Beginning of Wisdom: Reading Genesis* (New York: Free Press, 2003), 56 (emphasis added).

We have not yet looked into matters of historicity: that is, whether the text makes historical truth claims, and by what hermeneutic we can discern them, and what historical truth values the text has. This will be the topic of chapter 10. For the present, however, we can at least note that the existence of sources is not in itself fatal to historicity; that must depend on the nature of the sources themselves and the process by which the editor(s) unified them. On the other hand, we must acknowledge that most practitioners of source criticism do believe that their results cast doubts on the historical quality of the Pentateuch narratives. This is because the sources are deemed to be much later than the events described, written for specific agendas that are ideological rather than historical, and the sources are discerned by means of their contradictions and repetitions.[4] In fact, as we shall see below, the statement from Friedman with which I began this chapter needs some adjustment. If we wish to describe how scholarship has actually proceeded, we cannot simply say that "scholars . . . have worked on discovering how the Bible came to be"; we must acknowledge that they have sought to perfect a *naturalistic* account of how the Bible came to be. Small wonder, then, that religious traditionalists have opposed them.

There are alternative theories to both simple Mosaic authorship and the Documentary Hypothesis: for example, one may deny that one or more of the conventional sources ever existed as a document. Another alternative—a radical one to be sure—is that of R. N. Whybray, who analyzes and rejects conventional source criticism in favor of the idea that a single author, probably in the sixth century B.C. (the time of the Babylonian exile), produced what we know as the Pentateuch by combining preexisting folk traditions, songs, laws, perhaps some documents, and his own invention, in such a way that the sources are virtually unrecoverable:[5]

> The Pentateuch, then, it may be suggested, is an outstanding but characteristic example of the work of an ancient historian. . . . He had at his disposal a mass of material, most of which may have been

4. Compare, for example, S. R. Driver, *The Book of Genesis* (Westminster Commentaries; London: Methuen, 1904), xxxi-lxi: the Priestly document has no historical value, and it is very difficult to tell what value the Yahwist and the Elohist have.

5. R. N. Whybray, *The Making of the Pentateuch: A Methodological Study* (Journal for the Study of the Old Testament Supplement 53; Sheffield: Sheffield Academic Press, 1989), 242. His model of such a historian is the Greek Herodotus (c. 484–425 B.C.).

of quite recent origin and had not necessarily formed part of any ancient Israelite tradition. Following the canons of the historiography of his time, he radically reworked this material, probably with substantial additions of his own invention, making no attempt to produce a smooth narrative free from inconsistencies, contradictions and unevennesses. Judged by the standards of ancient historiography, his work stands out as a literary masterpiece.

(Whybray is impressed with the literary unity revealed by such studies as those of Robert Alter.)

Duane Garrett begins his 1991 book, *Rethinking Genesis*, with an obituary for conventional source criticism:[6]

The time has long passed for scholars of every theological persuasion to recognize that the Graf-Wellhausen theory, as a starting point for continued research, is dead. The Documentary Hypothesis and the arguments that support it have been effectively demolished by scholars from many different theological perspectives and areas of expertise. Even so, the ghost of Wellhausen hovers over Old Testament studies and symposiums like a thick fog. . . . One wonders if we will ever return to the day when discussions of Genesis will not be stilted by interminable references to P and J. There are indications that such a day is coming. Many scholars are exploring the inadequacies of the Documentary Hypothesis and looking toward new models for explaining the Pentateuch.

Garrett's obituary is probably premature; in 2003 *The Bible with Sources Revealed*, by Richard Elliott Friedman, appeared, vigorously defending his version of the Documentary Hypothesis and deriding those who have claimed that the hypothesis has been overthrown.[7] He contends that such critics have never responded to the "classic and current arguments that made the Documentary Hypothesis the central model of the field";[8] hence he proceeds to lay these out and show how they yield results for the entire Pentateuch.

The present commentary has a very limited scope with respect to the entire Pentateuch, and hence it is not feasible to examine the

6. Duane Garrett, *Rethinking Genesis: The Sources and Authorship of the First Book of the Pentateuch* (Grand Rapids: Baker, 1991), 13. One of those whom he cites as "looking toward new models" is Whybray.

7. Such claimants may be very conservative, such as Garrett (not named in the bibliography), or very radical, such as Whybray (who is named).

8. Friedman, *The Bible with Sources Revealed*, 1.

question of its origin and unity in exhaustive detail. However, in light of Friedman's presentation, we should set out the arguments (section A) and assess how well they work for our chapters in the light of both the literary studies here (section B) and the ancient Near Eastern background (section C).

A. Summary of Friedman's Documentary Hypothesis and His Arguments

Friedman contends that the Pentateuch as we know it developed through several stages.[9] First, the document known as J (for *Yahweh*, "the LORD," written *Jahwe* in German) was composed in the southern kingdom, Judah, somewhere between 922 and 722 B.C. (that is, during the divided kingdoms). During the same period the document known as E (for *Elohim*, "God") was written in the northern kingdom, Israel. It covers some of the same topics as J does, but its author believed that no one knew the proper divine name until God revealed it to Moses (Exod. 3:15; 6:3).

Some time after the northern kingdom fell (722 B.C.), someone compiled a history of the people of Israel using these two sources; this is called JE, and its compiler is RJE (redactor of J and E).

Soon after RJE, the Jerusalem priesthood produced the document known as P (for Priestly), as an alternative story to that of JE. The P stories overlap with those of JE and agree with E on when the divine name was revealed.

The last main source is D (for Deuteronomy). D is part of a larger work, called the Deuteronomistic History (including Deuteronomy, Joshua, Judges, Samuel, and Kings); the Deuteronomistic History

> contains sources that are as old as J and E or possibly even older, but the formation of the work took place in the reign of King Josiah of Judah, circa 622 BCE. It was later expanded into a slightly longer second edition; this took place during the exile that followed the destruction of the southern kingdom of Judah by Babylon in 587 BCE.

An unknown redactor (called R) put all of these together.

9. I am following Friedman, *The Bible with Sources Revealed*, 3–6 for the theory, and 7–31 for the arguments. I have simplified in places.

There are some differences between Friedman's version and some others that are called Documentary Hypotheses: for example, many think that P is last, written during the exile, or even later. However, Friedman accepts the results of such linguistic researchers as Avi Hurvitz, who argued that the language of P predates that of Ezekiel and is thus preexilic.

Another difference is in the extent of the sources. A century ago, S. R. Driver wrote of the Hexateuch (Genesis through Joshua), but Friedman contends that J comprises parts of Joshua, Judges, Samuel, and 1 Kings 1–2. He accepts, as Driver did, that P extends into Joshua, and we have already seen his view of the Deuteronomistic History.

According to Friedman, there are seven arguments for this hypothesis of Pentateuch origin (not all of them will come into play in Gen. 1–4).

The first is the date of the *language*: J and E represent the earliest stage of Biblical Hebrew, while P is later, and D is later still. All of them come from before the postexilic period.

Second is *terminology*: sources prefer identifiable terms, such as "be fruitful and multiply" (P).

The third argument is *consistent content*: the sources differ in when, for example, the divine name was revealed, and P lacks "blatant anthropomorphisms."[10] P is the source that is most concerned with things like ages, dates, measurements, and so on.

Fourth, we find *continuity of texts*: "When the sources are separated from one another, we can read each source as a flowing, sensible text."

The fifth argument is *connections with other parts of the Bible*: "The individual sources each have affinities with particular portions of the Bible." For example, Jeremiah has much in common with D, as does Ezekiel with P, Hosea with J and E, and the court history (most of 2 Samuel) with J.

Sixth, there are the *relationships among the sources, to each other and to history*: that is, the sources reflect the concerns of the groups in which they were putatively produced. Hence J is oriented to Judah, E to Israel.

10. Ibid., 12. This is a conventional characterization of P; compare Driver, *Book of Genesis*, xxv: "Anthropomorphic expressions are indeed in general either avoided by P, or reduced to those harmless figures without which it is hardly possible to speak of God at all."

Finally, there is *convergence*: "Several different lines of evidence converge," that is, give consistent results for the sources. Friedman considers this the most compelling of all. This allows him, for example, to account for the doublets, that is, for the occasions in which the same thing is given twice, supposedly from different sources (such as the two creation stories, one from P and the other from J; the two genealogies from Adam, one from J and the other from P).

B. Assessment of the Literary Details of Genesis 1–4

As I have already said, I cannot here carry out a full analysis of Friedman's (or anyone else's) case for the entire Pentateuch. I will instead focus on what we found in our chapters, to see if these arguments work for them. Friedman provides his color-coded translation of the books, with notes, and thus we can follow him very easily.

We begin by noting that, according to Friedman, Genesis 1:1–2:3 comes from P. He tells us, "The deity is mentioned thirty-five times in the creation account and in every case called 'God' (Hebrew: Elohim), never by the name YHWH." Then 2:4a, "These are the generations of the heavens and the earth when they were created," comes from R, the final redactor of the Pentateuch. "The Redactor derived the formula ['these are the generations'] from a text that was originally an independent work, The Book of Records (*toledot*), which begins at Gen. 5:1."[11]

Starting at Genesis 2:4b and running through 4:26, we have material from J, with a few additions from R. The most notable addition is the word *God* in the composite divine name: according to the theory, the J source originally had only "the LORD," and R added "God" each time after "the LORD." "It therefore appears to be an effort by the Redactor (R) to soften the transition from the P creation, which uses only 'God' (thirty-five times), to the coming J stories, which will use only the name YHWH." The other addition from R is 4:25–26a, describing the birth of Seth and Enosh. (The notice in 4:26b, "At that time people began to call upon the name of the LORD," belongs to J.) This conclusion follows from the view that

11. The Book of Records is taken to be a document separate from the other sources, "used by the Redactor to form a logical framework for the combined sources in Genesis."

The J genealogy traces Adam's line through Cain alone and mentions no other surviving children. The Book of Records [Gen. 5] genealogy traces Adam's line through Seth and never mentions Cain or Abel. The Redactor added this line [4:25–26a] explaining that Seth was born to Adam and Eve, thus reconciling the two sources.

We can recognize the distinction between P and J because of the differences in their material. For example, at 2:4b:

> The P creation story begins with "the skies and the earth" (1:1) whereas the J story begins here [at 2:4b] with "earth and skies," reversing the order. This is not a proof of anything, but it is notable because, from their very first words, the sources each reflect their perspectives. P is more heaven-centered, almost a picture from the sky looking down, while J is more human-centered (and certainly more anthropomorphic), more like a picture from the earth looking up.

Then at 2:23: "The order of creation in Gen. 1–2:3 (P) is first plants, then animals, then man and woman; but in the creation account in Gen. 2:4b–24 (J) the order is man, then plants, then animals, then woman."

Two other factors deserve our attention. The first has to do with the genealogy from Cain (4:17–24, J) and that from Seth (Gen. 5, the Book of Records): the fact that some names are the same or similar, while others are different, indicates that they both probably derive from "a common, more ancient source."

Then at 4:26b ("At that time people began to call upon the name of the LORD"): "Here the J narrative declares unequivocally that invoking the divine name YHWH began in this early generation of humans on earth. According to E and P, this does not begin until the time of Moses."

I have presented this picture from the work of Friedman, and if I had used S. R. Driver, some of the details would have been different. For example, Driver conceived of 2:4a as part of P, 4:25–26 as part of J, and Genesis 5 as part of P. He agreed, however, on the other points I have cited.[12]

These source-critical conclusions—whether Friedman's, or Driver's, or someone else's—run contrary to the literary and grammatical observations I have already made on the text.

---

12. He also shared the older perspective that P was the latest stratum.

To begin with, we have already seen in chapter 3 that the formula "these are the generations of" structures Genesis by indicating a new stage in the development of the plot. Genesis 1:1–2:3 stands outside this structure as a prologue; hence, I concluded, it is not surprising that its narrative style, which is exalted and formulaic, is different from that of the rest of the book, which is more like what we find in the rest of the Old Testament narrative books. The purpose of the prologue is to insist that there is one God who is the Maker and Ruler of all that there is, and that he made mankind in his image; to fulfill this purpose it must of course stress the divine transcendence. Thus there is no surprise that the author would use "God" for such a function.

Further, we saw that the structure of Genesis 2:4 argues against dividing the verse. There is a header ("these are the generations of") that marks this as a part of the main plot; then there is an elaborate chiasmus that unites the two pericopes (1:1–2:3 and 2:4–25), inviting us to read them harmoniously. The shift in divine name identifies the cosmic Creator with the covenant God of Israel—an astonishing privilege indeed to be his people! Friedman is probably not far off in his observation about the unusual divine name, "The Lord God," in 2:4–3:24, though I would not use quite his words. Rather than say it "softens the transition from the P creation," I would say that by blending the two names it makes the identity clear and allows the transition to using one or the other.

These observations about the parts of Genesis 2:4 also show that, whatever their original sources, the parts now function as a literary whole, and thus the sources are unrecoverable. This literary whole invites us to read the two pericopes in a complementary way, and if we do this we can, without any grammatical innovation, read 2:5–6 as giving the setting of the event of 2:7, referring not to the "earth" but to the "land" ("region"). Since the days are God's workdays and thus need not be the ordinary kind, we can find in here evidence that the six workdays were longer than an ordinary week, and thus that 2:5–25 is an elaboration on the event of 1:26–28.

This means that we should not call these two creation account*s*: there is one big-picture creation account, followed by a close-up on the way God created them "male and female."

It also means that we can resolve all the apparent discrepancies in order of events: Genesis 2:5–6 does not refer to the *creation* of plants but to the growing of plants in a particular place, "the land," according to the annual climate cycle. Further, 2:8–9 also refers to a specific place, the garden. And we also can, within the rules of grammar, harmonize 2:19 (the making of animals) with the sixth day of Genesis 1.

We have also seen that the assertion that the P account lacks anthropomorphisms is mistaken: the first pericope actually depends on an anthropomorphic presentation, where God is a craftsman going through his workweek, taking his rest each evening, and then enjoying his Sabbath. This merges with the anthropomorphic presentation of the second pericope, in which God "forms" the man like a potter and "builds" the woman. Further, we have already seen that, while the first pericope certainly does emphasize God's transcendence, it is far from presenting him as distant or aloof. In fact it invites us to enter into aspects of God's own experience, and to imitate his model.

In my examination of Genesis 4, I found that there is no way to prove that the genealogy of 4:17–22 has any common origin with that of Genesis 5 and that we can easily make sense of the text as it now stands. The literary effect of the similarities—and they are small anyhow—is to contrast the members of the two lineages.

It is also hard to see why we should separate Genesis 4:25–26a from the rest of the chapter. It follows the structure of the pericope (a man knew his wife and she bore a son), and Eve names the son in both verses 1 and 25, with the name being significant. The different rationales for the names seem as well to indicate a development in Eve's character. The mention of an "offspring" also links up with a major key word in Genesis.

The last item from Friedman's list is Genesis 4:26b, "At that time people began to call upon the name of the LORD." To find this as a reference to the name *the LORD* is a linguistic failure, because it lays more stress on the word *name* than the idiom involved warrants. This makes the verse neutral on when anyone knew the true God as "the LORD."

One's position on this depends in the final analysis on how one reads Exodus 6:3, "I appeared to Abraham, to Isaac, and to Jacob, as God Almighty [*El Shaddai*], but by my name the LORD [*Yahweh*] I did not make myself known to them." It is possible that this simply implies that the patriarchs did not know the name, but if this is so, then the final editor would surely have seen this as clearly as any modern. We should suppose that if he was intelligent—which he gives evidence of having been—he might possibly have retrojected the divine name into Genesis, expecting competent readers to catch the retrojection, using this verse as the key.[13] But it is also possible that when the verse says "by my name," it means "by the full implications of my name," in which case 6:2–8 unfolds the implications of the name. And it is also possible that, rather than "by my name the LORD I did not make myself known to them," the clause is better rendered "by my name the LORD did I not make myself known to them?"[14] Genesis 4:26b does not decide between these options.

These are the arguments of Friedman. In the course of our studies in the pericopes, we have also encountered other proposals for literary history, such as Westermann's view that 3:14–19 is a later addition and that 3:23 was originally independent of 3:22, 24 (see footnote on Gen. 3:23). I have given literary reasons for opposing such views.

Where does this leave us? Do these pericopes come from separate sources or not? There is no way to answer this question, since the putative sources no longer exist. But for each feature that is put forward to support the source theory, it turns out that literary and grammatical considerations supply a better explanation in terms of the overall flow of the narrative. In other words, if someone produced this text by stitching sources together, he left the seams smooth indeed.

Now it is true that this only applies to four chapters of Genesis, and not to the whole Pentateuch. Other discourse-oriented studies have had similar results, as in the flood story.[15] We would perhaps need to take each pericope on its own before we could make an overall statement, but there is background information from ancient Near Eastern history and literature that helps us to see our way forward.

13. This would be an anachronism, but it is in keeping with what we find in the Pentateuch: olden days are described in terms of the experience of the audience.

14. For discussion and bibliography on these options, see A. R. Millard, "Abraham, Akenaten, Moses, and Monotheism," in *He Swore an Oath: Biblical Themes from Genesis 12–50*, ed. R. S. Hess et al. (Grand Rapids: Baker, 1994), 119–29, at 124–25. Millard's point is that Egyptian evidence shows that we should not rule out the last two options summarily.

15. See, for example, the following works of Robert Longacre: "The Discourse Structure of the Flood Narrative," in *Society of Biblical Literature 1976 Seminar Papers*, ed. G. MacRae (Missoula: Scholars, 1976), 235–62; "Interpreting Biblical Stories," in *Discourse and Literature*, ed. Teun A. van Dijk (Amsterdam/Philadelphia: John Benjamins, 1985), 169–85; *Joseph: A Story of Divine Providence* (Winona Lake: Eisenbrauns, 2003).

C. Assessment from Ancient Near Eastern Background

Kenneth Kitchen, an Egyptologist, has compiled a long and impressive list of details to show that the Pentateuch fits into the milieu of the late second millennium B.C. (that is, the time of Moses): in its points of contact with the literature of the Near East, in its historical and geographical references, and in its covenant structure.[16] He shows, in a lively and at times feisty way, why the biblical picture of a Moses educated in Egypt (somewhere around 1260 B.C.) as the primary author of the Pentateuch is the best explanation of what we find when we compare the books with well-established conclusions (he calls them "facts," chiding biblical scholars for ignorance of them) from scholars of ancient Egypt, Mesopotamia, and Anatolia. There are a few difficulties that remain, such as the Hebrew seeming to be later than the time of Moses and a few notes that reflect a later editor. The best explanation for these is that "copies of older works such as Deuteronomy or Joshua would be recopied, modernizing outdated grammatical forms and spellings, a process universal in the ancient Near East during the period from 2500 [B.C.] to Greco-Roman times."[17] In this process of modernization older names might be replaced or glossed with the current names.

Since it would take a whole book to support these conclusions, and since Kitchen has already written that book, I will simply summarize a few of the main points. Let us begin with the time of the exodus.

Kitchen draws on the work of Greta Hort, who showed that the plagues in Egypt match known phenomena—though he does not

16. K. A. Kitchen, *On the Reliability of the Old Testament* (Grand Rapids: Eerdmans, 2003); chapters 6, 7, and 9 deal with the exodus, the patriarchs, and the proto-history, from which the quotations that follow are taken. James Barr, *Fundamentalism* (Philadelphia: Westminster Press, 1978), 130–31, dismisses Kitchen's earlier work because Kitchen claims not to appeal to a theological starting point and thus may be called "objectivist," and because Kitchen's work "so fully breathes the spirit of total fundamentalism." It may be that there is an edge to Kitchen's arguments, but (1) he defends his position against postmodernism in the preface to this new work; (2) the complaints are unfair to the breadth and detail of Kitchen's researches and arguments; and (3) simply identifying undue influences on someone (from Barr's perspective) hardly in itself undercuts the truthfulness of his case, which must be decided on its own merits. In the same way Friedman mentions Kitchen by name in his essay "Some Recent Non-Arguments concerning the Documentary Hypothesis," in *Texts, Temples, and Traditions: A Tribute to Menahem Haran*, ed. Michael V. Fox et al. (Winona Lake: Eisenbrauns, 1996), 87–101, at 88 n. 2, but he pays no mind to anything that Kitchen actually wrote.

17. Quoted from Kitchen, *On the Reliability of the Old Testament*, 305.

share her naturalistic explanation of the final one, the death of the firstborn, since he does not rule out miracle.[18] He shows that "the account of the plagues in Exodus 7–12 is a well-formulated unity. And, as some traditional critics already admit, it cannot meaningfully be split up between imaginary sources such as J, E, or P (for which no physical manuscripts exist) without making a nonsense out of the account of the plagues that only works as a unity." He also shows that the plagues narrative presents a literary pattern, with the first nine plagues grouped in threes and the tenth standing out on its own for emphasis. This pattern also argues against sources.

The name *Raamses* (Exod. 1:11) corresponds to a known Egyptian dynasty, to the town of *Pi-Ramesse*, and to the building activity of Raamses II. This is significant because "Pi-Ramesse was abandoned as a royal residence circa 1130 [B.C.]." A tradition originating later than this time would have used a different place name, such as Tanis (compare Ps. 78:12, from the Iron Age). "If Raamses (as opposed to Zoan, Tanis) had never previously been part of *early* Hebrew tradition, there would have been no cause to look for it or incorporate it later. . . . Thus the occurrence of Raamses is an early (thirteenth/twelfth century) marker in the exodus tradition, and that fact must be accepted." The tabernacle shrine and ritual also fit the Late Bronze Age, and not later.

Next we turn to the covenant form used. Kitchen has compiled a typology of the treaty, law, and covenant forms from the ancient Near East, showing how they were distinctive of particular periods: archaic treaties (2500–2300 B.C.); early law codes (2100–1700 B.C.); early treaties (1800–1700 B.C.); intermediate treaties (1600–1400 B.C.); middle treaties and covenant (1400–1200 B.C.); and late treaties (900–650 B.C.). "It is vitally important to understand that the documents of each phase are sharply different in format and full content from those in the phases before and after them. There is no ambiguity." After close analysis, he concludes, "Sinai and its two renewals—especially the version in Deuteronomy—belong squarely within phase V, within 1400–1200 [B.C.]." A later writer would not have been likely to be so accurate.[19]

18. For comments on the metaphysics of these plagues, see my discussion in *The God of Miracles: An Exegetical Examination of God's Action in the World* (Wheaton: Crossway, 2000), 130–31.
19. We may add to this the conclusion of Chaim Rabin, "Discourse Analysis and the Dating of Deuteronomy," in *Interpreting the Hebrew Bible*, ed. J. A. Emerton and S. C. Reif

Finally, in regard to the exodus, there is the question of whether that generation of Israel could have produced such literary material. As Kitchen puts it, "How could brickfield slaves produce international-format documents?" Not even private citizens would have had access to the skills needed for the job: "Their only role was to hear the content of a treaty . . . and obey through their own ruler." We have a candidate ready to hand: "somebody distressingly like that old 'hero' of Biblical tradition, Moses, is badly needed at this point, to make any sense of the situation as we have it. . . . On the basis of the series of features in Exodus to Deuteronomy that belong to the late second millennium *and not later* [Kitchen's italics], there is, again, no other viable option."

There is more, but let us move on to Genesis 1–11. The tales from this part of the Bible have analogies in literature from Mesopotamia (dealing with creation, the beginning of cities, the flood, and so on), all of which were composed in the period 2000–1600 B.C. (This is not the same as saying that Genesis derives from these, or vice versa: "the differences are so numerous as to preclude either the Mesopotamian or Genesis accounts having been copied directly from the other.") Such tales were no longer composed after 1600, and thus "it is logical to suppose that the framework and basic content of Gen. [1–]11 goes back to the patriarchal period"—although, as I have argued here, its manner of telling is specially suited to its place in the current Pentateuch.

D. Conclusions

And that is where we will leave this discussion. A simple way to summarize it is that the evidence favors an origin for Deuteronomy in the time of Moses, though updated in the ways mentioned. The rest of the Pentateuch is surely best explained as the front end of Deuteronomy, as Friedman's version of the Documentary Hypothesis sees; Genesis is best explained as the front end to Exodus (answering the "why us?" question); and Genesis 1–11 is best explained as the front end of the whole Pentateuch. (See chapter 3 above.) At each

---

(Cambridge: Cambridge University Press, 1982), 171–77: the rhetorical style of Deuteronomy does not match that of the great writing prophets, since it lacks their poetry, and therefore it must come from an earlier time when such a register was permissible for a great prophet.

stage of the way the content reflects the second millennium milieu of Moses far better than the first millennium of the Davidic monarchy and later. We cannot say that there were no sources—indeed, why should we doubt that Genesis 1–11 comes from such—but we are in a good position to say that whatever the process of stitching together, it shows high literary skill, producing a coherent whole; at least Genesis 1–4 displays such coherence. We also need not doubt that Moses is the primary author of the Pentateuch as we have it.[20]

20. Gordon Wenham, *Story as Torah* (Grand Rapids: Baker, 2000), 41, notes that "the Mosaic era certainly accounts for many of the key features in Genesis." In the face of observations from "critical orthodoxy," he argues (42) "none of these observations are problems for a date in the united monarchy period" (David and Solomon). None of these factors come into play for our pericopes, however, and we need not doubt that Genesis is substantially from Moses.

9

THE COMMUNICATIVE PURPOSE
OF GENESIS 1—4

I n the communication model I described in chapter 2, we have
an author operating on a picture of the world shared between
himself and his audience to produce an effect (called the *message*).
We can talk responsibly about an authorial intention as the effect
the author wanted to produce in his audience—the ways he wanted
them to respond to his text.

In my discussions of the four pericopes I have drawn conclusions
about the meanings of the texts along these lines. I do not believe that
the message from the author to the very first audience necessarily
exhausts the meaning, but I do think that is the right place to start.

In these final three chapters I intend to draw these various threads
together. This chapter will focus on the immediate communicative
situation of Genesis; the next chapter will look into questions of history and science, to see what claims are embedded in the intention
of the text; and the final chapter will look at how today's audience
should appropriate these messages.

In this chapter I will focus on different aspects of the context in
which these chapters first came. I will first consider the ideological
context, namely, how Genesis 1–4 relates to creation stories from
elsewhere in the ancient Near East. Then I will examine the literary

context, namely how the message of Genesis 1–4 fits into the whole of the Pentateuch. And finally I will consider the life setting of the audience: How will these chapters impact their approach to life in Israel?

A. In Reference to Ancient Near Eastern Background

It is well known that Genesis is not the only tale of origins from the ancient world. Indeed, many peoples around the globe have origin stories, and the questions they address are virtually universal: How did the world and man come about, and for what purpose, and how does our group fit into the whole? In particular, creation and flood stories from Mesopotamia have been discovered over the past 150 years, and many think that these are the best parallels to the Genesis stories. Comparable tales from Egypt do not seem to be promising parallels or influences on the biblical stories.[1] There are bits and pieces from Ugarit, and these may provide hints to the ideological background of the biblical stories, to the extent that they describe the beliefs of the Canaanites proper.[2]

If my focus were on how the text came to be, I would need to consider whether these other stories and ideas *influenced* the biblical material as sources. But since I am interested in how the text functions as an act of communication, the history of composition fades from view. On the other hand, these stories do provide the ideological background against which the biblical narrative speaks; they may even provide some literary conventions and motifs.

1. R. J. Clifford and John J. Collins, "Introduction: The Theology of Creation Traditions," in *Creation in the Biblical Traditions*, ed. R. J. Clifford and John J. Collins (Catholic Biblical Quarterly Monograph Series 24; Washington, D.C.: Catholic Biblical Association of America, 1992), 1–15, at 2.

2. It is common to suppose that Ugaritic and Canaanite are interchangeable, but Ugarit is outside the actual bounds of Canaan, as shown in A. R. Millard, "The Canaanites," in *Peoples of Old Testament Times*, ed. D. J. Wiseman (Oxford: Clarendon Press, 1973), 29–52. Millard argues (36) that it is best to distinguish Ugaritic language and literature from Canaanite. Certainly they overlapped considerably, but it is better to use the specific name Ugaritic and not to prejudice the matter at any given point. Note also A. F. Rainey, "A Canaanite at Ugarit," *Israel Exploration Journal* 13 (1963): 43–45, who cites evidence from Ugarit that shows that Canaanites were there regarded as foreigners: "Perhaps we should henceforth refrain from calling the people of Ugarit Canaanites since they did not consider themselves as such" (45).

According to Kitchen there are four examples of "primeval proto-history" from the ancient Near East: Genesis 1–11; the Sumerian King List (c. eighteenth century B.C.; lists dynasties before and after the flood); the Atrahasis Epic (c. eighteenth century B.C., possibly earlier); and the Sumerian Flood Tale (or Eridu Genesis; c. 1600 B.C.).[3] Kitchen compares their content using this chart (with "modern times" being the beginning of the second millennium B.C.):

Sumerian King List	Atrahasis Epic	Eridu Genesis	Genesis 1–11
1. Creation assumed; kingship came down from heaven	1. Creation assumed; gods create humans to do their work	1. Creation; cities are instituted	1. Creation (1–2)
2. Series of eight kings in five cities	2. Noisy humans alienate deities	2. [Alienation]	2. Alienation (3), genealogies (4–5)
3. The flood	3. The flood; ark	3. The flood; ark	3. The flood; ark (6–9)
4. Kingship again; dynasties follow to—	4. New start	4. New start	4. New start; then genealogies, down to—
5. "Modern times"	(5. Modern times, implied)	(5. Modern times, implied)	5. "Modern times"

We may add to this the story of Adapa from Mesopotamia, a man to whom many compare the biblical Adam.[4] In this story, Adapa was one day fishing in the Persian Gulf when the south wind suddenly overturned his boat. Adapa cursed the wind, breaking one of its wings so that it could not blow for seven days. Hence Anu, the sky god, summoned Adapa to give account for himself, but before Adapa went, the god Ea instructed him on how to conduct himself and warned him that

3. K. A. Kitchen, *On the Reliability of the Old Testament* (Grand Rapids: Eerdmans, 2003), 423–27.

4. Alexander Heidel, *The Babylonian Genesis: The Story of Creation* (Chicago: University of Chicago Press, 1951), gives a translation of the text at 147–53; he summarizes the story and compares it with Gen. 3 at 122–26, denying that the Adapa story is the Babylonian account of the fall.

in heaven they will offer him the food and water of death, which he must not eat or drink. Adapa followed Ea's instructions and found favor with Anu, who decided to offer him the food and water of life—which would have conferred immortality. But Adapa refused and went back to live among mankind, apparently bringing illness to those among whom he lived. (Perhaps Adapa was in some sense a representative of mankind, or at least of his own region.) There are serious differences between this tale and Genesis 3, to be sure, and we will mention a few below, but the two stories do bear some resemblance.

Because of these similar structures we should agree with Kitchen and see the Mesopotamian tales as the literary analogues of the biblical one.[5] This does not mean that we will find no reference to Egyptian and west Semitic themes in the details, of course—though, as a matter of fact, the explicit references to west Semitic tales occur in other texts besides ours.[6]

The chief problem with this proposed background is the question of whether the audience would have been familiar enough with the ideas for the allusions to have any force; and it appears that we can say yes. To begin with, the Mesopotamian origin of the family line of Israel is standard fare in the Bible (compare Gen. 11:31; 15:7; Josh. 24:2–3; Neh. 9:7), so it is fair to suppose that stories like the Mesopotamian ones could have been handed down over the generations. Second, in view of the discussion in chapter 8, we have in Moses someone whose education would have made him familiar with the actual texts; and third, the texts themselves had become known among the western Semites, perhaps in oral form, in the Amarna period (a century or so before Moses, by Kitchen's reckoning).[7]

The biblical account shows both similarities with, and differences from, the Mesopotamian tales. Both of these show the connection between the two kinds of account: the similarities show that Gen-

5. The fact that Kitchen, an Egyptologist, sees it this way is helpful, especially since we encounter strong claims of Egyptian influence on the creation story, such as Currid, 43–51 (with bibliography). Further, the Mosaic origin of the Pentateuch, for which Kitchen has made such a compelling case (see chapter 8), would lead us to expect Egyptian parallels. However, the literary milieu of the primeval proto-histories that Kitchen documents shows why we should find the closest parallels in Mesopotamia—although, of course, we may certainly find specific points of contact with other ideologies as well.

6. See, for example, Heidel, *Babylonian Genesis*, 102–14. For a possible exception, see below.

7. See W. G. Lambert, "A New Look at the Babylonian Background of Genesis," *Journal of Theological Studies* n.s. 16, no. 2 (1965): 287–300, at 299.

esis is discussing the same events, while the differences show the different worldviews behind the accounts.[8] For example, some of the Mesopotamian accounts say that man was made from clay combined with a divine element (such as blood of a god, or flesh and blood of a god, or a god's spittle), while Genesis 2:7 has man formed from mud into which God breathed.[9] Both groups of stories have a dark and watery beginning. In both kinds the creation leads to divine rest, but in Mesopotamia this is because the gods made man in order to relieve themselves of the need to work, while the Bible does not depict God as one who depends on his creatures for sustenance—his rest is that of enjoyment and blessing.

If Genesis echoes the Adapa story, these too are different: Adapa had a chance to gain immortality for himself and mankind (of whom he was *not* the first), but he missed it out of obedience to instructions given him by a god, while Adam *fell* from his pristine state of moral purity and life by disobeying God's command. The flood stories tell of quite similar events, but the ideologies behind them are strikingly different: in Mesopotamia the gods send the flood because they cannot stand the noise that humans make, while in the Bible God sends it for moral reasons.

A possible exception to the lack of references to western Semitic material is "the great *sea creatures*" (תַנִּינִם, *tannînîm*) of Genesis 1:21: the cognate term in Ugaritic refers to an aquatic "dragon" that fights the gods, but here in Genesis they are simply creations of the one God,[10] and under his blessing. Many commentators suppose that the strange references to the sun and moon in Genesis 1:16—they are called the "greater light" and the "lesser light" rather than their normal Hebrew names—serve the purpose of demoting the luminaries from being deities to being "nameless objects designed by the Creator God to serve humanity."[11] In chapter 4, section D, I argued

8. A handy summary can be found in A. R. Millard, "A New Babylonian 'Genesis' Story," *Tyndale Bulletin* 18 (1967): 3–18, at 15–18; see also Heidel, *Babylonian Genesis*, 82–140.

9. Millard, "A New Babylonian 'Genesis' Story," 15, points out that such a concept is widespread, being found in Egypt and China. Consider also the Stoic Epictetus (first century A.D.), *Discourses* 1.3.3: "On the one hand the body, which we have in common with the brutes, and on the other, reason and intelligence, which we have in common with the gods."

10. Heidel, *Babylonian Genesis*, 104, reads Gen. 1:21 as referring to "such sea monsters as the whale and the shark."

11. Waltke, 63.

that this unusual naming is more likely an aspect of the rhetorically high style of the narrative; after all, apart from God and man, hardly anything gets its usual name in Genesis 1.

So what shall we make of the relationship between Genesis 1–11 and the Mesopotamian stories? In what is now regarded as a classic essay, Gerhard Hasel described some of the differences between the biblical and Mesopotamian creation stories and concluded that the biblical one is actually a *polemic* against the pagan view.[12] Although the differences mentioned above support this general position, we must note with Cassuto:[13]

> The purpose of the Torah in this section [Gen. 1:1–2:3] is to teach us that the whole world and all that it contains were created by the word of One God, according to His will, which operates without restraint. It is thus opposed to the concepts current among the peoples of the ancient East who were Israel's neighbours; and in some respects it is also in conflict with certain ideas that had already found their way into the ranks of our [Israelite] people. The language, however, is tranquil, undisturbed by polemic or dispute; the controversial note is heard indirectly, as it were, through the deliberate, quiet utterances of Scripture, which sets the opposing views at nought by silence or by subtle hint.

Rather than call it a *polemic*, then, we may take the Genesis narrative as an *alternative story* to those in Mesopotamia—a story whose purpose is to shape Israel's view of God, the world, and mankind, and their place in it all. As Kitchen concluded:[14]

> Gen. 1–11 is the Hebrew answer on how to present "prehistory/ protohistory" before the time of their first fully "historical" people, the patriarchs Abraham to Jacob. Again, the approach they adopted was common to their neighbors, using the same basic tools and concepts of that time: the succession of human generations, and how to span them. Mesopotamia chose to expand "heroically" the too-few reigns available. The Hebrew genealogies became telescoped through time, keeping a representative number. . . .

12. Gerhard F. Hasel, "The Polemic Nature of the Genesis Cosmology," *Evangelical Quarterly* 46 (1974): 81–102.

13. Cassuto, 7.

14. Kitchen, *On the Reliability of the Old Testament*, 447.

Genesis connects this story with the one true and living God—that is to say, Genesis is offering the true story of mankind's past. Even if the Mesopotamian tradition got the broad structure "right," Genesis corrects many of the details; but even more, it provides the true interpretation of these events. This is crucial because the Pentateuch sees the call of Abram and the Mosaic covenant as the key to the rest of the world coming to enjoy God's blessing; and these events are rooted in the prehistory and spiritual condition of mankind.[15]

B. In Reference to the Pentateuch as a Whole

In chapter 3, I considered the role of Genesis 1–4 in relation to its literary context in the Pentateuch. I suggested that Genesis 1–11 sets the stage for the mission of Israel to live as God's treasured people and thereby to be the vehicle of blessing to the rest of the world. There is one God, who made all that there is and who made man in his own image (Gen. 1); he entered into a special relationship with the first human beings, a relationship that was broken (Gen. 2–3). Mankind began to spread over all the earth (Gen. 4–5). The stories of the flood and the tower of Babel have similar import: all mankind is accountable to the one God who made them (and not to any fancy

15. I have limited this discussion to the world shared between the author and his first audience. It would be valuable as well to consider the process by which it was received, especially as Greek-speaking authors compared these chapters of Genesis with other sophisticated stories, such as Plato's *Timaeus*. The points of contact between the Septuagint of Genesis and the *Timaeus* are striking: for example, the notion of one God who is maker of the world; the idea of a beginning for the cosmos (*Timaeus* 28B); the use of ποιέω (with γίνομαι as its passive) for the work of creation (*Timaeus* 28BC); the world being καλός, "good" (*Timaeus* 29A); the reference to ζῷα, "living creatures" (*Timaeus* 69C); the use of πλάσσω for "forming" man's body (*Timaeus* 42D); the origin of woman from man (*Timaeus* 91A). Perhaps the Septuagint translators chose their Greek words with the parallels in mind—though in most cases they used the right Greek words for the Hebrew. Of course there are significant differences as well. Genesis is a simple tale, while the *Timaeus* is quite philosophical; Genesis describes creation from nothing, the *Timaeus* does not; Genesis describes mankind made for relationship with God and with each other, and sees woman as man's companion who shares with him the image of God, while the *Timaeus* focuses on other concerns (man as knower), and sees woman as coming from cowardly men. But in view of these points of contact, it was perhaps inevitable that Christian theologians would try to mesh the two as a way of commending their faith and of developing their philosophical theology.

of their own devising), and God is fully capable of bringing his judgment down on any people anywhere. But judgment is really only the backcloth: all mankind belongs to him, and the Pentateuch focuses on God's merciful and persistent efforts at recovering not just one ethnic group but the whole of mankind.

But now let us consider how Genesis 1–4 lays down a worldview that undergirds the religion of the Pentateuch.

The first aspect of that worldview is God the Creator. In these chapters God introduces himself, telling his people and the rest of mankind the most basic things they need to know in order to live well. If he is the Creator of all things, then he alone is self-sufficient: everything that is not God derives its being from him and depends on him for continued existence. Therefore he alone is the proper object of worship and adoration. As the Creator, he has done more than simply get the whole world started: he is personal and therefore relational, and he has impressed his personal qualities on mankind, that they might know and love him.

God made a good world as the arena for man to live out his relationship with his Maker. Though mankind has fallen, the goodness of the creation remains, and it remains the arena for man's life—but now it is the arena for redemption. The ordinary activities of life, such as eating, working, procreating, and breathing, are *good*. Any pain that man finds in these stems not from badness of the activities but from the sinfulness of man. Physical ordinances are a fitting means for God to work out his purposes for his people: he ordains sacrifices, beautiful garments for his priests, and an elaborate shrine for corporate worship, with "smells and bells" in the liturgy. The people use their bodies, bowing, kneeling, prostrating themselves, raising hands, and so forth, in their acts of worship.

Indeed, the three main festivals of the liturgical calendar are connected with the agricultural calendar: Passover with the barley harvest, Pentecost with the wheat harvest and the first fruits, and Tabernacles (or Booths) with the autumn fruit harvest. It is no contradiction, however, that they are also connected with events in redemptive history: Passover with the exodus from Egypt, Tabernacles with the wandering in the wilderness, and—later, anyhow—Pentecost with the giving of the law at Sinai. The God who created is the same God who redeemed Israel and made a covenant with her, and faithful adherence to the covenant enables God's people to enjoy the creation.

Further, God's position as Creator gives him the right to regulate how his covenant partners use his creation, whether that be in the clean and unclean laws, or when sex is fitting for married couples, or how they are to give work and rest to the land and their animals.

This creational perspective also allows Israel to see God's moral demands in their proper light: they restore man to his right functioning and express the goodness and generosity of the Creator every bit as much as the redemptive rituals do.

The second aspect of that worldview is the need for redemption. The first parents of mankind fell, and God promised them a Deliverer (Gen. 3:15) and guarded the tree of life from them, with the implication that the covenant ordinances (sacrifices, etc.) were the way back to "Eden." Genesis 4 shows how this family began life outside the garden—and how sin, once unleashed, began to run its course among mankind. The religion of the Pentateuch is shot through with provisions for redemption, because this answers to man's need.

This redemptive feature of the Pentateuch ought to instill the people of Israel with a spirit of gratitude, with glad embrace of all its promises and requirements. Adam earned for himself and his descendants death, and yet God in his mercy has offered a way of life. Israel is just one ethnic group out of all mankind, with no greater claim than any other, and the same need as all; and God has appointed them to privilege, that they might be the channel of his blessing to the rest of mankind. They ought never to take this for granted.

This leads to a further aspect of the worldview: God is Maker, Possessor, and Ruler of the whole world and is not limited by any of the creation. He is equally powerful in Egypt and Mesopotamia as he is in Canaan. And the people who live in faraway places are just as accountable to him as are the people of Israel, and they have just as much need of his love and grace.

Finally, these chapters of Genesis show why history must be a part of the religion of Israel. God created man as a bodily being, which means he lives in space and time: he experiences the world sequentially—historically—and learns from his experiences. God, who is personal, made man for relationships—with himself and with each other; and he furthers his relationship with his people through history. God will make and keep promises to the patriarchs and to their offspring, bringing them down to Egypt and out from there; he reveals his faithfulness in the process. Indeed, the Ten Commandments begin with a historical statement, laying a gracious foundation for obedience: "I am the LORD your God, who brought you out of the land of Egypt, out of the house of slavery."

C. In Reference to Life in Israel

These chapters prepare the people of Israel for their lives inside the land of Israel (and outside, by implication).

For example, most of them will work the ground and herd livestock. They must begin by seeing this as an exercise of dominion, no matter how much pain is involved. These people would already have been familiar with the features of the world around them, such as: if they want barley, they must plant barley seeds; land animals are typically small creepy-crawlies, larger wild game or predators, or the ones you can domesticate. Certainly the first pericope does not aim to provide this as information; rather, its function is to place these various categories of experience in their proper context—things work this way because the one Creator designed them to do so.

The second pericope especially emphasizes humans in relationship with their Maker (the Lord God). The Creator has lavished all manner of good gifts upon them: good trees, work to do, companionship, and role relationships. The text depicts humanity in its pristine condition, with no lack, no barrier to their felicity in God, and no motivation for disobedience.

Any Israelite who read Genesis 1–2 would certainly ask why his or her life reflected so little of these things. Genesis 3 provides the explanation, and the curses of 3:16–19 describe what these people were familiar with. The function of these chapters would be to foster an intense inward ache, a yearning for restoration—which then would move the heart to lay hold of the covenant.

The people of Israel would also find in here a doctrine of covenant inclusion: namely, that God can establish his covenant with a *people* by way of a representative. He had done so through Adam and then again through Abram. The representative functions of Moses, the priests, and other leaders (including eventually kings) then make sense in this light. Further, each individual is a member of the people, which has implications: his or her own spiritual vitality derives from the vitality of the whole people and at the same time contributes to that vitality. Remembering the history of God's dealings with his people—which is usually corporate in its emphasis—therefore becomes a matter of personal importance, which motivates covenantal faithfulness. The individual is also prepared to see himself as part of a larger story as well: the Pentateuch holds out the promise of a day when the Gentiles would be ushered into God's light, and the individual is dignified with the opportunity to participate in that great project.

10

GENESIS 1–4, HISTORY, AND SCIENCE

In the previous chapter I argued that the factor of history is a basic part of the worldview and religion of the Pentateuch. In this chapter we will explore this matter more fully, so that we may decide to what extent we can responsibly appropriate the Pentateuch as Scripture.

First, we must clarify some preliminary distinctions and definitions. In particular, we must be clear on just what words such as "history" and "historical" mean; we must further distinguish between what we may call "historical truth *claims*" and "historical truth *value*."[1]

In ordinary English, to say that a story is historical is to say that we believe that its events actually took place. So if we say that an author has written history, we mean that he wants us to believe that his narrative relates things that really happened. The more professional or sophisticated the historian, the more he will try to show the way that events are causally related to one another. In modern times we have come to elevate scientific history, which often implies a neutral historian who only appeals to immanent causes—that is, never appealing to the supernatural to explain events. From this

---

1. These ideas are deeply indebted to V. Philips Long, *The Art of Biblical History* (Grand Rapids: Zondervan, 1994).

perspective, the ancient world has left us with nothing like scientific history, since its authors are partisan and refer to gods extensively.

The notion of scientific history suffers from serious philosophical problems: for example, historians are not neutral; and if we exclude supernatural causes from our descriptions, we must either show that they are not relevant or else be willing to leave gaps in our causal explanations. For this reason, we cannot equate scientific history with true history, unless we wish to give up on both.

In this work I am sticking with the ordinary language definition of "history."

Now we can distinguish between truth *claims* and truth *values*. The notion is simple and intuitive: a narrative can be historical in the sense that its author wants us to believe that its events really happened; it makes historical truth claims. But sometimes we say that a narrative is historical if we are confident that its events really did happen: we are focusing on its historical truth value.[2] To move from truth claim to truth value implies that we have some criterion for verifying a claim. What kinds of criteria make sense? Some only allow truth value to those events that we can verify by physical means, though they may be willing to allow corroboration from other historians. But this is an impoverished epistemology, because it leaves no place for the testimony of reliable witnesses. I have told my wife and children the story that explains why there is a wide scar on my left knee; they have no way to verify it, and they might find it difficult to track down those who were present when the events happened and who can corroborate or correct my story. Should they disbelieve me? Only if they have reason to doubt my memory or motives—which they do not. They are rational, and thus they believe me.

But what if we are unsure of how reliable the witness is—at least in this particular case? There is a kind of external verification that can help us, namely, the way the story comports with other things we have a right to believe. We further should consider how good a record the witness has in other stories that we have been able to verify.

Now we may also state the basic hermeneutical implication of these definitions and distinctions: to say that an account is historical does not settle every question of how we should correlate its

2. Compare Mark G. Brett, "Motives and Intentions in Genesis 1," *Journal of Theological Studies* n.s. 42, no. 1 (1991): 1–16, at 12 n. 25: "Clearly, one can grasp an author's point without being persuaded by it."

statements with the way *we* would describe things, since we have to take into account the communicative purpose of the text we are considering. In particular:

(1) "Historical" in this sense is not the same as "prose," and certainly does not imply that our account has no figurative or imaginative elements.

(2) "Historical" is not the same as "complete in detail" or "free from ideological bias," neither of which is possible.

(3) "Historical" is not the same as "told in exact chronological sequence" unless the text claims that for itself.

For example, Psalm 105:26–38 retells the story of the plagues in Egypt, but it tells them in a different order from that in Exodus, and it does not tell about all of the plagues. Is the psalm—a poem—thereby unhistorical? Or should we set it against Exodus, and maybe declare Exodus the product of a different tradition? Neither: they are two different types of writing, with different communicative purposes.

A. Historical Truth Claims

How would we assess the presence of historical truth claims in a narrative? We would consider such factors as the genre of the narrative and its characteristic use. Our pericopes are narrative prose, whose characteristic use in the Bible is to report events in space and time. We would then ask about the book in which it is set: Does the book show an interest in historical people and events? At the very least, we can say that the genealogies of Genesis show the link between the original pair and the generation that entered Egypt, and Genesis is part of the larger narrative of the Pentateuch, which has an interest in historical events. We should further look for explicit statements the narrator makes about historical precedents, circumstances, and consequences of the events he records. For example, here we find that Eve was to be the mother of all living (people), and this is evidenced in her parentage of the humans in Genesis 4–5. We further see that this pair were made morally upright and enjoyed a happy relationship with each other, the world, and God in Genesis 2, but as a result of the events in Genesis 3 they brought themselves into an unhappy condition; and this is the only possible explanation for the spread of sin we find in the chapters that follow. We would further consider how competent readers from the same culture (or at least from a culture that shows continuity with the original audience) have taken the narrative. In the case of the Bible this would include the rest of the Old Testament, extrabiblical Jewish material, and the New Testament. All of these take the material as history, and Josephus is representative: he applied the term ἱστορία ("history") to Genesis, which he contrasted to μυθολογία ("mythology") and ψευδῆ πλάσματα ("false inventions").[3]

We may add to all this the literary milieu in which these pericopes belong, namely, the Mesopotamian creation and flood stories, as discussed in the previous chapter. As Kitchen points out:[4] "As to definition [for the flood story], myth or 'protohistory,' it should be noted that the Sumerians and Babylonians had no doubts on that score. They included it squarely in the middle of their earliest historical tradition, with kings before it and kings after it." He further argues:[5]

> The ancient Near East did *not* historicize myth (i.e., read it as imaginary "history"). In fact, exactly the reverse is true—there was, rather, a trend to "mythologize" history, to celebrate actual historical events and people in mythological terms. . . . The ancients (Near Eastern and Hebrew alike) knew that propaganda based on real events was far more effective than that based on sheer invention.

Thus the very content invites us to recognize the historical impulse.

On the other hand, we must be cautious about too high a level of literalism in reading this material, since it seems to follow some of the conventions of the literature of which it is part. Hence, for example, some of the details of the order of events in Genesis 1:1–2:3 may well belong to the literary class rather than to the author's own distinctive claims, and the "forming" of the man (2:7)—not to mention the "building" of the woman (2:22)—may reflect the background conventions as well. This does not mean that we are left with no ability to discern claims, but we will have to ascertain just what

3. Josephus, *Antiquities* 1.15–16.
4. K. A. Kitchen, *On the Reliability of the Old Testament* (Grand Rapids: Eerdmans, 2003), 425–26.
5. Ibid., 262, 300.

the author was emphasizing. (As we shall see, in my judgment the author is concerned with the metaphysics of the events, namely, the supernatural causes.) Similarly, in Genesis 4 we have to allow for a level of anachronism.[6]

With these in view, we can list, in a broadstroke way, some of the most important historical truth claims found in these first four pericopes of Genesis.

To begin with, we find the assertion that the universe does not exist on its own; it had a beginning, which resulted from the creative work of God: "In the beginning God created the heavens and the earth." Further, the world did not organize itself; it took God's special activity to shape the earth into a place for mankind to live, to populate it with plants and animals, and to bring man into being. We see this special activity in the presence of the Spirit of God (Gen. 1:2), in the repeated "and God said" followed by the fulfillment, and in the divine consultation in the making of man.

Metaphysically, we may refer to this as supernatural: that is, God made the world, endowing its parts with natural properties (or causal powers) that he maintains in existence; and he may at any time bring about something that goes beyond the natural causal powers of his creatures. The Spirit and the word add something to the natures of the things they operate on.[7] The literary reading of Genesis 1:1–2:3 that I developed in chapter 4 shows why it is unlikely that the author makes a strong claim for the sequence of events and reminds us that he says little about the actual processes that produced the effects. When we combine this with the literary milieu of ancient creation accounts, we find confirmation for that reticence. On the other hand, the metaphysical claim is inescapable.

These reflections help us when we come to the "forming" of the man in Genesis 2:7. The picture of forming man like a potter using clay may well be one of the literary conventions of the creation story, and thus we should not press its details too far. At the same time—in reference to modern theories of man's origin—we can say that the text

6. Similarly, the climate implied in Gen. 2:5–6 is like that of the western Levant, notably of Israel. It is not clear whether this is a strong claim of the historical location of the event or simply a literary device that recounts the event in terms familiar to the audience.

7. For an exegetical defense of this metaphysic, see my *God of Miracles: Science and Faith*, chapters 11 and 14; "Miracles, Intelligent Design, and God-of-the-Gaps," *Perspectives on Science and Christian Faith* 55, no. 1 (2003): 22–29.

does *not* envision man as the natural descendant of another animal. It is less decisive when it comes to where the material part of man came from. It is emphatic, however, about the supernatural character of the process that produced the first man and his wife.[8]

And what of lengths of time? The author makes no comment on how long before the first creation day the universe began, but he does not assert that the first creation day is the first day of the universe as a whole, or even of the earth. The process of transforming the "unproductive, unfruitful and uninhabited world" into a fit place for mankind to live and love—the six creation days—took some length of time, longer than an ordinary week (in order to allow the climate cycle of Gen. 2:5–6 to be established).

From the description of the four rivers in Genesis 2:10–14, we may infer that the narrator has located Eden as a real place. We have seen that any effort to pin down just what and where the rivers Pishon and Gihon were leaves us only with probabilities. But when the author names the Tigris and Euphrates, he does touch on identifiable places. The garden was "in" this region (2:8).

Genesis 2 leaves us with a distinct human pair. From Genesis 2–3 we may further infer the following:

(1) All humans have this pair, Adam and Eve, as their ultimate ancestors.
(2) This pair were made morally upright and enjoyed a blissful relationship with each other, the world, and God.
(3) A Dark Power used an ordinary animal as a mouthpiece to deceive this pair and lead them into disobedience.
(4) This couple, and specifically the man, was the representative head of all their descendants in their moral relationship to God, and hence they brought upon themselves and their descendants sinfulness and divine judgment, which explains why no one now experiences the blissful relationships mentioned above.
(5) God promised to do something remedial for the humans, and our first parents apparently believed this promise.

8. For reflection on this question with reference to biological theories, consult my *Science and Faith*, 267–69.

God banished this pair from the garden, and thus they began to experience the hardships to which God sentenced them. At the same time, they remained under God's care and retained their humanity: they raised children, they worshiped, and their descendants displayed intelligence, creativity, and resourcefulness (Gen. 4:20–24). Because of their disobedience in the garden, sin multiplied and found new ways to express itself and to soil human life and the creation; but still some held on to their faith (4:25–26).

The people of Israel, who descended from Abram, were thus the heirs of Shem (Gen. 11:10–27), of Noah (5:32), and of Seth (5:6–28).

B. Historical Truth Value

How might we verify or confirm any of the historical truth claims listed in the previous section? By most modern reckoning, the origins of the universe and of mankind are hidden in distant antiquity, leaving us only a chain of inferences to set beside the scriptural record. Many popular figures, both of the secular and creationist varieties, are sure that the two are incompatible, and we must ditch either the biblical story or the scientific one.

It may come to that, but not just yet. First we must decide whether the two stories really do conflict; and in raising the question, we realize that to do so we have to compare *interpretations* of the data. I have given reasons against a literalistic reading of Genesis, and this literalistic reading is the one on which the supposed conflict is based. On the other hand, the secular science popularizers are also imposing an interpretation on the empirical data, namely, one that allows only natural causes. To address this we would have to show that a purely naturalistic story is inadequate to account for what we observe in ourselves and in the rest of the world, and in the historical events of the rest of the Bible. I will not do that here, since this is available elsewhere.[9]

9. For arguments and bibliography on the sciences, consult my *Science and Faith*. For the historical material, consult Kitchen, *On the Reliability of the Old Testament*, and F. F. Bruce, *The New Testament Documents: Are They Reliable?* (Downers Grove, Ill.: InterVarsity, 1981).

Instead, let us consider whether the biblical picture fits with a reasonable interpretation of the world around us and with what we know to be true of ourselves.

Should the universe look like it had a beginning? Theologians have not always agreed on the answer to this question. Aquinas, for example, argued that philosophy (which in his day included inferences from natural science) cannot prove that the universe *did* have a beginning, nor could it prove that it *did not*.[10] But that was in reference to the state of natural philosophy in his own day. The Christian philosopher Peter Kreeft comments on Aquinas:[11]

> The issue is important for the Middle Ages because Aristotle had apparently proved that the world was eternal, but Scripture had revealed that it had a beginning; thus philosophy and revealed theology, reason and faith, seemed to contradict each other, invalidating the central medieval enterprise of their marriage.
>
> In modern scientific cosmology, the "Steady State theory" was the equivalent of the Aristotelian eternal universe theory, and the "Big Bang" theory, which gives the world a temporal beginning, fits in nicely with the idea of the creation *of* time (rather than creation *in* time). The scientific evidence seems to have refuted the "Steady State" and confirmed the "Big Bang" pretty conclusively, thus also confirming once again that faith and reason never really contradict each other.

Consider as well what Ernan McMullin wrote:[12] "If the universe began in time through the act of the creator, from our vantage point it would look something like the big bang cosmologists are now talking about."

The Big Bang theory (actually, family of theories) is an inference from empirical data, and the issues that surround it are so closely tied to people's view of themselves that it is no surprise that not everyone accepts it. That it has survived serious scientific challenges so far is no guarantee that it will continue to do so. On the other hand, we

10. Aquinas, *Summa Theologica* 1.46.

11. Peter Kreeft, *A Summa of the Summa: The Essential Philosophical Passages of St. Thomas Aquinas'* Summa Theologica *Edited and Explained for Beginners* (San Francisco: Ignatius, 1990), 197 n. 15.

12. Cited in David Kelsey, "The Doctrine of Creation from Nothing," in *Evolution and Creation*, ed. Ernan McMullin (Notre Dame: University of Notre Dame Press, 1985), 176–96, at 190.

can at least say that it is compatible with the reading of Genesis for which I have argued here, and we cannot say that cosmology has falsified Genesis 1:1. Philosophically oriented cosmologists continue to affirm that the big question is, why is there something rather than nothing?—and, in view of the other factors we will mention below, an explanation that refers to a supernatural and purposeful cause is better than one that appeals to a purely natural and purposeless one.

Next, let us consider what makes living things work. They are far more than just conglomerates of chemicals; all are quite complex organizations, with a language system—DNA—at their core. All of our experience supports the idea that a language system can only arise from design: that is, by an intelligence imposing the arrangement on raw material.

And what shall we say of mankind? Human beings share many characteristics with the other animals: they have bodies, they eat and sleep and breed and get rid of waste. But they also have distinctive features: they reason, they have a will that can choose on a moral basis (going beyond simple survival or preference), they use language, they make and enjoy beauty, and they can enter into relationships governed by love and commitment. We have all heard claims that the same features can be found in other animals, to a lesser degree than what we find in man, but the claims typically founder on closer inspection.[13]

In all of this it is hard to avoid the point that G. K. Chesterton made so long ago:[14]

> No philosopher denies that a mystery still attaches to the two great
> transitions: the origin of the universe itself and the origin of the
> principle of life itself. Most philosophers have the enlightenment
> to add that a third mystery attaches to the origin of man himself.
> In other words, a third bridge was built across a third abyss of the

13. For examples, consider my *Science and Faith*, 278–80. See also Susan Milius, "Beast Buddies," *Science News* 164, no. 18 (November 1, 2003): 282–84, which describes aspects of animal behavior that are similar to what we call friendship; I would argue that it only works if we define friendship down, but at least the article concludes: "Harder to understand though, according to Silk, are the bonds so close and widespread in *Homo sapiens*. She says, 'None of our models of reciprocity [among nonhuman animals] can accommodate the psychology of human friendship.' "

14. G. K. Chesterton, *The Everlasting Man* (1925; repr., Garden City: Doubleday, 1955), 27.

unthinkable when there came into the world what we call reason and what we call will.

Three kinds of readers will be unsatisfied with my conclusions thus far. First, the young-earth creationists will think that I have shown a lack of nerve in failing to let the Bible teach that the world is young, simply settling for design. Second, the complementarists, who think that Genesis is more about *values* than about *history*, will think that I have claimed too much when I endorsed the evidence of design in the world. Third, skeptics will think I am being cagey when I think I am being careful. But it is a bad idea to trim one's exegesis, one way or the other, just to avoid falling foul of anyone's criticism. The exegetical arguments I have advanced, coupled with the philosophical arguments outlined here, stand or fall on their own merits. At least I am willing to put my beliefs into empirical harm's way!

And what shall we say of the fall account? If we deny that its events (or some string of events just like them) really happened, we will end up denying something we know to be true of ourselves and of everyone else: we are out of sorts, and we feel this to be *wrong*. The mathematician Blaise Pascal (1623–1662) keenly observed:[15]

> Man's greatness is so obvious that it can even be deduced from his wretchedness, for what is nature in animals we call wretchedness in man, thus recognizing that, if his nature is today like that of the animals, he must have fallen from some better state which was once his own.
>
> Who indeed would think himself unhappy not to be king except one who had been dispossessed? . . . Who would think himself unhappy if he had only one mouth and who would not if he had only one eye? It has probably never occurred to anyone to be distressed at not having three eyes, but those who have none are inconsolable.
>
> Man's greatness and wretchedness are so evident that the true religion must necessarily teach us that there is in man some great

15. Blaise Pascal, *Pensées*, ed. A. J. Krailsheimer (London: Penguin, 1995), nos. 117, 149. Cf. Peter Kreeft's annotated edition of Pascal, *Christianity for Modern Pagans* (San Francisco: Ignatius, 1993), 59, 65–66. The French original can be found in Blaise Pascal, *Pensées*, ed. Ch.-M. des Granges (Paris: Éditions Garnier Frères, 1964), nos. 409, 430 (using the Brunschvicg numbers). For insightful application of this line of reasoning, see Kreeft's section 2; and Douglas Groothuis, "Deposed Royalty: Pascal's Anthropological Argument," *Journal of the Evangelical Theological Society* 41, no. 2 (1998): 297–312.

principle of greatness and some great principle of wretchedness. It must also account for such amazing contradictions.

To make man happy it must show him that a God exists whom we are bound to love; that our true bliss is to be in him, and our sole ill is to be cut off from him. It must acknowledge that we are full of darkness which prevents us from knowing and loving him, and so, with our duty obliging us to love God and our concupiscence leading us astray, we are full of unrighteousness. It must account to us for the way in which we thus go against God and our own good. It must teach us the cure for our helplessness and the means of obtaining this cure. Let us examine all the religions of the world on that point and let us see whether any but the Christian religion meets it.

Anyone who wishes to be taken seriously must face this and account for it—and who has done better than Genesis?

This bad news about man has the cold touch of reality: it awakens us, and at the same time it opens the way to refreshment. As Chesterton wrote:[16]

> The Fall is a view of life. It is not only the only enlightening, but the only encouraging view of life. It holds, as against the only real alternative philosophies, those of the Buddhist or the Pessimist or the Promethean, that we have misused a good world, and not merely been entrapped into a bad one. It refers evil back to the wrong use of the will, and thus declares that it can eventually be righted by the right use of the will. Every other creed except that one is some form of surrender to fate. A man who holds this view of life will find it giving light on a thousand things; on which mere evolutionary ethics have not a word to say. For instance, on the colossal contrast between the completeness of man's machines and the continued corruption of his motives; on the fact that no social progress really seems to leave self behind; . . . on that proverb that says "the price of liberty is eternal vigilance," which is only what the theologians say of every other virtue, and is itself only a way of stating the truth of original sin; on those extremes of good and evil by which man exceeds all the animals by the measure of heaven and hell; on that sublime sense of loss that is in the very sound of all great poetry, and nowhere more than in the poetry of pagans and sceptics: "We look before and after, and pine for what is not";

16. G. K. Chesterton, *As I Was Saying*, ed. Robert Knille (Grand Rapids: Eerdmans, 1985), 160.

which cries against all prigs and progressives out of the very depths and abysses of the broken heart of man, that happiness is not only a hope, but also in some strange manner a memory; and that we are all kings in exile.

This way of looking at the world also equips us to begin to deal with the problem of evil: how can God be infinitely good, wise, and powerful, and at the same time tolerate evil in the world? I can only outline an approach here and defer a fuller discussion to another occasion. First, though, we must carefully define "evil": the literary reading I have offered does not agree that natural processes (such as animal predation, earthquakes, and hurricanes) are *in themselves* contrary to God's will or opposed to a good creation. But the fall has had its impact on all mankind, with the result that (1) we do not have the sympathetic feel for the natural world necessary to govern it to uniformly benign purposes; and (2) we do not govern ourselves by uniformly benign purposes; and (3) we have lost our closeness to God by which we can perceive his hand in every natural event. Second, we must see that to call the existence of pain and evil a problem is to acknowledge our inward sense that they are not right; and this means that we are implicitly recognizing a standard of rightness external to the world, to which the observed world does not measure up. This is as far as we can go with these chapters of Genesis; to fill out the picture we need the rest of redemptive history.[17]

C. World Picture, Worldview, and Good Faith Communication

Many contend that the Bible presents a "primitive" picture of the world—for example, it suggests that the sky is really a kind of hard canopy that keeps water from drowning us all. If we want to talk about biblical truth claims, they say, we will have to account for this feature (usually by sitting lightly on truth value).[18] The most

17. For more, see my *Science and Faith*, 226–28, 309–15.
18. Examples abound and do not all come from opponents of the Bible. One who publishes in conservative venues is Paul H. Seely, as in: "The Firmament and the Water Above, part I: The Meaning of *Raqia'* in Gen. 1:6–8," *Westminster Theological Journal* 53 (1991): 227–40; "The Firmament and the Water Above, part II: The Meaning of 'the Water above the Firmament' in Gen. 1:6–8," *Westminster Theological Journal* 54 (1992): 31–46; "The Geographical Meaning of 'Earth' and 'Seas' in Genesis 1:10," *Westminster Theological Journal* 59 (1997): 231–55.

common way of responding to this claim is to speak of phenomeno-logical language, that is, language that describes things in terms of what they look like to us. An obvious example of this is the English expression "sunrise": we all understand that the sun does not really rise, but even the world's foremost astronomers will use this expres-sion without embarrassment. Another example is the quasi-technical term "centrifugal force," referring to what one feels when twirling a stone on a string: it seems like the stone is pulling away from the center, hence the name. Actually, in Newtonian physics, if the stone is whirling at a constant rate, the only force is the one that the string applies to the stone, deflecting its motion from a straight line and pulling toward the center—it is actually a "centri*petal* force."[19]

We do not consider anyone deceptive or ill-informed who follows the conventional uses of phenomenological language, because we do not expect such language to be making strong claims about the inner workings of the things it describes; instead it allows us to refer to real events without getting bogged down in such questions.

Hence the question we must address is what kind of claim the language of an ancient account actually makes about the subject it describes. This can be difficult to assess when the original speakers are all dead, so we can instead resort to the notion of what I will call good faith communication.

In my communication model of chapter 2, I noted that an author and his audience share a picture of the world (knowledge, beliefs, values, experiences, language), and communication operates on that picture for various purposes. These purposes may include adding new things for the audience to know or believe; correcting the things that they thought they knew; reminding the audience of what they believe or have experienced, so that they will act upon it; evoking some aspect of their shared world picture so that they will celebrate or mourn it; reorienting their worldview. Note that here I distinguish between world *picture* and world*view*. The world picture is just that: what one imagines to be the shape of the world and the things in it, such as how large the earth is, what shape it has, where the land leaves off and the sea begins, what is under the ground and over the sky, and so on. The worldview—to be discussed in more detail in the

---

19. Physicist friends tell me that it gets even more complicated when we go from Newtonian mechanics (or special relativity) to general relativity. The point—that such expressions are a legitimate part of good faith communications—stands.

final chapter—is one's basic religious stance toward the world, such as whether it came from God or exists on its own, whether there is a universal moral code, and so on. The worldview is intended to be normative, while the world picture need not be; by this distinction I, as a modern who accepts contemporary cosmology as part of my world picture, can share a worldview with some ancient whose world picture involved a stationary earth with an orbiting sun.

Any act of communication will allude to some parts of this shared world picture. If the validity of the speaker's point depends on the truth value of the thing alluded to, then we may say that a good faith act of communication implies that the speaker is also affirming the alluded part. A traditional understanding of biblical authority actually supports this distinction: the words of the text serving as an act of communication, and not the structure of the author's thought, is where we find God speaking.

For example, consider Luke 20:27–40, where Sadducees question Jesus in order to show that the idea of a resurrection is absurd. They begin by saying, "Teacher, Moses wrote for us," and refer to Deuteronomy 25:5. In his reply Jesus accepts the premise that "Moses wrote" the passage and goes on to cite Exodus 3:6, in which "even Moses showed" that the dead are raised. The two sides shared a world picture in common, namely, one in which a prophet named Moses wrote the Pentateuch—a writing from which the Pentateuch receives its status as authoritative Scripture. Jesus' point about the resurrection being the teaching of the Pentateuch requires that Exodus 3:6 be just as Mosaic as Deuteronomy 25:5.[20]

Not every good faith act of communication requires that the speaker endorse what he alludes to. For example, I am not breaking faith with anyone when I refer to Sam and Frodo without asserting that *The Lord of the Rings* is historical—unless of course I had led my audience to believe that the account was historical when I knew it was not. In the same way, biblical authors refer to pagan myths. Whether or not the author himself believed the myth to be true has no impact on whether he made his point in good faith. It is enough to suppose that he is using the ideas in a different setting from their

20. See also Matt. 19:1–12, where Jesus refers to the Mosaic creation account (Gen. 1:27; 2:24) when Pharisees try to establish ethics from a law, Deut. 24:1–4. The Mosaic stamp on both passages is part of the shared picture of the world, which Jesus affirms in order to make his point.

original or evoking the emotional overtones of the mythic names, for the purpose of asserting the Lord's superiority over them all.[21]

Take another example: in 1 Timothy 4:7, Paul tells Timothy to avoid "profane and old wives' myths" (my trans.; Greek τοὺς βεβήλους καὶ γραώδεις μύθους; ESV, "irreverent, silly myths"). When he uses the adjective γραώδεις ("typical of old women"), he is using a set phrase, found in other Greek writers, referring to stories not worth the attention of serious people.[22] Now it may or may not have been the case that these Greek authors had a low view of women's intellectual abilities and that they thought older women have no capacity for serious discourse anyhow. But in no way does Paul's use of the expression commit him to such a view (especially since we can tell that he did not hold it—see 5:9–10; Titus 2:3; 2 Tim. 1:5),[23] nor does his point depend in any way on whether as a matter of statistics old wives actually tell such tales. Perhaps, if we pressed him, he would say that these tales appeal to a certain kind of woman who is not sweetened by divine grace and that comparable older men have their own kind of silliness, but this is no matter: we can identify the kind of tale he had in mind well enough.[24]

This indicates that we cannot simply assume either that the background ideas are or are not being endorsed just because an author uses them. We shall have to ask, therefore, whether the background ideas are bound up with the communicative intent.

For us to say that the Bible authors assert a certain world picture as being true, we would have to be sure that physical cosmology is part of their communicative purpose. As soon as we see this,

21. See J. N. Oswalt, "The Myth of the Dragon and Old Testament Faith," *Evangelical Quarterly* 49:3 (1977): 163–72. Oswalt also shows that some alleged allusions are not allusions at all.

22. For example, Plato (428–347 B.C.) in his *Theaetetus* 176B, dismisses a false motivation for virtue as "what is called old wives' chatter" (ὁ λεγόμενος γραῶν ὕθλος). The historian Strabo (c. 64 B.C.–A.D. 19) in his *Geography* 1.2.3, decries a man who makes Homer's poetical art out to be "old wives' mythology" (γραώδη μυθολογίαν).

23. The NASB rendering, "worldly fables fit only for old women," makes Paul sound like he did subscribe to such a view.

24. Nicholas Wolterstorff, *Divine Discourse: Philosophical Reflections on the Claim that God Speaks* (Cambridge: Cambridge University Press, 1995), 209–16, addresses cases in which the presuppositions of a sentence may actually be false but the communication act still be successful. A biblical example would be the supposed geocentric cosmology in passages such as Ps. 93:1. In the first place, this is incorrect exegesis of the biblical texts, as I show in my *Science and Faith*, chapter 6. Second, such cases do not apply in this study, since I am trying to ascertain what the biblical authors *did* believe and try to inculcate.

we are relieved of quite a few of the supposed primitive elements. For example, the statements about the world "not moving" (Pss. 93:1; 96:10; 104:5) have to do with various kinds of stability but not with physical immovability. Likewise, the phrase *pillars of the earth* appears in poetic contexts (1 Sam. 2:8; Ps. 75:3), as does the expression *corners of the earth* (Job 37:3; Isa. 11:12; 41:9; Rev. 7:1; 20:8); there is no reason to suppose that physical description is what these authors were seeking.

Some think that texts such as Exodus 20:4, "the water under the earth," refer to a subterranean ocean. It is more likely, in view of the parallel with Deuteronomy 4:18, that the idea is simply that the level of the water (the rivers, lakes, and seas where the fish dwell) is "lower than" the level of the land.

There is no evidence that the "expanse" (רָקִיעַ, *raqîaʻ*) *must* be describing a solid canopy as a physical entity; it is enough to take it as speaking *as if* the sky were such.[25] Looked at this way, "opening the windows of heaven" is a colorful way of describing a severe downpour (Gen. 7:11; 8:2), and a modern meteorologist could use the expression without being misunderstood (I have heard them speak of "raining buckets"). Delitzsch explains the term *expanse* thus:[26]

> The stem-word רָקַע [*r-q-ʻ*; that is, the verb from which רָקִיעַ is derived] means to tread . . . , then also to make thin, close and firm, and in this way to extend, to stretch out. The higher ethereal region, the so-called atmosphere, the sky, is here meant; it is represented as the semi-spherical vault of heaven stretched out over the earth and its waters.

We can see that this is right from the way that other biblical texts speak of the sky being "stretched out" (using the verb נָטָה, *natâ*).[27] The sky looks like that is what happened.

Phenomenological language is a useful category, then, because it is a feature of ordinary language and of poetic language, and this is

25. The cognate verb appears in Job 37:18: "Can you, like him, *spread out* the skies, hard as a cast metal mirror?" To assert that this poetical context asserts something about physical cosmology is to accept a severe burden of proof.

26. Delitzsch, 85–86. He goes on to quote a Latin author who points out that the term στερέωμα ("firmament") is used not by virtue of physical properties but by virtue of its effect, as if it were separating waters like a wall.

27. Job 9:8; Ps. 104:2; Isa. 40:22; 42:5; 44:24; 45:12; 51:13; Jer. 10:12; 51:15; Zech. 12:1.

what we regularly find in the Bible. It would of course be a fallacy to suppose that this kind of language has no philosophical implications, but the trick is to discern just what those will be. The biblical material speaks largely in terms of historical matters and of a worldview, and asserts that they are true.

This leaves us with the following: it may well be that some biblical statements reflect a world picture that we cannot share—say, on the size of the earth, or that the moon is a lamp rather than a reflector. But this does not mean that the world picture is part of the message being communicated. Most of these cases are more likely phenomenological language, which we know does not make claims even about the world picture. And a number of them (such as the supposed stationary earth) are simply matters of misinterpretation, which we can now correct.

D. What Kind of Science Does This Expect?

Usually when someone discusses Genesis and science, he is thinking about what is called creation science, the idea that we must see the world as being something less than 100,000 years old (most today would say between 6,000 and 10,000). Most creation scientists oppose evolution on a large scale, preferring instead to think of "created kinds," from which all of today's living things are descended.[28]

By my exegesis Genesis itself gives no support to this kind of creation science, as my discussions on the relation of Genesis 1:1 to 1:3, the length of the creation period, and the meaning of "kind" shows. Further, it is a tricky business to use an account like 1:1–2:3 for scientific purposes when its language is so far from what a scientist today would need. The description is broadstroke and suggestive, with no species of plant or animal getting its normal name (other than man). The plants are grouped into two categories: small plants that bear seeds, and larger woody plants ("trees") that bear fruit. The land animals are grouped into those which can be tamed and put to work ("livestock"), smaller things that creep on the ground ("creeping things"), and larger wild animals ("beasts of the earth").

---

28. The flood, taken to be worldwide, figures into almost every picture drawn by creation scientists as well. It is a multipurpose tool, explaining geological phenomena, fossils, and extinction. I am not addressing it at all in this work because it comes later in Genesis.

These categories hardly present an alternative taxonomy to the one that we use; they instead reflect the animals' relation to a peasant farmer. The heavenly light-bearers are described in terms of their function in man's liturgical calendar.

In today's Western culture, to call an account "scientific" can mean any of a number of things. It can mean it is more accurate than ordinary observation or that it is less clouded by human bias; it might mean that it is "cold," bled dry from all that makes the world interesting, or that it is reductionistic and materialistic, explaining even cherished phenomena such as love in terms of chemical reactions. This is a problem with the word *science* and its cognates in the modern world, and I do not propose to examine or solve it. I will simply state that at their best the sciences aim to describe features of the world around us systematically and critically.

From whatever perspective we bring to the word *scientific*, it should be clear that Genesis 1:1–2:3 is not a scientific account. By that I mean that it has used language geared to its communicative purpose, which was to tell the story in order to inculcate a particular view of God and the world—a view shot through with wonder, delight, and awe at the boundless energy and creativity of God. Hence, in saying that it is not scientific, I am far from agreeing that it is inferior, because the question would then be, inferior for what end?

At the same time, I have said that the passage is given to inculcate a view of the world, and this will have implications for the way one thinks about the world. Indeed, I would claim that it lays the foundation for all good science and philosophy, by telling us that the world came from a good and wise Creator, who made a good world for us to live in, enjoy, and rule. Consider how God keeps seeing things as "good." As Aquinas put it:[29]

> For he [God] brought things into being in order that his goodness might be communicated to creatures, and be represented by them; and because his goodness could not be adequately represented by one creature alone, he produced many and diverse creatures, that what was wanting to one in the representation of the divine goodness might be supplied by another. For goodness, which in God is simple and uniform, in creatures is manifold and divided; and hence the whole universe together [partakes of] the divine goodness and represents it better than any single creature whatever.

29. Aquinas, *Summa Theologica* 1.47.1 *respondeo*.

God, who is himself good and the source of all goodness, has shared some of his goodness with his creation. This implies that created things really exist, and really have causal powers (or "natures").

Further, God made man to have dominion over the world, which at first meant to rule it in wisdom and generosity like God's own. To manage the world this way man must be able to know its properties in order to use them to the best advantage. Our senses and intelligence allow us to say things about the world that are true—things we have learned by experience; they also allow us to admire and extol its beauty. God has made man and the world for each other. In other words, all the components necessary for good science follow from seeing the world as God's creation.

E. Conclusions

The first four pericopes of Genesis occur in a book, and belong to a class of literature, that purports to tell history. Being careful with the literary conventions allows us to discern several distinct historical truth claims. Properly considered, these claims about the world and ourselves fit well with honest conclusions from ordinary observation and from the sciences.

Many of these claims are not exactly what we would call new information: I expect that any Israelite already knew full well that plants and animals reproduce "each according to its kind" and that man has a unique role among the other animals. (The Greeks called man the "rational animal," and a believing Israelite would have agreed, so long as we define "rational" carefully.) The historical accounts of Genesis 1–4 put these readily available pieces of information into their proper framework: things work this way because God made them to do so, so that we could enjoy his world; we feel a need for his presence because he made us for that, too, and offers it through the covenant.

In the middle of the twentieth century it was common to contrast Hebrew thought with Greek: the one was dynamic, passionate, concerned with doing, while the other was static and intellectual. The contrast was ill-conceived; embracing the biblical account, which does indeed foster passionate faith and obedience to the Creator, also provides an intellectually robust stance toward the world.

11

SEEING THE WORLD
THROUGH THE EYES OF GENESIS 1–4

In this chapter I will consider how Genesis 1–4 can shape our view of the world today. I approach the text, not simply as a grammarian or as a student of the ancient Near East, but as a committed Christian believer. I was born in the middle of the twentieth century and have worked as an engineer, pastor, and seminary teacher.

I began by speaking of my distaste for the kinds of controversies that swirl around these chapters in Genesis. I hope that I have shown that these controversies, especially those among conservative Christians about the age of the earth and the history of life, are missing the focus of the texts themselves. That focus was to craft a view of the world in ancient Israel by telling the true narrative of the creation and fall of man. In chapter 10 I explained what it means to say that this narrative is true.

The literary setting of Genesis 1–4 is its place as the front end of the Pentateuch; the Pentateuch centers on the Mosaic covenant. In a canonical perspective, these pericopes are also the front end to the whole Bible. The uniform testimony of the New Testament authors was that their message *carried on* the revelation given earlier, rather than *replaced* it. In Romans 11:17 Paul describes Gentile believers in Christ as wild olive shoots grafted in among the branches of the olive tree, the olive tree being an image of the people of God throughout the ages.[1] Later in the letter (15:4) he tells this mixed Jew and Gentile church, "For whatever was written in former days was written for our instruction, that through endurance and through the encouragement of the Scriptures we might have hope." How then shall we receive the instruction and find hope? The pericopes should function among us in the same way as they did among their first readers, inculcating a worldview.

In this chapter we will first discuss the idea of a worldview; we will then list some of the key contributions Genesis 1–4 makes to a biblical worldview and consider the impact these contributions should have on how we practice some key Christian doctrines.

A. Worldview: The Idea

According to David Naugle's study, "Conceiving of Christianity as a worldview has been one of the most significant developments in the recent history of the church," and the first conservative Protestants to describe the faith this way were the Scot James Orr (1844–1913) and the Dutchman Abraham Kuyper (1837–1920).[2]

According to Naugle the chief objections to this would have come from the perspectives that play down the cognitive element in religion, stressing instead feelings and values. In reply to these objections we can simply note that Genesis has actually made truth claims, both about history and about metaphysics; it will not stay confined to feelings and values—vital as these are—but offers a ground for these feelings and values.[3]

1. The ancient people of God are like an olive tree in Jer. 11:16 and Hos. 14:6.
2. David K. Naugle, *Worldview: The History of a Concept* (Grand Rapids: Eerdmans, 2002), 4–25. These theologians' use of the word *worldview* had antecedents in European philosophy, however. And it is fair to say that others have talked about the *idea*, though they have used another term such as "philosophy (of life)." In 1905 G. K. Chesterton showed no sense of introducing a new term when he wrote: "But there are some people, nevertheless—and I am one of them—who think that the most practical and important thing about a man is still his view of the universe. We think that for a landlady considering a lodger, it is important to know his income, but still more important to know his philosophy" (Chesterton, *Heretics/Orthodoxy* [repr., Nashville: Thomas Nelson, 2000], 3).
3. References from Christian philosophers include Paul Herrick, *Reason and Worldview: An Introduction to Western Philosophy* (Orlando: Harcourt, 1999); and J. P. Moreland and William Lane Craig, *Philosophical Foundations for a Christian Worldview* (Downers Grove, Ill.: InterVarsity Press, 2003).

There does not seem to be one agreed-upon definition of the word *worldview*, or even on whether there is a *Christian* worldview as opposed to an Anglican, Baptist, Catholic, Lutheran, Methodist, Orthodox, or Reformed worldview.[4] Some even take worldviews to be antithetical to one another, raising problems of communication between adherents of differing worldviews. I find it more to our advantage if we can think of a Christian worldview as something broader than a specific doctrinal position (such as whom to baptize), something that—theoretically at least—all traditional Christians can claim.[5] We can then acknowledge that churches and individuals will always be inconsistent with this basic worldview to a greater or lesser extent.

In this light, I will take one's worldview as his basic stance toward the world. It contains both a cognitive element and a dispositional one and often is not fully articulated; we can (at least begin to) put a worldview into words by asking how the deepest self would answer the following questions:[6]

- Where does the world come from?
- Is the world good or bad? (How can we define good or bad?)
- What does it mean to be human?
- What is my connection to other people?
- How should people live?
- Should all people live by the same standards?
- What should we do with our failures to live by these standards?
- What is a reliable guide for answering these questions?
- Is there a single Big Story that ties everything together—or are there several, or none?
- What place does God have in it all?

4. An example would be Albert M. Wolters, *Creation Regained: Biblical Basis for a Reformational Worldview* (Grand Rapids: Eerdmans, 1985), 9–10. Indeed, Wolters asserts as true things that I, a fellow Reformed Christian, reject. Does that mean that there are different Reformed worldviews?

5. Naugle, *Worldview*, 52–54, agrees with this position.

6. An alternative way of describing a worldview comes in N. T. Wright, *The New Testament and the People of God* (Minneapolis: Fortress, 1992), 122–26. He says that a worldview typically does four things: (1) provides the stories through which people view reality; (2) answers the basic questions, who are we? where are we? what is wrong? and what is the solution? (3) provides cultural symbols; and (4) offers a praxis, a way-of-being-in-the-world. It is crucial to include the aspect of the story of which we see ourselves to be a part—though at times Wright tends to overemphasize this aspect as if it were the whole of the worldview.

Genesis 1–4 is crucial for a Christian's being able to answer these questions, along the lines we discussed in chapter 9. Even though the God question is at the end of this list, Genesis starts there—that is, not simply with creation but with the Creator.

The notion of worldview shows up often now, especially in analyses of apologetics and conversion. This is a positive development, but there are two common defects in these discussions to which I will simply declare my replies.

The first defect of these discussions is that they frequently imply that one adopts a worldview *as a whole*, and I do not know of anyone's experience that this describes. That is, most people who change worldviews do so because they begin to change their minds about various positions—say, about whether Jesus rose from the dead. The changes of mind can and should affect other beliefs but often do not unless a person is determined to pursue consistency. At some point the person may realize that he has a different worldview—though as a practical matter, most North American Christians have not been exposed to this way of describing their belief systems.

The second defect is the frequent implication that one just *chooses* a worldview and needs no further warrant. For Christians, this takes the form of *fideism*, which separates faith from rationality, and simply demands faith apart from reasons. The theological defense for this is the doctrine that "faith is the gift of God." But no biblical evangelist actually functions this way, as our examination of Acts 17:24–28 shows (chapter 4, section E.5). God's work of renewal does not create the evidence for the faith; instead it deals with the heart's resistance to the evidence.

B. The Biblical Worldview and Christian Doctrine

The worldview that Genesis 1–4 (and the Bible as a whole) inculcates centers on God and the grand narrative of creation, covenant, fall, redemption, and eventual consummation. I finished chapter 10 by drawing the conclusion that the biblical account provides an intellectually robust stance toward the world, and this means that, just as Genesis 1–4 was to shape the worldview of ancient Israel, it should serve to shape ours today. Now in this section I want to suggest ways in which a worldview that does justice to Genesis 1–4 will push us to allow certain doctrines to have their proper impact. Here

I can only outline and suggest, but I think these points flow freely from what I have found in these chapters of Genesis.

We must begin with God, as Genesis 1–2 does: the Creator, who calls us to join his people who love him and to serve mankind, has displayed his magnificence in the work of creation. This work is vast beyond our imaginations and intricate in all its details: a stunning achievement! But even though it is stunning, it is not God; it derives its beauty from him and therefore is not to be worshiped. God's power and goodness show that he is worthy of adoration and love from all his rational creatures; our sin and coldness toward him are worse than anything else we could describe and bring shame and disgrace upon us and everything we touch. And yet this God has made a way for people like us to come to him, to receive forgiveness, to delight in knowing him, to have our humanity restored to proper working order, to shine with his glory even now and forever. What we—and everyone else—need first and foremost is to live in his favor.

God the Creator has shown himself the Ruler of all as well. The fact that he gave real existence and causal powers to created things (Gen. 1:31, "very good") does not take away any of his sovereign rule: since he made things and keeps them in existence, the natural events are just as much his works as the supernatural ones. It is true that there is a difference in the way in which he shows his power in these, and it is often true that the supernatural events make God's presence more noticeable for us; therefore the distinction is valid and useful, but we must not allow it to obscure the fundamental fact of God's pervasive and all-encompassing rule.

Further, this worldview endorses our bodily existence, because it begins with a Creator who delighted in his material creation. Our bodies are not distinct from ourselves; quite the opposite, they are part of how we display the image of God (Gen. 1:26–27). Christians know that they must control their drives—for such things as food, sex, comfort—but at no point may they control them by calling them evil. Rather, in our evil we incline toward corrupt ways of expressing our humanness, and this calls for vigilance.

It follows, then, that our bodies are the arena in which we experience God's sanctifying work: we grow in holiness through *doing* the right things. A child learns spiritual lessons through the bodily pain that comes from the rod (Prov. 22:15; 23:13–14). The body is a fit place by its creation to be a temple of the indwelling Holy Spirit (1 Cor. 6:19), so it is to be kept pure. The bodily expression of love—the embrace that a husband gives his wife, the hugs that a parent gives a child, the clasped hands that friends exchange—is a good thing, and no concession to weakness or frail passion.

This aspect of the biblical worldview shows why the believer should take good care of his body as part of his obligation to God. It shows why there is a connection between our bodily health and our spiritual health, and why being overtired commonly makes us feel spiritually dull, and why brain injuries can deprive us of spiritual capacities.

The body is the vehicle by which we worship as well: in the Bible people pray and sing aloud, stand, kneel, raise their hands, prostrate themselves, use musical instruments, burn incense, perceive beauty, receive sacraments. Some Protestants have overreacted to abuses by stressing the action of the heart, as if it could *replace* the actions of the body (rather than *work with* them). The right reply is *abusus usum non tollit*, "abuse does not take away proper use."[7]

The goodness of our bodily life implies (see also chapter 9, section B) that our epistemology should have a place for learning by experience, since our bodies are rooted in space and time. I have heard that the ideal kind of certainty is that which comes from pure reasoning, such as in mathematics, but this is not the biblical ideal at all, nor is it how people conduct rewarding relationships based on trust. The Bible appeals to the people of God to *remember*, to call to mind their experiences of God's faithfulness to his promises—experiences, some of which are direct, and most of which are part of the shared corporate memory of the covenant. The exodus from Egypt and the resurrection of Jesus are empirical facts that build trust. This is the stuff that relationships are built upon.

If we accept that the goal of redemption is to restore fallen human nature to its proper created function (compare the discussion in chapter 5, section C.8), then we will see that our eschatology needs to affirm the goodness of our bodily life more clearly as well. When a believer dies, we may indeed confess that his or her soul has "gone to be with the Lord," but this is not the end, much less the ideal—it

7. An especially egregious overreaction comes from my own tradition: Heinrich Heppe, *Reformed Dogmatics*, trans. G. T. Thompson (repr., Grand Rapids: Baker, 1978), 609 §24.28, says: "Hence a man who is so strong in faith that he can be joyfully confident of his state of grace, can do without the sacraments." The whole article seems to imply that the sacraments are merely a concession to weak faith rather than an endorsement of our bodily nature.

is only a temporary arrangement. The full glory will be revealed in the resurrection of our bodies and the renewal of all creation as a place for us to live, love, and serve in boundless delight. Christians will continue to disagree over whether the biblical millennial position is optimistic (postmillennial) or pessimistic (most amillennial and premillennial views), but the ultimate eschatology is an optimistic one, because God has committed himself to seeing his creation display its holy beauty.[8]

As C. S. Lewis put it:[9]

> There is no good trying to be more spiritual than God. God never meant man to be a purely spiritual creature. That is why he uses material things like bread and wine to put the new life into us. We may think this rather crude and unspiritual. God does not: He invented eating. He likes matter. He invented it.

Related to this will be a proper appreciation of the beauty of human nature and its accomplishments. Whether it be by musical artistry, scientific insight, or dedicated craftsmanship, mankind is capable of producing things that take our breath away. The bravery shown by pagan Greeks to defend the pass at Thermopylae, or a "heathen" mother to nurture her baby, or my secular neighbor as he battles cancer, has every right to inspire me.

In the same way, the world God made is a beautiful place. Christians ought to enjoy that beauty without embarrassment (except the embarrassment that comes from receiving such an extravagant gift), and they ought as well to protect that beauty from human greed and carelessness.

Thus the fully Christian stance toward culture is not one of *retreat* but of *capture*. It is true that some cultures are badly defiled, and Christian faithfulness in them will reject a great deal of those cultures' goods; but our ideals are people like Joseph and Daniel, as well as Moses and the Hebrew midwives. This also means that the believing worldview fully embraces the life of the mind: the intellect is part of the image of God. It is genuinely human to be curious, to answer questions and solve problems, and to enjoy the process—even when the applicability of our results is hard to see.

8. This way of thinking should enable us to see one aspect of the healing miracles of Jesus: they display his intent to restore damaged human nature to its proper function.

9. C. S. Lewis, *Mere Christianity* (New York: Scribner, 1952), book 2, chapter 5.

The biblical worldview brings with it a high regard for human nature. Because God made man in his image and gave him dominion, he bestowed breath-taking dignity on mankind. The fall of Adam and Eve defiled all that, but did not take away the fundamental dignity of true humanness. To grasp this would yield respect toward everyone we meet and grief over anything that distorts the full expression of our humanity. It would also make us confident in communicating our Christian faith: there is a common human nature that we share with everyone, which equips all manner of people to understand and respond to the gospel. And we can see why a Christian should never withdraw from social witness dealing with such things as the right to life, racial discrimination, the proper definition of marriage, and even foreign policy. This witness seeks structures and laws that promote and protect the enjoyment of our common human nature, for *all* people, and especially for those who may be easily dominated (Prov. 24:11–12; 31:8–9).

Christians have often disagreed over whether laws and rules are good things, and some have offered love in place of law. But this is intolerable, not only in view of the explicit teaching of Jesus and Paul (Matt. 22:34–40; Rom. 13:8–10) but also in view of the creational perspective on God's moral demands that we found here. God redeems his people in order to restore them to their proper functioning, and he gives them the guidance of his moral laws as a gift to shape them, not as a standard to which they must live up or die. Moral law is a gift of the Creator's love. This means that we do not love people if we do not care to point them to the Creator's own moral code.

From this we can see evil and sin in their right perspective. They are foreign intruders into God's good world, and they express disdain for the goodness and authority of the Maker (3:1–5). Because of our first parents' sin, evil stains every aspect of our existence, and our good rests in redemption: forgiveness and the relentless rooting out of the evil in us and our children. But evil affects social structures as well: this means that such structures always need improving; it also means that the structures themselves are not the solution for human evil and can only restrain it to some degree. Thus police forces and armies are a necessary fact of human existence, and we must be prepared to use them, since not everyone will choose the good.

This worldview will also equip us with a perspective on moral maturity and innocence—which we often confuse with naïveté. This follows from the nature of the tree of knowing good and evil, about which I concluded that it was the appointed means by which the human pair would come to know good and evil, either from above, having mastered temptation, or from below, having become slaves to sin. The better we are, the more clearly we know good and evil, and the more skilled we are at discerning how temptation affects us, and at resisting it. Lewis, who seems to have understood basic things exceptionally well, wrote:[10]

> When a man is getting better he understands more and more clearly the evil that is still left in him. When a man is getting worse, he understands his badness less and less. . . . Good people know about both good and evil: bad people do not know about either. . . .
>
> Those who are seriously attempting chastity are more conscious, and soon know a great deal more about their own sexuality than anyone else. They come to know their desires as Wellington knew Napoleon, or as Sherlock Holmes knew Moriarty; as a rat-catcher knows rats or a plumber knows about leaky pipes. Virtue—even attempted virtue—brings light; indulgence brings fog.

Finally, the notion of covenant inclusion should play a larger part in our piety and doctrinal emphases than it does in the contemporary West. We share with the rest of mankind our origin in Adam, not only biologically but also covenantally. We who are believers were once in Adam but have been made to be in Christ—joined to him as our new covenantal representative. We have been made a part of his body, which is the people of God throughout the ages. This loyalty should have first place over all others, whether to race, or class, or country. My well-being, and that of my family, is tied to the well-being of the people of God: I derive benefit from the faithfulness of God's people, and I contribute benefit to others by my own faithfulness. When Paul tells me to rejoice with those who rejoice and weep with those who weep, that includes my brothers and sisters who suffer persecution, as well as those believers who came before me and who will follow after I die. I am not on my own; I am part of something bigger and grander.

And by this notion I can grasp how to profit from the historical and prophetical parts of the Bible, which are so often depressing and which so resist the individualizing moralism that we preachers are accustomed to bring to them. I can see them instead as part of the

10. Ibid., book 3, chapter 4, and book 3, chapter 5.

great narrative of redemptive history, unified by a theme: God calls, shapes, and preserves a people for his own. This speaks to me because it summons me to prayer and faithfulness; but it also reassures me, because God has been shaping this people *for me and my family to be a part of it*. Great indeed is his faithfulness, even to such as I!

C. Conclusions

The vehicle that God has chosen to convey this view of life and the world is narrative. As modern Westerners we might look for something more systematic, but we would be mistaken: even the secular world composes its grand narrative to convey its deepest message—in our case the story of the purely natural process that brought us here without aim or intention.[11] A missiologist has noted,[12] "Most tribal people have never learned from a systematized curriculum; they learn from stories." But I suspect that this is not limited to tribal people; it is likely a human universal—something about our bodily and therefore historical existence requires it. These narratives from the Bible offer us a place in God's great scheme, and we should gladly seize the opportunity.

No one can say all that there is to say about these pericopes of Genesis; there is always more to learn, more to read, more to conclude. Nor can anyone say all that there is about applying these pericopes to Christian faithfulness. That is no shortcoming, however. The more we study them, the more we appreciate their narrative art and theological import; and the more we give our imaginations to them, then the more our own lives will be shaped by the story they tell. For it is the true story of our beginning; it tells us the true story of how we got here, and of how we ought to live now. It is the beginning of the story of God's faithfulness to his people, and to each member of that people, which will carry us through to the end.

11. We must distinguish carefully between the *scientific* theories of how the universe and life arose, which may or may not be good inferences from the data, and the *ideological* uses to which those theories will be put (whether or not the theories lend themselves to such uses).

12. Don Pederson, "Biblical Narrative as an Agent for Worldview Change," *International Journal of Frontier Missions* 14, no. 4 (1997): 163–66.

Bibliography

Aalders, G. Charles. *Genesis*. Grand Rapids: Zondervan, 1981.

Akin, Daniel. "A Discourse Analysis of the Temptation of Jesus Christ as Recorded in Matthew 4:1–11." *Occasional Papers in Translation and Textlinguistics* 1, no. 1 (1987): 78–86.

Alexander, Joseph Addison. *The Gospel according to Matthew*. Reprint. Grand Rapids: Baker, 1980.

Alexander, T. Desmond. "From Adam to Judah: The Significance of the Family Tree in Genesis." *Evangelical Quarterly* 61, no. 1 (1989): 5–19.

———. *From Paradise to the Promised Land: An Introduction to the Pentateuch*. Grand Rapids: Baker, 2002.

———. "Further Observations on the Term 'Seed' in Genesis." *Tyndale Bulletin* 48, no. 2 (1997): 363–67.

———. "Genealogies, Seed and the Compositional Unity of Genesis." *Tyndale Bulletin* 44, no. 2 (1993): 255–70.

———. "Messianic Ideology in the Book of Genesis." Pages 19–39 in *The Lord's Anointed: Interpretation of Old Testament Messianic Texts*. Edited by P. E. Satterthwaite, R. S. Hess, G. J. Wenham. Carlisle: Paternoster, 1995.

———. "The Old Testament View of Life after Death." *Themelios* 11, no. 2 (1986): 41–46.

Alexander, T. Desmond, and David W. Baker, eds. *Dictionary of the Old Testament: Pentateuch*. Downers Grove, Ill.: InterVarsity Press, 2003.

Alter, Robert. *The Art of Biblical Narrative*. New York: Basic Books, 1981.

———. *Genesis: Translation and Commentary*. New York: Norton, 1996.

Amit, Yairah. "Biblical Utopianism: A Mapmaker's Guide to Eden." *Union Seminary Quarterly Review* 44 (1990): 11–17.

Andersen, Francis I. "On Reading Genesis 1–3." Pages 137–50 in *Backgrounds for the Bible*. Edited by M. P. O'Connor, and D. N. Freedman. Winona Lake: Eisenbrauns, 1987.

Anderson, Bernhard W. *Creation versus Chaos: The Reinterpretation of Mythical Symbolism in the Bible*. New York: Association Press, 1967.

———. *From Creation to New Creation*. Minneapolis: Augsburg Fortress, 1994.

———, ed. *Creation in the Old Testament*. Philadelphia: Fortress, 1984.

Anderson, Gary. "The Interpretation of Genesis 1:1 in the Targums." *Catholic Biblical Quarterly* 52, no. 1 (1990): 21–29.

Atwell, James A. "An Egyptian Source for Genesis 1." *Journal of Theological Studies* n.s. 51, no. 2 (2000): 441–77.

Azevedo, Joaquim. "At the Door of Paradise: A Contextual Interpretation of Gen. 4:7." *Biblische Notizen* 100 (1999): 45–59.

Baker, David W. "Further Examples of the *Waw Explicativum*." *Vetus Testamentum* 30, no. 2 (1980): 129–36.

Bar-Efrat, S. "Some Observations on the Analysis of Structure in Biblical Narrative." *Vetus Testamentum* 30 (1980): 154–73.

Barkey, Michael B., ed. *Environmental Stewardship in the Judeo-Christian Tradition: Jewish, Catholic, and Protestant Wisdom on the Environment*. Grand Rapids: Acton Institute, 2000.

Barr, James. "Adam: Single Man, or All Humanity?" Pages 3–12 in *Hesed ve-Emet: Studies in Honor of Ernest S. Frerichs*. Edited by Jodi Magness, and Seymour Gitin. Atlanta: Scholars, 1998.

———. *Fundamentalism*. Philadelphia: Westminster Press, 1978.

———. *The Garden of Eden and the Hope of Immortality*. Minneapolis: Fortress, 1992.

———. "The Image of God in the Book of Genesis—A Study of Terminology." *Bulletin of the John Rylands Library* 51 (1968): 11–26.

———. "Was Everything That God Created Really Good? A Question on the First Verse of the Bible." *God in the Fray: A Tribute to Walter Brueggemann*. Edited by Tod Linafelt and Timothy Beal. Minneapolis: Fortress, 1998.

———. "Why the World Was Created in 4004 B.C.: Archbishop Ussher and Biblical Chronology." *Bulletin of the John Rylands Library* 67, no. 2 (1985): 575–608.

Bartholomew, Craig. "Covenant and Creation: Covenant Overload or Covenantal Deconstruction." *Calvin Theological Journal* 30 (1995): 11–33.

Batto, Bernard. "The Institution of Marriage in Genesis 2 and Atrahasis." *Catholic Biblical Quarterly* 62, no. 4 (2000): 621–31.

Beattie, D. R. G. "What Is Genesis 2–3 About?" *Expository Times* 92, no. 1 (1980): 8–10.

Beauchamp, P., et al., ed. *La création dans l'orient ancien*. Paris: Les Éditions du Cerf, 1987.

Bergant, Dianne, and Carroll Stuhlmueller. "Creation according to the Old Testament." Pages 153–75 in *Evolution and Creation*. Edited by Ernan McMullin. Notre Dame: University of Notre Dame Press, 1985.

Berry, R. J. "This Cursed Earth: Is 'the Fall' Credible?" *Science and Christian Belief* 11, no. 1 (1999): 29–49.

Bimson, John. *New Bible Atlas*. Downers Grove, Ill.: InterVarsity Press, 1985.

Bird, Phyllis A. " 'Male and Female He Created Them': Gen. 1:27b in the Context of the Priestly Account of Creation." *Harvard Theological Review* 74, no. 2 (1981): 129–59.

Black, David Alan, ed. *Linguistics and New Testament Interpretation*. Nashville: Broadman, 1992.

Blocher, Henri. *In the Beginning*. Downers Grove, Ill.: InterVarsity Press, 1984.

Bloom, John. "On Human Origins: A Survey." *Christian Scholars Review* 27, no. 2 (1997): 181–203.

Boorer, Sue. "The Kerygmatic Intention of the Priestly Writer." *Australian Biblical Review* 25 (1977): 12–20.

Bowling, Andrew C. "Another Brief Overview of the Hebrew Verb." *Journal of Translation and Textlinguistics* 9, no. 1 (1997): 48–69.

Brandon, S. G. F. "The Origin of Death in Some Ancient Near Eastern Religions." *Religious Studies* 1 (1966): 217–28.

Brett, Mark. "Motives and Intentions in Genesis 1." *Journal of Theological Studies* n.s. 42 (1991): 1–16.

Brown, William P. "Divine Act and the Art of Persuasion in Genesis 1." *History and Interpretation: Essays in Honour of John H. Hayes*. Edited by M. P. Graham et al. Sheffield: Sheffield Academic Press, 1993.

Brown, William P., and S. Dean McBride, eds. *God Who Creates: Essays in Honor of W. Sibley Towner*. Grand Rapids: Eerdmans, 2000.

Brueggemann, Walter. "The Kerygma of the Priestly Writers." *Zeitschrift für die Alttestamentliche Wissenschaft* 84 (1972): 397–414.

———. *Genesis*. Atlanta: John Knox Press, 1982.

Bryan, David T. "A Reevaluation of Gen. 4 and 5 in Light of Recent Studies in Genealogical Fluidity." *Zeitschrift für die Alttestamentliche Wissenschaft* 99, no. 2 (1987): 180–86.

Buccelati, Giorgio. "Adapa, Genesis, and the Notion of Faith." *Ugarit Forschungen* 5 (1973): 61–66.

Bullmore, Michael. "The Four Most Important Biblical Passages for a Christian Environmentalism." *Trinity Journal* n.s. 19, no. 2 (1998): 139–62.

Buth, Randall. "The Hebrew Verb in Current Discussions." *Journal of Translation and Textlinguistics* 5, no. 2 (1992): 91–105.

Calvin, John. *Genesis*. Translated by John King. Calvin Translation Society. Grand Rapids: Baker, 1979 (original 1563).

Cameron, Nigel. "Genesis and Evolution." *Themelios* 7, no. 3 (1982): 28–31.

Carmichael, Calum M. *The Story of Creation: Its Origin and Its Interpretation in Philo and the Fourth Gospel*. Ithaca: Cornell University Press, 1996.

Cassuto, Umberto. *Commentary on the Book of Genesis*. Translated by Israel Abrahams. Jerusalem: Magnes, 1961 (Hebrew original, 1944).

Castellino, G. R. "Genesis iv 7." *Vetus Testamentum* 10, no. 4 (1960): 442–45.

Clifford, R. J., and John J. Collins, eds. *Creation in the Biblical Traditions*. Catholic Biblical Quarterly Monograph Series 24. Washington, D.C.: Catholic Biblical Association of America, 1992.

Clines, David. "The Image of God in Man." *Tyndale Bulletin* 19 (1968): 53–103.

———. "אָדָם, the Hebrew for 'Human, Humanity': A Response to James Barr." *Vetus Testamentum* 53, no. 3 (2003): 297–310.

Clouser, Roy A. "Genesis on the Origin of the Human Race." *Perspectives on Science and Christian Faith* 43, no. 1 (1991): 2–13.

Collins, C. John. "Ambiguity and Theology in Ruth: Ruth 1:21 and 2:20." *Presbyterion* 19, no. 2 (1993): 97–102.

———. "Galatians 3:16: What Kind of Exegete Was Paul?" *Tyndale Bulletin* 54, no. 1 (2003): 75–86.

———. "Discourse Analysis and the Interpretation of Gen. 2:4–7." *Westminster Theological Journal* 61 (1999): 269–76.

———. "From Literary Analysis to Theological Exposition: The Book of Jonah." *Journal of Translation and Textlinguistics* 7, no. 1 (1995): 28–44.

———. *The God of Miracles: An Exegetical Examination of God's Action in the World*. Wheaton: Crossway, 2000.

————. *The God of Miracles: An Exegetical Examination of God's Action in the World*. Leicester: Inter-Varsity Press, 2001.

————. *Homonymous Verbs in Biblical Hebrew: An Investigation of the Role of Comparative Philology*. Ph.D. diss., University of Liverpool, 1988.

————. "How Old Is the Earth? Anthropomorphic Days in Genesis 1:1–2:3." *Presbyterion* 20, no. 2 (1994): 109–30.

————. "The (Intelligible) Masoretic Text of Malachi 2:16 or, How Does God Feel about Divorce?" *Presbyterion* 20, no. 1 (1994): 36–40.

————. "Miracles, Intelligent Design, and God-of-the-Gaps." *Perspectives on Science and Christian Faith* 55, no. 1 (2003): 22–29.

————. "Reading Genesis 1:1–2:3 as an Act of Communication: Discourse Analysis and Literal Interpretation." Pages 131–51 in *Did God Create in Six Days?* Edited by Joseph Pipa Jr. and David Hall. Taylors, S.C.: Southern Presbyterian Press, 1999.

————. "The Refrain of Genesis 1: A Critical Review of Its Rendering in the English Bible." (forthcoming).

————. *Science and Faith: Friends or Foes?* Wheaton: Crossway, 2003.

————. "A Syntactical Note on Genesis 3:15: Is the Woman's Seed Singular or Plural?" *Tyndale Bulletin* 48, no. 1 (1997): 141–48.

————. "The *Wayyiqtol* as 'Pluperfect': When and Why." *Tyndale Bulletin* 46, no. 1 (1995): 117–40.

————. "What Happened to Adam and Eve? A Literary-Theological Approach to Genesis 3." *Presbyterion* 27, no. 1 (2001): 12–44.

————. "When Should We Translate *Poieô* 'to Make' as 'to Reckon'?" *Selected Technical Articles Related to Translation* 16 (1986): 12–32.

Copan, Paul. "Is *Creatio ex Nihilo* a Post-Biblical Invention? An Examination of Gerhard May's Proposal." *Trinity Journal* n.s. 17 (1996): 77–93.

Cotter, David W. *Genesis*. Berit Olam. Collegeville: Liturgical Press, 2003.

Craig, Kenneth M., Jr. "Questions outside Eden (Genesis 4.1–16): Yahweh, Cain and Their Rhetorical Interchange." *Journal for the Study of the Old Testament* 86 (1999): 107–28.

Cranfield, C. E. B. *Romans*. International Critical Commentary. Edinburgh: T & T Clark, 1975.

Currid, John D. "An Examination of the Egyptian Background of the Genesis Cosmogony." *Biblische Zeitschrift* 35, no. 1 (1991): 18–40.

————. *Genesis, vol. 1 (1:1–25:18)*. EP Study Commentary. Darlington, UK: Evangelical Press, 2003.

Davies, Philip R. "Making It: Creation and Contradiction in Genesis." *The Bible in Human Society: Essays in Honour of John Rogerson*. Edited by M. Daniel Carroll R. Sheffield: Sheffield Academic Press, 1995.

Day, Allan J. "Adam, Anthropology and the Genesis Record—Taking Genesis Seriously in the Light of Contemporary Science." *Science and Christian Belief* 10, no. 2 (1998): 115–43.

Delitzsch, Franz. *A New Commentary on Genesis*. Edinburgh: T & T Clark, 1888.

Dillmann, August. *Genesis*. Edinburgh: T & T Clark, 1897 (German original, 1892).

Driver, S. R. *The Book of Genesis*. Westminster Commentary. London: Methuen, 1904.

Dumbrell, William J. "Creation, Covenant and Work." *Evangelical Quarterly* 13 (1984): 137–56.

———. "Genesis 2:1–3: Biblical Theology of Creation Covenant." *Evangelical Quarterly* 25, no. 3 (2001): 219–30.

Ellington, John. "Man and Adam in Genesis 1–5." *Bible Translator* 30, no. 2 (1979): 201–5.

Emmrich, Martin. "The Temptation Narrative of Genesis 3:1–6: A Prelude to the Pentateuch and the History of Israel." *Evangelical Quarterly* 73, no. 1 (2001): 3–20.

Engnell, Ivan. " 'Knowledge' and 'Life' in the Creation Story." Pages 103–19 in *Wisdom in Israel and in the Ancient Near East*. Edited by M. Noth and D. Winton Thomas. Vetus Testamentum Supplement. Leiden: Brill, 1960.

Feldman, Louis H. *Flavius Josephus, Translation and Commentary, vol. 3: Judean Antiquities 1–4*. Edited by Steve Mason. Leiden: Brill, 2000.

Firmage, Edwin. "Genesis 1 and the Priestly Agenda." *Journal for the Study of the Old Testament* 82 (1999): 97–114.

Fischer, Dick. "In Search of the Historical Adam, part 1." *Perspectives on Science and Christian Faith* 45, no. 4 (1993): 241–51.

———. "In Search of the Historical Adam, part 2." *Perspectives on Science and Christian Faith* 46, no. 1 (1994): 47–57.

Fisher, Loren. "Creation at Ugarit and in the Old Testament." *Vetus Testamentum* 15 (1965): 313–24.

Foh, Susan. "What Is the Woman's Desire?" *Westminster Theological Journal* 37 (1975): 376–83.

Fokkelman, Jan. *Reading Biblical Narrative: An Introductory Guide*. Louisville: Westminster John Knox Press, 1999 (Dutch original 1995).

Freedman, R. David. "Woman, a Power Equal to Man." *Biblical Archaeology Review* 9, no. 1 (1983): 56–58.

Fretheim, Terence. "Is Genesis 3 a Fall Story?" *Word and World* 14, no. 2 (1994): 144–53.

Friedman, Richard Elliott. *The Bible with Sources Revealed: A New View into the Five Books of Moses*. New York: HarperCollins, 2003.

―――. "Some Recent Non-Arguments concerning the Documentary Hypothesis." Pages 87–101 in *Texts, Temples, and Traditions: A Tribute to Menahem Haran*. Edited by Michael V. Fox. Winona Lake: Eisenbrauns, 1996.

Futato, Mark. "Because It Had Rained: A Study of Gen. 2:5–7 with Implications for Gen. 2:4–25 and Gen. 1:1–2:3." *Westminster Theological Journal* 60 (1998): 1–21.

Gaffin, Richard. *Resurrection and Redemption: A Study in Paul's Soteriology*. Phillipsburg, N.J.: Presbyterian and Reformed, 1987.

Galambush, Julie. "*'adam* from *'adamâ, 'ishshâ* from *'ish*: Derivation and Subordination in Genesis 2.4b–3.24." *History and Interpretation*. Edited by M. P. Graham et al. Sheffield: Sheffield Academic Press, 1993.

Garlington, Don B. "Jesus, the Unique Son of God: Tested and Faithful." *Bibliotheca Sacra* 150 (1994): 284–308.

Garrett, Duane. *Rethinking Genesis: The Sources and Authorship of the First Book of the Pentateuch*. Grand Rapids: Baker, 1991.

Gleason, Henry A., Jr. "Some Contributions of Linguistics to Biblical Studies." *Hartford Quarterly* 4 (1963): 47–56.

Godfrey, W. Robert. *God's Pattern for Creation: A Covenantal Reading of Genesis 1*. Phillipsburg, N.J.: P&R, 2003.

Goulder, M. D. "Exegesis of Genesis 1–3 in the New Testament." *Journal of Jewish Studies* 43, no. 2 (1992): 226–29.

Green, William Henry. "Primeval Chronology." Pages 13–28 in *Classical Evangelical Essays in Old Testament Interpretation*. Edited by Walter Kaiser. Grand Rapids: Baker, 1972.

Gros Louis, Kenneth R. R., ed. *Literary Interpretations of Biblical Narratives*. Nashville: Abingdon, 1974.

―――, ed. *Literary Interpretations of Biblical Narratives, vol. 2*. Nashville: Abingdon, 1982.

Grundtke, Christopher. "A Tempest in a Teapot? Genesis iii 8 Again." *Vetus Testamentum* 51, no. 4 (2001): 548–51.

Gunkel, Hermann. *Genesis*. Macon: Mercer University Press, 1997 (German original, 1910).

Gunn, D. M., and D. N. Fewell. *Narrative in the Hebrew Bible*. Oxford: Clarendon Press, 1993.

Habel, N. C., and Shirley Wurst, eds. *The Earth Story in Genesis. The Earth Bible*. Sheffield: Sheffield Academic Press, 2000.

Hagopian, David G., ed. *The Genesis Debate: Three Views on the Days of Creation*. Mission Viejo, Calif.: Crux Press, 2001.

Hallberg, Calinda. "Storyline and Theme in a Biblical Narrative: 1 Samuel 3." *Occasional Papers in Translation and Textlinguistics* 3, no. 1 (1989): 1–35.

Hallo, William W. "New Moons and Sabbaths: A Case-Study in the Contrastive Approach." *Hebrew Union College Annual* 48 (1977): 1–18.

Hamilton, Victor P. *Genesis 1–17*. New International Commentary on the Old Testament. Grand Rapids: Eerdmans, 1990.

Harris, R. Laird. "The Mist, the Canopy, and the Rivers of Eden." *Bulletin of the Evangelical Theological Society* 11, no. 4 (1968): 177–79.

Hart, Ian. "Genesis 1:1–2:3 as a Prologue to the Book of Genesis." *Tyndale Bulletin* 46, no. 2 (1995): 315–36.

Hartley, John. *Genesis*. New International Biblical Commentary. Peabody: Hendrickson, 2000.

Hasel, Gerhard. "The Meaning of 'Let us' in Gn 1:26." *Andrews University Seminary Studies* 13, no. 1 (1975): 58–66.

———. "The Meaning of the Chronogenealogies of Genesis 5 and 11." *Origins* 7, no. 2 (1980): 53–70.

———. "The Polemic Nature of the Genesis Cosmology." *Evangelical Quarterly* 46 (1974): 81–102.

———. "Recent Translations of Genesis 1:1: A Critical Look." *Bible Translator* 22, no. 4 (1971): 154–67.

Hasel, Gerhard, and Michael Hasel. "The Hebrew Term *'ed* in Gen. 2,6 and Its Connection in Ancient Near Eastern Literature." *Zeitschrift für die Alttestamentliche Wissenschaft* 112 (2000): 321–40.

Hauser, Alan J. "Linguistic and Thematic Links between Genesis 4:1–16 and Genesis 2–3." *Journal of the Evangelical Theological Society* 23, no. 4 (1980): 297–305.

Hays, Richard. *Echoes of Scripture in the Letters of Paul*. New Haven: Yale, 1989.

Heidel, Alexander. *The Babylonian Genesis*. Chicago: University of Chicago Press, 1951.

———. *The Gilgamesh Epic and Old Testament Parallels*. Chicago: University of Chicago, 1949.

Heins, Barbara D. "From Leprosy to Shalom and Back Again: A Discourse Analysis of 2 Kings 5." *Occasional Papers in Translation and Textlinguistics* 2, no. 1 (1988): 20–31.

Helm, Paul. "Arguing about Origins." *Themelios* 4, no. 1 (1978): 20–24.

Hendel, Ronald. " 'The Flame of the Whirling Sword': A Note on Genesis 3:24." *Journal of Biblical Literature* 104, no. 4 (1985): 671–74.

Hertz, J. H. *The Pentateuch and Haftorahs*. London: Soncino Press, 1980.

Hess, Richard. "Genesis 1–2 and Recent Studies of Ancient Texts." *Science and Christian Belief* 7 (1995): 141–49.

———. "Genesis 1–2 in Its Literary Context." *Tyndale Bulletin* 41, no. 1 (1990): 143–53.

———. "The Roles of the Woman and the Man in Genesis 3." *Themelios* 18, no. 3 (1993): 15–18.

———. "Splitting the Adam." Pages 1–15 in *Studies in the Pentateuch*. Edited by J. A. Emerton. Vetus Testamentum Supplement 41. Leiden: Brill, 1991.

Hess, Richard, and David Tsumura, eds. *'I Studied Inscriptions from before the Flood': Ancient Near Eastern, Literary, and Linguistic Approaches to Genesis 1–11*. Winona Lake: Eisenbrauns, 1994.

Hinschberger, Regine. "Image et resemblance dans la tradition sacerdotale (Gn 1,26–28; 5,1–3; 9,6b)." *Revue des sciences religieuses* 59, no. 3–4 (1985): 185–99.

Hollenbach, Bruce, and Jim Watters. "Study Guide on Pragmatics and Discourse." *Notes on Translation* 12, no. 1 (1998): 13–35.

Houk, Cornelius B. "Statistical Analysis of Genesis Sources." *Journal for the Study of the Old Testament* 27, no. 1 (2002): 75–105.

House, Paul. *Old Testament Theology*. Downers Grove, Ill.: InterVarsity, 1998.

Huffmon, Herbert B. "Cain, the Arrogant Sufferer." Pages 109–13 in *Biblical and Related Studies Presented to Samuel Iwry*. Edited by A. Kort and S. Morschauser. Winona Lake: Eisenbrauns, 1985.

Hugenberger, Gordon. *Marriage as a Covenant: Biblical Law and Ethics as Developed from Malachi*. Grand Rapids: Baker, 1998 (1994).

Hutter, Manfred. "Adam als Gärtner und König (Gen. 2:8, 15)." *Biblische Zeitschrift* 30, no. 2 (1986): 258–62.

Hvidberg, Flemming. "The Canaanitic Background of Gen.. i-iii." *Vetus Testamentum* 10, no. 3 (1960): 285–94.

Johnston, Philip. " 'Left in Hell'?" Pages 213–22 in *The Lord's Anointed*. Edited by P. E. Satterthwaite. Grand Rapids: Baker, 1995.

Joines, Karen Randolph. "The Serpent in Gen. 3." *Zeitschrift für die Alttestamentliche Wissenschaft* 87, no. 1 (1975): 1–11.

Jónsson, Gunnlaugur A. *The Image of God: Genesis 1:26–28 in a Century of Old Testament Research*. Coniectanea Biblica, Old Testament Series 26. Lund: Almqvist & Wiksell, 1988.

Kahl, Brigitte. "And She Called His Name Seth . . . (Gen. 4:25): The Birth of Critical Knowledge and the Unread End of Eve's Story." *Union Seminary Quarterly Review* 53 (1999): 19–28.

Karlberg, Mark. "The Original State of Adam: Tensions within Reformed Theology." *Evangelical Quarterly* 59, no. 4 (1987): 291–309.

Kass, Leon. *The Beginning of Wisdom: Reading Genesis*. New York: Free Press, 2003.

Kaufman, S. A. "Reflections on the Assyrian-Aramaic Bilingual from Tell Fakhariyeh." *Maarav* 3, no. 2 (1982): 137–75.

Keil, C. F. *The First Book of Moses (Genesis)*. Keil and Delitzsch. Grand Rapids: Eerdmans, 1981 (reprint of 1875 English transation from German).

Kelly, Douglas F. *Creation and Change: Genesis 1.1–2.4 in the Light of Changing Scientific Paradigms*. Fearn, Ross-shire: Christian Focus, 1997.

Kelsey, David. "The Doctrine of Creation from Nothing." Pages 176–96 in *Evolution and Creation*. Edited by Ernan McMullin. Notre Dame: University of Notre Dame Press, 1985.

Kempf, Stephen A. "Genesis 3:14–19: Climax of the Discourse?" *Journal of Translation and Textlinguistics* 6 (1993): 354–77.

———. "Introducing the Garden of Eden: The Structure and Function of Genesis 2:4b–7." *Journal of Translation and Textlinguistics* 7, no. 4 (1996): 33–53.

Kidner, Derek. *Genesis*. Tyndale Old Testament Commentary. Downers Grove, Ill.: InterVarsity Press, 1967.

———. "Genesis 2:5, 6: Wet or Dry?" *Tyndale Bulletin* 17 (1966): 109–14.

———. *Proverbs*. Tyndale Old Testament Commentary. Downers Grove, Ill.: InterVarsity Press, 1964.

———. *Psalms 73–150*. Tyndale Old Testament Commentary. Downers Grove, Ill.: InterVarsity, 1973.

Kiel, Yehudah. *Sefer Bere'shit [Genesis]*. Da'at Miqra. Jerusalem: Mossad Harav Kook, 1997.

Kilgallen, John J. "The Power Struggle between Man and Woman (Gen. 3,16b)." *Biblica* 77, no. 2 (1996): 197–209.

Kitchen, K. A. *On the Reliability of the Old Testament*. Grand Rapids: Eerdmans, 2003.

Klein, Ralph W. "The Message of P." Pages 57–66 in *Die Botschaft und die Boten: Festschrift für Hans Walter Wolff zum 70. Geburtstag*. Edited by J. Jeremias, and L. Perlitt. Neukirchen-Vluyn: Neukirchener, 1981.

Kline, Meredith G. "Because It Had Not Rained." *Westminster Theological Journal* 20 (1958): 146–57.

————. "Genesis." Pages 79–114 in *The New Bible Commentary: Revised*. Edited by Donald Guthrie et al. Grand Rapids: Eerdmans, 1970.

————. "Response to Collins et al." *Perspectives on Science and Christian Faith* 48, no. 3 (1996): 209–10.

————. "Space and Time in the Genesis Cosmogony." *Perspectives on Science and Christian Faith* 48, no. 1 (1996): 2–15.

Krasovec, Joze. "Punishment and Mercy in the Primeval History (Gen. 1–11)." *Ephemerides Theologicae Lovanienses* 70, no. 1 (1994): 5–33.

Kselman, John S. "The Book of Genesis: A Decade of Scholarly Research." *Interpretation* 45 (1991): 380–92.

————. "The Recovery of Poetic Fragments from the Pentateuchal Priestly Source." *Journal of Biblical Literature* 97 (1978): 161–73.

Külling, Samuel R. "The Dating of the So-Called 'P-sections' in Genesis." *Journal of the Evangelical Theological Society* 15, no. 2 (1972): 67–76.

Lambert, W. G. "A New Look at the Babylonian Background of Genesis." *Journal of Theological Studies* n.s. 16, no. 2 (1965): 287–300.

Lane, William. "The Initiation of Creation." *Vetus Testamentum* 13, no. 1 (1963): 63–73.

Larsson, Gerhard. "The Chronology of the Pentateuch: A Comparison of the MT and LXX." *Journal of Biblical Literature* 102, no. 3 (1983): 401–9.

Lauer, Stuart. "Was the Tree of Life Always off Limits? A Critique of Vos's Answer." *Kerux* 16, no. 3 (2001): 42–50.

Lavallee, Louis. "Augustine on the Creation Days." *Journal of the Evangelical Theological Society* 32, no. 4 (1989): 457–64.

Layton, Scott C. "Remarks on the Canaanite Origin of Eve." *Catholic Biblical Quarterly* 59, no. 1 (1997): 22–32.

Letham, Robert. " 'In the Space of Six Days': The Days of Creation from Origen to the Westminster Assembly." *Westminster Theological Journal* 61 (1999): 149–74.

Leupold, H. C. *Exposition of Genesis*. Grand Rapids: Baker, 1980.

Levenson, Jon D. *Creation and the Persistence of Evil*. San Francisco: Harper & Row, 1988.

Levin, Saul. "The More Savory Offering: A Key to the Problem of Gen. 4:3–5." *Journal of Biblical Literature* 98, no. 1 (1979): 85.

Lewis, Jack P. "The Days of Creation: An Historical Survey of Interpretations." *Journal of the Evangelical Theological Society* 32, no. 4 (1989): 433–55.

————. "The Offering of Abel (Gen. 4:4): A History of Interpretation." *Journal of the Evangelical Theological Society* 37, no. 4 (1994): 481–96.

Liddell, Henry George, and Robert Scott. *A Greek-English Lexicon*. Oxford: Clarendon Press, 1996.

Livingstone, David. "Preadamites: The History of an Idea from Heresy to Orthodoxy." *Scottish Journal of Theology* 40 (1987): 41–66.

Loewenstamm, S. E. "Beloved Is Man in That He Was Created in the Image." Pages 48–50 in *Comparative Studies in Biblical and Ancient Oriental Literatures*. Edited by S. E. Loewenstamm. Neukirchen-Vluyn: Neukirchener, 1980.

———. "The Development of the Term 'First' in the Semitic Languages." Pages 13–16 in *Comparative Studies in Biblical and Ancient Oriental Literatures*. Edited by S. E. Loewenstamm. Neukirchen-Vluyn: Neukirchener, 1980.

———. "The Seven Day-Unit in Ugaritic Epic Literature." *Israel Exploration Journal* 15 (1965): 121–33.

Long, V. Philips. *The Art of Biblical History*. Grand Rapids: Zondervan, 1994.

———. *The Reign and Rejection of King Saul*. Atlanta: Scholars, 1989.

———. "Scenic, Succinct, Subtle: An Introduction to the Literary Artistry of 1 and 2 Samuel." *Presbyterion* 19, no. 1 (1993): 32–47.

Longacre, Robert. "Discourse Perspective on the Hebrew Verb: Affirmation and Restatement." Pages 177–89 in *Linguistics and Biblical Hebrew*. Edited by Walter Bodine. Winona Lake: Eisenbrauns, 1992.

———. "The Discourse Structure of the Flood Narrative." Pages 235–62 in *Society of Biblical Literature 1976 Seminar Papers*. Edited by G. MacRae. Missoula: Scholars, 1976.

———. "Interpreting Biblical Stories." Pages 169–85 in *Discourse and Literature*. Edited by Teun A. van Dijk. Amsterdam/Philadelphia: John Benjamins, 1985.

———. *Joseph: A Story of Divine Providence*. Winona Lake: Eisenbrauns, 2003.

Lucas, E. C. "Some Scientific Issues Related to the Understanding of Genesis 1–3." *Themelios* 12, no. 2 (1987): 46–51.

Lust, J. "A Gentle Breeze or a Roaring Thunderous Sound?" *Vetus Testamentum* 25, no. 1 (1975): 110–15.

Manns, Frederic. "Col.. 1,15–20: Midrash chrétien de Gen.. 1,1." *Revue des sciences religieuses* 53 (1979): 100–110.

Marston, Justin. "Jewish Understandings of Genesis 1 to 3." *Science and Christian Belief* 12, no. 2 (2000): 127–50.

Marzel, Yitzhaq. "The Tree of the Knowledge of Good and Evil—Recognition of Life and Death." *Bet Miqra* 29 (1983–84): 352–60.

McEvenue, Sean. *The Narrative Style of the Priestly Writer*. Rome: Biblical Institute Press, 1971.

————. "Reading Genesis with Faith and Reason." *Word and World* 14, no. 2 (1994): 136–43.

Merrill, Eugene. "Covenant and the Kingdom: Genesis 1–3 as Foundation for Biblical Theology." *Criswell Theological Review* 1, no. 2 (1987): 295–308.

Milgrom, Jacob. "Sex and Wisdom: What the Garden of Eden Story Is Saying." *Bible Review* 10, no. 6 (1994): 21, 52.

Millard, A. R. "Abraham, Akenaten, Moses, and Monotheism." *He Swore an Oath: Biblical Themes in Genesis 12–50*. Edited by Richard Hess et al. Grand Rapids: Baker, 1994.

————. "The Etymology of Eden." *Vetus Testamentum* 34, no. 1 (1984): 103–6.

————. "A New Babylonian 'Genesis' story." *Tyndale Bulletin* 18 (1967): 3–18.

————. "Story, History, and Theology." *Faith, Tradition, and History: Old Testament Historiography in Its Near Eastern Context*. Edited by A. R. Millard et al. Winona Lake: Eisenbrauns, 1994.

Miller, Patrick D., Jr. "*Yeled* in the Song of Lamech." *Journal of Biblical Literature* 85, no. 4 (1966): 477–78.

Miller, J. M. "The Descendants of Cain: Notes on Genesis 4." *Zeitschrift für die Alttestamentliche Wissenschaft* 86, no. 2 (1974): 164–74.

————. "In the 'Image' and 'Likeness' of God." *Journal of Biblical Literature* 91 (1972): 289–304.

Milne, D. J. W. "Genesis 3 in the Letter to the Romans." *Reformed Theological Review* 39, no. 1 (1980): 10–18.

Mitchell, T. C. "The Old Testament Usage of *Neshamâ*." *Vetus Testamentum* 11, no. 2 (1961): 177–87.

Moberly, R. W. L. "Story in the Old Testament." *Themelios* 11, no. 3 (1986): 77–82.

————. "Did the Serpent Get It Right?" *Journal of Theological Studies* 39, no. 1 (1988): 1–27.

Moreland, J. P., and John Mark Reynolds, eds. *Three Views on Creation and Evolution*. Grand Rapids: Zondervan, 1999.

Mueller, Hans-Peter. "Parallelen zu Gen. 2f. und Ez 28 aus dem Gilgamesch-Epos." *Zeitschrift für die Althebraistik* 3, no. 2 (1990): 167–78.

Munday, John C., Jr. "Eden's Geography Erodes Flood Geology." *Westminster Theological Journal* 58 (1996): 123–54.

Naidoff, Bruce. "A Man to Work the Soil: A New Interpretation of Genesis 2–3." *Journal for the Study of the Old Testament* 5 (1978): 2–14.

Narrowe, Morton H. "Another Look at the Tree of Good and Evil." *Jewish Bible Quarterly* 26, no. 3 (1998): 184–88.

Newman, Robert, and Herman Eckelmann. *Genesis One and the Origin of the Earth*. Downers Grove, Ill.: InterVarsity Press, 1977.

Newman, Robert C. "Scientific Problems for Scientism." *Presbyterion* 21, no. 2 (1995): 73–88.

Niccacci, Alviero. "Analysis of Biblical Narrative." Pages 175–98 in *Biblical Hebrew and Discourse Linguistics*. Edited by R. D. Bergen. Dallas: Summer Institute of Linguistics, 1994.

Nichols, Anthony. "Explicitness in Translation and the Westernization of Scripture." *Reformed Theological Review* 47, no. 3 (1988): 78–88.

Niehaus, Jeffrey. "In the Wind of the Storm: Another Look at Genesis iii 8." *Vetus Testamentum* 44, no. 2 (1994): 263–67.

Och, Bernard. "The Garden of Eden." *Judaism* 37 (1988): 143–56.

Olley, John W. "Further Observations on *Mîn*, 'Kind.'" *Science and Christian Belief* 11, no. 1 (1999): 69–72.

Orlinsky, Harry. "The Plain Meaning of Genesis 1:1–3." *Biblical Archaeologist* 46, no. 4 (1983): 207–9.

Ortlund, Raymond C., Jr. "Male-Female Equality and Male Headship: Genesis 1–3." Pages 95–112 in *Recovering Biblical Manhood and Womanhood*. Edited by John Piper and Wayne Grudem. Wheaton: Crossway, 1991.

———. *Whoredom: God's Unfaithful Wife in Biblical Theology*. Grand Rapids: Eerdmans, 1996.

Oswalt, J. N. "The Myth of the Dragon and Old Testament Faith." *Evangelical Quarterly* 49, no. 3 (1977): 163–72.

Page, Sydney. *Powers of Evil: A Biblical Study of Satan and Demons*. Grand Rapids: Baker, 1995.

Paran, Meir. *Forms of the Priestly Style in the Pentateuch: Patterns, Linguistic Usages, Syntactic Structures*. Jerusalem: Magnes, 1989.

Parunak, H. Van Dyke. "Oral Typesetting: Some Uses of Biblical Structure." *Biblica* 62, no. 2 (1981): 153–68.

Pederson, Don. "Biblical Narrative as an Agent for Worldview Change." *International Journal of Frontier Missions* 14, no. 4 (1997): 163–66.

Pipa, Joseph, Jr. "From Chaos to Cosmos: A Critique of the Non-Literal Interpretations of Genesis 1:1–2:3." Pages 153–98 in *Did God Create in Six Days?* Edited by Joseph Pipa Jr. and David Hall. Taylors, S.C.: Southern Presbyterian Press, 1999.

Plaut, W. Gunther. *The Torah*. New York: Union of American Hebrew Congregations, 1981.

Polak, Frank. "The Oral and the Written: Syntax, Stylistics and the Development of Biblical Prose Narrative." *Journal of the Ancient Near Eastern Society* 26 (1998): 59–105.

———. "Poetic Style and Parallelism in the Creation Account (Genesis 1.2–2.3)." Pages 2–31 in *Creation in Jewish and Christian Tradition*. Edited by Henning Graf Reventlow and Yair Hoffman. Sheffield: Sheffield Academic Press, 2002.

Quick, Philip A. "Resumptive Repetition: A Two-Edged Sword." *Journal of Translation and Textlinguistics* 6, no. 4 (1993): 289–316.

Rabin, Chaim. "Discourse Analysis and the Dating of Deuteronomy." Pages 171–77 in *Interpreting the Hebrew Bible*. Edited by J. A. Emerton and Stefan C. Reif. Cambridge: Cambridge University Press, 1982.

Radday, Yehuda T. "The Four Rivers of Paradise." *Hebrew Studies* 23 (1982): 23–31.

Rainey, A. F. "A Canaanite at Ugarit." *Israel Exploration Journal* 13 (1963): 43–45.

Ramaroson, Leonard. "A propos de Gn 4,7." *Biblica* 49, no. 2 (1968): 233–37.

Reis, Pamela Tamarkin. "What Cain Said: A Note on Genesis 4.8." *Journal for the Study of the Old Testament* 27, no. 1 (2002): 107–13.

Revell, E. J. "Concord with Compound Subjects and Related Uses of Pronouns." *Vetus Testamentum* 43 (1993): 69–87.

———. "The System of the Verb in Standard Biblical Prose." *Hebrew Union College Annual* 60 (1989): 1–37.

Reyburn, William, and Euan Fry. *Handbook on Genesis*. UBS Handbook Series. New York: United Bible Societies, 1997.

Robertson, O. Palmer. "Current Reformed Thinking on the Nature of the Divine Covenants." *Westminster Theological Journal* 40 (1977): 63–76.

Robinson, Robert B. "Literary Functions of the Genealogies of Genesis." *Catholic Biblical Quarterly* 48, no. 4 (1986): 595–608.

Rogerson, John. "Slippery Words, V. Myth." *Expository Times* 90 (1978): 10–14.

Rogland, Max. "*Ad litteram*: Some Dutch Reformed Theologians on the Creation Days." *Westminster Theological Journal* 63 (2001): 211–33.

Rooker, Mark. "Genesis 1:1–3: Creation or Re-Creation?" *Bibliotheca Sacra* 149 (1992): 316–23.

———. "Genesis 1:1–3: Creation or Re-Creation? (Part 2)." *Bibliotheca Sacra* 149 (1992): 411–27.

Ross, Hugh. *The Genesis Question*. Colorado Springs: NavPress, 1998.

Rudolph, David J. "Festivals in Genesis 1:14." *Tyndale Bulletin* 54, no. 2 (2003): 23–40.

Russell, Colin. *The Earth, Humanity and God*. London: University College of London Press, 1994.

Ryken, Leland, and Tremper Longman III, eds. *A Complete Literary Guide to the Bible*. Grand Rapids: Zondervan, 1993.

Sacks, Robert D. *A Commentary on the Book of Genesis*. Lewiston: Edwin Mellen, 1990.

Sailhamer, John. *Genesis*. Expositor's Bible Commentary. Grand Rapids: Zondervan, 1990.

———. *Genesis Unbound*. Sisters: Questar, 1996.

Sandmel, Samuel. "Genesis 4:26b." *Hebrew Union College Annual* 32 (1961): 19–29.

Sauer, James A. "The River Runs Dry." *Biblical Archaeology Review* 22, no. 4 (1996): 52–57.

Sawyer, J. F. A. "The Meaning of בצלם אלהים ('in the Image of God') in Genesis I–XI." *Journal of Theological Studies* n.s. 25, no. 2 (1974): 418–26.

Schaeffer, Francis. *Genesis in Space and Time*. Downers Grove, Ill.: Inter-Varsity Press, 1972.

Schmitt, J. J. "Like Eve, Like Adam: משל in Gen. 3,16." *Biblica* 72, no. 1 (1991): 1–22.

Seely, Paul. "The Basic Meaning of *Mîn*, 'Kind.' " *Science and Christian Belief* 9, no. 1 (1997): 47–56.

———. "The Firmament and the Water Above, part I: The Meaning of *Raqia'* in Gen. 1:6–8." *Westminster Theological Journal* 53 (1991): 227–40.

———. "The Firmament and the Water Above, part II: The Meaning of 'the Water above the Firmament' in Gen. 1:6–8." *Westminster Theological Journal* 54 (1992): 31–46.

———. "The Geographical Meaning of 'Earth' and 'Seas' in Genesis 1:10." *Westminster Theological Journal* 59 (1997): 231–55.

Shea, William H. "Adam in Ancient Mesopotamian Traditions." *Andrews University Seminary Studies* 15 (1977): 27–41.

Ska, Jean Louis. "De la relative indépendence de l'écrit sacerdotal." *Biblica* 76 (1995): 396–415.

———. "Je vais lui faire un allié qui soit son homologue' (Gn 2,18): A propos du terme *'ezer*—'aide.' " *Biblica* 65, no. 2 (1984): 233–38.

———. *"Our Fathers Have Told Us": Introduction to the Analysis of Hebrew Narratives*. Rome: Editrice Pontificio Istituto Biblico, 1990.

Skinner, John. *Genesis*. International Critical Commentary. Edinburgh: T & T Clark, 1930.

Slivniak, Dmitri. "The Garden of Double Messages: Deconstructing Hierarchical Oppositions in the Garden Story." *Journal for the Study of the Old Testament* 27, no. 4 (2003): 439–60.

Spina, Frank Anthony. "The 'Ground' for Cain's Rejection (Gen. 4): *'adamâ* in the Context of Gen. 1–11." *Zeitschrift für die Alttestamentliche Wissenschaft* 104, no. 3 (1992): 319–32.

Spurrell, G. J. *Notes on the Text of the Book of Genesis*. Oxford: Clarendon Press, 1896.

Steinmann, Andrew. "אחד as an Ordinal Number and the Meaning of Genesis 1:5." *Journal of the Evangelical Theological Society* 45, no. 4 (2002): 577–84.

Stek, John. " 'Covenant' Overload in Reformed Theology." *Calvin Theological Journal* 29 (1994): 12–41.

———. "What Says the Scripture?" Pages 203–65 in *Portraits of Creation*. Edited by Howard J. Van Till, Robert E. Snow, John H. Stek, Davis A. Young. Grand Rapids: Eerdmans, 1990.

Sternberg, Meir. *The Poetics of Biblical Narrative: Ideological Literature and the Drama of Reading*. Bloomington: Indiana University Press, 1985.

Stordalen, Terje. *Echoes of Eden: Genesis 2–3˙and Symbolism of the Eden Garden in Biblical Hebrew Literature*. Leuven: Peeters, 2000.

———. "Genesis 2,4: Restudying a *Locus Classicus*." *Zeitschrift für die Alttestamentliche Wissenschaft* 104, no. 2 (1992): 163–77.

———. "Man, Soil, Garden: Basic Plot in Genesis 2–3 Reconsidered." *Journal for the Study of the Old Testament* 53 (1992): 3–26.

Talmon, Shemaryahu. "The Presentation of Synchroneity and Simultaneity in Biblical Narrative." Pages 9–26 in *Studies in Hebrew Narrative Art*. Edited by J. Heinemann and S. Werses. Scripta Hierosolymitana. Jerusalem: Magnes, 1978.

Tosato, Angelo. "On Genesis 2:24." *Catholic Biblical Quarterly* 52, no. 3 (1990): 389–409.

Trible, Phyllis. "Eve and Adam: Genesis 2–3 Reread." *Andover Newton Quarterly* 13, no. 4 (1973): 251–58.

Tsumura, David. *The Earth and the Waters in Genesis 1 and 2: A Linguistic Investigation*. Sheffield: Sheffield Academic Press, 1989.

van Wolde, Ellen. "The Story of Cain and Abel: A Narrative Study." *Journal for the Study of the Old Testament* 52 (1991): 25–41.

———. "The Text as an Eloquent Guide: Rhetorical, Linguistic and Literary Features in Genesis 1." *Literary Structure and Rhetorical Strategies in the Hebrew Bible*. Edited by L. J. de Regt et al. Assen: Van Gorcum, 1996.

Vawter, Bruce. *A Path through Genesis*. New York: Sheed & Ward, 1956.

Vermes, Geza. "Genesis 1–3 in Post-Biblical Hebrew and Aramaic Litera-
    ture before the Mishnah." *Journal of Jewish Studies* 43, no. 2 (1992):
    221–25.

Vermeylen, Jacques. "La descendance de Caïn et la descendance d'Abel (Gen.
    4,17–26 + 5,28b–29)." *Zeitschrift für die Alttestamentliche Wissenschaft*
    103, no. 2 (1991): 175–93.

Wallace, Howard. *The Eden Narrative*. Atlanta: Scholars Press, 1985.

Walsh, Jerome T. "Genesis 2:4b–3:24: A Synchronic Approach." *Journal of
    Biblical Literature* 96, no. 2 (1977): 161–77.

Waltke, Bruce K. "The Creation account in Genesis 1:1–3: Part I, Introduc-
    tion to Biblical Cosmogony." *Bibliotheca Sacra* 32 (1975): 25–36.

———. "The Creation account in Genesis 1:1–3: Part II, The Restitution
    Theory." *Bibliotheca Sacra* 32 (1975): 136–44.

———. "The Creation account in Genesis 1:1–3: Part III, The Initial Chaos
    Theory and the Precreation Chaos Theory." *Bibliotheca Sacra* 32 (1975):
    216–28.

———. "The Creation account in Genesis 1:1–3: Part IV, The Theology of
    Genesis 1." *Bibliotheca Sacra* 32 (1975): 327–42.

———. "The First Seven Days: What Is the Creation Account Trying to Tell
    Us?" *Christianity Today* 32 (1988): 42–46.

———. *Genesis: A Commentary*. Grand Rapids: Zondervan, 2001.

———. "The Literary Genre of Genesis, Chapter One." *Crux* 27, no. 4 (1991):
    2–10.

Walton, John. *Genesis*. NIV Application Commentary. Grand Rapids: Zonder-
    van, 2001.

Warfield, Benjamin B. *Biblical and Theological Studies*. Philadelphia: Pres-
    byterian and Reformed, 1968.

———. "On the Antiquity and the Unity of the Human Race." *Princeton
    Theological Review* 9 (1911): 1–25.

Weeks, Noel. "The Hermeneutical Problem of Genesis 1–11." *Themelios* 4,
    no. 1 (1978): 12–19.

Weinfeld, Moshe. "Sabbath, Temple, and the Enthronement of the Lord—the
    Problem of the *Sitz im Leben* of Genesis 1:1–2:3." Pages 501–12 in *Mé-
    langes bibliques et orientaux en l'honneur de M. Henri Cazelles*. Edited
    by A. Caquot and M. Delcor. Alter Orient und Altes Testament 212.
    Neukirchen-Vluyn: Neukirchener, 1981.

Wenham, Gordon J. "The Gap between Law and Ethics in the Bible." *Journal
    of Jewish Studies* 48, no. 1 (1997): 17–29.

———. *Genesis 1–15*. Word Biblical Commentary. Waco: Word, 1987.

————. "Original Sin in Genesis 1–11." *Churchman* 104, no. 4 (1990): 309–28.

————. "The Priority of P." *Vetus Testamentum* 49, no. 2 (1999): 240–58.

————. *Story as Torah: Reading the Old Testament Ethically*. Grand Rapids: Baker, 2000.

Wernberg-Möller, P. "Is There an Old Testament Theology?" *Hibbert Journal* 59 (1960–61): 21–29.

Westermann, Claus. *Genesis 1–11*. Minneapolis: Augsburg, 1984 (German original, 1974).

Whybray, R. N. "The Immorality of God: Reflections on Some Passages in Genesis, Job, Exodus and Numbers." *Journal for the Study of the Old Testament* 72 (1996): 89–120.

————. *The Making of the Pentateuch: A Methodological Study*. Sheffield: Sheffield Academic Press, 1989.

Wifall, Walter. "God's Accession Year according to P." *Biblica* 62 (1981): 527–34.

Wilkinson, David. *The Message of Creation*. The Bible Speaks Today. Downers Grove, Ill.: InterVarsity Press, 2002.

Williams, A. J. "The Relationship of Genesis 3:20 to the Serpent." *Zeitschrift für die Alttestamentliche Wissenschaft* 89, no. 3 (1977): 357–74.

Wise, Kurt P. *Faith, Form, and Time: What the Bible Teaches and Science Confirms about Creation and the Age of the Universe*. Nashville: Broadman & Holman, 2002.

Wright, Christopher J. H. *Living as the People of God: The Relevance of Old Testament Ethics*. Leicester: Inter-Varsity Press, 1983.

————. *Walking in the Ways of the Lord: The Ethical Authority of the Old Testament*. Downers Grove, Ill.: InterVarsity Press, 1995.

Wright, David F. "Woman before and after the Fall: A Comparison of Luther's and Calvin's Interpretation of Genesis 1–3." *Churchman* 98, no. 2 (1984): 126–35.

Wright, D. P. "Holiness, Sex, and Death in the Garden of Eden." Biblica 77, no. 3 (1996): 305–29.

Wright, N. T. *Climax of the Covenant*. Minneapolis: Fortress, 1993.

————. *Jesus and the Victory of God*. Minneapolis: Fortress, 1996.

————. *The New Testament and the People of God*. Minneapolis: Fortress, 1992.

————. *The Resurrection of the Son of God*. Minneapolis: Fortress, 2003.

Wyatt, Nicolas. "The Darkness of Genesis i 2." *Vetus Testamentum* 43, no. 4 (1993): 543–54.

———. "Interpreting the Creation and Fall Story in Genesis 2–3." *Zeitschrift für die Alttestamentliche Wissenschaft* 93, no. 1 (1981): 10–21.

Young, Davis A. "The Antiquity and the Unity of the Human Race Revisited." *Christian Scholars Review* 24, no. 4 (1995): 380–96.

———. "The Contemporary Relevance of Augustine's View of Creation." *Perspectives on Science and Christian Faith* 40, no. 1 (1988): 42–45.

Young, Edward J. "The Relation of the First Verse of Genesis One to Verses Two and Three." *Westminster Theological Journal* 21, no. 2 (1959): 133–46.

Youngblood, Ronald. "Moses and the King of Siam." *Journal of the Evangelical Theological Society* 16, no. 4 (1973): 215–22.

INDEX OF BIBLICAL AND
EXTRABIBLICAL REFERENCES

10:8—164n44
11:1—24n42
14:6—269n1

Joel

2:3—186

Amos

4:13—80
5:26—65
9:5–6—80

Jonah

1:5–6—107n30
1:9—174n67
2:10—193n12

Micah

7:17—163n41

Zechariah

12:1—264n27
13:5—104n5

Malachi

2:11—144
2:14—113, 142
2:14–16—143–44
4:4—37

NEW TESTAMENT
Matthew

1:8—205
2:15—24n42
3:1—24
3:3—24
3:7—187
3:13–17—24
3:16—45n17
3:17—187
4:1—26
4:1–11—18, 23, 24, 28,
   29, 186, 188
4:2—27
4:3—26, 27
4:4—26
4:5—26

4:6—26, 27
4:7—22n36, 26, 27
4:8—26
4:8–9—27
4:10—25, 26, 27
4:11—26, 27
5—185
5:21–24—215
7:16—165n44
8:29—24n42
10:16—150n2
11:11—159
11:27—24n42
14:33—24n42
16:16—24n42
16:23—25
17:5—24n42
18:21–22—219
19:1–12—262n20
19:3–5—121
19:3–9—144
19:4–5—108n36
19:7–8—37
22:34–40—276
23:33—156n33, 187
23:35—217, 218
24:36—24n42
26:63—24n42
27:43—24n42
27:54—24n42
28:18—24
28:18–20—28
28:19—24n42
28:19–20—29

Mark

1:12–13—186
10:2–8—121
10:2–9—144

Luke

2:9–14—60, 61
3:7—187
3:23—187
3:38—187, 217
4:1–13—186
4:13—187

7:28—159
11:51—217, 218
20:27–40—262
23:43—105n15, 186
24:31—151n7

John

1:1—95
1:1–5—94
1:14—31n50
5:1–18—92
5:17—125
5:22—92n121
5:30—92n121
8:34—92n121
8:44—171

Acts

1:8—88
6:7—88
7:17—88
9:31—88
12:24—88
13:47—88
14:8–18—97
14:15—98, 99
17:2—184
17:16–34—97–98
17:22–31—132
17:24–25—99
17:24–28—272
17:26—167
17:26–27—130
19:20—88

Romans

1:21–25—81
1:23—82
1:26—82
4:3–5—29
5:12–14—166n47
5:12–19—155, 176,
   180–82
5:12–21—114
6:11—181n81
6:16—181n81
6:21—181n81

INDEX OF SUBJECTS AND NAMES

C. John Collins (S.M., Massachusetts Institute of Technology; M.Div., Faith Evangelical Lutheran Seminary; Ph.D., University of Liverpool) is professor of Old Testament and department chairman at Covenant Theological Seminary. His professional experience spans both science and biblical studies, and he is a member of the American Scientific Affiliation and the Society of Biblical Literature.

Collins is author of *The God of Miracles* and *Science and Faith*, as well as numerous published articles and conference papers in the areas of biblical linguistics, Old Testament exegesis and theology, and the Bible and science. Among his work as a Bible translator, he has served as chairman of the Old Testament Committee for the English Standard Version of the Bible.